A Programming Approach

# The Little SAS® Book

## a primer
### FOURTH EDITION

*Lora D. Delwiche* and *Susan J. Slaughter*

The correct bibliographic citation for this manual is as follows: Delwiche, Lora D., and Susan J. Slaughter. 2008. *The Little SAS® Book: A Primer, Fourth Edition.* Cary, NC: SAS Institute Inc.

**The Little SAS® Book: A Primer, Fourth Edition**

ISBN 978-1-59994-725-9
ISBN 978-1-59994-875-1 (electronic book)

SAS Institute Inc., SAS Campus Drive, Cary, North Carolina 27513.

1st printing, July 2008
2nd printing, May 2009
3rd printing, May 2010
4th printing, May 2011
5th printing, November 2011

SAS® Publishing provides a complete selection of books and electronic products to help customers use SAS software to its fullest potential. For more information about our e-books, e-learning products, CDs, and hard-copy books, visit the SAS Publishing Web site at **support.sas.com/publishing** or call 1-800-727-3228.

# Contents

# Acknowledgments

As hard as we have worked on this book, we could never have done it alone. Many people at SAS helped make this book what it is. To our many hard-working reviewers: Janice Bloom, Amber Elam, Phil Gibbs, Chris Hemedinger, Elizabeth Maldonado, Lelia McConnell, Julie McKnight, Martin Mincey, Jason Moore, Sandy Owens, and Cynthia Zender, we say, "Thanks for hanging in there with us." Special thanks go to reviewers Bob Rodriguez, Sanjay Matange, and Dan Heath, "Without you, we couldn't have included ODS Graphics in this edition." To our copyeditor, Mike Boyd, and our designer, Patrice Cherry, "Thanks for making us look good." To our technical publishing specialists, Jennifer Dilley and Candy Farrell, "Thanks for rectifying all those wayward footnotes, squeezing in those last few sentences, and finding those missing images." And last but not least we would like to thank—faster than a speeding deadline, stronger than Microsoft Word, able to leap tall drafts in a single bound—our editor-in-chief, Julie Platt; managing editor, Mary Beth Steinbach; and acquisitions editor, Stephenie Joyner.

Outside the walls of SAS many other people also contributed to this book. In particular we would like to thank our readers. We love meeting you at conferences even if we seem a little shy. Without you, of course, there would be no reason to keep writing. Most of all we would like to thank our families for their understanding and support.

# Introducing SAS Software

SAS software is used by millions of people all over the world—in over 100 countries, at over 44,000 sites. SAS (pronounced sass) is both a company and software. When people say SAS, they sometimes mean the software running on their computers and sometimes mean the company.

People often ask what SAS stands for. Originally the letters S-A-S stood for Statistical Analysis System (not to be confused with Scandinavian Airlines System, San Antonio Shoemakers, or the Society for Applied Spectroscopy). SAS products have become so diverse that several years back SAS officially dropped the name Statistical Analysis System, now outgrown, and became simply SAS.

**SAS products**   The roots of SAS software reach back to the 1970s when it started out as a software package for statistical analysis, but SAS didn't stop there. By the mid-1980s SAS had already branched out into graphics, online data entry, and compilers for the C programming language. In the 1990s the SAS family tree grew to include tools for visualizing data, administering data warehouses, and building interfaces to the World Wide Web. In the new century, SAS has continued to grow with products designed for cleansing messy data, discovering and developing drugs, and detecting money laundering. Just as AT&T is now more than telephones and telegraphs, SAS is more than statistics.

While SAS has a diverse family of products, most of these products are integrated; that is, they can be put together like building blocks to construct a seamless system. For example, you might use SAS/ACCESS software to read data stored in an external database such as Oracle, analyze it using SAS/ETS software (business modeling and forecasting), use ODS Graphics to produce sophisticated plots, and then forward the results in e-mail messages to your colleagues, all in a single computer program. To find out more about products available from SAS, see the Web site

www.sas.com.

**Operating environments**   SAS software runs in a wide range of operating environments. You can take a program written on a personal computer and run it on a mainframe after changing only the file-handling statements specific to each operating environment. And because SAS programs are as portable as possible, SAS programmers are as portable as possible, too. If you know SAS in one operating environment, you can switch to another operating environment without having to relearn SAS.

**SAS OnDemand for Academics**   SAS OnDemand for Academics is available for use with courses at colleges and universities. With this product, you can access the power of SAS software through the Internet. You simply download a client software application and use it to perform your work. Processing takes place on a SAS server hosted by SAS Institute Inc. Then the results are returned from the server to your PC.

**SASware Ballot**   SAS puts a high percentage of its revenue into research and development, and each year SAS users help determine how that money will be spent by voting on the SASware Ballot. The ballot is a list of suggestions for new features and enhancements. All SAS users are eligible to vote and thereby influence the future development of SAS software. You can even make your own suggestions for the SASware Ballot by sending e-mail to

suggest@sas.com.

For further information about the SASware Ballot see the SAS Customer Support Web site at

support.sas.com.

# About This Book

**Who needs this book** This book is for all new SAS users in business, government, and academia, or for anyone who will be conducting data analysis using SAS software. You need no prior experience with SAS, but if you have some experience you may still find this book useful for learning techniques you missed or for reference.

**What this book covers** This book introduces you to the SAS language with lots of practical examples, clear and concise explanations, and as little technical jargon as possible. Most of the features covered here come from Base SAS, which contains the core of features used by all SAS programmers. One exception is chapter 8 which includes procedures from SAS/STAT and SAS/GRAPH. Other exceptions appear in chapters 2 and 9 which cover importing and exporting data from other types of software; some methods require SAS/ACCESS Interface to PC Files.

We have tried to include every feature of Base SAS that a beginner is likely to need. Some of you will be surprised that certain topics, such as macros, are included because macros are normally considered advanced. But they appear here because sometimes new users need them. However, that doesn't mean that you need to know everything in this book. On the contrary, this book is designed so you can read just those sections you need to solve your problems. Even if you read this book from cover to cover, you may find yourself returning to refresh your memory as new programming challenges arise.

**What this book does not cover** To use this book you need no prior knowledge of SAS, but you must know something about your local computer and operating environment. The SAS language is virtually the same from one operating environment to another, but some differences are unavoidable. For example, every operating environment has a different way of storing and accessing files. Also, some operating environments have more of a capacity for interactive computing than others. Your employer may have rules limiting the size of files you can print. This book addresses operating environments as much as possible, but no book can answer every question about your local system. You must have either a working knowledge of your operating environment or someone you can turn to with questions.

This book is not a replacement for the SAS Help and Documentation, or the many SAS publications. Sooner or later you'll need to go to these and other sources to learn details not covered in this book. Appendix A, "Where to Go from Here," lists many resources available to SAS users including the SAS Customer Support Web site, SAS training courses, SAS users groups, and SAS Technical Support for those really tough questions.

We cover only a few of the many SAS statistical procedures. Fortunately, the statistical procedures share many of the same statements, options, and output, so these few can serve as an introduction to the others. Once you have read chapter 8, we think that other statistical procedures will feel familiar.

Unfortunately, a book of this type cannot provide a thorough introduction to statistical concepts such as degrees of freedom, or crossed and nested effects. There are underlying assumptions about your data that must be met for the tests to be valid. Experimental design and careful selection of the models are critical. Interpretation of the results can often be difficult and subjective. We assume that readers who are interested in statistical computing already know something about statistics. People who want to use statistical procedures but are unfamiliar with these concepts should consult a statistician, seek out an introductory statistics text, or, better yet, take a course in statistics.

**Modular sections**  Our goal in writing this book is to make learning SAS as easy and enjoyable as possible. Let's face it—SAS is a big topic. You may have already spent some time scratching your head in front of a shelf full of SAS publications, or staring at a screen full of documentation until your eyes become blurry. We can't condense all of SAS into this little book, but we can condense topics into short, readable sections.

This entire book is composed of two-page sections, each section a complete topic. This way, you can easily skip over topics which do not apply to you. Of course, we think *every* section is important, or we would not have included it. You probably don't need to know everything in this book, however, to complete your job. By presenting topics in short digestible sections, we believe that learning SAS will be easier and more fun—like eating three meals a day instead of one giant meal a week.

**Graphics**  Wherever possible, graphic illustrations either identify the contents of the section or help explain the topic. A box with rough edges indicates a raw data file, and a box with nice smooth edges indicates a SAS data set. The squiggles inside the box indicate data—any old data—and a period indicates a missing value. The arrow between boxes of these types means that the section explains how to get from data that look like the one box to data that look like the other. Some sections have graphics which depict printed output. These graphics look like a stack of papers with headers printed at the top of the page.

**Typographical conventions**  SAS doesn't care whether your programs are written in uppercase or lowercase, so you can write your programs any way you want. In this book, we have used uppercase and lowercase to tell you something. The statements on the left below show the syntax, or general form, while the statements on the right show an example of actual statements as they might appear in a SAS program.

**Syntax**
```
PROC PRINT DATA = data-set-name;
   VAR variable-list;
```

**Example**
```
PROC PRINT DATA = bigcats;
   VAR Lions Tigers;
```

Notice that the keywords PROC PRINT, DATA, and VAR are the same on both sides and that the descriptive terms *data-set-name* and *variable-list* on the syntax side have been replaced with an actual data set name and variable names in the example.

In this book, all SAS keywords appear in uppercase letters. A keyword is an instruction to SAS and must be spelled correctly. Anything written in lowercase italics is a description of what goes in that spot in the statement, not what you actually type. Anything in lowercase or mixed case letters (and not in italics) is something that the programmer has made up such as a variable name, a name for a SAS data set, a comment, or a title. See section 1.2 for further discussion of the significance of case in SAS names.

**Indention**  This book contains many SAS programs, each complete and executable. Programs are formatted in a way which makes them easy for you to read and understand. You do not have to format your programs this way, as SAS is very flexible, but attention to some of these details will make your programs easier to read. Easy-to-read programs are time-savers for you, or the consultant you hire at $100 per hour, when you need to go back and decipher the program months or years later.

The structure of programs is shown by indenting all statements after the first in a step. This is a simple way to make your programs more readable, and it's a good habit to form. SAS doesn't really care where statements start or even if they are all on one line. In the following program, the INFILE and INPUT statements are indented, indicating that they belong with the DATA statement:

```
* Read animals' weights from file. Print the results.;
DATA animals;
    INFILE 'c:\MyRawData\Zoo.dat';
    INPUT Lions Tigers;
RUN;

PROC PRINT DATA = animals;
RUN;
```

Last, we have tried to make this book as readable as possible and, we hope, even enjoyable. Once you master the contents of this small book you will no longer be a beginning SAS programmer.

**Data and programs used in this book**  You can access the example data and programs by linking to the author pages for this book at http://support.sas.com/authors. From this Web site, select Example Code and Data to display the SAS data and programs that are included in the book.

# What's New

This fourth edition of *The Little SAS Book: A Primer* includes some SAS features added since SAS 9.1 and a few features that are not new, but nonetheless new to this book.

A major new feature with SAS 9.2 is ODS Graphics. ODS Graphics is a whole new way of creating graphs using SAS. We added 11 new sections on ODS Graphics to this edition including ODS Graphics concepts, the SGPLOT procedure, and producing ODS Graphics in statistical procedures.

Other new topics we added to the book are the WHERE= data set option, computed variables in PROC REPORT, and grouping in procedures with user-defined formats. In addition, we added 16 new functions, and more on viewing SAS data sets using Viewtable.

Most of the features in this edition are available with SAS 9.1.3; a few are new with SAS 9.2. We have tried to point out whenever a feature is new. So unless otherwise noted, you can assume that everything in this book is available in SAS 9.1.3.

Here, listed by section, are the new topics:

## ODS Graphics (new with SAS 9.2)

| Section | Feature |
| --- | --- |
| 8.1 | **Basic concepts** for understanding ODS Graphics |
| 8.2 to 8.6 | **PROC SGPLOT** for producing stand-alone bar charts, histograms, box plots, scatter plots, series plots, and fitted curves |
| 8.8 | **ODS Graphics for PROC UNIVARIATE** for creating distribution, probability, and quantile plots |
| 8.11 | **ODS Graphics for PROC FREQ** for creating frequency, deviation, kappa, and odds ratio plots |
| 8.13 | **ODS Graphics for PROC CORR** for creating scatter plots with prediction ellipses, and matrix plots |
| 8.15 | **ODS Graphics for PROC REG** for creating fit and residual plots as well as many types of diagnostic plots |
| 8.16 | **ODS Graphics for PROC ANOVA** for creating box plots |

## Other features new with SAS 9.2

| Section | Feature |
| --- | --- |
| 2.3, 2.17 | **Support for JMP, Paradox, Stata, and SPSS** files in the Import Wizard and PROC IMPORT |
| 4.3 | **SORTSEQ=LINGUISTIC** option in PROC SORT sorts upper- and lowercase letters together |
| 4.9, 4.13, 4.21 | **MODE** statistic is now available in PROC MEANS, PROC TABULATE, and PROC REPORT |
| 5.9 | **SPANROWS** option in PROC REPORT combines cells in the same group into a single cell |

| 6.2, 6.4 | **Name prefix and numbered range data set lists** for specifying lists of data set names in SET or MERGE statements |
| 9.2, 9.4 | **Support for JMP, Paradox, Stata, and SPSS** files in the Export Wizard and PROC EXPORT |
| 10.9 | **PUTLOG** statement writes to the SAS log even if a FILE statement is in the DATA step |

## Also new with this edition

| **Section** | **Feature** |
| 2.8 | **ANYDTDTE.** informat allows for reading data with mixed date styles in a single variable |
| 2.16 | **DATAROWS=** statement for delimited files in PROC IMPORT tells which row in the file contains the first data row |
| 2.16 | **GUESSINGROWS=** statement for delimited files in PROC IMPORT tells how many rows to use to determine variable types |
| 2.17 | **RANGE=** statement for Microsoft Excel files in PROC IMPORT specifies what part of the sheet contains the data |
| 2.22 | **LABEL=** data set option specifies a label for the data set |
| 3.3 | **ANYALNUM, ANYALPHA, ANYDIGIT, ANYSPACE, CAT, CATS, CATX, COMPRESS, INDEX, PROPCASE,** and **TRANWRD** character functions |
| 3.4 | **N** and **NMISS** numeric functions and **WEEKDAY** and **YEAR** date functions |
| 3.12 | **Name prefix variable lists** for specifying lists of variable names all starting with the same characters |
| 4.3 | **DUPOUT=** option in PROC SORT specifies a data set to contain the duplicate observations eliminated when the data are sorted |
| 4.22 | **Compute blocks** in PROC REPORT for calculating new variables to appear in PROC REPORT output |
| 4.23 | **Grouping data in procedures** with user-defined formats |
| 5.4, 5.5, 5.6 | **ODS NOPROCTITLE** statement tells SAS not to include procedure titles in ODS output |
| 5.5, 5.6 | **ODS STARTPAGE=** option controls where page breaks are added to ODS output |
| 6.13 | **WHERE=** data set option to control which observations are processed when reading or writing data sets |
| 10.6 | **?? format modifier** suppresses the invalid data message in the SAS log if SAS encounters invalid data for the variable |

**1**

**"An honest tale speeds best being plainly told."**

WILLIAM SHAKESPEARE, *KING RICHARD III*

From *King Richard III* by William Shakespeare. Public domain.

# CHAPTER 1

# Getting Started Using SAS Software

# 1.1  The SAS Language

Many software applications are either menu driven, or command driven (enter a command—see the result). SAS is neither. With SAS, you use statements to write a series of instructions called a SAS program. The program communicates what you want to do and is written using the SAS language. There are some menu-driven front ends to SAS, for example SAS Enterprise Guide software, which make SAS appear like a point-and-click program. However, these front ends still use the SAS language to write programs for you. You will have much more flexibility using SAS if you learn to write your own programs using the SAS language. Maybe learning a new language is the last thing you want to do, but be assured that although there are parallels between SAS and languages you know (be they English or JAVA), SAS is much easier to learn.

**SAS programs**   A SAS program is a sequence of statements executed in order. A statement gives information or instructions to SAS and must be appropriately placed in the program. An everyday analogy to a SAS program is a trip to the bank. You enter your bank, stand in line, and when you finally reach the teller's window, you say what you want to do. The statements you give can be written down in the form of a program:

```
I would like to make a withdrawal.
   My account number is 0937.
   I would like $200.
   Give me five 20s and two 50s.
```

Note that you first say what you want to do, then give all the information the teller needs to carry out your request. The order of the subsequent statements may not be important, but you must start with the general statement of what you want to do. You would not, for example, go up to a bank teller and say, "Give me five 20s and two 50s." This is not only bad form, but would probably make the teller's heart skip a beat or two. You must also make sure that all the subsequent statements belong with the first. You would not say, "I want the largest box you have" when making a withdrawal from your checking account. That statement belongs with "I would like to open a safe deposit box." A SAS program is an ordered set of SAS statements like the ordered set of instructions you use when you go to the bank.

**SAS statements**   As with any language, there are a few rules to follow when writing SAS programs. Fortunately for us, the rules for writing SAS programs are much fewer and simpler than those for English.

The most important rule is

## Every SAS statement ends with a semicolon.

This sounds simple enough. But while children generally outgrow the habit of forgetting the period at the end of a sentence, SAS programmers never seem to outgrow forgetting the semicolon at the end of a SAS statement. Even the most experienced SAS programmer will at least occasionally forget the semicolon. You will be two steps ahead if you remember this simple rule.

**Layout of SAS programs**    There really aren't any rules about how to format your SAS program. While it is helpful to have a neat looking program with each statement on a line by itself and indentions to show the various parts of the program, it isn't necessary.

♦    SAS statements can be in upper- or lowercase.

♦    Statements can continue on the next line (as long as you don't split words in two).

♦    Statements can be on the same line as other statements.

♦    Statements can start in any column.

So you see, SAS is so flexible that it is possible to write programs so disorganized that no one can read them, not even you. (Of course, we don't recommend this.)

**Comments**    To make your programs more understandable, you can insert comments into your programs. It doesn't matter what you put in your comments—SAS doesn't look at it. You could put your favorite cookie recipe in there if you want. However, comments are usually used to annotate the program, making it easier for someone to read your program and understand what you have done and why.

There are two styles of comments you can use: one starts with an asterisk (*) and ends with a semicolon (;). The other style starts with a slash asterisk (/*) and ends with an asterisk slash (*/). The following SAS program shows the use of both of these style comments:

```
* Read animals' weights from file;
DATA animals;
    INFILE 'c:\MyRawData\Zoo.dat';
    INPUT Lions Tigers;
PROC PRINT DATA = animals;   /* Print the results */
RUN;
```

Since some operating environments interpret a slash asterisk (/*) in the first column as the end of a job, be careful when using this style of comment not to place it in the first column. For this reason, we chose the asterisk-semicolon style of comment for this book.

**Programming tips**    People who are just learning a programming language often get frustrated because their programs do not work correctly the first time they write them. Writing programs should be done in small steps. Don't try to tackle a long complicated program all at once. If you start small, build on what works, and always check your results along the way, you will increase your programming efficiency. Sometimes programs that do not produce errors are still incorrect. This is why it is vital to check your results as you go even when there are no errors. If you do get errors, don't worry. Most programs simply don't work the first time, if for no other reason than you are human. You forget a semicolon, misspell a word, have your fingers in the wrong place on the keyboard. It happens. Often one small mistake can generate a whole list of errors. If you build your programs piece by piece, programs are much easier to correct when something goes wrong.

## 1.2 SAS Data Sets

Before you run an analysis, before you write a report, before you do anything with your data, SAS must be able to read your data. Before SAS can analyze your data, the data must be in a special form called a SAS data set.[1] Getting your data into a SAS data set is usually quite simple as SAS is very flexible and can read almost any data. Once your data have been read into a SAS data set, SAS keeps track of what is where and in what form. All you have to do is specify the name and location of the data set you want, and SAS figures out what is in it.

**Variables and observations** Data, of course, are the primary constituent of any data set. In traditional SAS terminology the data consist of variables and observations. Adopting the terminology of relational databases, SAS data sets are also called tables, observations are also called rows, and variables are also called columns. Below you see a rectangular table containing a small data set. Each line represents one observation, while Id, Name, Height, and Weight are variables. The data point Charlie is one of the values of the variable Name and is also part of the second observation.

**Variables (Also Called Columns)**

|  | Id | Name | Height | Weight |
|---|---|---|---|---|
| 1 | 53 | Susie | 42 | 41 |
| 2 | 54 | Charlie | 46 | 55 |
| 3 | 55 | Calvin | 40 | 35 |
| 4 | 56 | Lucy | 46 | 52 |
| 5 | 57 | Dennis | 44 | . |
| 6 | 58 |  | 43 | 50 |

Observations (Also Called Rows)

**Data types** Raw data come in many different forms, but SAS simplifies this. In SAS there are just two data types: numeric and character. Numeric fields are, well, numbers. They can be added and subtracted, can have any number of decimal places, and can be positive or negative. In addition to numerals, numeric fields can contain plus signs (+), minus signs (-), decimal points (.), or E for scientific notation. Character data are everything else. They may contain numerals, letters, or special characters (such as $ or !) and can be up to 32,767 characters long.

If a variable contains letters or special characters, it must be character data. However, if it contains only numbers, then it may be numeric or character. You should base your decision on how you will use the variable.[2] Sometimes data that consist solely of numerals make more sense as character data than as numeric. ZIP codes, for example, are made up of numerals, but it just doesn't make sense to add, subtract, multiply, or divide ZIP codes. Such numbers make more sense as character data. In the previous data set, Name is obviously a character variable, and Height and Weight are numeric. Id, however, could be either numeric or character. It's your choice.

---

[1] There are exceptions. If your data are in a format written by another software product, you may be able to read your data directly without creating a SAS data set. For database management systems and spreadsheets, you may be able to use SAS/ACCESS software. See chapter 2 for more information. For SPSS, see appendix B.

[2] If disk space is a problem, you may also choose to base your decision on storage size. You can use the LENGTH statement, discussed in section 10.15, to control the storage size of variables.

**Missing data** Sometimes despite your best efforts, your data may be incomplete. The value of a particular variable may be missing for some observations. In those cases, missing character data are represented by blanks, and missing numeric data are represented by a single period (.). In the preceding data set, the value of Weight for observation 5 is missing, and its place is marked by a period. The value of Name for observation 6 is missing and is just left blank.

**Size of SAS data sets** Prior to SAS 9.1, SAS data sets could contain up to 32,767 variables. Beginning with SAS 9.1, the maximum number of variables in a SAS data set is limited by the resources available on your computer—but SAS data sets with more than 32,767 variables cannot be used with earlier versions of SAS. The number of observations, no matter which version of SAS you are using, is limited only by your computer's capacity to handle and store them.

**Rules for SAS names** You make up names for the variables in your data and for the data sets themselves. It is helpful to make up names that identify what the data represent, especially for variables. While the variable names A, B, and C might seem like perfectly fine, easy-to-type names when you write your program, the names Sex, Height, and Weight will probably be more helpful when you go back to look at the program six months later. Follow these simple rules when making up names for variables and data set members:

♦   Names must be 32 characters or fewer in length.[3]

♦   Names must start with a letter or an underscore ( _ ).

♦   Names can contain only letters, numerals, or underscores ( _ ). No %$!*&#@, please.[4]

♦   Names can contain upper- and lowercase letters.

This last point is an important one. SAS is insensitive to case so you can use uppercase, lowercase or mixed case—whichever looks best to you. SAS doesn't care. The data set name heightweight is the same as HEIGHTWEIGHT or HeightWeight. Likewise, the variable name BirthDate is the same as BIRTHDATE and birThDaTe. However, there is one difference for variable names. SAS remembers the case of the first occurrence of each variable name and uses that case when printing results. That is why, in this book, we use mixed case for variable names but lowercase for other SAS names.

**Documentation stored in SAS data sets** In addition to your actual data, SAS data sets contain information about the data set such as its name, the date that you created it, and the version of SAS you used to create it. SAS also stores information about each variable, including its name, label (if any), type (numeric or character), length (or storage size), and position within the data set. This information is sometimes called the descriptor portion of the data set, and it makes SAS data sets self-documenting.

---

[3] Beginning with SAS 9, format names can also be 32 characters long, and informat names can be 31 characters (including the $ for character values). Prior to SAS 9, format names could be 8 characters while informat names could be 7 characters (also including the $). Librefs and filerefs must be 8 characters or fewer in length, and member names for versioned data sets must be 28 characters or fewer.

[4] It is possible to use special characters, including spaces, in variable names if you use the system option VALIDVARNAMES=ANY and a name literal of the form '*variable-name*'N. See the SAS Help and Documentation for details.

## 1.3  The Two Parts of a SAS Program

SAS programs are constructed from two basic building blocks: DATA steps and PROC steps. A typical program starts with a DATA step to create a SAS data set and then passes the data to a PROC step for processing. Here is a simple program that converts miles to kilometers in a DATA step and prints the results with a PROC step:

**DATA step**
```
DATA distance;
    Miles = 26.22;
    Kilometers = 1.61 * Miles;
```

**PROC step**
```
PROC PRINT DATA = distance;
RUN;
```

DATA and PROC steps are made up of statements. A step may have as few as one or as many as hundreds of statements. Most statements work in only one type of step—in DATA steps but not PROC steps, or vice versa. A common mistake made by beginners is to try to use a statement in the wrong kind of step. You're not likely to make this mistake if you remember that DATA steps read and modify data while PROC steps analyze data, perform utility functions, or print reports.

DATA steps start with the DATA statement, which starts, not surprisingly, with the word DATA. This keyword is followed by a name that you make up for a SAS data set. The DATA step above produces a SAS data set named DISTANCE. In addition to reading data from external, raw data files, DATA steps can include DO loops, IF-THEN/ELSE logic, and a large assortment of numeric and character functions. DATA steps can also combine data sets in just about any way you want, including concatenation and match-merge.

Procedures, on the other hand, start with a PROC statement in which the keyword PROC is followed by the name of the procedure (PRINT, SORT, or MEANS, for example). Most SAS procedures have only a handful of possible statements. Like following a recipe, you use basically the same statements or ingredients each time. SAS procedures do everything from simple sorting and printing to analysis of variance and 3D graphics. Other SAS procedures perform utility functions such as importing data files and data entry.

A step ends when SAS encounters a new step (marked by a DATA or PROC statement), a RUN statement, or, if you are running in batch mode, the end of the program.[1] RUN statements tell SAS to run all the preceding lines of the step and are among those rare, global statements that are not part of a DATA or PROC step. In the program above, SAS knows that the DATA step has ended when it reaches the PROC statement. The PROC step ends with a RUN statement, which coincides with the end of the program.

---

[1] If you use SAS long enough, you may run into an exception. Steps can also terminate with a QUIT, STOP, or ABORT statement.

While a typical program starts with a DATA step to input or modify data and then passes the data to a PROC step, that is certainly not the only pattern for mixing DATA and PROC steps. Just as you can stack building blocks in any order, you can arrange DATA and PROC steps in any order. A program could even contain only DATA steps or only PROC steps.

To review, the table below outlines the basic differences between DATA and PROC steps:

| **DATA steps** | **PROC steps** |
| --- | --- |
| ▷ begin with DATA statements | ▷ begin with PROC statements |
| ▷ read and modify data | ▷ perform specific analysis or function |
| ▷ create a SAS data set | ▷ produce results or report |

As you read this table, keep in mind that it is a simplification. Because SAS is so flexible, the differences between DATA and PROC steps are, in reality, more blurry. The table above is not meant to imply that PROC steps never create SAS data sets (most do), or that DATA steps never produce reports (they can). Nonetheless, you will find it much easier to write SAS programs if you understand the basic functions of DATA and PROC steps.

## 1.4 The DATA Step's Built-in Loop

DATA steps read and modify data, and they do it in a way that is flexible, giving you lots of control over what happens to your data. However, DATA steps also have an underlying structure, an implicit, built-in loop. You don't tell SAS to execute this loop: SAS does it automatically. Memorize this:

### DATA steps execute line by line and observation by observation.

This basic concept is rarely stated explicitly. Consequently, new users often grow into old users before they figure this out on their own.

The idea that DATA steps execute line by line is fairly straightforward and easy to understand. It means that, by default, SAS executes line one of your DATA step before it executes line two, and line two before line three, and so on. That seems common sense, and yet new users frequently run into problems because they try to use a variable before they create it. If a variable named Z is the product of X and Y, then you better make sure that the statements creating X and Y come before the statements creating Z.

What is not so obvious is that while DATA steps execute line by line, they also execute observation by observation. That means SAS takes the first observation and runs it all the way through the DATA step (line by line, of course) before looping back to pick up the second observation. In this way, SAS sees only one observation at a time.

Imagine a SAS program running in slow motion: SAS reads observation number one from your input data set. Then SAS executes your DATA step using that observation. If SAS reaches the end of the DATA step without encountering any serious errors, then SAS writes the current observation to a new, output data set and returns to the beginning of the DATA step to process the next observation. After the last observation has been written to the output data set, SAS terminates the DATA step and moves on to the next step, if there is one. End of slow motion; please return to normal gigahertz.

This diagram illustrates how an observation flows through a DATA step:

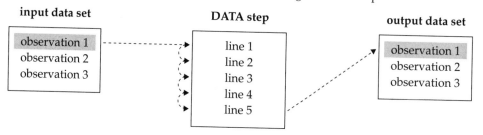

SAS reads observation number one and processes it using line one of the DATA step, then line two, and so on until SAS reaches the end of the DATA step. Then SAS writes the observation in the output data set. This diagram shows the first execution of the line-by-line loop. Once SAS finishes with the first observation, it loops back to the top of the DATA step and picks up observation two. When SAS reaches the last observation, it automatically stops.[1]

Here is an analogy. DATA step processing is a bit like voting. When you arrive at your polling place, you stand in line behind other people who have come to vote. When you reach the front of the line you are asked standard questions: "What is your name? Where do you live?" Then you sign your name, and you cast your vote. In this analogy, the people are observations, and the voting process is the DATA step. People vote one at a time (or observation by observation). Each voter's choices are secret, and peeking at your neighbor's ballot is definitely frowned upon. In addition, each person completes each step of the process in the same order (line by line). You cannot cast your vote before you give your name and address. Everything must be done in the proper order.

---

[1] If this seems a bit too structured, don't worry. You can override the line-by-line and observation-by-observation structure in a number of ways. For example, you can use the RETAIN statement, discussed in section 3.10, to make data from the previous observation available to the current observation. You can also use the OUTPUT statement, discussed in sections 6.9 and 6.10, to control when observations are written to the output data set.

## 1.5  Choosing a Mode for Submitting SAS Programs

So far we have talked about writing SAS programs, but simply writing a program does not give you any results. Just like writing a letter to your representative in Congress does no good unless you mail it, a SAS program does nothing until you submit or execute it. You can execute a SAS program several ways, but not all methods are available for all operating environments. Check in the SAS Help and Documentation for your operating environment to find out which methods are available to you. The method you choose for executing a SAS program will depend on your preferences and on what is most appropriate for your application and your environment. If you are using SAS at a large site with many users, then ask around and find out which is the most accepted method of executing SAS. If you are using SAS on your own personal computer, then choose the method that suits you.

**SAS windowing environment**  If you type SAS at your system prompt, or click on the SAS icon, you will most likely get into the SAS windowing environment. In this interactive environment, you can write and edit SAS programs, submit programs for processing, and view and print your results. In addition, there are many SAS windows for performing different tasks such as managing SAS files, customizing the interface, accessing SAS Help, and importing or exporting data. Exactly what your windowing environment looks like depends on the type of computer you are using, the operating environment on the computer, and what options are in effect when you start up SAS. If you are using a personal computer, then the SAS windowing environment will look similar to other programs on your computer, and many of the features will be familiar to you.

**SAS Enterprise Guide**  If you have SAS Enterprise Guide software,[1] which runs only under Windows, you may choose to submit your programs from within SAS Enterprise Guide. To do this, open a Code window where you can enter your SAS program or open an existing SAS program. Then you can choose to run your code on the local machine, or on a remote server where SAS is installed. To run your SAS program on a remote server, you must have SAS Integration Technologies software installed. Also, SAS Enterprise Guide can write SAS code for you through its extensive menu system.

**Noninteractive mode**  Noninteractive mode is where your SAS program statements are in a file on your system, and you start up SAS specifying that you want to execute that file. SAS immediately starts to process your file and ties up your computer, or window, until it is finished. The results are usually placed in a file or files, and you are returned to your system prompt.

---

[1] Beginning with SAS 9, SAS Enterprise Guide software is included with Base SAS software for Windows. SAS Enterprise Guide software is also available with SAS Version 8, but is licensed separately.

Noninteractive mode is useful in many situations. This mode is good if you want your program to execute immediately, but you do not want to or cannot use a windowing environment. Noninteractive mode is usually started by typing SAS at your system prompt (shown here as $), followed by the filename containing your program statements:

```
$ SAS MyFile.sas
```

**Batch or background mode**  With batch or background mode, your SAS program is in a file. You submit the file for processing with SAS. Your SAS program may start executing immediately, or it could be put in a queue behind other jobs. Batch processing is used a lot on mainframe computers. You can continue to work on your computer while your job is being processed, or better yet, you can go to the baseball game and let the computer work in your absence. Batch processing is usually less expensive than other methods and is especially good for large jobs which can be set up to execute during off-hours when the rates are at their lowest. When your job is complete, the results will be placed in a file or files, which you can display or print at any time.

To find out how to submit SAS programs for batch processing, check the SAS Help and Documentation for your operating environment or with other SAS users at your site. Even sites with the same operating environment may have different ways of submitting jobs in batch mode.

**Remote submit**  If you have SAS/CONNECT software, it is possible to write and develop your SAS programs on one system, then submit them for processing on another. Using this method, you write your program on your local machine, establish a connection to the remote machine, and run the program on the remote machine. Then the results are delivered back to your local machine. You might want to do this if your remote machine is much more powerful than your local machine, and you are running very large programs. Also, you might need to access large or shared data files on the remote machine.

**Interactive line mode**  This mode is mentioned only because you might see it in the SAS documentation, and you might get into it by accident. In interactive line mode, you are prompted for SAS statements one line at a time. There is no easy way to correct mistakes once you have entered them, so unless you are an excellent typist, and an excellent programmer, interactive line mode is exceedingly frustrating.

If you do find yourself in this mode (you will know when you get a 1? as a prompt), you can get out by typing ENDSAS; and pressing ENTER. For example

```
1? ENDSAS;
```

## 1.6 Windows and Commands in the SAS Windowing Environment

It used to be that SAS looked pretty much the same on all platforms, and you couldn't change its appearance. But now SAS adopts the look and feel of your operating environment, and there are many ways in which you can customize your SAS environment. This is good for you because many aspects of the SAS windowing environment will be familiar, and if you don't like the default view, you can change it. It makes writing about it more difficult, because we can't tell you exactly what your SAS session will look like and how it will behave. However, there are many common elements between the various operating environments, and you will probably already be familiar with those elements which are different.

### The SAS Windows

There are five basic SAS windows: the Results and Explorer windows, and three programming windows: Editor, Log, and Output. It is possible to bring up SAS without all these windows, and sometimes the windows are not immediately visible (for example, in the Windows operating environment, the Output window comes up behind the Editor and Log windows), but all these windows do exist in your SAS session. There are also many other SAS windows that you may use for tasks such as getting help, changing SAS system options, and customizing your SAS session. The following figure shows the default view for a Microsoft Windows SAS session, with pointers to the five main SAS windows.

**Editor**  This window is a text editor. You can use it to type in, edit, and submit SAS programs as well as edit other text files such as raw data files. In Windows operating environments, the default editor is the Enhanced Editor. The Enhanced Editor is syntax sensitive and color codes your programs making it easier to read them and find mistakes. The Enhanced Editor also allows you to collapse and expand the various steps in your program. For other operating environments, the default editor is the Program Editor whose features vary with the version of SAS and operating environment.

**Log** The Log window contains notes about your SAS session, and after you submit a SAS program, any notes, errors, or warnings associated with your program as well as the program statements themselves will appear in the Log window.

**Output** If your program generates any printable results, then they will appear in the Output window.

**Results** The Results window is like a table of contents for your Output window; the results tree lists each part of your results in an outline form.

**Explorer** The Explorer window gives you easy access to your SAS files and libraries.

## The SAS Commands

There are SAS commands for performing a variety of tasks. Some tasks are probably familiar, such as opening and saving files, cutting and pasting text, and accessing Help. Other commands are specific to the SAS System, such as submitting a SAS program, or starting up a SAS application. You may have up to three ways to issue commands: menus, the toolbar, or the SAS command bar (or command line). The following figure shows the location of these three methods of issuing SAS commands in the Windows operating environment default view.

**Menus** Most operating environments will have pull-down menus located either at the top of each window, or at the top of your screen. If your menus are at the top of your screen, then the menus will change when you activate the different windows (usually by clicking on them). You may also have, for each window, context-sensitive pop-up menus that appear when you press the right or center button of your mouse.

**Toolbar** The toolbar, if you have one, gives you quick access to commands that are already accessible through the pull-down menus. Not all operating environments have a toolbar.

**SAS command bar** The command bar is a place that you can type in SAS commands. In some operating environments the command bar is located with the toolbar (as shown here); in other operating environments you may have a command line with each of the SAS windows (usually indicated by `Command=>`). Most of the commands that you can type in the command bar are also accessible through the pull-down menus or the toolbar.

**Controlling your windows** The Window pull-down menu gives you choices on how the windows are placed on your screen. You can also activate any of the programming windows by selecting it from the Window pull-down menu, typing the name of the window in the command line area of your SAS session, or simply clicking on the window.

##  1.7    Submitting a Program in the SAS Windowing Environment

Naturally after going to the trouble of writing SAS programs, you want to see some results. As we have already discussed, there are several ways of submitting SAS programs. If you use the SAS windowing environment, then you can edit and submit programs, and see results all within the windowing environment.

**Getting your program into the editor**  The first thing you need to do is get your program into the Editor window. You can either type your program into the editor, or you can bring the program into the Editor window from a file. The commands for editing in the editor and for opening files should be familiar. SAS tries to follow conventions that are common for your operating environment. For example, to open a file in the editor, you can select Open from the File pull-down menu. For some operating environments you may have an Open icon on the toolbar, and you may also have the option of pasting your file into the editor from the clipboard.

**Submitting your program**  Once your program appears in the editor, you execute it (either the whole program, or a part you have highlighted) using the SUBMIT command. Depending on your operating environment, you have a few choices on how to execute the SUBMIT command.

Use the Submit icon on the toolbar.

Make the Editor window active and enter SUBMIT in the command line area of your SAS session.

Make the Editor window active and select Submit from the Run pull-down menu.

The figure to the right shows a program in the Enhanced Editor in the Windows operating environment ready to be submitted using the Submit icon on the toolbar.

**Viewing the SAS Log and Output** If you are using the Enhanced Editor (Windows operating environment), after you submit your program, the program remains in the Enhanced Editor window and the results of your program go into the Log and Output windows. If you are using the Program Editor (all other operating environments) then your results also go into the Log and Output windows, but your program disappears from the Program Editor window. At first it may be a shock for you to see your program disappear in front of your eyes. Don't worry; the program you spent so long writing is not gone forever. If your program produced any output, then you will also get new entries in the Results window. The Results window is like a table of contents for your SAS output and is discussed in more detail in section 1.9. This figure is an example of what your screen might look like after you submit a program from the Enhanced Editor.

You may not see all three of the programming windows (Editor, Log, and Output) at the same time. In some operating environments, the windows are placed one on top of the other. You can bring a window to the top by clicking on it, typing its name in the command line area, or selecting it from the Window menu.

### Getting your program back

Unfortunately for most of us, our programs do not run perfectly every time. If you have an error in your program, you will most likely want to edit the program and run it again. If you are using the Enhanced Editor, then your program will remain in the window after you submit it. However, if you are using the Program Editor window, you will need to get your program back in the Program Editor window using the RECALL command. You have two choices for executing the RECALL command.

Make the Program Editor the active window, then enter RECALL in the command line area of your SAS session.

Make the Program Editor the active window, then select `Recall Last Submit` from the Run pull-down menu.

The RECALL command will bring back the last block of statements you submitted. If you use the RECALL command again, it will insert the block of statements submitted before the last one, and so on and so on, until it retrieves all the statements you submitted.

# 1.8  Reading the SAS Log

Every time you run a SAS job, SAS writes messages in your log. Many SAS programmers ignore the SAS log and go straight to the output. That's understandable, but dangerous. It is possible—and sooner or later it happens to all of us—to get bogus results that look fine in the output. The only way to know they are bad is to check the SAS log. Just because it runs doesn't mean it's right.

**Where to find the SAS log**  The location of the SAS log varies depending on the operating environment you use, the mode you use (SAS windowing environment, noninteractive, or batch), and local settings. If you submit a program in the windowing environment, you will, by default, see the SAS log in your Log window as in the following figure.

If you submit your program in batch or noninteractive mode, the log will be written to a file that you can view or print using your operating environment's commands for viewing and printing. The name given to the log file is generally some permutation of the name you gave the original program. For example, if you named your SAS program Marathon.sas, then it is a good bet that your log file will be Marathon.log. At some installations the log and output files are written to a single file, so don't be surprised if you find them together.

**What the log contains**  People tend to think of the SAS log as either a rehash of their program or as just a lot of gibberish. OK, we admit, there is some technical trivia in the SAS log, but there is also plenty of important information. Here is a simple program that converts miles to kilometers and prints the result:

```
* Create a SAS data set named distance;
* Convert miles to kilometers;
DATA distance;
   Miles = 26.22;
   Kilometers = 1.61 * Miles;
RUN;
* Print the results;
PROC PRINT DATA = distance;
RUN;
```

If you run this program, SAS will produce a log similar to this:

```
❶ NOTE: Copyright (c) 2002-2008 by SAS Institute Inc., Cary, NC, USA.
   NOTE: SAS (r) Proprietary Software Version 9.2 (TS1M0)
         Licensed to XYZ Inc., Site 0099999001.
   NOTE: This session is executing on the W32_VSPRO  platform.

   NOTE: SAS initialization used:
         real time               1.40 seconds
         cpu time                0.96 seconds

❷ 1     * Create a SAS data set named distance;
   2     * Convert miles to kilometers;
   3     DATA distance;
   4        Miles = 26.22;
   5        Kilometers = 1.61 * Miles;
   6     RUN;

❸ NOTE: The data set WORK.DISTANCE has 1 observations and 2 variables.
❹ NOTE: DATA statement used (Total process time):
         real time               0.03 seconds
         cpu time                0.03 seconds

❷ 7     * Print the results;
   8     PROC PRINT DATA = distance;
   9     RUN;

   NOTE: There were 1 observations read from the data set WORK.DISTANCE
❹ NOTE: PROCEDURE PRINT used (Total process time):
         real time               0.01 seconds
         cpu time                0.00 seconds
```

The SAS log above is a blow-by-blow account of how SAS executes the program.

❶ It starts with notes about the version of SAS and your SAS site number.

❷ It contains the original program statements with line numbers added on the left.

❸ The DATA step is followed by a note containing the name of the SAS data set created (WORK.DISTANCE), and the number of observations (1) and variables (2). A quick glance is enough to assure you that you did not lose any observations or accidentally create a lot of unwanted variables.

❹ Both DATA and PROC steps produce a note about the computer resources used. At first you probably won't care in the least. But if you run on a multi-user system or have long jobs with large data sets, these statistics may start to pique your interest. If you ever find yourself wondering why your job takes so long to run, a glance at the SAS log will tell you which steps are the culprits.

If there were error messages, they would appear in the log, indicating where SAS got confused and what action it took. You may also find warnings and other types of notes which sometimes indicate errors and other times just provide useful information.

## 1.9 ▶ Viewing Your Results in the Output Window

How you view or print your output depends on how you submit your program. If you submit your program in the SAS windowing environment, then your output will, by default, go to the Output window. If you choose another way to submit your program, either batch or noninteractive, then your output will probably be in a file on your computer. Use your operating environment's commands to view and print the output file (also called the listing). For example, if you execute your SAS program in noninteractive mode on a UNIX system, then your output will be in a file with an extension .lst. To view the file, you can use either the `cat` or `more` commands, and to print the file you would use your system's command for printing files (usually you would type either `lp` or `lpr`).

**The Output window**    After submitting your program in the SAS windowing environment, your results will go to the Output window. If you have the SAS Explorer option turned on (some operating environments have this turned on by default, while others do not), then you will also see a listing of the different parts of your output in your Results window. The following figure shows what your Output window might look like after submitting a simple program under Windows.

**Printing or saving the contents of the Output window**    If you want to print or save the entire contents of the Output window, first make the Output window active by clicking in it, then select either `Print` or `Save As` from the File pull-down menu. If you are not using a personal computer, then your environment may not be set up for printing from within SAS. If you cannot print from within SAS, then save the output to a file and use your system's command for printing files.

**The Results window**    When you have a lot of output, the Results window can be very helpful. The Results window is like a table of contents for your output. It lists each procedure that produces output, and if you open, or expand, the procedure in the Results tree, you can see each part of the procedure output. The following figure shows what your screen might look like if you ran the ANOVA (Analysis of Variance) procedure.

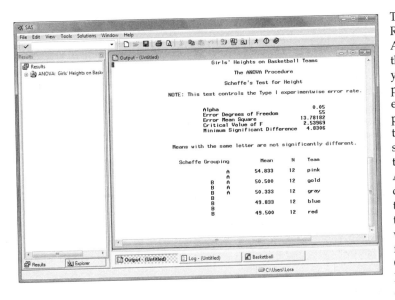

There is one entry in the Results window for the ANOVA procedure. Notice that in the Output window, you see the end of the procedure's output. If you expand the ANOVA procedure in the results tree, by clicking the plus (+) signs, then you will see all the different parts of the ANOVA output. Double-click the output you want to see, and it will appear at the top of the Output window. The following figure shows what your Output window would look like after you double-click on the `Overall ANOVA` item in the Results window.

## Printing or saving parts of the output

Using the Results window, it is possible to print or save just the parts of the output you want. First highlight the item you want in the Results window, then bring up the context-sensitive menu. In the Windows operating environment you do this with the right mouse button; in other operating environments, it may be the middle or right mouse button. Then select either `Print` or `Save As` from the pop-up menu. You may also be able to print or save from the File pull-down menu once you highlight the output part you want. If your SAS environment is not set up for printing from within SAS, then save your results to a file and use your operating environment's command for printing files.

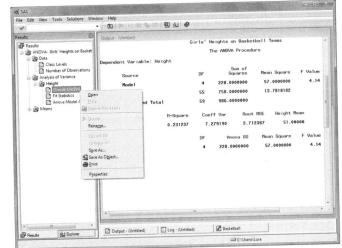

## 1.10  Creating HTML Output

If you are using the SAS windowing environment, then you can create output in Hypertext Markup Language (HTML) format with just a few clicks of your mouse.[1]

**The Preferences window**  To turn on HTML output (in Windows, UNIX, or OpenVMS[2]), select `Options-Preferences` from the Tools menu. This opens the Preferences window. Click the Results tab to bring it to the front. Here is what the Results portion of the Preferences window looks like in Windows.

When you first open this window, you will see a check next to `Create Listing`. Listing is the default type of output, and it is what you see in the Output window if you are using the SAS windowing environment, or in the output or listing file if you are running in batch mode. You can turn on HTML output by clicking the box next to `Create HTML`. To turn off the listing or HTML output, just click to un-check it.

In the Preferences window, you can also select a style for HTML output by clicking the arrow next to the Style box and scrolling through the list of styles provided with SAS. When you are done with the Preferences window, click the OK button.

**The Results Viewer and Results windows**  Once you have turned on HTML output, then every time you run a program, your output will automatically appear in the Results Viewer window. The following figure shows what you see after running two simple procedures: MEANS and PRINT. Two windows are showing: the Results Viewer window displaying the HTML output, and the Results window listing all the pieces of output in tree form.

---

[1] If you are not using the SAS windowing environment, you can still produce HTML output by using ODS statements (see chapter 5).

[2] If you are using z/OS, you will need to modify your registry settings in order to generate HTML interactively. Contact your site's SAS Support Personnel for more information.

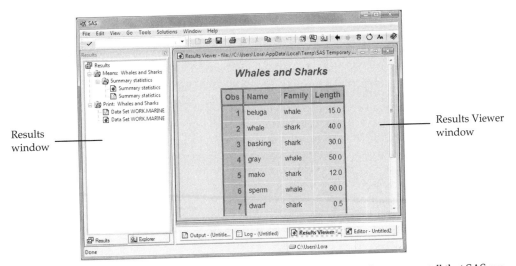

Results window

Results Viewer window

The Results Viewer window shows you only one piece of output at a time, but you can tell that SAS ran both procedures by looking at the list in the Results window. You can expand the list by clicking the plus (+) signs, or collapse it by clicking the minus (-) signs. Since both the listing and HTML output were turned on, each procedure produced two pieces of output: one for listing, and one for HTML. You can display any piece of output by double-clicking its name in the Results window.

To save a piece of output in a file, make the Results Viewer window active by clicking it, then click the File menu, and choose Save As.... To print a piece of output, select Print from the File menu.

The preceding screen used the DEFAULT style which is the default for HTML output. To see the same output with a different style, just choose a different style in the Preferences window, and re-run your program. Here is the output from the same program using the D3D style.

## 1.11  SAS Data Libraries

Before you can use a SAS data set, you have to tell SAS where to find it. You do that by setting up a SAS library. A SAS library is simply a location where SAS data sets (as well as other types of SAS files) are stored. Depending on your operating environment, a SAS library might be a folder or directory on your computer, or it might be a physical location like a hard drive, flash drive, or CD. To set up a library, all you have to do is make up a name for your library and tell SAS where it is. There are several ways to do this including using the LIBNAME statement (covered in sections 2.19 to 2.20) and using the New Library window in the SAS windowing environment.

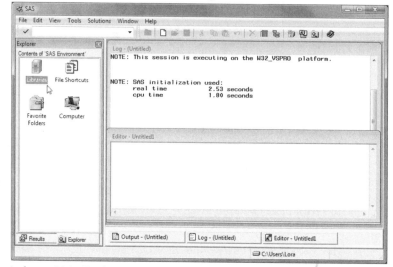

When you start the SAS windowing environment, you see the basic SAS windows including the SAS Explorer window on the left. (If the Explorer window is under the Results window, click its tab to bring it forward.) If you double-click the Libraries icon, Explorer will open the Active Libraries window showing all the libraries that are currently defined. To go back to the previous window within Explorer, choose Up one level from the View menu, or click in the Explorer window to make it active and then click the Up One Level button on the toolbar.

**The Active Libraries window**  When you open the Active Libraries window, you will see at least three libraries: SASHELP, SASUSER, and WORK. You may have other libraries for specific SAS products (such as the MAPS library for SAS/GRAPH software), or libraries that have been set up by you or someone you work with. The SASHELP library contains information that controls your SAS session along with sample SAS data sets. The WORK library is a temporary storage location for SAS data sets. It is also the default library. If you create a SAS data set without specifying a library, SAS will put it in the WORK library, and then delete it when you end your session. If you make changes to the default settings for the SAS windowing environment, this information will be stored in the SASUSER library. You can also store SAS data sets, SAS programs, and other SAS files in the SASUSER library. However, many people prefer to create a new library for their SAS files.

**Creating a new library**  You can create new SAS libraries using the New Library window. To open this window, either left-click in the Active Libraries window (to make it active) and choose New from the File menu, or right-click in the Active Libraries window and choose New from the pop-up menu.

In the New Library window, type the name of the library you want to create. This name is called a libref which is short for library reference. A libref must be 8 characters or fewer; start with a letter or underscore; and contain only letters, numerals, or underscores. In this window, the name BIKES has been typed in as the libref. In the Path field, enter the complete path to the folder or directory where you want your data sets to be stored, or choose the Browse… button to navigate to the location. If you don't want to define your library reference every time you start up SAS, then check the Enable at startup box. Click OK and then your new library reference will appear in the Active Libraries window.

Here is the Active Libraries window showing the newly created BIKES library.

# 1.12   Viewing Data Sets in the Viewtable Window

In addition to listing your current libraries and creating new libraries, you can also use SAS Explorer to open SAS data sets for viewing in Viewtable. When you are writing programs it is always a good idea to check the data sets you create to make sure they are correct. Viewtable is one way you can look at your SAS data sets.

Start by double-clicking the Libraries icon in the Explorer window as shown in the previous section. This will open the Active Libraries window showing all the libraries that are currently defined on your system. If you double-click a library icon, SAS will open a Contents window showing you all the SAS files in that particular library.

To go back to the previous window within Explorer, choose `Up one level` from the View menu, or click in the Explorer window to make it active and then click the Up One Level button on the toolbar.

**The Contents window**   This window shows the contents of a library. SAS data sets are represented by an icon showing a little table of data and a red ball, so the library shown on the right contains three data sets named CUSTOMERS, MODELS, and ORDERS. If you double-click a data set, SAS will open a Viewtable window showing that data set. (If you don't yet have any SAS data sets of your own, you can view sample data sets that are provided with SAS in the SASHELP library. The CLASS data set in the SASHELP library is a good one to view.)

**The Viewtable window**   This window allows you to create, browse, and edit data sets. When you first open SAS data sets, the data are in browse mode so you cannot make any changes. To switch to edit mode, select `Edit Mode` from the Edit menu. Creating and editing data sets using Viewtable is discussed in more detail in section 2.2. This picture shows the data set named MODELS from the BIKES library.

| | Model Name | Type of Bicycle | List Price | Frame Composition |
|---|---|---|---|---|
| 1 | Black Bora | Track | $796.00 | Aluminum |
| 2 | Delta Breze | Road | $399.00 | CroMoly |
| 3 | Jet Stream | Track | $1,130.00 | CroMoly |
| 4 | Mistral | Road | $1,995.00 | Carbon Comp |
| 5 | Nor'easter | Mountain | $899.00 | Aluminum |
| 6 | Santa Ana | Mountain | $459.00 | Aluminum |
| 7 | Scirocco | Mountain | $2,256.00 | Titanium |
| 8 | Trade Wind | Road | $759.00 | Aluminum |

VIEWTABLE: Bikes.Models

**Changing column headings**  By default, Viewtable uses variable labels for column headings or, if a variable does not have a label, the variable name is displayed. Sometimes you may want to see the actual variable names instead of the labels. To do this, click the Viewtable window to make it active, then select Column Names from the View menu. Here is the MODELS SAS data set showing the column (also called variable) names instead of the labels.

| | Model | Type | Price | Frame |
|---|---|---|---|---|
| 1 | Black Bora | Track | $796.00 | Aluminum |
| 2 | Delta Breze | Road | $399.00 | CroMoly |
| 3 | Jet Stream | Track | $1,130.00 | CroMoly |
| 4 | Mistral | Road | $1,995.00 | Carbon Comp |
| 5 | Nor'easter | Mountain | $899.00 | Aluminum |
| 6 | Santa Ana | Mountain | $459.00 | Aluminum |
| 7 | Scirocco | Mountain | $2,256.00 | Titanium |
| 8 | Trade Wind | Road | $759.00 | Aluminum |

VIEWTABLE: Bikes.Models

**Column options**  If you right-click a column heading, several options will appear in the pop-up menu. You can control colors, fonts, and view the column attributes. You can choose to sort the data by the values in the column. If you are not in edit mode, then you are given the option of creating a new data set containing the sorted data. You can also hide or hold columns. If you choose to hide a column, the data will not be visible in the current Viewtable session. To unhide a column, select Hide/Unhide from the Data menu item to open the Hide/Unhide window. In this window you can change the visibility of all columns. When you choose to hold a column, it and every column to the left of it will always be visible, even when you scroll to the right.

VIEWTABLE: Bikes.Models

| | Model | | ice | Frame |
|---|---|---|---|---|
| 1 | Black Bora | Colors... | $796.00 | Aluminum |
| 2 | Delta Breze | Fonts... | $399.00 | CroMoly |
| 3 | Jet Stream | Sort | $1,130.00 | CroMoly |
| 4 | Mistral | Hide | $1,995.00 | Carbon Comp |
| 5 | Nor'easter | Hold | $899.00 | Aluminum |
| 6 | Santa Ana | Column Description | $459.00 | Aluminum |
| 7 | Scirocco | Column Attributes... | $2,256.00 | Titanium |
| 8 | Trade Wind | | $759.00 | Aluminum |

## 1.13   Viewing the Properties of Data Sets with SAS Explorer

The Properties window for a SAS data set contains some very useful information, such as the date and time the data set was created, the number of observations, all the variable names, and the attributes of the variables. The Properties window contains information similar to the output produced by the CONTENTS procedure described in section 2.22.

**Opening the Properties window**  To open the Properties window, start by double-clicking the Libraries icon in the Explorer window and then double-clicking the library containing the SAS data set. SAS will display the contents of the library in the Explorer window. Right-click the icon for the data set, and select Properties from the pop-up menu. This opens the Properties window with the General tab on top.[1]

**The General tab**   This window displays information about the data set such as the date it was created and the number of rows (or observations) and columns (or variables).

---

**The Columns tab** If you click the Columns tab, SAS displays information about the columns (or variables) in that data set. The variable name, type, and length are displayed along with any formats or informats assigned to the variable. The variable labels are also displayed in this window, but to see them, you need to scroll to the right.

You can also sort any of these columns alphabetically by clicking the column heading, or use the Find feature to look for specific variables. This window shows the variables sorted by name. If you have lots of variables in your data set, using the Sort and Find features can make your work easier.

# 1.14  Using SAS System Options

System options are parameters you can change that affect SAS—how it works, what the output looks like, how much memory is used, error handling, and a host of other things. SAS makes many assumptions about how you want it to work. This is good. You do not want to specify every little detail each time you use SAS. However, you may not always like the assumptions SAS makes. System options give you a way to change some of these assumptions.

Not all options are available for all operating environments. A list of options specific to your operating environment appears in the SAS Help and Documentation. You can see a list of system options and their current values by opening the SAS System Options window or by using the OPTIONS procedure. To use the OPTIONS procedure, submit the following SAS program and view the results in the SAS log:

```
PROC OPTIONS;
RUN;
```

There are four ways to specify system options. Some options can be specified using only some of these methods. The SAS Help and Documentation for your operating environment tells you which methods are valid for each system option:

1. Your system administrator (this could be you if you are using a PC) can create a SAS configuration file which contains settings for the system options. This file is accessed by SAS every time SAS is started.

2. Specify system options at the time you start up SAS from your system's prompt (called the invocation).

3. Change selected options in the SAS System Options window if you are using the SAS windowing environment.

4. Use the OPTIONS statement as a part of your SAS program.

The methods are listed here in order of increasing precedence; method 2 will override method 1, method 3 will override method 2, and so forth. If you are using the SAS windowing environment, methods 3 and 4, the SAS System Options window and OPTIONS statement, will override each other—so whichever was used last will be in effect. Only the last two methods are covered here. The first two methods are very system dependent; to find out more about these methods see the SAS Help and Documentation for your operating environment.

**OPTIONS statement**  The OPTIONS statement is part of a SAS program and affects all steps that follow it. It starts with the keyword OPTIONS and follows with a list of options and their values. For example

```
OPTIONS LINESIZE = 80 NODATE;
```

The OPTIONS statement is one of the special SAS statements which do not belong to either a PROC or a DATA step. This global statement can appear anywhere in your SAS program, but it usually makes the most sense to let it be the first line in your program. This way you can easily see which options are in effect. If the OPTIONS statement is in a DATA or PROC step, then it affects that step and the following steps. Any subsequent OPTIONS statements in a program override previous ones.

## The SAS System Options
**window** You can view and change SAS system options through the SAS System Options window. Open it either by typing OPTIONS in the command line area on your screen, or by selecting it from the Tools pull-down menu. To change the value of an option, first locate the option by clicking on the appropriate category on the left side of the screen. A list of options and their current values will appear on the right side of the screen. Right-click the option itself to modify the value or set it to the default.

**Common options** The following are some common system options you might want to use:

| | |
|---|---|
| CENTER \| NOCENTER | Controls whether output is centered or left-justified. Default: CENTER. |
| DATE \| NODATE | Controls whether or not today's date will appear at the top of each page of output. Default: DATE. |
| LINESIZE = *n* | Controls the maximum length of output lines. Possible values for *n* are 64 to 256. Default varies. |
| NUMBER \| NONUMBER | Controls whether or not page numbers appear on each page of SAS output. Default: NUMBER. |
| ORIENTATION = PORTRAIT ORIENTATION = LANDSCAPE | Specifies the orientation for printing output. Default: PORTRAIT |
| PAGENO = *n* | Starts numbering output pages with *n*. Default is 1. |
| PAGESIZE = *n* | Controls the maximum number of lines per page of output. Possible values for *n* are 15 to 32767. Default varies. |
| RIGHTMARGIN = *n* LEFTMARGIN = *n* TOPMARGIN = *n* BOTTOMMARGIN = *n* | Specifies size of margin (such as 0.75in or 2cm) to be used for printing output. Default: 0.00in. |
| YEARCUTOFF = *yyyy* | Specifies the first year in a hundred-year span for interpreting two-digit dates. Default: 1920. |

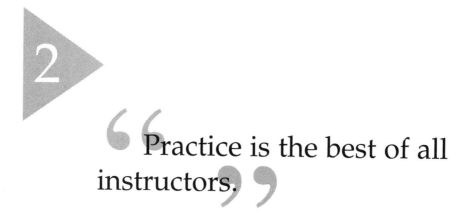

**2**

" Practice is the best of all instructors. "

PUBLIUS SYRUS, CIRCA 42 B.C

" We all learned by doing, by experimenting (and often failing), and by asking questions. "

JAY JACOB WIND

From *Bartlett's Familiar Quotations* 13th edition, by John Bartlett, copyright 1955 by Little Brown & Company. Public domain.
From the SAS L Listserv, March 15, 1994. Reprinted by permission of the author.

# CHAPTER 2

# Getting Your Data into SAS

## 2.1 Methods for Getting Your Data into SAS

Data come in many different forms. Your data may be handwritten on a piece of paper, or typed into a raw data file on your computer. Perhaps your data are in a database file on your personal computer, or in a database management system (DBMS) on the mainframe computer at your office. Wherever your data reside, there is a way for SAS to use them. You may need to convert your data from one form to another, or SAS may be able to use your data in their current form. This section outlines several methods for getting your data into SAS. Most of these methods are covered in this book, but a few of the more advanced methods are merely mentioned so that you know they exist. We do not attempt to cover all methods available for getting your data into SAS, as new methods are continually being developed, and creative SAS users can always come up with clever methods that work for their own situations. But there should be at least one method explained in this book that will work for you.

Methods for getting your data into SAS can be put into four general categories:

- ◆ entering data directly into SAS data sets

- ◆ creating SAS data sets from raw data files

- ◆ converting other software's data files into SAS data sets

- ◆ reading other software's data files directly.

Naturally, the method you choose will depend on where your data are located, and what software tools are available to you.

**Entering data directly into SAS data sets** Sometimes the best method for getting your data into SAS is to enter the data directly into SAS data sets through your keyboard.

- ◆ The Viewtable window, discussed in section 2.2, is included with Base SAS software. Viewtable allows you to enter your data in a tabular format. You can define variables, or columns, and give them attributes such as name, length, and type (character or numeric).

- ◆ SAS Enterprise Guide software, which is included with Base SAS for Windows, has a data entry window that is very similar to the Viewtable window. As with Viewtable, you can define variables and give them attributes.

- ◆ SAS/FSP software, short for Full Screen Product, allows you to design custom data entry screens. It also has the capability for detecting data entry errors as they happen. The SAS/FSP product is licensed separately from Base SAS software.

**Creating SAS data sets from raw data files** Much of this chapter is devoted to reading raw data files (also referred to as text, ASCII, sequential, or flat files). You can always read a raw data file since the DATA step is an integral part of Base SAS software. And, if your data are not already in a raw data file, chances are you can convert your data into a raw data file. There are two general methods for reading raw data files:

- ◆ The DATA step is so versatile that it can read almost any type of raw data file. This method is covered in this chapter starting with section 2.4.

♦   The Import Wizard, covered in section 2.3 and its cousin the IMPORT procedure, covered in section 2.16, are available for UNIX, OpenVMS, and Windows operating environments. These are simple methods for reading particular types of raw data files including comma-separated values (CSV) files, and other delimited files.

## Converting other software's data files into SAS data sets  Each software application has its own form for data files. While this is useful for software developers, it is troublesome for software users—especially when your data are in one application, but you need to analyze them with another. There are several options for converting data from applications into SAS data sets:

♦   The IMPORT procedure and the Import Wizard can be used to convert Microsoft Excel, Lotus, dBase, Stata, SPSS, JMP, Paradox, and Microsoft Access files into SAS data sets if you have SAS/ACCESS Interface to PC Files installed on your computer. This is covered in sections 2.3 and 2.17.

♦   If you don't have SAS/ACCESS software, then you can always create a raw data file from your application and read the raw data file with either the DATA step or the IMPORT procedure. Many applications can create CSV files, which are easily read using the Import Wizard or IMPORT procedure (covered in sections 2.3 and 2.16) or the DATA step (covered in section 2.15).

♦   Dynamic Data Exchange (DDE), covered in section 2.18, is available only for those working in the Windows operating environment. To use DDE, you must have the other Windows application (Microsoft Excel for example) running on your computer at the same time as SAS. Then using DDE and the DATA step, you can convert data into SAS data sets.

## Reading other software's data files directly  Under certain circumstances you may be able to read data without converting to a SAS data set. This method is particularly useful when you have many people updating data files, and you want to make sure that you are using the most current data.

♦   The SAS/ACCESS products allow you to read data without converting your data into SAS data sets. There are SAS/ACCESS products for most of the popular database management systems including ORACLE, DB2, INGRES, and SYBASE. This method of data access is not covered in this book.

♦   We already mentioned using SAS/ACCESS Interface to PC Files to convert several PC file types to SAS data sets, but you can also use the Excel and Access engines to read these types of files directly without converting. See the SAS Help and Documentation for more information on these engines.

♦   There are also data engines that allow you to read data directly but are part of Base SAS software. The SPSS engine is covered in appendix B. There are also engines for OSIRIS, old versions of SAS data sets, and SAS data sets in transport format. Check the SAS Help and Documentation for your operating environment for a complete list of available engines.

Given all these methods for getting your data into SAS, you are sure to find at least one method that will work for you—probably more.

## 2.2 Entering Data with the Viewtable Window

The Viewtable window which is part of Base SAS software[1] is an easy way to create new data sets, or browse and edit existing data sets. True to its name, the Viewtable window displays tables (another name for data sets) in a tabular format. To open the Viewtable window, select `Table Editor` from the Tools menu. An empty Viewtable window will appear.

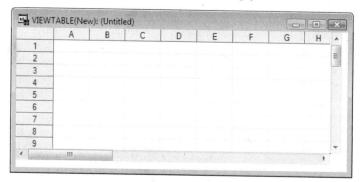

This table contains no data. Instead you see rows (or observations) labeled with numbers and columns (or variables) labeled with letters. You can start typing data into this default table, and SAS will automatically figure out if your columns are numeric or character. However, it's a good idea to tell SAS about your data so each column is set up the way you want. You do this with the Column Attributes window.

**Column Attributes window**  The letters at the tops of columns are default variable names. By right-clicking a letter, you can choose to open a Column Attributes window for that column. This window contains default values which you can replace with the values you desire. If you plan to enter date values, then you should choose a date informat so that dates entered will be automatically converted to SAS date values.[2] See sections 2.7 and 2.8 for more on informats. If you also choose a date format, then the dates will be displayed as readable dates. See sections 4.5 and 4.6 for more on formats. When you are satisfied with the values, click Apply. To switch to a new column, click that column in the Viewtable window. When you are finished changing column attributes click Close.

---

[1] If you are using a non-graphical monitor, then SAS uses FSVIEW to display your tables, so you also need SAS/FSP software which is licensed separately.

[2] SAS date values are the number of days since January 1, 1960.

**Entering data** Once you have defined your columns you are ready to type in your data. To move the cursor, click a field, or use tab and arrow keys. Here is a table with column attributes defined and data entered.

**Saving your table** To save a table, select `Save As...` from the File menu. Select a library, and then specify the member name of your table. The libraries displayed correspond to locations (such as directories) on your computer. If you want to save your table in a different location, you can add another library by clicking the New Library icon. Type in a name for the new library and its path. Then click OK. Specify the member name by typing it in the `Member Name` field.

**Opening an existing table** To browse or edit an existing table, first select `Table Editor` from the Tools menu to open the Viewtable window. Then select `Open` from the File menu. Click the library you want and then the table name. If the table you want to open is not in any of the existing libraries, click the New Library icon. Type in a name for the new library and its path. Then click OK. To switch from browse mode (the default) to edit mode, select `Edit Mode` from the Edit menu. You can also open an existing table by navigating to it in the SAS Explorer window, and double-clicking it.

**Other features** The Viewtable window has many other features including sorting, printing, adding and deleting rows, and viewing multiple rows (the default, called Table View) or viewing one row at a time (called Form View). You can control these features using either menus or icons.

**Using your table in a SAS program** Tables that you create in Viewtable can be used in programs just as tables created in programs can be used in Viewtable. For example, if you saved your table in the SASUSER library and named it COFFEE, you could print it with this program:

```
PROC PRINT DATA=Sasuser.coffee;
RUN;
```

## 2.3    Reading Files with the Import Wizard

Using the Import Wizard,[1] you can convert a variety of data file types into SAS data sets by simply answering a few questions. The Import Wizard will scan your file to determine variable types[2] and will, by default, use the first row of data for the variable names. The Import Wizard can read all types of delimited files including comma-separated values (CSV) files which are a common file type for moving data between applications. And, if you have SAS/ACCESS Interface to PC Files, then you can also read a number of popular PC file types.[3]

Start the Import Wizard by choosing `Import Data...` from the File menu.

Select the type of file you are importing by choosing from the list of standard data sources such as comma-separated values (*.csv) files.

Now, specify the location of the file that you want to import. By default, SAS uses the first row in the file as the variable names for the SAS data set, and starts reading data in the second row. The `Options...` button takes you to another screen where you can change this default action.

---

[1] The Import Wizard is available in the Windows, UNIX, and OpenVMS operating environments.

[2] By default the Import Wizard will scan the first 20 rows for delimited files and the first 8 rows for Microsoft Excel files. If you have all missing data in these rows, or the data are not representative of the entire file, then the Import Wizard (and the IMPORT procedure) may not read the file correctly. See sections 2.16 and 2.17 for more information.

[3] Under Windows and UNIX you can read dBase files, and starting with SAS 9.2, SPSS, Stata, JMP, and Paradox files. Under Windows you can read Excel and Lotus files, and under 32-bit Windows you can also read Microsoft Access files.

The next screen asks you to choose the SAS library and member name for the SAS data set that will be created. If you choose the WORK library, then the SAS data set will be deleted when you exit SAS. If you choose a different library, then the SAS data set will remain even after you exit SAS. There is no way to define a library from within the Import Wizard, so make sure your library is defined before entering the Import Wizard. You can define libraries using the New Library window discussed in section 1.11 (or using a LIBNAME statement as discussed in section 2.20). After choosing a library, enter a member name for the SAS data set.

In the last window, the Import Wizard gives you the option of saving the PROC IMPORT statements used for importing the file.

For some types of files, the Import Wizard asks additional questions. For example, if you are importing Microsoft Access files, then you will be asked for the database name and the table you want to import. You will also be given an opportunity to enter user ID and password information if applicable.

### Using imported data in a SAS program
Data that you import through the Import Wizard can be used in any SAS program. For example, if you saved your data in the WORK library and named it BANDS, you could print it with this program:

```
PROC PRINT DATA=WORK.bands;
RUN;
```

Or, since WORK is the default library, you could also use:

```
PROC PRINT DATA=bands;
RUN;
```

## 2.4 Telling SAS Where to Find Your Raw Data

If your data are in raw data files (also referred to as text, ASCII, sequential, or flat files), using the DATA step to read the data gives you the most flexibility. The first step toward reading raw data files is telling SAS where to find the raw data. Your raw data may be either internal to your SAS program, or in a separate file. Either way, you must tell SAS where to find your data.

A raw data file can be viewed using simple text editors or system commands. For PC users, raw data files will either have no program associated with them, or they will be associated with simple editors like Microsoft Notepad. In some operating environments, you can use commands to list the file, such as the `cat` or `more` commands in UNIX. Spreadsheet files are examples of data files that are not raw data. If you try using a text editor to look at a spreadsheet file, you will probably see lots of funny special characters you can't find on your keyboard. It may cause your computer to beep and chirp, making you wish you had that private office down the hall. It looks nothing like the nice neat rows and columns you see when you use your spreadsheet software to view the same file.

**Internal raw data** If you type raw data directly in your SAS program, then the data are internal to your program. You may want to do this when you have small amounts of data, or when you are testing a program with a small test data set. Use the DATALINES statement to indicate internal data. The DATALINES statement must be the last statement in the DATA step. All lines in the SAS program following the DATALINES statement are considered data until SAS encounters a semicolon. The semicolon can be on a line by itself or at the end of a SAS statement which follows the data lines. Any statements following the data are part of a new step. If you are old enough to remember punching computer cards, you might like to use the CARDS statement instead. The CARDS statement and the DATALINES statement are synonymous. The following SAS program illustrates the use of the DATALINES statement. (The DATA statement simply tells SAS to create a SAS data set named USPRESIDENTS, and the INPUT statement tells SAS how to read the data. The INPUT statement is discussed in sections 2.5 through 2.15.)

```
* Read internal data into SAS data set uspresidents;
DATA uspresidents;
   INPUT President $ Party $ Number;
   DATALINES;
Adams F 2
Lincoln R 16
Grant R 18
Kennedy D 35
   ;
RUN;
```

**External raw data files** Usually you will want to keep data in external files, separating the data from the program. This eliminates the chance that data will accidentally be altered when you are editing your SAS program. Use the INFILE statement to tell SAS the filename and path, if appropriate, of the external file containing the data. The INFILE statement follows the DATA statement and must precede the INPUT statement. After the INFILE keyword, the file path and name are enclosed in quotation marks. Examples from several operating environments follow:

| | |
|---|---|
| Windows: | INFILE 'c:\MyDir\President.dat'; |
| UNIX: | INFILE '/home/mydir/president.dat'; |
| Open VMS: | INFILE '[username.mydir]president.dat'; |
| z/OS: | INFILE 'MYID.PRESIDEN.DAT'; |

Suppose the following data are in a file called President.dat in the directory MyRawData on the C drive (Windows):

```
Adams F 2
Lincoln R 16
Grant R 18
Kennedy D 35
```

The following program shows the use of the INFILE statement to read the external data file:

```
* Read data from external file into SAS data set;
DATA uspresidents;
   INFILE 'c:\MyRawData\President.dat';
   INPUT President $ Party $ Number;
RUN;
```

**The SAS log** Whenever you read data from an external file, SAS gives some very valuable information about the file in the SAS log. The following is an excerpt from the SAS log after running the previous program. Always check this information after you read a file as it could indicate problems. A simple comparison of the number of records read from the infile with the number of observations in the SAS data set can tell you a lot about whether SAS is reading your data correctly.

```
NOTE: The infile 'c:\MyRawData\President.dat' is:
      File Name=c:\MyRawData\President.dat,
      RECFM=V,LRECL=256
NOTE: 4 records were read from the infile 'c:\MyRawData\President.dat'.
      The minimum record length was 9.
      The maximum record length was 12.
NOTE: The data set WORK.USPRESIDENTS has 4 observations and 3 variables.
```

**Long records** In some operating environments, SAS assumes external files have a record length of 256 or less. (The record length is the number of characters, including spaces, in a data line.) If your data lines are long, and it looks like SAS is not reading all your data, then use the LRECL= option in the INFILE statement to specify a record length at least as long as the longest record in your data file.

```
INFILE 'c:\MyRawData\President.dat' LRECL=2000;
```

Check the SAS log to see that the maximum record length is as long as you think it should be.

## 2.5   Reading Raw Data Separated by Spaces

If the values in your raw data file are all separated by at least one space,[1] then using list input (also called free formatted input) to read the data may be appropriate. List input is an easy way to read raw data into SAS, but with ease come a few limitations. You must read all the data in a record—no skipping over unwanted values. Any missing data must be indicated with a period. Character data, if present, must be simple: no embedded spaces, and no values greater than 8 characters in length.[2] If the data file contains dates or other values which need special treatment, then list input may not be appropriate. This may sound like a lot of restrictions, but a surprising number of data files can be read using list input.

The INPUT statement, which is part of the DATA step, tells SAS how to read your raw data. To write an INPUT statement using list input, simply list the variable names after the INPUT keyword in the order they appear in the data file. Generally, variable names must be 32 characters or fewer, start with a letter or an underscore, and contain only letters, underscores, or numerals. If the values are character (not numeric), then place a dollar sign ($) after the variable name. Leave at least one space between names, and remember to place a semicolon at the end of the statement. The following is an example of a simple list style INPUT statement.

```
INPUT Name $ Age Height;
```

This statement tells SAS to read three data values. The $ after Name indicates that it is a character variable, whereas the Age and Height variables are both numeric.

**Example**   Your hometown has been overrun with toads this year. A local resident, having heard of frog jumping in California, had the idea of organizing a toad jump to cap off the annual town fair. For each contestant you have the toad's name, weight, and the jump distance from three separate attempts. If the toad is disqualified for any jump, then a period is used to indicate missing data. Here is what the data file ToadJump.dat looks like:

```
Lucky 2.3 1.9 . 3.0
Spot 4.6 2.5 3.1 .5
Tubs 7.1 . . 3.8
Hop 4.5 3.2 1.9 2.6
Noisy 3.8 1.3 1.8
1.5
Winner 5.7 . . .
```

This data file does not look very neat, but it does meet all the requirements for list input: the character data are 8 characters or fewer and have no embedded spaces, all values are separated by at least one space, and missing data are indicated by a period. Notice that the data for Noisy have spilled over to the next data line. This is no problem since, by default, SAS will go to the next data line to read more data if there are more variables in the INPUT statement than there are values in the data line.

---

[1] SAS can read files with other delimiters such as commas or tabs using list input. See sections 2.14 and 2.15.

[2] It is possible to override this constraint using the LENGTH statement, discussed in section 10.13, which can change the length of character variables from the default of 8 to anything between 1 and 32,767.

Here is the SAS program that will read the data:

```
* Create a SAS data set named toads;
* Read the data file ToadJump.dat using list input;
DATA toads;
    INFILE 'c:\MyRawData\ToadJump.dat';
    INPUT ToadName $ Weight Jump1 Jump2 Jump3;
RUN;
* Print the data to make sure the file was read correctly;
PROC PRINT DATA = toads;
    TITLE 'SAS Data Set Toads';
RUN;
```

The variables ToadName, Weight, Jump1, Jump2, and Jump3 are listed after the keyword INPUT in the same order as they appear in the file. A dollar sign ($) after ToadName indicates that it is a character variable; all the other variables are numeric. A PROC PRINT statement is used to print the data values after reading them to make sure they are correct. The PRINT procedure, in its simplest form, prints the values for all variables and all observations in a SAS data set. The TITLE statement after the PROC PRINT tells SAS to put the text enclosed in quotation marks on the top of each page of output. If you had no TITLE statement in your program, SAS would put the words "The SAS System" at the top of each page.

Here are the results of the PRINT procedure. It is important to always check data sets you create to make sure they are correct. You can also use Viewtable (discussed in section 1.12) to view data.

```
                    SAS Data Set Toads                          1

           Toad
   Obs     Name      Weight    Jump1    Jump2    Jump3

    1      Lucky       2.3       1.9       .        3.0
    2      Spot        4.6       2.5      3.1       0.5
    3      Tubs        7.1        .        .        3.8
    4      Hop         4.5       3.2      1.9       2.6
    5      Noisy       3.8       1.3      1.8       1.5
    6      Winner      5.7        .        .         .
```

Because SAS had to go to a second data line to get the data for Noisy's final jump, the following note appears in the SAS log:

```
NOTE: SAS went to a new line when INPUT statement reached past the end of a line.
```

If you find this note in your SAS log when you didn't expect it, then you may have a problem. If so, look in section 10.4 which discusses this note in more detail.

## 2.6   Reading Raw Data Arranged in Columns

Some raw data files do not have spaces (or other delimiters) between all the values or periods for missing data—so the files can't be read using list input. But if each of the variable's values is always found in the same place in the data line, then you can use column input as long as all the values are character or standard numeric. Standard numeric data contain only numerals, decimal points, plus and minus signs, and E for scientific notation. Numbers with embedded commas or dates, for example, are not standard.

Column input has the following advantages over list input:

♦   spaces are not required between values

♦   missing values can be left blank

♦   character data can have embedded spaces

♦   you can skip unwanted variables.

Survey data are good candidates for column input. Most answers to survey questionnaires are single digits (0 through 9). If a space is entered between each value, then the file will be twice the size and require twice the typing of a file without spaces. Data files with street addresses, which often have embedded blanks, are also good candidates for column input. The street Martin Luther King Jr. Boulevard should be read as one variable not five, as it would be with list input. Data which can be read with column input can often also be read with formatted input or a combination of input styles (discussed in sections 2.7, 2.8, and 2.9).

With column input, the INPUT statement takes the following form: after the INPUT keyword, list the first variable's name. If the variable is character, leave a space; then place a $. After the $, or variable name if it is numeric, leave a space; then list the column or range of columns for that variable. The columns are positions of the characters or numbers in the data line and are not to be confused with columns like those you see in a spreadsheet. Repeat this for all the variables you want to read. The following shows a simple INPUT statement using column style:

```
INPUT Name $ 1-10 Age 11-13 Height 14-18;
```

The first variable, Name, is character and the data values are in columns 1 through 10. The Age and Height variables are both numeric, since they are not followed by a $, and data values for both of these variables are in the column ranges listed after their names.

**Example**   The local minor league baseball team, the Walla Walla Sweets, is keeping records about concession sales. A ballpark favorite are the sweet onion rings which are sold at the concession stands and also by vendors in the bleachers. The ballpark owners have a feeling that in games with lots of hits and runs more onion rings are sold in the bleachers than at the concession stands. They think they should send more vendors out into the bleachers when the game heats up, but need more evidence to back up their feelings.

For each home game they have the following information: name of opposing team, number of onion ring sales at the concession stands and in the bleachers, the number of hits for each team, and the final score for each team. The following is a sample of the data file named OnionRing.dat. For your reference, a column ruler showing the column numbers has been placed above the data:

```
----+----1----+----2----+----3----+----4
Columbia Peaches      35  67  1 10  2  1
Plains Peanuts       210      2  5  0  2
Gilroy Garlics       151035 12 11  7  6
Sacramento Tomatoes  124  85 15  4  9  1
```

Notice that the data file has the following characteristics, all making it a prime candidate for column input. All the values line up in columns, the team names have embedded blanks, missing values are blank, and in one case there is not a space between data values. (Those Gilroy Garlics fans must really love onion rings.)

The following program shows how to read these data using column input:

```
* Create a SAS data set named sales;
* Read the data file OnionRing.dat using column input;
DATA sales;
   INFILE 'c:\MyRawData\OnionRing.dat';
   INPUT VisitingTeam $ 1-20 ConcessionSales 21-24 BleacherSales 25-28
        OurHits 29-31 TheirHits 32-34 OurRuns 35-37 TheirRuns 38-40;
RUN;
* Print the data to make sure the file was read correctly;
PROC PRINT DATA = sales;
   TITLE 'SAS Data Set Sales';
RUN;
```

The variable VisitingTeam is character (indicated by a $) and reads the visiting team's name in columns 1 through 20. The variables ConcessionSales and BleacherSales read the concession and bleacher sales in columns 21 through 24 and 25 through 28, respectively. The number of hits for the home team, OurHits, and the visiting team, TheirHits, are read in columns 29 through 31 and 32 through 34, respectively. The number of runs for the home team, OurRuns, is read in columns 35 through 37, while the number of runs for the visiting team, TheirRuns, is in columns 38 through 40.

Here are the results of the PRINT procedure. You can also use Viewtable to view the data.

```
                      SAS Data Set Sales                          1

              Concession Bleacher  Our Their  Our Their
 Obs   VisitingTeam     Sales     Sales  Hits  Hits Runs  Runs

  1   Columbia Peaches    35        67     1    10    2    1
  2   Plains Peanuts     210         .     2     5    0    2
  3   Gilroy Garlics      15      1035    12    11    7    6
  4   Sacramento Tomatoes 124       85    15     4    9    1
```

## 2.7   Reading Raw Data Not in Standard Format

```
01/01/60  1,002          0  1002
01/03/60  2,012   ➡️     2  2012
02/01/60  4,336         31  4336
```

Sometimes raw data are not straightforward numeric or character. For example, we humans easily read the number 1,000,001 as one million and one, but your trusty computer sees it as a character string. While the embedded commas make the number easier for us to interpret, they make the number impossible for the computer to recognize without some instructions. In SAS, informats are used to tell the computer how to interpret these types of data.

Informats are useful anytime you have non-standard data. (Standard numeric data contain only numerals, decimal points, minus signs, and E for scientific notation.) Numbers with embedded commas or dollar signs are examples of non-standard data. Other examples include data in hexadecimal or packed decimal formats. SAS has informats for reading these types of data as well.

Dates[1] are perhaps the most common non-standard data. Using date informats, SAS will convert conventional forms of dates like 10-31-2007 or 31OCT07 into a number, the number of days since January 1, 1960. This number is referred to as a SAS date value. (Why January 1, 1960? Who knows? Maybe 1960 was a good year for the SAS founders.) This turns out to be extremely useful when you want to do calculations with dates. For example, you can easily find the number of days between two dates by subtracting one from the other.

There are three general types of informats: character, numeric, and date. A table of selected SAS informats appears in section 2.8. The three types of informats have the following general forms:

| **Character** | **Numeric** | **Date** |
|---|---|---|
| $informat*w*. | informat*w.d* | informat*w*. |

The $ indicates character informats, INFORMAT is the name of the informat, *w* is the total width, and *d* is the number of decimal places (numeric informats only). The period is very important part of the informat name. Without a period, SAS may try to interpret the informat as a variable name, which by default, cannot contain any special characters except the underscore. Two informats do not have names: $*w*., which reads standard character data, and *w.d*, which reads standard numeric data.

Use informats by placing the informat after the variable name in the INPUT statement; this is called formatted input. The following INPUT statement is an example of formatted input:

```
INPUT Name $10. Age 3. Height 5.1 BirthDate MMDDYY10.;
```

The columns read for each variable are determined by the starting point and the width of the informat. SAS always starts with the first column; so the data values for the first variable, Name, which has an informat of $10., are in columns 1 through 10. Now the starting point for the second variable is column 11, and SAS reads values for Age in columns 11 through 13. The values for the third variable, Height, are in columns 14 through 18. The five columns include the decimal place and the decimal point itself (150.3 for example). The values for the last variable, BirthDate, start in column 19 and are in a date form.

---

[1] Using dates in SAS is discussed in more detail in section 3.8.

**Example**  This example illustrates the use of informats for reading data. The following data file, Pumpkin.dat, represents the results from a local pumpkin-carving contest. Each line includes the contestant's name, age, type (carved or decorated), the date the pumpkin was entered, and the scores from each of five judges.

```
Alicia Grossman   13 c 10-28-2008 7.8 6.5 7.2 8.0 7.9
Matthew Lee        9 D 10-30-2008 6.5 5.9 6.8 6.0 8.1
Elizabeth Garcia  10 C 10-29-2008 8.9 7.9 8.5 9.0 8.8
Lori Newcombe      6 D 10-30-2008 6.7 5.6 4.9 5.2 6.1
Jose Martinez      7 d 10-31-2008 8.9 9.510.0 9.7 9.0
Brian Williams    11 C 10-29-2008 7.8 8.4 8.5 7.9 8.0
```

The following program reads these data. Please note there are many ways to input these data, so if you imagined something else, that's OK.

```
* Create a SAS data set named contest;
* Read the file Pumpkin.dat using formatted input;
DATA contest;
    INFILE 'c:\MyRawData\Pumpkin.dat';
    INPUT Name $16. Age 3. +1 Type $1. +1 Date MMDDYY10.
        (Score1 Score2 Score3 Score4 Score5) (4.1);
RUN;
* Print the data set to make sure the file was read correctly;
PROC PRINT DATA = contest;
    TITLE 'Pumpkin Carving Contest';
RUN;
```

The variable Name has an informat of $16., meaning that it is a character variable 16 columns wide. Variable Age has an informat of three, is numeric, three columns wide, and has no decimal places. The +1 skips over one column. Variable Type is character, and it is one column wide. Variable Date has an informat MMDDYY10. and reads dates in the form 10-31-2007 or 10/31/2007, each 10 columns wide. The remaining variables, Score1 through Score5, all require the same informat, 4.1. By putting the variables and the informat in separate sets of parentheses, you only have to list the informat once.

Here are the results of the PRINT procedure. You can also use Viewtable to view the data.

```
                    Pumpkin Carving Contest                          1

    Obs       Name       Age Type  Date² Score1 Score2 Score3 Score4 Score5

     1   Alicia Grossman  13   c   17467   7.8    6.5    7.2    8.0    7.9
     2   Matthew Lee       9   D   17469   6.5    5.9    6.8    6.0    8.1
     3   Elizabeth Garcia 10   C   17468   8.9    7.9    8.5    9.0    8.8
     4   Lori Newcombe     6   D   17469   6.7    5.6    4.9    5.2    6.1
     5   Jose Martinez     7   d   17470   8.9    9.5   10.0    9.7    9.0
     6   Brian Williams   11   C   17468   7.8    8.4    8.5    7.9    8.0
```

---

[2] Notice that these dates are printed as the number of days since January 1, 1960. Section 4.5 discusses how to format these values into readable dates.

## 2.8    Selected Informats

| Informat | Definition | Width range | Default width |
|---|---|---|---|
| **Character** | | | |
| $CHAR*w*. | Reads character data—does not trim leading or trailing blanks | 1–32,767 | 8 or length of variable |
| $HEX*w*. | Converts hexadecimal data to character data | 1–32,767 | 2 |
| $*w*. | Reads character data—trims leading blanks | 1–32,767 | none |
| **Date, Time, and Datetime**[1] | | | |
| ANYDTDTE*w*. | Reads dates in various date forms | 5–32 | 9 |
| DATE*w*. | Reads dates in form: *ddmmmyy* or *ddmmmyyyy* | 7–32 | 7 |
| DATETIME*w*. | Reads datetime values in the form: *ddmmmyy hh:mm:ss.ss* | 13–40 | 18 |
| DDMMYY*w*. | Reads dates in form: *ddmmyy* or *ddmmyyyy* | 6–32 | 6 |
| JULIAN*w*. | Reads Julian dates in form: *yyddd* or *yyyyddd* | 5–32 | 5 |
| MMDDYY*w*. | Reads dates in form: *mmddyy* or *mmddyyyy* | 6–32 | 6 |
| TIME*w*. | Reads time in form: *hh:mm:ss.ss* (hours:minutes:seconds—24-hour clock) | 5–32 | 8 |
| **Numeric** | | | |
| COMMA*w.d* | Removes embedded commas and $, converts left parentheses to minus sign | 1–32 | 1 |
| HEX*w*. | Converts hexadecimal to floating-point values if *w* is 16. Otherwise, converts to fixed-point. | 1–16 | 8 |
| IB*w.d* | Reads integer binary data | 1–8 | 4 |
| PD*w.d* | Reads packed decimal data | 1–16 | 1 |
| PERCENT*w*. | Converts percentages to numbers | 1–32 | 6 |
| *w.d* | Reads standard numeric data | 1–32 | none |

[1] SAS date values are the number of days since January 1, 1960. Time values are the number of seconds past midnight, and datetime values are the number of seconds past midnight January 1, 1960.

| Informat | Input data | INPUT statement | Results |
|----------|-----------|-----------------|---------|
| **Character** | | | |
| $CHAR*w*. | my cat<br>   my cat | INPUT Animal $CHAR10.; | my cat<br>   my cat |
| $HEX*w*. | 6C6C | INPUT Name $HEX4.; | ll  (ASCII)or<br>%%  (EBCDIC)[2] |
| $*w*. | my cat<br>   my cat | INPUT Animal $10.; | my cat<br>my cat |
| **Date, Time, and Datetime** | | | |
| ANYDTDTE*w*. | 1jan1961<br><br>01/01/61 | INPUT Day ANYDTDTE10.; | 366<br><br>366 |
| DATE*w*. | 1jan1961<br>1 jan 61 | INPUT Day DATE10.; | 366<br>366 |
| DATETIME*w*. | 1jan1960 10:30:15<br>1jan1961,10:30:15 | INPUT Dt DATETIME18.; | 37815<br>31660215 |
| DDMMYY*w*. | 01.01.61<br>02/01/61 | INPUT Day DDMMYY8.; | 366<br>367 |
| JULIAN*w*. | 61001<br>1961001 | INPUT Day JULIAN7.; | 366<br>366 |
| MMDDYY*w*. | 01-01-61<br>01/01/61 | INPUT Day MMDDYY8.; | 366<br>366 |
| TIME*w*. | 10:30<br>10:30:15 | INPUT Time TIME8.; | 37800<br>37815 |
| **Numeric** | | | |
| COMMA*w.d* | $1,000,001<br>(1,234) | INPUT Income COMMA10.; | 1000001<br>-1234 |
| HEX*w*. | F0F3 | INPUT Value HEX4.; | 61683 |
| IB*w.d* | [3] | INPUT Value IB4.; | 255 |
| PD*w.d* | [3] | INPUT Value PD4.; | 255 |
| PERCENT*w*. | 5%<br>(20%) | INPUT Value PERCENT5.; | 0.05<br>-0.2 |
| *w.d* | 1234<br>-12.3 | INPUT Value 5.1; | 123.4<br>-12.3 |

[2] The EBCDIC character set is used on most IBM mainframe computers, while the ASCII character set is used on most other computers. So, depending on the computer you are using, you will get one or the other.

[3] These values cannot be printed.

## 2.9   Mixing Input Styles

Each of the three major input styles has its own advantages. List style is the easiest; column style is a bit more work; and formatted style is the hardest of the three. However, column and formatted styles do not require spaces (or other delimiters) between variables and can read embedded blanks. Formatted style can read special data such as dates. Sometimes you use one style, sometimes another, and sometimes the easiest way is to use a combination of styles. SAS is so flexible that you can mix and match any of the input styles for your own convenience.

**Example**   The following raw data contain information about U.S. national parks: name, state (or states as the case may be), year established, and size in acres:

```
Yellowstone              ID/MT/WY 1872      4,065,493
Everglades               FL 1934            1,398,800
Yosemite                 CA 1864              760,917
Great Smoky Mountains NC/TN 1926              520,269
Wolf Trap Farm           VA 1966                  130
```

You could write the INPUT statement for these data in many ways—that is the point of this section. The following program shows one way to do it:

```
* Create a SAS data set named nationalparks;
* Read a data file NatPark.dat mixing input styles;
DATA nationalparks;
   INFILE 'c:\MyRawData\NatPark.dat';
   INPUT ParkName $ 1-22 State $ Year @40 Acreage COMMA9.;
RUN;
PROC PRINT DATA = nationalparks;
   TITLE 'Selected National Parks';
RUN;
```

Notice that the variable ParkName is read with column style input, State and Year are read with list style input, and Acreage is read with formatted style input. Here is the result of the PRINT procedure. You can also use Viewtable to view the data.

| | Selected National Parks | | | 1 |
|---|---|---|---|---|
| Obs | ParkName | State | Year | Acreage |
| 1 | Yellowstone | ID/MT/WY | 1872 | 4065493 |
| 2 | Everglades | FL | 1934 | 1398800 |
| 3 | Yosemite | CA | 1864 | 760917 |
| 4 | Great Smoky Mountains | NC/TN | 1926 | 520269 |
| 5 | Wolf Trap Farm | VA | 1966 | 130 |

Sometimes programmers run into problems when they mix input styles. When SAS reads a line of raw data it uses a pointer to mark its place, but each style of input uses the pointer a little differently. With list style input, SAS automatically scans to the next non-blank field and starts reading. With column style input, SAS starts reading in the exact column you specify. But with formatted input, SAS just starts reading—wherever the pointer is, that is where SAS reads.

Sometimes you need to move the pointer explicitly, and you can do that by using the column pointer, @*n*, where *n* is the number of the column SAS should move to.

In the preceding program, the column pointer @40 tells SAS to move to column 40 before reading the value for Acreage. If you removed the column pointer from the INPUT statement, as shown in the following statement, then SAS would start reading Acreage right after Year:

```
INPUT ParkName $ 1-22 State $ Year Acreage COMMA9.;
```

The resulting output would look like this:

```
                     Selected National Parks                        1

    Obs     ParkName                State      Year    Acreage

     1      Yellowstone             ID/MT/WY   1872     4065
     2      Everglades              FL         1934      .
     3      Yosemite                CA         1864      .
     4      Great Smoky Mountains   NC/TN      1926      5
     5      Wolf Trap Farm          VA         1966      .
```

Because Acreage was read with formatted input, SAS started reading right where the pointer was. Here is the data file with a column ruler for counting columns at the top and asterisks marking the place where SAS started reading the values of Acreage:

```
----+----1----+----2----+----3----+----4----+----5
Yellowstone            ID/MT/WY 1872 *  4,065,493
Everglades             FL 1934 *        1,398,800
Yosemite               CA 1864 *          760,917
Great Smoky Mountains  NC/TN 1926 *       520,269
Wolf Trap Farm         VA 1966 *              130
```

The COMMA9. informat told SAS to read nine columns, and SAS did that even when those columns were completely blank.

The column pointer, @*n*, has other uses too and can be used anytime you want SAS to skip backwards or forwards within a data line. You could use it, for example, to skip over unneeded data, or to read a variable twice using different informats.

# 2.10  Reading Messy Raw Data

Sometimes you need to read data that just don't line up in nice columns or have predictable lengths. When you have these types of messy files, ordinary list, column, or formatted input simply aren't enough. You need more tools in your bag: tools like the @'character' column pointer and the colon modifier.

**The @'*character*' column pointer**  In section 2.9 we showed you how you can use the @ column pointer to move to a particular column before reading data. However, sometimes you don't know the starting column of the data, but you do know that it always comes after a particular character or word. For these types of situations, you can use the @'*character*' column pointer. For example, suppose you have a data file that has information about dog ownership. Nothing in the file lines up, but you know that the breed of the dog always follows the word Breed:. You could read the dog's breed using the following INPUT statement:

```
INPUT @'Breed:' DogBreed $;
```

**The colon modifier**  The above INPUT statement will work just fine as long as the dog's breed name is 8 characters or less (the default length for a character variable). So if the dog is a Shepherd you're fine, but if the dog is a Rottweiler, all you will get is Rottweil. If you assign the variable an informat in the INPUT statement such as $20. to tell SAS that the variable's field is 20 characters, then SAS will read for 20 columns whether or not there is a space in those columns.[1] So the DogBreed variable may include unwanted characters which appear after the dog's breed on the data line. If you only want SAS to read until it encounters a space,[2] then you can use a colon modifier on the informat. To use a colon modifier, simply put a colon (:) before the informat (e.g. :$20. instead of $20.).

For example, given this line of raw data,

```
My dog Sam  Breed: Rottweiler  Vet Bills: $478
```

the following table shows the results you would get using different INPUT statements:

| Statements | Value of variable DogBreed |
| --- | --- |
| `INPUT @'Breed:' DogBreed $;` | Rottweil |
| `INPUT @'Breed:' DogBreed $20.;` | Rottweiler Vet Bill |
| `INPUT @'Breed:' DogBreed :$20.;` | Rottweiler |

---

[1] It is also possible to define a variable's length in a LENGTH or INFORMAT statement instead of in an INPUT statement. When a variable's length is defined before the INPUT statement, then SAS will read until it encounters a space or reaches the length of the variable—the same behavior as using the colon modifier. The INFORMAT statement is covered in section 2.21 and the LENGTH statement is covered in section 10.13.

[2] A space is the default delimiter. This method works for files with other delimiters as well. See sections 2.15 and 2.16 for more information on reading delimited data.

**Example**  Web logs are a good example of messy data. The following data lines are part of a web log for a dog care business website. The data lines start with the IP address of the computer accessing the web page followed by other information including the date the file was accessed and the file name.

```
130.192.70.235 - - [08/Jun/2008:23:51:32 -0700] "GET /rover.jpg HTTP/1.1" 200 66820
128.32.236.8 - - [08/Jun/2008:23:51:40 -0700] "GET /grooming.html HTTP/1.0" 200 8471
128.32.236.8 - - [08/Jun/2008:23:51:40 -0700] "GET /Icons/brush.gif HTTP/1.0" 200 89
128.32.236.8 - - [08/Jun/2008:23:51:40 -0700] "GET /H_poodle.gif HTTP/1.0" 200 1852
118.171.121.37 - - [08/Jun/2008:23:56:46 -0700] "GET /bath.gif HTTP/1.0" 200 14079
128.123.121.37 - - [09/Jun/2008:00:57:49 -0700] "GET /lobo.gif HTTP/1.0" 200 18312
128.123.121.37 - - [09/Jun/2008:00:57:49 -0700] "GET /statemnt.htm HTTP/1.0" 200 238
128.75.226.8 - - [09/Jun/2008:01:59:40 -0700] "GET /Icons/leash.gif HTTP/1.0" 200 98
```

We are interested in the date the files were accessed and the filename. You can see that because the IP address is not always the same number of characters, the date does not line up in the same column all the time. Also, not only does the filename not line up in columns, but the length of the filename is highly variable. Here is a SAS program that can read this file:

```
DATA weblogs;
   INFILE 'c:\MyWebLogs\dogweblogs.txt';
   INPUT @'[' AccessDate DATE11. @'GET' File :$20.;
RUN;
PROC PRINT DATA = weblogs;
   TITLE 'Dog Care Web Logs';
RUN;
```

This INPUT statement uses @'[' to position the column pointer to read the date, then uses @'GET' to position the column pointer to read the filename. Because the filename is more than 8 characters, but not always the same number of characters, an informat with a colon modifier :$20. is used to read the filename.

Here are the results of the PRINT procedure. You can also use Viewtable to view the data.

```
                    Dog Care Web Logs                        1


          Obs      AccessDate[3]      File


           1        17691            /rover.jpg
           2        17691            /grooming.html
           3        17691            /Icons/brush.gif
           4        17691            /H_poodle.gif
           5        17691            /bath.gif
           6        17692            /lobo.gif
           7        17692            /statemnt.htm
           8        17692            /Icons/leash.gif
```

---

[3] Notice that these dates are printed as the number of days since January 1, 1960. Section 4.5 discusses how to format these values into readable dates.

# 2.11   Reading Multiple Lines of Raw Data per Observation

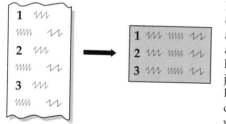

In a typical raw data file each line of data represents one observation, but sometimes the data for each observation are spread over more than one line. Since SAS will automatically go to the next line if it runs out of data before it has read all the variables in an INPUT statement, you could just let SAS take care of figuring out when to go to a new line. But if you know that your data file has multiple lines of raw data per observation, it is better for you to explicitly tell SAS when to go to the next line than to make SAS figure it out. That way you won't get that suspicious SAS-went-to-a-new-line note in your log. To tell SAS when to skip to a new line, you simply add line pointers to your INPUT statement.

The line pointers, slash (/) and pound-*n* (#*n*), are like road signs telling SAS, "Go this way." To read more than one line of raw data for a single observation, you simply insert a slash into your INPUT statement when you want to skip to the next line of raw data. The #*n* line pointer performs the same action except that you specify the line number. The *n* in #*n* stands for the number of the line of raw data for that observation; so #2 means to go to the second line for that observation, and #4 means go to the fourth line. You can even go backwards using the #*n* line pointer, reading from line 4 and then from line 3, for example. The slash is simpler, but #*n* is more flexible.

**Example**   A colleague is trying to plan his next summer vacation, but he wants to go someplace where the weather is just right. He obtains data from a meteorology database. Unfortunately, he has not quite figured out how to export from this database and makes a rather odd file.

The file contains information about temperatures for the month of July for Alaska, Florida, and North Carolina. (If your colleague chooses the last state, maybe he can visit SAS headquarters.) The first line contains the city and state, the second line lists the normal high temperature and normal low (in degrees Fahrenheit), and the third line contains the record high and low:

```
Nome AK
55 44
88 29
Miami FL
90 75
97 65
Raleigh NC
88 68
105 50
```

The following program reads the weather data from a file named Temperature.dat:

```
* Create a SAS data set named highlow;
* Read the data file using line pointers;
DATA highlow;
    INFILE 'c:\MyRawData\Temperature.dat';
    INPUT City $ State $
          / NormalHigh NormalLow
          #3 RecordHigh RecordLow;
RUN;
PROC PRINT DATA = highlow;
    TITLE 'High and Low Temperatures for July';
RUN;
```

The INPUT statement reads the values for City and State from the first line of data. Then the slash tells SAS to move to column 1 of the next line of data before reading NormalHigh and NormalLow. Likewise, the #3 tells SAS to move to column 1 of the third line of data for that observation before reading RecordHigh and RecordLow. As usual, there is more than one way to write this INPUT statement. You could replace the slash with #2 or replace #3 with a slash.

These notes appear in the log:

```
NOTE: 9 records were read from the infile 'c:\MyRawData\Temperature.dat'.
      The minimum record length was 5.
      The maximum record length was 10.

NOTE: The data set WORK.HIGHLOW has 3 observations and 6 variables.
```

Notice that while nine records were read from the infile, the SAS data set contains just three observations. Usually this would set off alarms in your mind, but here it confirms that indeed three data lines were read for every observation just as planned. You should always check your log, particularly when using line pointers.

Here are the results of the PRINT procedure. You can also view the data using Viewtable.

```
                     High and Low Temperatures for July              1

                            Normal    Normal    Record    Record
        Obs    City     State    High      Low       High      Low

         1     Nome      AK       55        44        88        29
         2     Miami     FL       90        75        97        65
         3     Raleigh   NC       88        68       105        50
```

## 2.12   Reading Multiple Observations per Line of Raw Data

There ought to be a Murphy's law of data: whatever form data can take, it will. Normally SAS assumes that each line of raw data represents no more than one observation. When you have multiple observations per line of raw data, you can use double trailing at signs (@@) at the end of your INPUT statement. This line-hold specifier is like a stop sign telling SAS, "Stop, hold that line of raw data." SAS will hold that line of data, continuing to read observations until it either runs out of data or reaches an INPUT statement that does not end with a double trailing @.

**Example**  Suppose you have a colleague who is planning a vacation and has obtained a file containing data about rainfall (in inches) for the three cities he is considering. The file contains the name of each city, the state, average rainfall for the month of July, and average number of days with measurable precipitation in July. The raw data look like this:

```
Nome AK 2.5 15 Miami FL 6.75
18 Raleigh NC . 12
```

Notice that in this data file the first line stops in the middle of the second observation. The following program reads these data from a file named Precipitation.dat and uses an @@ so SAS does not automatically go to a new line of raw data for each observation:

```
* Input more than one observation from each record;
DATA rainfall;
   INFILE 'c:\MyRawData\Precipitation.dat';
   INPUT City $ State $ NormalRain MeanDaysRain @@;
RUN;
PROC PRINT DATA = rainfall;
   TITLE 'Normal Total Precipitation and';
   TITLE2 'Mean Days with Precipitation for July';
RUN;
```

These notes will appear in the log:

```
NOTE: 2 records were read from the infile 'c:\MyRawData\Precipitation.dat'
      The minimum record length was 18.
      The maximum record length was 28.

NOTE: SAS went to a new line when INPUT statement reached past the
      end of a line.

NOTE: The data set WORK.RAINFALL has 3 observations and
      4 variables.
```

While only two records were read from the raw data file, the RAINFALL data set contains three observations. The log also includes a note saying SAS went to a new line when the INPUT statement reached past the end of a line. This means that SAS came to the end of a line in the middle of an observation and continued reading with the next line of raw data. Normally these messages would indicate a problem, but in this case they are exactly what you want.

Here are the results of the PRINT procedure. You can also use Viewtable to view the data.

```
              Normal Total Precipitation and                    1
            Mean Days with Precipitation for July


                                      Normal      Mean
            Obs    City     State      Rain     DaysRain

             1     Nome      AK        2.50        15
             2     Miami     FL        6.75        18
             3     Raleigh   NC         .          12
```

## 2.13   Reading Part of a Raw Data File

At some time you may find that you need to read a small fraction of the records in a large data file. For example, you might be reading U.S. census data and want only female heads-of-household who have incomes above $225,000 and live in Walla Walla, Washington. You could read all the records in the data file and then throw out the unneeded ones, but that would waste time.

Luckily, you don't have to read all the data before you tell SAS whether to keep an observation. Instead, you can read just enough variables to decide whether to keep the current observation, then end the INPUT statement with an at sign (@), called a trailing at. This tells SAS to hold that line of raw data. While the trailing @ holds that line, you can test the observation with an IF statement to see if it's one you want to keep. If it is, then you can read data for the remaining variables with a second INPUT statement. Without the trailing @, SAS would automatically start reading the next line of raw data with each INPUT statement.

The trailing @ is similar to the column pointer, @*n*, introduced in section 2.9. By specifying a number after the @ sign, you tell SAS to move to a particular column. By using an @ without specifying a column, it is as if you are telling SAS, "Stay tuned for more information. Don't touch that dial!" SAS will hold that line of data until it reaches either the end of the DATA step, or an INPUT statement that does not end with a trailing @.

**Example**   You want to read part of a raw data file containing local traffic data for freeways and surface streets. The data include information about the type of street, name of street, the average number of vehicles per hour traveling that street during the morning, and the average number of vehicles per hour for the evening. Here are the raw data:

```
freeway 408                            3684 3459
surface Martin Luther King Jr. Blvd.   1590 1234
surface Broadway                       1259 1290
surface Rodeo Dr.                      1890 2067
freeway 608                            4583 3860
freeway 808                            2386 2518
surface Lake Shore Dr.                 1590 1234
surface Pennsylvania Ave.              1259 1290
```

Suppose you want to see only the freeway data at this point so you read the raw data file, Traffic.dat, with this program:

```
* Use a trailing @, then delete surface streets;
DATA freeways;
   INFILE 'c:\MyRawData\Traffic.dat';
   INPUT Type $ @;
   IF Type = 'surface' THEN DELETE;
   INPUT Name $ 9-38 AMTraffic PMTraffic;
RUN;
PROC PRINT DATA = freeways;
   TITLE 'Traffic for Freeways';
   RUN;
```

Notice that there are two INPUT statements. The first reads the character variable Type and then ends with an @. The trailing @ holds each line of data while the IF statement tests it. The second INPUT statement reads Name (in columns 9 through 38), AMTraffic, and PMTraffic. If an observation has a value of surface for the variable Type, then the second INPUT statement never executes. Instead SAS returns to the beginning of the DATA step to process the next observation and does not add the unwanted observation to the FREEWAYS data set. (Do not pass go, do not collect $200.)

When you run this program, the log will contain the following two notes, one saying that eight records were read from the input file and another saying that the new data set contains only three observations:

```
NOTE: 8 records were read from the infile 'c:\MyRawData\Traffic.dat'.
      The minimum record length was 47.
      The maximum record length was 47.

NOTE: The data set WORK.FREEWAYS has 3 observations and 4 variables.
```

The other five observations had a value of surface for the variable Type and were deleted by the IF statement. Here is the result of the PRINT procedure. You can also view the data in Viewtable.

```
                    Traffic for Freeways                        1

          Obs     Type      Name    AMTraffic    PMTraffic
           1      freeway    408      3684        3459
           2      freeway    608      4583        3860
           3      freeway    808      2386        2518
```

**Trailing @ versus double trailing @** The double trailing @, discussed in the previous section, is similar to the trailing @. Both are line-hold specifiers; the difference is how long they hold a line of data for input. The trailing @ holds a line of data for subsequent INPUT statements, but releases that line of data when SAS returns to the top of the DATA step to begin building the next observation. The double trailing @ holds a line of data for subsequent INPUT statements even when SAS starts building a new observation. In both cases, the line of data is released if SAS reaches a subsequent INPUT statement that does not contain a line-hold specifier.

# 2.14   Controlling Input with Options in the INFILE Statement

So far in this chapter, we have seen ways to use the INPUT statement to read many different types of raw data. When reading raw data files, SAS makes certain assumptions. For example, SAS starts reading with the first data line and, if SAS runs out of data on a line, it automatically goes to the next line to read values for the rest of the variables. Most of the time this is OK, but some data files can't be read using the default assumptions. The options in the INFILE statement change the way SAS reads raw data files. The following options are useful for reading particular types of data files. Place these options after the filename in the INFILE statement.

**FIRSTOBS=**   The FIRSTOBS= option tells SAS at what line to begin reading data. This is useful if you have a data file that contains descriptive text or header information at the beginning, and you want to skip over these lines to begin reading the data. The following data file, for example, has a description of the data in the first two lines:

```
Ice-cream sales data for the summer
Flavor      Location   Boxes sold
Chocolate   213        123
Vanilla     213        512
Chocolate   415        242
```

The following program uses the FIRSTOBS= option to tell SAS to start reading data on the third line of the file:

```
DATA icecream;
   INFILE 'c:\MyRawData\IceCreamSales.dat' FIRSTOBS = 3;
   INPUT Flavor $ 1-9 Location BoxesSold;
RUN;
```

**OBS=**   The OBS= option can be used anytime you want to read only a part of your data file. It tells SAS to stop reading when it gets to that line in the raw data file. Note that it does not necessarily correspond to the number of observations. If, for example, you are reading two raw data lines for each observation, then an OBS=100 would read 100 data lines, and the resulting SAS data set would have 50 observations. The OBS= option can be used with the FIRSTOBS= option to read lines from the middle of the file. For example, suppose the ice-cream sales data had a remark at the end of the file that was not part of the data.

```
Ice-cream sales data for the summer
Flavor      Location   Boxes sold
Chocolate   213        123
Vanilla     213        512
Chocolate   415        242
Data verified by Blake White
```

With FIRSTOBS=3 and OBS=5, SAS will start reading this file on the third data line and stop reading after the fifth data line.

```
DATA icecream;
   INFILE 'c:\MyRawData\IceCreamSales2.dat' FIRSTOBS = 3 OBS=5;
   INPUT Flavor $ 1-9 Location BoxesSold;
RUN;
```

**MISSOVER** By default, SAS will go to the next data line to read more data if SAS has reached the end of the data line and there are still more variables in the INPUT statement that have not been assigned values. The MISSOVER option tells SAS that if it runs out of data, don't go to the next data line. Instead, assign missing values to any remaining variables. The following data file illustrates where this option may be useful. This file contains test scores for a self-paced course. Since not all students complete all the tests, some have more scores than others.

```
Nguyen    89 76 91 82
Ramos     67 72 80 76 86
Robbins   76 65 79
```

The following program reads the data for the five test scores, assigning missing values to tests not completed:

```
DATA class102;
    INFILE 'c:\MyRawData\AllScores.dat' MISSOVER;
    INPUT Name $ Test1 Test2 Test3 Test4 Test5;
RUN;
```

**TRUNCOVER** You need the TRUNCOVER option when you are reading data using column or formatted input and some data lines are shorter than others. If a variable's field extends past the end of the data line, then, by default, SAS will go to the next line to start reading the variable's value. This option tells SAS to read data for the variable until it reaches the end of the data line, or the last column specified in the format or column range, whichever comes first. The next file contains addresses and must be read using column or formatted input because the street names have embedded blanks. Note that the data lines are all different lengths:

```
John Garcia      114   Maple Ave.
Sylvia Chung    1302   Washington Drive
Martha Newton     45   S.E. 14th St.
```

This program uses column input to read the address file. Because some of the addresses stop before the end of the variable Street's field (columns 22 through 37), you need the TRUNCOVER option. Without the TRUNCOVER option, SAS would try to go to the next line to read the data for Street on the first and third records.

```
DATA homeaddress;
    INFILE 'c:\MyRawData\Address.dat' TRUNCOVER;
    INPUT Name $ 1-15 Number 16-19 Street $ 22-37;
RUN;
```

TRUNCOVER is similar to MISSOVER. Both will assign missing values to variables if the data line ends before the variable's field starts. But when the data line ends in the middle of a variable field, TRUNCOVER will take as much as is there, whereas MISSOVER will assign the variable a missing value.

## 2.15   Reading Delimited Files with the DATA Step

Delimited files are raw data files that have a special character separating data values. Many programs can save data as delimited files, often with commas or tab characters for delimiters. SAS gives you two options for the INFILE statement that make it easy to read delimited data files: the DLM= option and the DSD option.

**The DLM= option**   If you read your data using list input, the DATA step expects your file to have spaces between your data values. The DELIMITER=, or DLM=, option in the INFILE statement allows you to read data files with other delimiters. The comma and tab characters are common delimiters found in data files, but you could read data files with any delimiter character by just enclosing the delimiter character in quotation marks after the DLM= option (i.e., DLM='&'). If your delimiter is a string of characters, then use the DLMSTR= option.

**Example**   The following file is comma-delimited where students' names are followed by the number of books they read for each week in a summer reading program:

```
Grace,3,1,5,2,6
Martin,1,2,4,1,3
Scott,9,10,4,8,6
```

This program uses list input to read the books data file specifying the comma as the delimiter:

```
DATA reading;
   INFILE 'c:\MyRawData\Books.dat' DLM = ',';
   INPUT Name $ Week1 Week2 Week3 Week4 Week5;
RUN;
```

If the same data had tab characters between values instead of commas, then you could use the following program to read the file. This program uses the DLM='09'X option. In ASCII, 09 is the hexadecimal equivalent of a tab character, and the notation '09'X means a hexadecimal 09. If your computer uses EBCDIC (IBM mainframes) instead of ASCII, then use DLM='05'X.

```
DATA reading;
   INFILE 'c:\MyRawData\Books.txt' DLM = '09'X;
   INPUT Name $ Week1 Week2 Week3 Week4 Week5;
RUN;
```

By default, SAS interprets two or more delimiters in a row as a single delimiter. If your file has missing values, and two delimiters in a row indicate a missing value, then you will also need the DSD option in the INFILE statement.

**The DSD option**   The DSD (Delimiter-Sensitive Data) option for the INFILE statement does three things for you. First, it ignores delimiters in data values enclosed in quotation marks. Second, it does not read quotation marks as part of the data value. Third, it treats two delimiters in a row as a missing value. The DSD option assumes that the delimiter is a comma. If your delimiter is not a comma, then you can use the DLM= option with the DSD option to specify the delimiter. For example, to read a tab-delimited ASCII file with missing values indicated by two consecutive tab characters use

```
INFILE 'file-specification' DLM='09'X DSD;
```

**CSV files**  Comma-separated values files, or CSV files, are a common type of file that can be read with the DSD option. Many programs, such as Microsoft Excel, can save data in CSV format. These files have commas for delimiters and consecutive commas for missing values; if there are commas in any of the data values, then those values are enclosed in quotation marks.

**Example**  The following example illustrates how to read a CSV file using the DSD option. Jerry's Coffee Shop employs local bands to attract customers. Jerry keeps records of the number of customers for each band, for each night they play in his shop. The band's name is followed by the date and the number of customers present at 8 p.m., 9 p.m., 10 p.m., and 11 p.m.

```
Lupine Lights,12/3/2007,45,63,70,
Awesome Octaves,12/15/2007,17,28,44,12
"Stop, Drop, and Rock-N-Roll",1/5/2008,34,62,77,91
The Silveyville Jazz Quartet,1/18/2008,38,30,42,43
Catalina Converts,1/31/2008,56,,65,34
```

Notice that one group's name has embedded commas, and is enclosed in quotation marks. Also, the last group has a missing data point for the 9 p.m. hour as indicated by two consecutive commas. Use the DSD option in the INFILE statement to read this data file. It is also prudent, when using the DSD option, to add the MISSOVER option if there is any chance that you have missing data at the end of your data lines (as in the first line of this data file). The MISSOVER option tells SAS that if it runs out of data, don't go to the next data line to continue reading. Here is the program that will read this data file:

```
DATA music;
   INFILE 'c:\MyRawData\Bands.csv' DLM = ',' DSD MISSOVER;
   INPUT BandName :$30. GigDate :MMDDYY10. EightPM NinePM TenPM ElevenPM;
RUN;
PROC PRINT DATA = music;
   TITLE 'Customers at Each Gig';
RUN;
```

Notice that for BandName and GigDate we use colon modified informats. The colon modifier tells SAS to read for the length of the informat (30 for BandName and 10 for GigDate), or until it encounters a delimiter, whichever comes first. Because the names of the bands are longer than the default length of 8 characters, we use the :$30. informat for BandName to read up to 30 characters.

Here are the results of the PROC PRINT. You can also view the data in the Viewtable window.

| | | Customers at Each Gig | | | | 1 |
|---|---|---|---|---|---|---|
| Obs | BandName | Gig Date[1] | Eight PM | Nine PM | Ten PM | Eleven PM |
| 1 | Lupine Lights | 17503 | 45 | 63 | 70 | . |
| 2 | Awesome Octaves | 17515 | 17 | 28 | 44 | 12 |
| 3 | Stop, Drop, and Rock-N-Roll | 17536 | 34 | 62 | 77 | 91 |
| 4 | The Silveyville Jazz Quartet | 17549 | 38 | 30 | 42 | 43 |
| 5 | Catalina Converts | 17562 | 56 | . | 65 | 34 |

---

[1] Notice that these dates are printed as the number of days since January 1, 1960. Section 4.5 discusses how to format these values into readable dates.

## 2.16   Reading Delimited Files with the IMPORT Procedure

We suspect that by now you have realized that with SAS there is usually more than one way to accomplish the same result. In the previous section we showed you how to read delimited data files using the DATA step; now we are going to show you how to read delimited files a different way: using the IMPORT procedure.[1]

There are a few things that PROC IMPORT does for you that make it easy to read certain types of data files. PROC IMPORT will scan your data file (the first 20 rows by default) and automatically determine the variable types (character or numeric), will assign lengths to the character variables, and can recognize some date formats. PROC IMPORT will treat two consecutive delimiters in your data file as a missing value, will read values enclosed by quotation marks, and assign missing values to variables when it runs out of data on a line. Also, if you want, you can use the first line in your data file for the variable names.

The general form of the IMPORT procedure is

```
PROC IMPORT DATAFILE = 'filename' OUT = data-set;
```

where the file you want to read follows the DATAFILE= option, and the name of the SAS data set you want to create follows the OUT= option. SAS will determine the file type by the extension of the file as shown in the following table.

| Type of File | Extension | DBMS Identifier |
| --- | --- | --- |
| Comma-delimited | .csv | CSV |
| Tab-delimited | .txt | TAB |
| Delimiters other than commas or tabs | | DLM |

If your file does not have the proper extension, or your file is of type DLM, then you must use the DBMS= option in the PROC IMPORT statement. Use the REPLACE option if you already have a SAS data set with the name you specified in the OUT= option, and you want to overwrite it. Here is the general form of PROC IMPORT with both the REPLACE and the DBMS options:

```
PROC IMPORT DATAFILE = 'filename' OUT = data-set
       DBMS = identifier REPLACE;
```

**Optional statements**   Some types of files need a few more instructions to be read correctly. If the data do not start in the first line of the file, use the DATAROWS statement. If the delimiter is not a comma, tab, or space, use the DELIMITER statement. If your file contains only data and no headings, use the GETNAMES=NO statement to assign default variable names. Lastly, if your data file has all missing values or non-representative data in the first 20 data rows, you may need the GUESSINGROWS statement to make sure variables are assigned the correct data type and length.

DATAROWS = *n*;                              Start reading data in row *n*. Default is 1.

DELIMITER = *'delimiter-character'*;   Delimiter for DLM files. Default is space.

---

[1] The IMPORT procedure is available on UNIX, OpenVMS, and Windows only.

GETNAMES=NO;

Do not get variable names from the first line of input file. Default is YES. If NO, then variables are named VAR1, VAR2, VAR3, and so on.

GUESSINGROWS = *n*;

Use *n* rows to determine variable types. Default is 20.

The following shows the general form of PROC IMPORT with the GETNAMES=NO statement:

```
PROC IMPORT DATAFILE = 'filename' OUT = data-set;
   GETNAMES = NO;
```

**Example**  The following example uses data about Jerry's Coffee Shop where Jerry employs local bands to attract customers. Jerry keeps records of the number of customers present throughout the evening for each band.  The data are the band name, followed by the gig date, and the number of customers present at 8 p.m., 9 p.m., 10 p.m., and 11 p.m. Notice that one of the bands, "Stop, Drop, and Rock-N-Roll," has commas in the name of the band. When a data value contains the delimiter, then the value must be enclosed in quotation marks.

```
Band Name,Gig Date,Eight PM,Nine PM,Ten PM,Eleven PM
Lupine Lights,12/3/2007,45,63,70,
Awesome Octaves,12/15/2007,17,28,44,12
"Stop, Drop, and Rock-N-Roll",1/5/2008,34,62,77,91
The Silveyville Jazz Quartet,1/18/2008,38,30,42,43
Catalina Converts,1/31/2008,56,,65,34
```

Here is the program that will read this data file and print out the SAS data set after importing:

```
PROC IMPORT DATAFILE ='c:\MyRawData\Bands2.csv' OUT = music REPLACE;
RUN;
PROC PRINT DATA = music;
   TITLE 'Customers at Each Gig';
RUN;
```

Here are the results of the PROC PRINT.  Notice that GigDate is a readable date.  This is because IMPORT automatically assigns informats and formats to some forms of dates.  (See section 4.5 for a discussion of formats.)  Also note that PROC IMPORT used the first data row for variable names and that spaces in names were replaced with underscores to conform to standard SAS naming rules for variables. You can also use Viewtable to view the data.

```
                   Customers at Each Gig                      1

Obs    Band_Name                        Gig_Date     Eight_PM

 1     Lupine Lights                    12/03/2007      45
 2     Awesome Octaves                  12/15/2007      17
 3     Stop, Drop, and Rock-N-Roll      01/05/2008      34
 4     The Silveyville Jazz Quartet     01/18/2008      38
 5     Catalina Converts                01/31/2008      56

Obs      Nine_PM        Ten_PM      Eleven_PM

 1          63            70             .
 2          28            44            12
 3          62            77            91
 4          30            42            43
 5           .            65            34
```

## 2.17 Reading PC Files with the IMPORT Procedure

If you have SAS/ACCESS Interface to PC Files, then you can use the IMPORT procedure to import several types of PC files in the Windows and UNIX operating environments. File types you can read include: Microsoft Excel, Lotus (not on UNIX), dBase, Microsoft Access, and starting with SAS 9.2, JMP, Paradox, SPSS, and Stata. An alternative method of reading some types of PC files in the Windows operating environment which does not require SAS/ACCESS is Dynamic Data Exchange (DDE) which is covered in the next section.

Here is the general form of the IMPORT procedure for reading PC files except Microsoft Access:

```
PROC IMPORT DATAFILE = 'filename' OUT = data-set
     DBMS = identifier  REPLACE;
```

where *filename* is the file you want to read and *data-set* is the name of the SAS data set you want to create. The REPLACE option tells SAS to replace the SAS data set named in the OUT= option if it already exists. If your data file has the proper extension, as shown in the following table, then you may not need the DBMS= option. Of course, it never hurts to specify the DBMS.

| Type of File | Extension | DBMS Identifier |
|---|---|---|
| Microsoft Excel | .xls | EXCEL |
| | | XLS |
| dBase | .dbf | DBF |
| JMP | .jmp | JMP |
| Lotus | .wk4 | WK4 |
| Paradox | .db | PARADOX |
| SPSS Save file | .sav | SAV |
| Stata | .dta | DTA |

**Microsoft Excel Files** For Excel 97 through 2003,[1] you can use the default EXCEL identifier (32-bit Windows only), or the XLS identifier. The XLS identifier looks at all rows in the file to determine the column type, whereas the EXCEL identifier only looks at the first 8 data rows by default.

If you have more than one sheet in your file, then you can specify which sheet to read using the following statement:

```
SHEET="sheet-name";
```

If you want to read only specific cells in the sheet, you can specify a range. The range can be a named range (if defined), or you can specify the upper-left and lower-right cells for the range as follows:

```
RANGE="sheet-name$UL:LR";
```

By default, the IMPORT procedure will take the variable names from the first row of the spreadsheet (also with Lotus). If you do not want this, then you can add the following statement to the procedure and SAS will name the variables F1, F2, and so on.

```
GETNAMES=NO;
```

---

[1] For Microsoft Excel5 files, you can use either the EXCEL5 (Windows only) or the XLS DBMS identifier. Excel 2007 files are supported starting with SAS 9.2 Phase 2.

**Microsoft Access Files**  If you want to read Microsoft Access files, then instead of using the DATAFILE= option, you need a DATATABLE= option and the DATABASE= statement as follows:[2]

```
PROC IMPORT DATATABLE = 'table-name' OUT = data-set DBMS = identifier
      REPLACE;
   DATABASE =   'database-path';
```

The following are the DBMS identifiers for Microsoft Access. If you want to read a Microsoft Access 97 file, then you must specify the DBMS identifier. The ACCESS DBMS identifier is valid for Microsoft Access files 2000 through 2003.

| Type of File | Extension | DBMS Identifier[2] |
|---|---|---|
| Microsoft Access | .mdb | ACCESS |
| | | ACCESS97 |

**Example**  Suppose you have the following Microsoft Excel spreadsheet which contains data about onion ring sales for the local minor league baseball team games. The visiting team name is followed by the sales in the concession stands and in the bleachers, then the number of hits and runs for each team.

| | A | B | C | D | E | F | G |
|---|---|---|---|---|---|---|---|
| | | C Sales | B Sales | Our Hits | Their Hits | Our Runs | Their Runs |
| 1 | VisitingTeam | | | | | | |
| 2 | Columbia Peaches | 35 | 67 | 1 | 10 | 2 | 1 |
| 3 | Plains Peanuts | 210 | | 2 | 5 | 0 | 2 |
| 4 | Gilroy Garlics | 15 | 1035 | 12 | 11 | 7 | 6 |
| 5 | Sacramento Tomatoes | 124 | 85 | 15 | 4 | 9 | 1 |
| 6 | | | | | | | |
| 7 | | | | | | | |

A1 — 'VisitingTeam — Sheet1

The following program reads the Microsoft Excel file using the IMPORT procedure.

```
* Read an Excel spreadsheet using PROC IMPORT;
PROC IMPORT DATAFILE = 'c:\MyExcelFiles\OnionRing.xls' DBMS=XLS OUT = sales;
RUN;
PROC PRINT DATA = sales;
   TITLE 'SAS Data Set Read From Excel File';
RUN;
```

Here are the results of the PROC PRINT. You can also use Viewtable to view the data.

```
                       SAS Data Set Read From Excel File                          1

                                                      Their_              Their_
 Obs   Visiting_Team        C_Sales   B_Sales   Our_Hits    Hits    Our_Runs   Runs

  1    Columbia Peaches        35        67         1        10        2         1
  2    Plains Peanuts         210         .         2         5        0         2
  3    Gilroy Garlics          15      1035        12        11        7         6
  4    Sacramento Tomatoes    124        85        15         4        9         1
```

[2] Additional options may be needed if your Microsoft Access database is password-protected. To read Microsoft Access files under the UNIX operating environment, you will need the PC Files Server installed, and use the ACCESSCS identifier. Access 2007 files are supported starting with SAS 9.2 Phase 2. See the SAS Help and Documentation for more information.

## 2.18   Reading PC Files with DDE

One method for reading PC files is Dynamic Data Exchange (DDE). DDE has some advantages and disadvantages when compared to other methods of reading PC files. DDE can only be used in the Windows operating environment, and the application (such as Microsoft Excel) must be running on the computer while SAS is accessing the file. Additionally, both SAS and the application must be running on the same computer. But DDE does allow you to directly access data stored in PC files and it does not require any additional SAS products to be licensed. There are several ways to access data through DDE. We will present three methods:

♦   copying data to the clipboard

♦   specifying the DDE triplet

♦   starting the PC application from SAS, then reading the data.

**Copying data to the clipboard**  If you don't want to be bothered with determining the DDE triplet, then you can just copy the rows and columns that you want to read into SAS onto the clipboard. Then you use the CLIPBOARD keyword in the DDE FILENAME statement. For example, suppose you have the following spreadsheet open in Microsoft Excel.

| | A | B | C | D | E | F | G |
|---|---|---|---|---|---|---|---|
| 1 | Visiting Team | C Sales | B Sales | Our Hits | Their Hits | Our Runs | Their Runs |
| 2 | Columbia Peaches | 35 | 67 | 1 | 10 | 2 | 1 |
| 3 | Plains Peanuts | 210 | | 2 | 5 | 0 | 2 |
| 4 | Gilroy Garlics | 15 | 1035 | 12 | 11 | 7 | 6 |
| 5 | Sacramento Tomatoes | 124 | 85 | 15 | 4 | 9 | 1 |

A2   ▾   *fx*   'Columbia Peaches

Sheet1

Copy the rows and columns you want to read into SAS (A2 to G5) onto the clipboard, then, without closing Microsoft Excel, submit the following SAS program:

```
* Read an Excel spreadsheet using DDE;
FILENAME baseball DDE 'CLIPBOARD';
DATA sales;
   INFILE baseball NOTAB DLM='09'x DSD MISSOVER;
   LENGTH VisitingTeam $ 20;
   INPUT VisitingTeam CSales BSales OurHits TheirHits OurRuns TheirRuns;
RUN;
```

The FILENAME statement defines a fileref (BASEBALL) as type DDE and specifies that you want to read the contents of the clipboard. By default, DDE assumes there are spaces between your data values. So, if you have embedded spaces in your data, then you will need the NOTAB and the DLM='09'x options in the INFILE statement. These two options tell SAS to put a tab character (NOTAB) between values and define the tab character as the delimiter (DLM='09'x). In addition, if you have missing values in your data, you will want to add the DSD and MISSOVER options to the INFILE statement. The DSD option treats two delimiters in a row as missing data and the MISSOVER options tells SAS not to go to the next data line to continue reading data if it runs out of data on the current line.

**Specifying the DDE triplet** The clipboard method is easy, but it requires you to take the extra step of copying the data to the clipboard before you run the SAS program. If you know the DDE triplet for the data you want to read, then you can just specify the triplet in the FILENAME statement. However figuring out what the DDE triplet is can be a little tricky. Each application has its own way of specifying a DDE triplet. In general, the DDE triplet takes on the following form:

*application | topic ! item*

Specific information about DDE triplets can be found in the documentation for the PC application. However, there is a way to find out the DDE triplet for your data from within SAS. First, copy the data you want onto the clipboard, then toggle to your SAS session. From the Solutions menu, select Accessories. Then select DDE Triplet. A window will appear that will give the DDE triplet for the data that you copied to the clipboard. For example, the DDE triplet for the spreadsheet shown is

```
Excel|C:\MyFiles\[BaseBall.xls]sheet1!R2C1:R5C7
```

So, to read the same data by specifying the DDE triplet, you would use the following FILENAME statement and the rest of the program is the same:

```
FILENAME baseball DDE 'Excel|C:\MyFiles\[BaseBall.xls]sheet1!R2C1:R5C7';
```

**Starting the application from SAS** With both the previous examples, the PC application must first be running before you can run the SAS program. Since this is sometimes inconvenient, you may want to start the application from within SAS, then read the data using DDE. You need to add two things to your SAS program to do this. First, you need the NOXWAIT and NOXSYNC systems options, then you need to use the X statement. Here is an example program:

```
* Read an Excel spreadsheet using DDE;
OPTIONS NOXSYNC NOXWAIT;
X '"C:\MyFiles\BaseBall.xls"';
FILENAME baseball DDE 'Excel|C:\MyFiles\[BaseBall.xls]sheet1!R2C1:R5C7';
DATA sales;
   INFILE baseball NOTAB DLM='09'x DSD MISSOVER;
   LENGTH VisitingTeam $ 20;
   INPUT VisitingTeam CSales BSales OurHits TheirHits OurRuns TheirRuns;
RUN;
```

The NOXWAIT and the NOXSYNC options tell SAS not to wait for input from the user, and to return control back to SAS after executing the command. The X statement simply tells Windows to execute the program or open the file that follows in quotation marks. Notice that there are two sets of quotation marks around the filename. If you have embedded spaces in the path for your filename, then you need to enclose the filename in two sets of quotation marks. Note that using this method, you must specify the DDE triplet in the FILENAME statement.

## 2.19   Temporary versus Permanent SAS Data Sets

SAS data sets are available in two varieties: temporary and permanent. A temporary SAS data set is one that exists only during the current job or session and is automatically erased by SAS when you finish. If a SAS data set is permanent, that doesn't mean that it lasts for eternity, just that it remains when the job or session is finished.

Each type of data set has its own advantages. Sometimes you want to keep a data set for later use, and sometimes you don't. In this book, most of our examples use temporary data sets because we don't want to clutter up your disks. But, in general, if you use a data set more than once, it is more efficient to save it as a permanent SAS data set than to create a new temporary SAS data set every time you want to use the data.

**SAS data set names**   All SAS data sets have a two-level name such as WORK.BIKESALES, with the two levels separated by a period. The first level of a SAS data set name, WORK in this case, is called its libref (short for SAS data library reference). A libref is like an arrow pointing to a particular location. Sometimes a libref refers to a physical location, such as a flash drive or CD, while other times it refers to a logical location such as a directory or folder. The second level, BIKESALES, is the member name that uniquely identifies the data set within the library.

Both the libref and member name follow the standard rules for valid SAS names. They must start with a letter or underscore and contain only letters, numerals, or underscores. However, librefs cannot be longer than 8 characters while member names can be up to 32 characters long.

You never explicitly tell SAS to make a data set temporary or permanent, it is just implied by the name you give the data set when you create it. Most data sets are created in DATA steps, but PROC steps can also create data sets. If you specify a two-level name (and the libref is something other than WORK), then your data set will be permanent. If you specify just one level of the data set name (as we have in most of the examples in this book), then your data set will be temporary. SAS will use your one-level name as the member name and automatically append the libref WORK. By definition, any SAS data set with a libref of WORK is a temporary data set and will be erased by SAS at the end of your job or session. Here are some sample DATA statements and the characteristics of the data sets they create:

| DATA statement | Libref | Member name | Type |
|---|---|---|---|
| DATA ironman; | WORK | ironman | temporary |
| DATA WORK.tourdefrance; | WORK | tourdefrance | temporary |
| DATA Bikes.doublecentury; | Bikes | doublecentury | permanent |

**Temporary SAS data sets**   The following program creates and then prints a temporary SAS data set named DISTANCE:

```
DATA distance;
   Miles = 26.22;
   Kilometers = 1.61 * Miles;
RUN;
PROC PRINT DATA = distance;
RUN;
```

Notice that the libref WORK does not appear in the DATA statement. Because the data set has just a one-level name, SAS assigns the default library, WORK, and uses DISTANCE as the member name within that library. The log contains this note with the complete, two-level name:

```
NOTE: The data set WORK.DISTANCE has 1 observations and 2 variables.
```

**Permanent SAS data sets**  Before you can use a libref, you need to define it. You can define libraries using the New Library window in SAS Explorer (covered in section 1.11). You can also use the LIBNAME statement (covered in section 2.20) or you can let SAS define the libref for you using direct referencing (covered in section 2.21).[1]

The BIKES library, defined in the New Library window shown in the figure on the right, points to the 'Ruiz Racing Bicycles' folder under the 'MySASLib' folder, on the C drive (Windows).

Librefs defined using the New Library window will appear in the Active Libraries window of the SAS Explorer as shown in the figure on the left. If you double-click the library icon, all the SAS data sets in the library will be listed in the Contents window for the library.

The following program is the same as the preceding one except that it creates a permanent SAS data set. Notice that a two-level name appears in the DATA statement.

```
DATA Bikes.distance;
   Miles = 26.22;
   Kilometers = 1.61 * Miles;
RUN;
PROC PRINT DATA = Bikes.distance;
RUN;
```

This time the log contains this note:

```
NOTE: The data set BIKES.DISTANCE has 1 observations and 2 variables.
```

This is a permanent SAS data set because the libref is not WORK.

---

[1] With batch processing under z/OS, you may also use Job Control Language (JCL).  The DDname is your libref.

## 2.20  Using Permanent SAS Data Sets with LIBNAME Statements

A libref is a nickname that corresponds to the location of a SAS data library. When you use a libref as the first level in the name of a SAS data set, SAS knows to look for that data set in that location. This section shows you how to define a libref using the LIBNAME statement which is the most universal (and therefore most portable) method of creating a libref. You can also define a libref using the New Library window (covered in section 1.11) or for some computers, operating environment control language.[1] The basic form of the LIBNAME statement is

```
LIBNAME libref 'your-SAS-data-library';
```

After the keyword LIBNAME, you specify the libref and then the location of your permanent SAS data set in quotation marks. Librefs must be 8 characters or shorter; start with a letter or underscore; and contain only letters, numerals, or underscores. Here is the general form of LIBNAME statements for individual operating environments:

| | |
|---|---|
| Windows: | `LIBNAME libref 'drive:\directory';` |
| UNIX: | `LIBNAME libref '/home/path';` |
| Open VMS: | `LIBNAME libref '[userid.directory]';` |
| z/OS: | `LIBNAME libref 'data-set-name';` |

**Creating a permanent SAS data set**    The following example creates a permanent SAS data set containing information about magnolia trees. For each type of tree the raw data file includes the scientific name, common name, maximum height, age at first blooming when planted from seed, whether evergreen or deciduous, and color of flowers.

```
M. grandiflora Southern Magnolia 80 15 E white
M. campbellii                     80 20 D rose
M. liliiflora  Lily Magnolia      12  4 D purple
M. soulangiana Saucer Magnolia    25  3 D pink
M. stellata    Star Magnolia      10  3 D white
```

This program sets up a libref named PLANTS pointing to the MySASLib directory on the C drive (Windows). Then it reads the raw data from a file called Mag.dat, creating a permanent SAS data set named MAGNOLIA which is stored in the PLANTS library.

```
LIBNAME plants 'c:\MySASLib';
DATA plants.magnolia;
    INFILE 'c:\MyRawData\Mag.dat';
    INPUT ScientificName $ 1-14 CommonName $ 16-32 MaximumHeight
        AgeBloom Type $ Color $;
RUN;
```

---

[1] With batch processing under z/OS, you may use Job Control Language (JCL). The DDname is your libref.

The log contains this note showing the two-level data set name:

```
NOTE: The data set PLANTS.MAGNOLIA has 5 observations and 6 variables.
```

Librefs defined using LIBNAME statements will appear in the Active Libraries window of the SAS Explorer. If you double-click the library icon, all the SAS data sets in the library will be listed in the Contents window for the library.

If you print a directory of files on your computer, you will not see a file named PLANTS.MAGNOLIA. That is because operating environments have their own systems for naming files. When run under Windows, UNIX, or Open VMS, this data set will be called `magnolia.sas7bdat`. Under z/OS, the filename would be the *data-set-name* specified in the LIBNAME statement.

**Reading a permanent SAS data set**   To use a permanent SAS data set, you can include a LIBNAME statement in your program and refer to the data set by its two-level name. For instance, if you wanted to go back later and print the permanent data set created in the last example, you could use the following statements:

```
LIBNAME example 'c:\MySASLib';
PROC PRINT DATA = example.magnolia;
    TITLE 'Magnolias';
RUN;
```

This time the libref in the LIBNAME statement is EXAMPLE instead of PLANTS, but it points to the same location as before, the MySASLib directory on the C drive. The libref can change, but the member name, MAGNOLIA, stays the same.

The output looks like this:

```
                                Magnolias                                    1

                                        Maximum   Age
    Obs   ScientificName    CommonName   Height   Bloom  Type  Color

     1    M. grandiflora  Southern Magnolia    80     15    E    white
     2    M. campbellii                        80     20    D    rose
     3    M. liliiflora   Lily Magnolia        12      4    D    purple
     4    M. soulangiana  Saucer Magnolia      25      3    D    pink
     5    M. stellata     Star Magnolia        10      3    D    white
```

## 2.21  Using Permanent SAS Data Sets by Direct Referencing

If you don't want to be bothered with setting up librefs and defining SAS libraries, but you still want to use permanent SAS data sets, then you can use direct referencing. Direct referencing still uses SAS libraries, but instead of defining the library yourself, you let SAS do it for you.

Using direct referencing is easy, just take your operating environment's name for a file, enclose it in quotation marks, and put it in your program. The quotation marks tell SAS that this is a permanent SAS data set. Here is the general form of the DATA statement for creating permanent SAS data sets under different operating environments:

| | |
|---|---|
| Windows: | DATA '*drive:\directory\filename*'; |
| UNIX: | DATA '*/home/path/filename*'; |
| Open VMS: | DATA '*[userid.directory]filename*'; |
| z/OS: | DATA '*data-set-name*'; |

For directory-based operating environments, if you leave out the directory or path, then SAS uses the current working directory. For example, this statement would create a permanent SAS data set named TREES in your current working directory.

```
DATA 'trees';
```

For UNIX and Open VMS operating environments, by default, your current directory is the directory where you started SAS. You can change the current directory for the SAS session by choosing Change Directory from the Options menu of the Tools pull-down menu. Under Windows the name of the current working directory is displayed at the bottom of the SAS window. You can change the directory for the current SAS session by double-clicking the directory name which will open the Change Folder window.

**Example**  The following example creates a permanent SAS data set containing information about magnolia trees. For each type of tree the raw data file includes the scientific name, common name, maximum height, age at first blooming when planted from seed, whether evergreen or deciduous, and color of flowers.

```
M. grandiflora Southern Magnolia 80 15 E white
M. campbellii                     80 20 D rose
M. liliiflora  Lily Magnolia      12  4 D purple
M. soulangiana Saucer Magnolia    25  3 D pink
M. stellata    Star Magnolia      10  3 D white
```

This program reads the raw data from a file called Mag.dat, creating a permanent SAS data set named MAGNOLIA. The MAGNOLIA data set is stored in the MySASLib directory on the C drive (Windows).

```
DATA 'c:\MySASLib\magnolia';
   INFILE 'c:\MyRawData\Mag.dat';
   INPUT ScientificName $ 1-14 CommonName $ 16-32 MaximumHeight
      AgeBloom Type $ Color $;
RUN;
```

If you look in your SAS log you will see this note:

```
NOTE: The data set c:\MySASLib\magnolia has 5 observations and 6 variables.
```

This is a permanent SAS data set, so SAS will not erase it. If you list the files in the MySASLib directory, you will see a file named magnolia.sas7bdat. Notice that SAS automatically appended a file extension, even though no extension appeared in the SAS program.

When you put quotation marks around your data set name, you are using direct referencing, and SAS creates a permanent SAS data set. Since you haven't specified a libref, SAS makes up a libref for you. You don't need to know the name of the libref that SAS makes up, but it is there and, you can see it in the Active Libraries window. This is what the Active Libraries window looks like after running the previous program. SAS has created a library named WC000001 which contains the MAGNOLIA data set.

**Reading SAS data sets using direct referencing**   To read a permanent SAS data set using direct referencing, simply enclose the path and name for the data set in quotation marks wherever you would use a SAS data set name. For example, to print the MAGNOLIA data set, you could use the following statements:

```
PROC PRINT DATA = 'c:\MySASLib\magnolia';
   TITLE 'Magnolias';
RUN;
```

The output looks like this:

```
                              Magnolias                                    1

                                         Maximum   Age
 Obs   ScientificName     CommonName      Height   Bloom  Type  Color

  1    M. grandiflora   Southern Magnolia    80      15    E    white
  2    M. campbellii                         80      20    D    rose
  3    M. liliiflora    Lily Magnolia        12       4    D    purple
  4    M. soulangiana   Saucer Magnolia      25       3    D    pink
  5    M. stellata      Star Magnolia        10       3    D    white
```

## 2.22    Listing the Contents of a SAS Data Set

To use a SAS data set, all you need to do is tell SAS the name and location of the data set you want, and SAS will figure out what is in it. SAS can do this because SAS data sets are self-documenting, which is another way of saying that SAS automatically stores information about the data set (also called the descriptor portion) along with the data. You can't display a SAS data set on your computer screen using a word processor. However, there is an easy way to get a description of a SAS data set; you simply run the CONTENTS procedure.

PROC CONTENTS is a simple procedure. In most cases you just type the keywords PROC CONTENTS and specify the data set you want with the DATA= option:

```
PROC CONTENTS DATA = data-set;
```

If you omit the DATA= option, then by default SAS will use the most recently created data set.

**Example**  The following DATA step creates a data set so we can run PROC CONTENTS:

```
DATA funnies (LABEL = 'Comics Character Data');
   INPUT Id Name $ Height Weight DoB MMDDYY8. @@;
   LABEL Id  = 'Identification no.'
      Height = 'Height in inches'
      Weight = 'Weight in pounds'
      DoB    = 'Date of birth';
   INFORMAT DoB MMDDYY8.;
   FORMAT DoB WORDDATE18.;
   DATALINES;
53 Susie    42   41   07-11-81 54 Charlie  46   55   10-26-54
55 Calvin   40   35   01-10-81 56 Lucy     46   52   01-13-55
   ;
* Use PROC CONTENTS to describe data set funnies;
PROC CONTENTS DATA = funnies;
RUN;
```

Note that the DATA step above includes a LABEL= data set option[1] on the DATA statement and a LABEL statement. The LABEL= data set option gives a label for the entire data set while the LABEL statement assigns labels to individual variables. These optional labels, which can be up to 256 characters long, allow you to document your data in more detail than is possible with just variable or data set names. For variables, if you specify a LABEL statement in a DATA step, then the descriptions will be stored in the data set and will be printed by PROC CONTENTS. You can also use LABEL statements in PROC steps to customize your reports, but then the labels apply only for the duration of the PROC step and are not stored in the data set.

INFORMAT and FORMAT statements also appear in this program. You can use these optional statements to associate informats or formats with variables. Just as informats give SAS special instructions for reading a variable, formats give SAS special instructions for writing a variable. If you specify an INFORMAT or FORMAT statement in a DATA step, then the name of that informat or format will be saved in the data set and printed by PROC CONTENTS. FORMAT statements, like LABEL statements, can be used in PROC steps to customize your reports, but then the name of the format is not stored in the data set.[2]

---

[1] See section 6.11 for more information on data set options.

[2] Sections 4.5 and 4.6 discuss standard SAS formats more thoroughly.

The output from PROC CONTENTS is like a table of contents for your data set:

```
                         The CONTENTS Procedure

  ❶ Data Set Name    WORK.FUNNIES            ❷ Observations          4
    Member Type      DATA                    ❸ Variables             5
    Engine           V9                        Indexes               0
  ❹ Created          Monday, May 5, 2008 09:23 AM   Observation Length    40
    Last Modified    Monday, May 5, 2008 09:23 AM   Deleted Observations  0
    Protection                                 Compressed            NO
    Data Set Type                              Sorted                NO
  ❺ Label            Comics Character Data
    Data Representation  WINDOWS_32
    Encoding wlatin1     wlatin1 Western (Windows)

              -----Engine/Host Dependent Information-----
    Data Set Page Size          4096
    Number of Data Set Pages    1
    First Data Page             1
    Max Obs per Page            101
    Obs in First Data Page      4
    Number of Data Set Repairs  0
    File Name                   C:\Users\Lora\AppData\Local\Temp\SAS
                                Temporary Files\_TD5468\funnies.sas7bdat
    Release Created             9.0201M0
    Host Created                W32_VSPRO

              -----Alphabetic List of Variables and Attributes-----
    #   Variable ❶Type ❷Len   ❸Format      ❹Informat ❺Label

    5   DoB      Num    8    WORDDATE18.   MMDDYY8.  Date of birth
    3   Height   Num    8                            Height in inches
    1   Id       Num    8                            Identification no.
    2   Name     Char   8
    4   Weight   Num    8                            Weight in pounds
```

The output starts with information about your data set and then describes each variable.

**For the data set**
❶ Data set name
❷ Number of observations
❸ Number of variables
❹ Date created
❺ Data set label (if any)

**For each variable**
❶ Type (numeric or character)
❷ Length (storage size in bytes)
❸ Format for printing (if any)
❹ Informat for input (if any)
❺ Variable label (if any)

**3**

"Contrariwise," continued Tweedledee," if it was so, it might be; and if it were so, it would be; but as it isn't, it ain't. That's logic."

LEWIS CARROLL

From *Alice Through the Looking Glass* by Lewis Carroll. Public domain.

# CHAPTER 3

## Working with Your Data

## 3.1  Creating and Redefining Variables

If someone were to compile a list of the most popular things to do with SAS software, creating and redefining variables would surely be near the top. Fortunately, SAS is flexible and uses a common sense approach to these tasks. You create and redefine variables with assignment statements using this basic form:

```
variable = expression;
```

On the left side of the equal sign is a variable name, either new or old. On the right side of the equal sign may appear a constant, another variable, or a mathematical expression. Here are examples of these basic types of assignment statements:

| Type of expression | Assignment statement |
| --- | --- |
| numeric constant | Qwerty = 10; |
| character constant | Qwerty = 'ten'; |
| a variable | Qwerty = OldVar; |
| addition | Qwerty = OldVar + 10; |
| subtraction | Qwerty = OldVar - 10; |
| multiplication | Qwerty = OldVar * 10; |
| division | Qwerty = OldVar / 10; |
| exponentiation | Qwerty = OldVar ** 10; |

Whether the variable Qwerty is numeric or character depends on the expression that defines it. When the expression is numeric, Qwerty will be numeric; when it is character, Qwerty will be character.

When deciding how to interpret your expression, SAS follows the standard mathematical rules of precedence: SAS performs exponentiation first, then multiplication and division, followed by addition and subtraction. You can use parentheses to override that order. Here are two similar SAS statements showing that a couple of parentheses can make a big difference:

| Assignment statement | Result |
| --- | --- |
| x = 10 * 4 + 3 ** 2; | x = 49 |
| x = 10 * (4 + 3 ** 2); | x = 130 |

While SAS can read expressions with or without parentheses, people often can't. If you use parentheses, your programs will be a lot easier to read.

**Example**  The following raw data are from a survey of home gardeners. Gardeners were asked to estimate the number of pounds they harvested for four crops: tomatoes, zucchini, peas, and grapes.

```
Gregor  10  2  40     0
Molly   15  5  10  1000
Luther  50 10  15    50
Susan   20  0   .    20
```

This program reads the data from a file called Garden.dat and then modifies the data:

```
* Modify homegarden data set with assignment statements;
DATA homegarden;
    INFILE 'c:\MyRawData\Garden.dat';
    INPUT Name $ 1-7 Tomato Zucchini Peas Grapes;
    Zone = 14;
    Type = 'home';
    Zucchini = Zucchini * 10;
    Total = Tomato + Zucchini + Peas + Grapes;
    PerTom = (Tomato / Total) * 100;
RUN;
PROC PRINT DATA = homegarden;
    TITLE 'Home Gardening Survey';
RUN;
```

This program contains five assignment statements. The first creates a new variable, Zone, equal to a numeric constant, 14. The variable Type is set equal to a character constant, home. The variable Zucchini is multiplied by 10 because that just seems natural for zucchini. Total is the sum for all the types of plants. PerTom is not a genetically engineered tomato but the percentage of harvest which were tomatoes. The report from PROC PRINT contains all the variables, old and new:

```
                    Home Gardening Survey                        1

 Obs  Name    Tomato Zucchini Peas Grapes Zone Type  Total  PerTom

  1   Gregor    10      20     40     0    14   home    70   14.2857
  2   Molly     15      50     10   1000   14   home  1075    1.3953
  3   Luther    50     100     15     50   14   home   215   23.2558
  4   Susan     20       0      .     20   14   home     .       .
```

Notice that the variable Zucchini appears only once because the new value replaced the old value. The other four assignment statements each created a new variable. When a variable is new, SAS adds it to the data set you are creating. When a variable already exists, SAS replaces the original value with the new one. Using an existing name has the advantage of not cluttering your data set with a lot of similar variables. However, you don't want to overwrite a variable unless you are really sure you won't need the original value later.

The variable Peas had a missing value for the last observation. Because of this, the variables Total and PerTom, which are calculated from Peas, were also set to missing and this message appeared in the log:

```
NOTE: Missing values were generated as a result of performing an operation on
      missing values.
```

This message is a flag that often indicates an error. However, in this case it is not an error but simply the result of incomplete data collection.[1]

---

[1] If you want to add only non-missing values, you can use the SUM function discussed in section 10.7.

## 3.2 Using SAS Functions

Sometimes a simple expression, using only arithmetic operators, does not give you the new value you are looking for. This is where functions are handy, simplifying your task because SAS has already done the programming for you. All you need to do is plug the right values into the function and out comes the result—like putting a dollar in a change machine and getting back four quarters.

SAS has hundreds of functions in general areas including:

| | |
|---|---|
| Character | Macro |
| Character String Matching | Mathematical |
| Date and Time | Probability |
| Descriptive Statistics | Random Number |
| Distance | State and ZIP Code |
| Financial | Variable Information |

The next two sections give a sample of the most common SAS functions.

Functions perform a calculation on, or a transformation of, the arguments given in parentheses following the function name. SAS functions have the following general form:

```
function-name(argument, argument, ...)
```

All functions must have parentheses even if they don't require any arguments. Arguments are separated by commas and can be variable names, constant values such as numbers or characters enclosed in quotation marks, or expressions. The following statement computes Birthday as a SAS date value using the function MDY and the variables MonthBorn, DayBorn, and YearBorn. The MDY function takes three arguments, one each for the month, day, and year:

```
Birthday = MDY(MonthBorn, DayBorn, YearBorn);
```

Functions can be nested, where one function is the argument of another function. For example, the following statement calculates NewValue using two nested functions, INT and LOG:

```
NewValue = INT(LOG(10));
```

The result for this example is 2, the integer portion of the natural log of the numeric constant 10 (2.3026). Just be careful when nesting functions that each parenthesis has a mate.

**Example** Data from a pumpkin carving contest illustrate the use of several functions. The contestants' names are followed by their age, type of pumpkin (carved or decorated), date of entry, and the scores from five judges:

```
Alicia Grossman    13 c 10-28-2008 7.8 6.5 7.2 8.0 7.9
Matthew Lee         9 D 10-30-2008 6.5 5.9 6.8 6.0 8.1
Elizabeth Garcia   10 C 10-29-2008 8.9 7.9 8.5 9.0 8.8
Lori Newcombe       6 D 10-30-2008 6.7 5.6 4.9 5.2 6.1
Jose Martinez       7 d 10-31-2008 8.9 9.510.0 9.7 9.0
Brian Williams     11 C 10-29-2008 7.8 8.4 8.5 7.9 8.0
```

The following program reads the data, creates two new variables (AvgScore and DayEntered) and transforms another (Type):

```
DATA contest;
    INFILE 'c:\MyRawData\Pumpkin.dat';
    INPUT Name $16. Age 3. +1 Type $1. +1 Date MMDDYY10.
          (Scr1 Scr2 Scr3 Scr4 Scr5) (4.1);
    AvgScore = MEAN(Scr1, Scr2, Scr3, Scr4, Scr5);
    DayEntered = DAY(Date);
    Type = UPCASE(Type);
RUN;
PROC PRINT DATA = contest;
    TITLE 'Pumpkin Carving Contest';
RUN;
```

The variable AvgScore is created using the MEAN function, which returns the mean of the non-missing arguments. This differs from simply adding the arguments together and dividing by their number, which would return a missing value if any of the arguments were missing.

The variable DayEntered is created using the DAY function, which returns the day of the month. SAS has all sorts of functions for manipulating dates, and what's great about them is that you don't have to worry about things like leap year—SAS takes care of that for you.

The variable Type is transformed using the UPCASE function. SAS is case sensitive when it comes to variable values; a 'd' is not the same as 'D'. The data file has both lowercase and uppercase letters for the variable Type, so the function UPCASE is used to make all the values uppercase.

Here are the results:

| | | | | | | | | | | Avg | Day |
|---|---|---|---|---|---|---|---|---|---|---|---|
| Obs | Name | Age | Type | Date[1] | Scr1 | Scr2 | Scr3 | Scr4 | Scr5 | Score | Entered |
| 1 | Alicia Grossman | 13 | C | 17467 | 7.8 | 6.5 | 7.2 | 8.0 | 7.9 | 7.48 | 28 |
| 2 | Matthew Lee | 9 | D | 17469 | 6.5 | 5.9 | 6.8 | 6.0 | 8.1 | 6.66 | 30 |
| 3 | Elizabeth Garcia | 10 | C | 17468 | 8.9 | 7.9 | 8.5 | 9.0 | 8.8 | 8.62 | 29 |
| 4 | Lori Newcombe | 6 | D | 17469 | 6.7 | 5.6 | 4.9 | 5.2 | 6.1 | 5.70 | 30 |
| 5 | Jose Martinez | 7 | D | 17470 | 8.9 | 9.5 | 10.0 | 9.7 | 9.0 | 9.42 | 31 |
| 6 | Brian Williams | 11 | C | 17468 | 7.8 | 8.4 | 8.5 | 7.9 | 8.0 | 8.12 | 29 |

Pumpkin Carving Contest                                    1

---

[1] Notice that these dates are printed as the number of days since January 1, 1960. Section 4.5 discusses how to format these values into readable dates.

# 3.3    Selected SAS Character Functions

| Function name | Syntax[1] | Definition |
|---|---|---|
| **Character** | | |
| ANYALNUM | ANYALNUM(*arg,start*) | Returns position of first occurrence of any alphabetic character or numeral at or after optional start position |
| ANYALPHA | ANYALPHA(*arg,start*) | Returns position of first occurrence of any alphabetic character at or after optional start position |
| ANYDIGIT | ANYDIGIT(*arg,start*) | Returns position of first occurrence of any numeral at or after optional start position |
| ANYSPACE | ANYSPACE(*arg,start*) | Returns position of first occurrence of a white space character at or after optional start position |
| CAT | CAT(*arg-1,arg-2,...arg-n*) | Concatenates two or more character strings together leaving leading and trailing blanks |
| CATS | CATS(*arg-1,arg-2,...arg-n*) | Concatenates two or more character strings together stripping leading and trailing blanks |
| CATX | CATX('*separator-string*', *arg-1,arg-2,...arg-n*) | Concatenates two or more character strings together stripping leading and trailing blanks and inserting a separator string between arguments |
| COMPRESS | COMPRESS(*arg*, '*char*') | Removes spaces or optional characters from character string |
| INDEX | INDEX(*arg*, '*string*') | Returns starting position for string of characters |
| LEFT | LEFT(*arg*) | Left aligns a SAS character expression |
| LENGTH | LENGTH(*arg*) | Returns the length of an argument not counting trailing blanks (missing values have a length of 1) |
| PROPCASE | PROPCASE(*arg*) | Converts first character in word to uppercase and remaining characters to lowercase |
| SUBSTR | SUBSTR(*arg,position,n*) | Extracts a substring from an argument starting at *position* for *n* characters or until end if no $n$ [2] |
| TRANSLATE | TRANSLATE(*source,to-1, from-1,...to-n,from-n*) | Replaces *from* characters in *source* with *to* characters (one to one replacement only—you can't replace one character with two, for example) |
| TRANWRD | TRANWRD(*source,from,to*) | Replaces *from* character string in *source* with *to* character string |
| TRIM | TRIM(*arg*) | Removes trailing blanks from character expression |
| UPCASE | UPCASE(*arg*) | Converts all letters in argument to uppercase |

[1] *arg* is short for argument, which means a literal value, variable name, or expression.

| Function name | Example | Result | Example | Result |
|---|---|---|---|---|
| **Character** | | | | |
| ANYALNUM | a='123 E St, #2 ';<br>x=ANYALNUM(a); | x=1 | a='123 E St, #2 ';<br>y=ANYALNUM(a,10); | y=12 |
| ANYALPHA | a='123 E St, #2 ';<br>x=ANYALPHA(a); | x=5 | a='123 E St, #2 ';<br>y=ANYALPHA(a,10); | y=0 |
| ANYDIGIT | a='123 E St, #2 ';<br>x=ANYDIGIT(a); | x=1 | a='123 E St, #2 ';<br>y=ANYDIGIT(a,10); | y=12 |
| ANYSPACE | a='123 E St, #2 ';<br>x=ANYSPACE(a); | x=4 | a='123 E St, #2 ';<br>y=ANYSPACE(a,10); | y=10 |
| CAT | a=' cat';b='dog ';<br>x=CAT(a,b); | x=' catdog ' | a='cat ';b=' dog';<br>y=CAT(a,b); | y='cat  dog' |
| CATS | a=' cat';b='dog ';<br>x=CATS(a,b); | x='catdog' | a='cat ';b=' dog';<br>y=CATS(a,b); | y='catdog' |
| CATX | a=' cat';b='dog ';<br>x=CATX(' ',a,b); | x='cat dog' | a=' cat';b='dog ';<br>y=CATX('&',a,b); | y='cat&dog' |
| COMPRESS | a=' cat & dog';<br>x=COMPRESS(a); | x='cat&dog' | a=' cat & dog';<br>y=COMPRESS(a,'&'); | y=' cat  dog' |
| INDEX | a='123 E St, #2';<br>x=INDEX(a,'#'); | x=11 | a='123 E St, #2';<br>y=INDEX(a,'St'); | y=7 |
| LEFT | a='  cat';<br>x=LEFT(a); | x='cat  ' | a='  my cat';<br>y=LEFT(a); | y='my cat  ' |
| LENGTH | a='my cat';<br>x=LENGTH(a); | x=6 | a=' my cat ';<br>y=LENGTH(a); | y=7 |
| PROPCASE | a='MyCat';<br>x=PROPCASE(a); | x='Mycat' | a='TIGER';<br>y=PROPCASE(a); | y='Tiger' |
| SUBSTR | a='(916)734-6281';<br>x=SUBSTR(a,2,3); | x='916' | y=SUBSTR('1cat',2); | y='cat' |
| TRANSLATE | a='6/16/99';<br>x=TRANSLATE<br>(a,'-','/'); | x='6-16-99' | a='my cat can';<br>y=TRANSLATE<br>(a, 'r','c'); | y='my rat ran' |
| TRANWRD | a='Main Street';<br>x=TRANWRD<br>(a,'Street','St'); | x='Main St' | a='my cat can';<br>y=TRANWRD<br>(a,'cat','rat'); | y='my rat can' |
| TRIM | a='my  '; b='cat';<br>x=TRIM(a)\|\|b;[3] | x='mycat  ' | a='my cat '; b='s';<br>y=TRIM(a)\|\|b; | y='my cats ' |
| UPCASE | a='MyCat';<br>x=UPCASE(a); | x='MYCAT' | y=UPCASE('Tiger'); | y='TIGER' |

[2] SUBSTR has a different function when on the left side of an equal sign.

[3] The concatenation operator | | concatenates character strings.

# 3.4 Selected SAS Numeric Functions

| Function name | Syntax[1] | Definition |
|---|---|---|
| **Numeric** | | |
| INT | INT(*arg*) | Returns the integer portion of argument |
| LOG | LOG(*arg*) | Natural logarithm |
| LOG10 | LOG10(*arg*) | Logarithm to the base 10 |
| MAX | MAX(*arg-1,arg-2,...arg-n*) | Largest non-missing value |
| MEAN | MEAN(*arg-1,arg-2,...arg-n*) | Arithmetic mean of non-missing values |
| MIN | MIN(*arg-1,arg-2,...arg-n*) | Smallest non-missing value |
| N | N(*arg-1,arg-2,...arg-n*) | Number of non-missing values |
| NMISS | NMISS(*arg-1,arg-2,...arg-n*) | Number of missing values |
| ROUND | ROUND(*arg, round-off-unit*) | Rounds to nearest round-off unit |
| SUM | SUM(*arg-1,arg-2,...arg-n*) | Sum of non-missing values |
| **Date** | | |
| DATEJUL | DATEJUL(*julian-date*) | Converts a Julian date to a SAS date value[2] |
| DAY | DAY(*date*) | Returns the day of the month from a SAS date value |
| MDY | MDY(*month,day,year*) | Returns a SAS date value from month, day, and year values |
| MONTH | MONTH(*date*) | Returns the month (1–12) from a SAS date value |
| QTR | QTR(*date*) | Returns the yearly quarter (1–4) from a SAS date value |
| TODAY | TODAY() | Returns the current date as a SAS date value |
| WEEKDAY | WEEKDAY(date) | Returns day of week (1=Sunday) from SAS date value |
| YEAR | YEAR(date) | Returns year from a SAS date value |

[1] *arg* is short for argument, which means a literal value, variable name, or expression.
[2] A SAS date value is the number of days since January 1, 1960.

| Function name | Example | Result | Example | Result |
|---|---|---|---|---|
| **Numeric** | | | | |
| INT | x=INT(4.32); | x=4 | y=INT(5.789); | y=5 |
| LOG | x=LOG(1); | x=0.0 | y=LOG(10); | y=2.30259 |
| LOG10 | x=LOG10(1); | x=0.0 | y=LOG10(10); | y=1.0 |
| MAX | x=MAX(9.3,8,7.5); | x=9.3 | y=MAX(-3,.,5); | y=5 |
| MEAN | x=MEAN(1,4,7,2); | x=3.5 | y=MEAN(2,.,3); | y=2.5 |
| MIN | x=MIN(9.3,8,7.5); | x=7.5 | y=MIN(-3,.,5); | y=-3 |
| N | x=N(1,.,7,2); | x=3 | y=N(.,4,.,.); | y=1 |
| NMISS | x=NMISS(1,.,7,2); | x=1 | y=NMISS(.,4,.,.); | y=3 |
| ROUND | x=ROUND(12.65); | x=13 | y=ROUND(12.65,.1); | y=12.7 |
| SUM | x=SUM(3,5,1); | x=9.0 | y=SUM(4,7,.); | y=11 |
| **Date** | | | | |
| DATEJUL | a=60001;<br>x=DATEJUL(a); | x=0 | a=60365;<br>y=DATEJUL(a); | y=364 |
| DAY | a=MDY(4,18,2008);<br>x=DAY(a); | x=18 | a=MDY(9,3,60);<br>y=DAY(a); | y=3 |
| MDY | x=MDY(1,1,1960); | x=0 | m=2; d=1; y=60;<br>Date=MDY(m,d,y); | Date=31 |
| MONTH | a=MDY(4,18,2008);<br>x=MONTH(a); | x=4 | a=MDY(9,3,60);<br>y=MONTH(a); | y=9 |
| QTR | a=MDY(4,18,2008);<br>x=QTR(a); | x=2 | a=MDY(9,3,60);<br>y=QTR(a); | y=3 |
| TODAY | x=TODAY(); | x=*today's date* | y=TODAY()-1; | y=*yesterday's date* |
| WEEKDAY | a=MDY(4,13,2008);<br>x=WEEKDAY(a); | x=1 | a=MDY(4,18,2008);<br>y=WEEKDAY(a); | y=6 |
| YEAR | a=MDY(4,13,2008);<br>x=YEAR(a); | x=2008 | a=MDY(1,1,1960);<br>y=YEAR(a); | y=1960 |

## 3.5 ▸ Using IF-THEN Statements

Frequently, you want an assignment statement to apply to some observations, but not all—under some conditions, but not others. This is called conditional logic, and you do it with IF-THEN statements:

```
IF condition THEN action;
```

The *condition* is an expression comparing one thing to another, and the *action* is what SAS should do when the expression is true, often an assignment statement. For example

```
IF Model = 'Mustang' THEN Make = 'Ford';
```

This statement tells SAS to set the variable Make equal to Ford whenever the variable Model equals Mustang. The terms on either side of the comparison may be constants, variables, or expressions. Those terms are separated by a comparison operator, which may be either symbolic or mnemonic. The decision of whether to use symbolic or mnemonic operators depends on your personal preference and the symbols available on your keyboard. Here are the basic comparison operators:

| Symbolic | Mnemonic | Meaning |
|---|---|---|
| = | EQ | equals |
| ¬ =, ^ =, or ~ = | NE | not equal |
| > | GT | greater than |
| < | LT | less than |
| > = | GE | greater than or equal |
| < = | LE | less than or equal |

The IN operator also makes comparisons, but it works a bit differently. IN compares the value of a variable to a list of values. Here is an example:

```
IF Model IN ('Corvette', 'Camaro') THEN Make = 'Chevrolet';
```

This statement tells SAS to set the variable Make equal to Chevrolet whenever the value of Model is Corvette or Camaro.

A single IF-THEN statement can only have one action. If you add the keywords DO and END, then you can execute more than one action. For example

```
IF condition THEN DO;          IF Model = 'Mustang' THEN DO;
   action;                        Make = 'Ford';
   action;                        Size = 'compact';
END;                           END;
```

The DO statement causes all SAS statements coming after it to be treated as a unit until a matching END statement appears. Together, the DO statement, the END statement, and all the statements in between are called a DO group.

You can also specify multiple conditions with the keywords AND and OR:

```
IF condition AND condition THEN action;
```

For example

```
IF Model = 'Mustang' AND Year < 1975 THEN Status = 'classic';
```

Like the comparison operators, AND and OR may be symbolic or mnemonic:

| Symbolic | Mnemonic | Meaning |
|---|---|---|
| & | AND | all comparisons must be true |
| \|, ¦, or ! | OR | only one comparison must be true |

Be careful with long strings of comparisons; they can be a logical maze.

**Example** The following data about used cars contain values for model, year, make, number of seats, and color:

```
Corvette 1955 .      2 black
XJ6      1995 Jaguar 2 teal
Mustang  1966 Ford   4 red
Miata    2002 .      . silver
CRX      2001 Honda  2 black
Camaro   2000 .      4 red
```

This program reads the data from a file called UsedCars.dat, uses a series of IF-THEN statements to fill in missing data, and creates a new variable, Status:

```
DATA sportscars;
    INFILE 'c:\MyRawData\UsedCars.dat';
    INPUT Model $ Year Make $ Seats Color $;
    IF Year < 1975 THEN Status = 'classic';
    IF Model = 'Corvette' OR Model = 'Camaro' THEN Make = 'Chevy';
    IF Model = 'Miata' THEN DO;
       Make = 'Mazda';
       Seats = 2;
    END;
RUN;
PROC PRINT DATA = sportscars;
    TITLE "Eddy's Excellent Emporium of Used Sports Cars";
RUN;
```

This program contains three IF-THEN statements. The first is a simple IF-THEN that creates the new variable Status based on the value of Year. That is followed by a compound IF-THEN using an OR. The last IF-THEN uses DO and END. The output looks like this:

```
                 Eddy's Excellent Emporium of Used Sports Cars        1

    Obs    Model      Year    Make      Seats    Color     Status

     1     Corvette   1955    Chevy       2      black     classic
     2     XJ6        1995    Jaguar      2      teal
     3     Mustang    1966    Ford        4      red       classic
     4     Miata      2002    Mazda       2      silver
     5     CRX        2001    Honda       2      black
     6     Camaro     2000    Chevy       4      red
```

## 3.6 Grouping Observations with IF-THEN/ELSE Statements

| red | | red | warm | |
| orange | | orange | warm | |
| yellow | | yellow | warm | |
| green | | green | cool | |
| blue | | blue | cool | |
| purple | | purple | cool | |

One common use of IF-THEN statements is for grouping observations. Perhaps a variable has too many different values and you want to print a more compact report, or perhaps you are going to run an analysis based on specific groups of interest. There are many possible reasons for grouping data, so sooner or later you'll probably need to do it.

The simplest and most common way to create a grouping variable is with a series of IF-THEN statements.[1] By adding the keyword ELSE to your IF statements, you can tell SAS that these statements are related.

IF-THEN/ELSE logic takes this basic form:

```
IF condition THEN action;
   ELSE IF condition THEN action;
   ELSE IF condition THEN action;
```

Notice that the ELSE statement is simply an IF-THEN statement with an ELSE tacked onto the front. You can have any number of these statements.

IF-THEN/ELSE logic has two advantages when compared to a simple series of IF-THEN statements without any ELSE statements. First, it is more efficient, using less computer time; once an observation satisfies a condition, SAS skips the rest of the series. Second, ELSE logic ensures that your groups are mutually exclusive so you don't accidentally have an observation fitting into more than one group.

Sometimes the last ELSE statement in a series is a little different, containing just an action, with no IF or THEN. Note the final ELSE statement in this series:

```
IF condition THEN action;
   ELSE IF condition THEN action;
   ELSE action;
```

An ELSE of this kind becomes a default which is automatically executed for all observations failing to satisfy any of the previous IF statements. You can only have one of these statements, and it must be the last in the IF-THEN/ELSE series.

**Example** Here are data from a survey of home improvements. Each record contains three data values: owner's name, description of the work done, and cost of the improvements in dollars:

```
Bob       kitchen cabinet face-lift    1253.00
Shirley   bathroom addition           11350.70
Silvia    paint exterior                     .
Al        backyard gazebo             3098.63
Norm      paint interior               647.77
Kathy     second floor addition      75362.93
```

---

[1] Other ways to create grouping variables include using a SELECT statement, or using a PUT function with a user-defined format from PROC FORMAT.

This program reads the raw data from a file called Home.dat and then assigns a grouping variable called CostGroup. This variable has a value of high, medium, low, or missing, depending on the value of Cost:

```
* Group observations by cost;
DATA homeimprovements;
    INFILE 'c:\MyRawData\Home.dat';
    INPUT Owner $ 1-7 Description $ 9-33 Cost;
    IF Cost = . THEN CostGroup = 'missing';
        ELSE IF Cost < 2000 THEN CostGroup = 'low';
        ELSE IF Cost < 10000 THEN CostGroup = 'medium';
        ELSE CostGroup = 'high';
RUN;
PROC PRINT DATA = homeimprovements;
    TITLE 'Home Improvement Cost Groups';
RUN;
```

Notice that there are four statements in this IF-THEN/ELSE series, one for each possible value of the variable CostGroup. The first statement deals with observations that have missing data for the variable Cost. Without this first statement, observations with a missing value for Cost would be incorrectly assigned a CostGroup of low. SAS considers missing values to be smaller than non-missing values, smaller than any printable character for character variables, and smaller than negative numbers for numeric variables. Unless you are sure that your data contain no missing values, you should allow for missing values when you write IF-THEN/ELSE statements.

The results look like this:

```
                    Home Improvement Cost Groups                    1


                                                            Cost
                                                   Cost     Group
    Obs    Owner     Description

     1     Bob       kitchen cabinet face-lift    1253.00   low
     2     Shirley   bathroom addition           11350.70   high
     3     Silvia    paint exterior                  .      missing
     4     Al        backyard gazebo              3098.63   medium
     5     Norm      paint interior                647.77   low
     6     Kathy     second floor addition       75362.93   high
```

## 3.7 ▸ Subsetting Your Data

Often programmers find that they want to use some of the observations in a data set and exclude the rest. The most common way to do this is with a subsetting IF statement in a DATA step.[1] The basic form of a subsetting IF is

```
IF expression;
```

Consider this example:

```
IF Sex = 'f';
```

At first subsetting IF statements may seem odd. People naturally ask, "IF Sex = 'f', then what?" The subsetting IF looks incomplete, as if a careless typist pressed the delete key too long. But it is really a special case of the standard IF-THEN statement. In this case the action is merely implied. If the expression is true, then SAS continues with the DATA step. If the expression is false, then no further statements are processed for that observation; that observation is not added to the data set being created; and SAS moves on to the next observation. You can think of the subsetting IF as a kind of on-off switch. If the condition is true, then the switch is on and the observation is processed. If the condition is false, then that observation is turned off.

If you don't like subsetting IFs, there is another alternative, the DELETE statement. DELETE statements do the opposite of subsetting IFs. While the subsetting IF statement tells SAS which observations to include, the DELETE statement tells SAS which observations to exclude:

```
IF expression THEN DELETE;
```

The following two statements are equivalent (assuming there are only two values for the variable Sex, and no missing data):

```
IF Sex = 'f';        IF Sex = 'm' THEN DELETE;
```

**Example**   The members of a local amateur playhouse want to choose a Shakespearean comedy for this spring's play. You volunteer to compile a list of titles using an online encyclopedia. For each play your data file contains title, approximate year of first performance, and type of play:

```
A Midsummer Night's Dream 1595  comedy
Comedy of Errors          1590  comedy
Hamlet                    1600  tragedy
Macbeth                   1606  tragedy
Richard III               1594  history
Romeo and Juliet          1596  tragedy
Taming of the Shrew       1593  comedy
Tempest                   1611  romance
```

---

[1] For more on subsetting IF statements see sections 2.13 and 6.9. Other ways to subset data include the WHERE statement (section 4.2 and appendix D), and WHERE= option (section 6.13).

This program reads the data from a raw data file called Shakespeare.dat and then uses a subsetting IF statement to select only comedies:

```
* Choose only comedies;
DATA comedy;
    INFILE 'c:\MyRawData\Shakespeare.dat';
    INPUT Title $ 1-26 Year Type $;
    IF Type = 'comedy';
RUN;
PROC PRINT DATA = comedy;
    TITLE 'Shakespearean Comedies';
RUN;
```

The output looks like this:

```
                        Shakespearean Comedies                1

          Obs    Title                      Year     Type

           1     A Midsummer Night's Dream   1595     comedy
           2     Comedy of Errors            1590     comedy
           3     Taming of the Shrew         1593     comedy
```

These notes appear in the log stating that although eight records were read from the input file, the data set WORK.COMEDY contains only three observations:

```
NOTE: 8 records were read from the infile 'c:\MyRawData\Shakespeare.dat'
NOTE: The data set WORK.COMEDY has 3 observations and 3 variables.
```

It is always a good idea to check the SAS log when you subset observations to make sure that you ended up with what you expected.

In the program above, you could substitute the statement

```
    IF Type = 'tragedy' OR Type = 'romance' OR Type = 'history' THEN DELETE;
```

for the statement

```
    IF Type = 'comedy';
```

But you would have to do a lot more typing. Generally, you use the subsetting IF when it is easier to specify a condition for including observations, and use the DELETE statement when is easier to specify a condition for excluding observations.

## 3.8  Working with SAS Dates

Dates can be tricky to work with. Some months have 30 days, some 31, some 28, and don't forget leap year. SAS dates simplify all this. A SAS date is a numeric value equal to the number of days since January 1, 1960. The table below lists four dates and their values as SAS dates:

| Date | SAS date value |
|------|---------------|
| January 1, 1959 | -365 |
| January 1, 1960 | 0 |
| January 1, 1961 | 366 |
| January 1, 2008 | 17532 |

SAS has special tools for working with dates: informats for reading dates, functions for manipulating dates, and formats for printing dates.[1] A table of selected date informats, formats, and functions appears in the next section.

**Informats**  To read variables that are dates, you use formatted style input. SAS has a variety of date informats for reading dates in many different forms. All of these informats convert your data to a number equal to the number of days since January 1, 1960. The INPUT statement below tells SAS to read a variable named BirthDate using the ANYDTDTE9. informat:[2]

```
INPUT BirthDate ANYDTDTE9.;
```

**Setting the default century for input**  When SAS sees a date with a two-digit year like 07/04/76, SAS has to decide in which century the year belongs. Is the year 1976, 2076, or perhaps 1776? The system option YEARCUTOFF= specifies the first year of a hundred-year span for SAS to use. The default value for this option is 1920, but you can change this value with the OPTIONS statement. To avoid problems, you may want to specify the YEARCUTOFF= option whenever you input data containing two-digit years. This statement tells SAS to interpret two-digit dates as occurring between 1950 and 2049:

```
OPTIONS YEARCUTOFF = 1950;
```

**Dates in SAS expressions**  Once a variable has been read with a SAS date informat, it can be used in arithmetic expressions like other numeric variables. For example, if a library book is due in three weeks, you could find the due date by adding 21 days to the date it was checked out:

```
DueDate = CheckDate + 21;
```

You can use a date as a constant in a SAS expression. Put the date in DATE*w*. format (such as 01JAN60). Then add quotation marks followed by the letter D. The assignment statement below creates a variable named EarthDay08, which is equal to the SAS date value for April 22, 2008:

```
EarthDay08 = '22APR2008'D;
```

---

[1] SAS also has informats, functions, and formats for working with time values (the number of seconds since midnight), and datetime values (the number of seconds since midnight, you guessed it, January 1, 1960).

[2] ANYDTDTE*w*. is a special informat that can read dates in almost any form. If a date is ambiguous such as 01-02-03, then SAS uses the value of the DATESTYLE= system option to determine the order of month, day and year. The default value of DATESTYLE= is MDY (month, then day, then year).

**Functions** SAS date functions perform many handy operations. The WEEKDAY function, for example, returns a number indicating the day of the week (with Sunday equal to 1). Suppose a library is closed on Mondays. You could use the WEEKDAY function to find books that are due on Monday, and then extend the due dates to Tuesday.

```
IF WEEKDAY(DueDate) = 2 THEN DueDate = DueDate + 1;
```

**Formats** If you print a SAS date value, SAS will by default print the actual value—the number of days since January 1, 1960. Since this is not very meaningful to most people, SAS has a variety of formats for printing dates in different forms.[3] The FORMAT statement below tells SAS to print the variable BirthDate using the WORDDATE18. format:

```
FORMAT BirthDate WORDDATE18.;
```

**Example** A local library has a data file containing details about library cards. Each record contains the card holder's name, birthdate, the date that the card was issued, and the due date for the last book borrowed.

```
A. Jones      1-1-60     9-15-06    29Feb08
M. Rincon     05/10/1949 29feb2008  23MAY2008
Z. Grandage   03181988   31 10 2007 31may08
K. Kaminaka   052903     2008024    12JUN08
```

The program below reads the raw data, and then computes the variable DaysOverDue by subtracting DueDate from the current date. Then an IF statement uses a date constant to identify cards issued after January 1, 2008.

```
DATA librarycards;
   INFILE 'c:\MyRawData\Library.dat' TRUNCOVER;
   INPUT Name $11. + 1 BirthDate MMDDYY10. +1 IssueDate ANYDTDTE10.
      DueDate DATE11.;
   DaysOverDue = TODAY() - DueDate;
   IF IssueDate > '01JAN2008'D THEN NewCard = 'yes';
RUN;
PROC PRINT DATA = librarycards;
   FORMAT Issuedate MMDDYY8. DueDate WEEKDATE17.;
   TITLE 'SAS Dates without and with Formats';
RUN;
```

Here is the output from PROC PRINT. Notice that the variable BirthDate is printed without a date format, while IssueDate and DueDate use formats. Because DaysOverDue is computed using the TODAY() function, its value will change depending on the day the program is run. The value of DaysOverDue is negative for books due in the future.

```
                 SAS Dates without and with Formats                   1

              Birth    Issue                       Days    New
Obs   Name    Date     Date          DueDate     OverDue   Card

 1  A. Jones       0  09/15/06   Fri, Feb 29, 2008    84
 2  M. Rincon  -3888  02/29/08   Fri, May 23, 2008     0    yes
 3  Z. Grandage 10304  10/31/07  Sat, May 31, 2008    -8
 4  K. Kaminaka 15854  01/24/08  Thu, Jun 12, 2008   -20    yes
```

---

[3] For more information on formats, see section 4.5.

# 3.9    Selected Date Informats, Functions, and Formats

| Informats | Definition | Width range | Default width |
|---|---|---|---|
| ANYDTDTE*w*. | Reads dates in various date forms | 5–32 | 9 |
| DATE*w*. | Reads dates in form: *ddmmmyy* or *ddmmmyyyy* | 7–32 | 7 |
| DDMMYY*w*. | Reads dates in form: *ddmmyy* or *ddmmyyyy* | 6–32 | 6 |
| JULIAN*w*. | Reads Julian dates in form: *yyddd* or *yyyyddd* | 5–32 | 5 |
| MMDDYY*w*. | Reads dates in form: *mmddyy* or *mmddyyyy* | 6–32 | 6 |

| Functions | Syntax | Definition |
|---|---|---|
| DATEJUL | DATEJUL(*julian-date*) | Converts a Julian date to a SAS date value[1] |
| DAY | DAY(*date*) | Returns the day of the month from a SAS date value |
| MDY | MDY(*month,day,year*) | Returns a SAS date value from month, day, and year values |
| MONTH | MONTH(*date*) | Returns the month (1–12) from a SAS date value |
| QTR | QTR(*date*) | Returns the yearly quarter (1–4) from a SAS date value |
| TODAY | TODAY() | Returns the current date as a SAS date value |
| WEEKDAY | WEEKDAY(date) | Returns day of week (1=Sunday) from SAS date value |
| YEAR | YEAR(date) | Returns year from a SAS date value |

| Formats | Definition | Width range | Default width |
|---|---|---|---|
| DATE*w*. | Writes SAS date values in form: *ddmmmyy* | 5–11 | 7 |
| DAY*w*. | Writes the day of the month from a SAS date value | 2–32 | 2 |
| EURDFDD*w*. | Writes SAS date values in form: *dd.mm.yy* | 2–10 | 8 |
| JULIAN*w*. | Writes a Julian date from a SAS date value | 5–7 | 5 |
| MMDDYY*w*. | Writes SAS date values in form: *mmddyy* or *mmddyyyy* | 2–10 | 8 |
| WEEKDATE*w*. | Writes SAS date values in form: *day-of-week, month-name dd, yy or yyyy* | 3–37 | 29 |
| WORDDATE*w*. | Writes SAS date values in form: *month-name dd, yyyy* | 3–32 | 18 |

[1] A SAS date value is the number of days since January 1, 1960

| Informats | Input data | INPUT statement | Results |
|---|---|---|---|
| ANYDTDTE*w*. | 1jan1961<br>01/01/61 | INPUT Day ANYDTDTE10.; | 366<br>366 |
| DATE*w*. | 1jan1961 | INPUT Day DATE10.; | 366 |
| DDMMYY*w*. | 01.01.61<br>02/01/61 | INPUT Day DDMMYY8.; | 366<br>367 |
| JULIAN*w*. | 61001 | INPUT Day JULIAN7.; | 366 |
| MMDDYY*w*. | 01-01-61 | INPUT Day MMDDYY8.; | 366 |

| Functions | Example | Result | Example | Results |
|---|---|---|---|---|
| DATEJUL | a=60001;<br>x=DATEJUL(a); | x=0 | a=60365;<br>y=DATEJUL(a); | y=364 |
| DAY | a=MDY(4,18,99);<br>x=DAY(a); | x=18 | a=MDY(9,3,60);<br>y=DAY(a); | y=3 |
| MDY | x=MDY(1,1,60); | x=0 | m=2; d=1; y=60;<br>Date=MDY(m,d,y); | Date=31 |
| MONTH | a=MDY(4,18,1999);<br>x=MONTH(a); | x=4 | a=MDY(9,3,60);<br>y=MONTH(a); | y=9 |
| QTR | a=MDY(4,18,99);<br>x=QTR(a); | x=2 | a=MDY(9,3,60);<br>y=QTR(a); | y=3 |
| TODAY | x=TODAY(); | x=today's<br>date | x=TODAY()-1;<br>a=MDY(4,18,2008); | x=yesterday's<br>date |
| WEEKDAY | a=MDY(4,13,2008);<br>x=WEEKDAY(a); | x=1 | y=WEEKDAY(a);<br>a=MDY(1,1,1960); | y=6 |
| YEAR | a=MDY(4,13,2008);<br>x=YEAR(a); | x=2008 | y=YEAR(a); | y=1960 |

| Formats | Input data | PUT statement[2] | Results |
|---|---|---|---|
| DATE*w*. | 8966 | PUT Birth DATE7.;<br>PUT Birth DATE9.; | 19JUL84<br>19JUL1984 |
| DAY*w*. | 8966 | PUT Birth DAY2.;<br>PUT Birth DAY7.; | 19<br>19 |
| EURDFDD*w*. | 8966 | PUT Birth EURDFDD8.<br>PUT Birth EURDFDD10.; | 19.07.84<br>19.07.1984 |
| JULIAN*w*. | 8966 | PUT Birth JULIAN5.;<br>PUT Birth JULIAN7.; | 84201<br>1984201 |
| MMDDYY*w*. | 8966 | PUT Birth MMDDYY8.;<br>PUT Birth MMDDYY6.; | 07/19/84<br>071984 |
| WEEKDATE*w*. | 8966 | PUT Birth WEEKDATE15.;<br>PUT Birth WEEKDATE29.; | Thu, Jul 19, 84<br>Thursday, July 19, 1984 |
| WORDDATE*w*. | 8966 | PUT Birth WORDDATE12.;<br>PUT Birth WORDDATE18.; | Jul 19, 1984<br>July 19, 1984 |

[2] Formats can be used in PUT statements and PUT functions in DATA steps, and in FORMAT statements in either DATA or PROC steps.

## 3.10   Using the RETAIN and Sum Statements

When reading raw data, SAS sets the values of all variables equal to missing at the start of each iteration of the DATA step. These values may be changed by INPUT or assignment statements, but they are set back to missing again when SAS returns to the top of the DATA step to process the next observation. RETAIN and sum statements change this. If a variable appears in a RETAIN statement, then its value will be retained from one iteration of the DATA step to the next. A sum statement also retains values from the previous iteration of the DATA step, but then adds to it the value of an expression.

**RETAIN statement**   Use the RETAIN statement when you want SAS to preserve a variable's value from the previous iteration of the DATA step. The RETAIN statement can appear anywhere in the DATA step and has the following form, where all variables to be retained are listed after the RETAIN keyword:

```
RETAIN variable-list;
```

You can also specify an initial value, instead of missing, for the variables. All variables listed before an initial value will start the first iteration of the DATA step with that value:

```
RETAIN variable-list initial-value;
```

**Sum statement**   A sum statement also retains values from the previous iteration of the DATA step, but you use it for the special cases where you simply want to cumulatively add the value of an expression to a variable. A sum statement, like an assignment statement, contains no keywords. It has the following form:

```
variable + expression;
```

No, there is no typo here and no equal sign either. This statement adds the value of the expression to the variable while retaining the variable's value from one iteration of the DATA step to the next. The variable must be numeric and has the initial value of zero. This statement can be re-written using the RETAIN statement and SUM function as follows:

```
RETAIN variable 0;
variable = SUM(variable, expression);
```

As you can see, a sum statement is really a special case of using RETAIN.

**Example**   This example illustrates the use of both the RETAIN and sum statements. The minor league baseball team, the Walla Walla Sweets, has the following data about their games. The date the game was played and the team played are followed by the number of hits and runs for the game:

```
6-19 Columbia Peaches      8   3
6-20 Columbia Peaches     10   5
6-23 Plains Peanuts        3   4
6-24 Plains Peanuts        7   2
6-25 Plains Peanuts       12   8
6-30 Gilroy Garlics        4   4
7-1  Gilroy Garlics        9   4
7-4  Sacramento Tomatoes  15   9
7-4  Sacramento Tomatoes  10  10
7-5  Sacramento Tomatoes   2   3
```

The team wants two additional variables in their data set. One shows the cumulative number of runs for the season, and the other shows the maximum number of runs in a game to date. The following program uses a sum statement to compute the cumulative number of runs, and the RETAIN statement and MAX function to determine the maximum number of runs in a game to date:

```
* Using RETAIN and sum statements to find most runs and total runs;
DATA gamestats;
    INFILE 'c:\MyRawData\Games.dat';
    INPUT Month 1 Day 3-4 Team $ 6-25 Hits 27-28 Runs 30-31;
    RETAIN MaxRuns;
    MaxRuns = MAX(MaxRuns, Runs);
    RunsToDate + Runs;
RUN;
PROC PRINT DATA = gamestats;
    TITLE "Season's Record to Date";
RUN;
```

The variable MaxRuns is set equal to the maximum of its value from the previous iteration of the DATA step (since it appears in the RETAIN statement) or the value of the variable Runs. The variable RunsToDate adds the number of runs per game, Runs, to itself while retaining its value from one iteration of the DATA step to the next. This produces a cumulative record of the number of runs.

Here are the results:

```
                          Season's Record to Date                          1

                                                      Max     Runs
    Obs   Month   Day        Team         Hits  Runs  Runs   ToDate

     1      6      19    Columbia Peaches    8    3     3       3
     2      6      20    Columbia Peaches   10    5     5       8
     3      6      23    Plains Peanuts      3    4     5      12
     4      6      24    Plains Peanuts      7    2     5      14
     5      6      25    Plains Peanuts     12    8     8      22
     6      6      30    Gilroy Garlics      4    4     8      26
     7      7       1    Gilroy Garlics      9    4     8      30
     8      7       4    Sacramento Tomatoes 15   9     9      39
     9      7       4    Sacramento Tomatoes 10  10    10      49
    10      7       5    Sacramento Tomatoes  2   3    10      52
```

## 3.11 Simplifying Programs with Arrays

Sometimes you want to do the same thing to many variables. You may want to take the log of every numeric variable or change every occurrence of zero to a missing value. You could write a series of assignment statements or IF statements, but if you have a lot of variables to transform, using arrays will simplify and shorten your program.

An array is an ordered group of similar items. You might think your local mall has a nice array of stores to choose from. In SAS, an array is a group of variables. You can define an array to be any group of variables you like, as long as they are either all numeric or all character. The variables can be ones that already exist in your data set, or they can be new variables that you want to create.

Arrays are defined using the ARRAY statement in the DATA step. The ARRAY statement has the following general form:

```
ARRAY name (n) $ variable-list;
```

In this statement, *name* is a name you give to the array, and *n* is the number of variables in the array. Following the (*n*) is a list of variable names. The number of variables in the list must equal the number given in parentheses. (You may use { } or [ ] instead of parentheses if you like.) This is called an explicit array, where you explicitly state the number of variables in the array. The $ is needed if the variables are character and is only necessary if the variables have not previously been defined.

The array itself is not stored with the data set; it is defined only for the duration of the DATA step. You can give the array any name, as long as it does not match any of the variable names in your data set or any SAS keywords. The rules for naming arrays are the same as those for naming variables (must be 32 characters or fewer and start with a letter or underscore followed by letters, numerals, or underscores).

To reference a variable using the array name, give the array name and the subscript for that variable. The first variable in the variable list has subscript 1, the second has subscript 2, and so forth. So if you have an array defined as

```
ARRAY store (4) Macys Penneys Sears Target;
```

STORE(1) is the variable Macys, STORE(2) is the variable Penneys, STORE(3) is the variable Sears, and STORE(4) is the variable Target. This is all just fine, but simply defining an array doesn't do anything for you. You want to be able to use the array to make things easier for you.

**Example**   The radio station WBRK is conducting a survey asking people to rate ten different songs. Songs are rated on a scale of 1 to 5, where 1 = change the station when it comes on, and 5 = turn up the volume when it comes on. If listeners had not heard the song or didn't care to comment on it, a 9 was entered for that song. The following are the data collected:

```
Albany      54 4 3 5 9 9 2 1 4 4 9
Richmond    33 5 2 4 3 9 2 9 3 3 3
Oakland     27 1 3 2 9 9 9 3 4 2 3
Richmond    41 4 3 5 5 5 2 9 4 5 5
Berkeley    18 3 4 9 1 4 9 3 9 3 2
```

The listener's city of residence, age, and their responses to all ten songs are listed. The following program changes all the 9s to missing values. (The variables are named using the first letters of the words in the song's title.)

```
* Change all 9s to missing values;
DATA songs;
   INFILE 'c:\MyRawData\WBRK.dat';
   INPUT City $ 1-15 Age domk wj hwow simbh kt aomm libm tr filp ttr;
   ARRAY song (10) domk wj hwow simbh kt aomm libm tr filp ttr;
   DO i = 1 TO 10;
      IF song(i) = 9 THEN song(i) = .;
   END;
RUN;
PROC PRINT DATA = songs;
   TITLE 'WBRK Song Survey';
RUN;
```

An array, SONG, is defined as having ten variables, the same ten variables that appear in the INPUT statement representing the ten songs. Next comes an iterative DO statement. All statements between the DO statement and the END statement are executed, in this case, ten times, once for each variable in the array.

The variable I is used as an index variable and is incremented by 1 each time through the DO loop. The first time through the DO loop, the variable I has a value of 1 and the IF statement would read `IF song(1)=9 THEN song(1)=.;`, which is the same as `IF domk=9 THEN domk=.;`. The second time through, I has a value of 2 and the IF statement would read `IF song(2)=9 THEN song(2)=.;`, which is the same as `IF wj=9 THEN wj=.;`. This continues through all ten variables in the array.

Here are the results:

```
                         WBRK Song Survey                                  1

 Obs   City    Age domk wj hwow simbh kt aomm libm tr filp ttr  i

  1   Albany    54   4   3   5    .    .   2    1   4   4    .  11
  2   Richmond  33   5   2   4    3    .   2    .   3   3    3  11
  3   Oakland   27   1   3   2    .    .   .    3   4   2    3  11
  4   Richmond  41   4   3   5    5    5   2    .   4   5    5  11
  5   Berkeley  18   3   4   .    1    4   .    3   .   3    2  11
```

Notice that the array members SONG(1) to SONG(10) did not become part of the data set, but the variable I did. You could have written ten IF statements instead of using arrays and accomplished the same result. In this program it would not have made a big difference, but if you had 100 songs in your survey instead of ten, then using arrays would clearly be a better solution.

## 3.12    Using Shortcuts for Lists of Variable Names

As the title states, this section is about shortcuts, shorthand ways of writing lists of variable names. While writing SAS programs, you will often need to write a list of variable names. When defining ARRAYS, using functions like MEAN or SUM, or using SAS procedures, you must specify which variables to use. Now, if you only have a handful of variables, you might not feel a need for a shortcut. But if, for example, you need to define an array with 100 elements, you might be a little grumpy after typing in the 49th variable name knowing you still have 51 more to go. You might even think, "There must be an easier way." Well, there is.

You can use an abbreviated list of variable names most anywhere you can use a regular variable list. In functions, abbreviated lists must be preceded by the keyword OF (for example, SUM(OF Cat8 - Cat12)). Otherwise, you simply replace the regular list of variables with the abbreviated one.

**Numbered range lists**    Variables which start with the same characters and end with consecutive numbers can be part of a numbered range list. The numbers can start and end anywhere as long as the number sequence between is complete. For example, the following INPUT statement shows a variable list and its abbreviated form:

| **Variable list** | **Abbreviated list** |
|---|---|
| `INPUT Cat8 Cat9 Cat10 Cat11 Cat12;` | `INPUT Cat8 - Cat12;` |

**Name range lists**    Name range lists depend on the internal order, or position, of the variables in the SAS data set. This is determined by the order of appearance of the variables in the DATA step. For example, given the following DATA step, the internal variable order would be Y A C H R B:

```
DATA example;
   INPUT y a c h r;
   b = c + r;
RUN;
```

To specify a name range list, put the first variable, then two hyphens, then the last variable. The following PUT statements show the variable list and its abbreviated form using a named range:

| **Variable list** | **Abbreviated list** |
|---|---|
| `PUT y a c h r b;` | `PUT y -- b;` |

If you are not sure of the internal order, you can find out using PROC CONTENTS with the POSITION option. The following program will list the variables in the permanent SAS data set DISTANCE sorted by position:

```
LIBNAME mydir 'c:\MySASLib';
PROC CONTENTS DATA = mydir.distance POSITION;
RUN;
```

Use caution when including name range lists in your programs. Although they can save on typing, they may also make your programs more difficult to understand and debug.

**Name prefix lists**    Variables which start with the same characters can be part of a name prefix list, and can be used in some SAS statements and functions. For example:

| **Variable list** | **Abbreviated list** |
|---|---|
| `DogBills = SUM(DogVet,DogFood,Dog_Care);` | `DogBills = SUM(OF Dog:);` |

**Special SAS name lists** The special name lists, _ALL_, _CHARACTER_, and _NUMERIC_ can also be used any place you want either all the variables, all the character variables, or all the numeric variables in a SAS data set. These name lists are useful when you want to do something like compute the mean of all the numeric variables for an observation (MEAN(OF _NUMERIC_)), or list the values of all variables in an observation (PUT _ALL_;).

**Example** The radio station WBRK wants to modify the program from the previous section, which changes all 9s to missing values. Now, instead of changing the original variables, they use the following program to create new variables (Song1 through Song10) which will have the new missing values. This program also computes the average score using the MEAN function.

```
DATA songs;
   INFILE 'c:\MyRawData\WBRK.dat';
   INPUT City $ 1-15 Age domk wj hwow simbh kt aomm libm tr filp ttr;
   ARRAY new (10) Song1 - Song10;
   ARRAY old (10) domk -- ttr;
   DO i = 1 TO 10;
      IF old(i) = 9 THEN new(i) = .;
         ELSE new(i) = old(i);
   END;
   AvgScore = MEAN(OF Song1 - Song10);
PROC PRINT DATA = songs;
   TITLE 'WBRK Song Survey';
RUN;
```

Note that both ARRAY statements use abbreviated variable lists; array NEW uses a numbered range list and array OLD uses a name range list. Inside the iterative DO loop, the Song variables (array NEW) are set equal to missing if the original variable (array OLD) had a value of 9. Otherwise, they are set equal to the original values. After the DO loop, a new variable, AvgScore, is created using an abbreviated variable list in the function MEAN. The output includes variables from both the OLD array (domk, wj, ... ttr) and NEW array (Song1 - Song10):

```
                                WBRK Song Survey                              1

                                                                          A
                                                                          v
                                                            S             g
                          s                 S S S S S S S S o             S
          C           d   h i   a l   f     o o o o o o o o o n           c
  O       i       A o     w m   o i     i t n n n n n n n n n g           o
  b       t       g m w o b k m b t l t g g g g g g g g g g 1             r
  s       y       e k j w h t m m r p r 1 2 3 4 5 6 7 8 9 0 i             e

  1 Albany   54 4 3 5 9 9 2 1 4 4 9 4 3 5 . . 2 1 4 4 . 11 3.28571
  2 Richmond 33 5 2 4 3 9 2 9 3 3 3 5 2 4 3 . 2 . 3 3 3 11 3.12500
  3 Oakland  27 1 3 2 9 9 9 3 4 2 3 1 3 2 . . . 3 4 2 3 11 2.57143
  4 Richmond 41 4 3 5 5 5 2 9 4 5 5 4 3 5 5 2 . 4 5 5 11 4.22222
  5 Berkeley 18 3 4 9 1 4 9 3 9 3 2 3 4 . 1 4 . 3 . 3 2 11 2.85714
```

4

"Once in a while the simple things work right off."

PHIL GALLAGHER

From the SAS L Listserve, 1994. Reprinted by permission of the author.

CHAPTER **4**

# Sorting, Printing, and Summarizing Your Data

# 4.1 Using SAS Procedures

```
PROC whatever
DATA=      _____
BY         _____
TITLE      _____
FOOTNOTE _____
LABEL      _____
```

Using a procedure, or PROC, is like filling out a form. Someone else designed the form, and all you have to do is fill in the blanks and choose from a list of options. Each PROC has its own unique form with its own list of options. But while each procedure is unique, there are similarities too. This section discusses some of those similarities.

All procedures have required statements, and most have optional statements. PROC PRINT, for example, requires only two words:

```
PROC PRINT;
```

However, by adding optional statements you could make this procedure a dozen lines or even longer.

**PROC statement** All procedures start with the keyword PROC followed by the name of the procedure, such as PRINT or CONTENTS. Options, if there are any, follow the procedure name. The DATA= option tells SAS which data set to use as input for that procedure. In this case, SAS will use a temporary SAS data set named BANANA:

```
PROC CONTENTS DATA = banana;
```

The DATA= option is, of course, optional. If you skip it, then SAS will use the most recently created data set, which is not necessarily the same as the most recently used. Sometimes it is easier to specify the data set you want than to figure out which data set SAS will use by default. To use a permanent SAS data set, issue a LIBNAME statement to set up a libref pointing to the location of your data set, and put the data set's two-level name in the DATA= option, as discussed in section 2.20,

```
LIBNAME tropical 'c:\MySASLib';
PROC CONTENTS DATA = tropical.banana;
```

or refer to it directly by placing your operating environment's name for the permanent SAS data set between quotation marks, as discussed in section 2.21.

```
PROC CONTENTS DATA = 'c:\MySASLib\banana';
```

**BY statement** The BY statement is required for only one procedure, PROC SORT. In PROC SORT the BY statement tells SAS how to arrange the observations. In all other procedures, the BY statement is optional, and tells SAS to perform a separate analysis for each combination of values of the BY variables rather than treating all observations as one group. For example, this statement tells SAS to run a separate analysis for each state:

```
BY State;
```

All procedures, except PROC SORT, assume that your data are already sorted by the variables in your BY statement. If your observations are not already sorted, then use PROC SORT to do the job.

**TITLE and FOOTNOTE statements**   You have seen TITLE statements many times in this book. FOOTNOTE works the same way, but prints at the bottom of the page. These global statements are not technically part of any step. You can put them anywhere in your program, but since they apply to the procedure output it generally makes sense to put them with the procedure. The most basic TITLE statement consists of the keyword TITLE followed by your title enclosed in quotation marks. SAS doesn't care if the two quotation marks are single or double as long as they are the same:

```
TITLE 'This is a title';
```

If you find that your title contains an apostrophe, use double quotation marks around the title, or replace the single apostrophe with two:

```
TITLE "Here's another title";
TITLE 'Here''s another title';
```

You can specify up to ten titles or footnotes by adding numbers to the keywords TITLE and FOOTNOTE:

```
FOOTNOTE3 'This is the third footnote';
```

Titles and footnotes stay in effect until you replace them with new ones or cancel them with a null statement. The following null statement would cancel all current titles:

```
TITLE;
```

When you specify a new title or footnote, it replaces the old title or footnote with the same number and cancels those with a higher number. For example, a new TITLE2 cancels an existing TITLE3, if there is one.

**LABEL statement**   By default, SAS uses variable names to label your output, but with the LABEL statement you can create more descriptive labels, up to 256 characters long, for each variable. This statement creates labels for the variables ReceiveDate and ShipDate:

```
LABEL ReceiveDate = 'Date order was received'
      ShipDate = 'Date merchandise was shipped';
```

When a LABEL statement is used in a DATA step, the labels become part of the data set; but when used in a PROC, the labels stay in effect only for the duration of that step.

**Customizing output**   You have a lot of control over the output produced by procedures. Using system options, you can set many features such as centering, dates, line size, and page size (section 1.14). With the Output Delivery System, you can also change the overall style of your output, produce output in different formats (such as HTML or RTF), or change almost any detail of your output (section 1.10 and chapter 5).

**Output data sets**   Most procedures produce some kind of report, but sometimes you would like the results of the procedure saved as a SAS data set so you can perform further analysis. You can create SAS data sets from any procedure output using the ODS OUTPUT statement (section 5.3). Some procedures can also write a SAS data set using an OUTPUT statement or OUT= option.

## 4.2 Subsetting in Procedures with the WHERE Statement

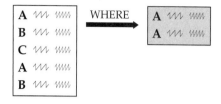

One optional statement for any PROC that reads a SAS data set is the WHERE statement. The WHERE statement tells a procedure to use a subset of the data. There are other ways to subset data, as you probably remember, so you could get by without ever using the WHERE statement.[1] However, the WHERE statement is a shortcut. While subsetting IFs work only in DATA steps, the WHERE statement works in PROC steps too.

Unlike subsetting in a DATA step, using a WHERE statement in a procedure does not create a new data set. That is one of the reasons why WHERE statements are sometimes more efficient than other ways of subsetting.

The basic form of a WHERE statement is

```
WHERE condition;
```

Only observations satisfying the condition will be used by the PROC. This may look familiar since it is similar to a subsetting IF. The left side of that condition is a variable name, and the right side is a variable name, a constant, or a mathematical expression. Mathematical expressions can contain the standard arithmetic symbols for addition (+), subtraction (-), multiplication (*), division (/), and exponentiation (**). Between the two sides of the expression, you can use comparison and logical operators; those operators may be symbolic or mnemonic. Here are the most frequently used operators:

| Symbolic | Mnemonic | Example |
|---|---|---|
| = | EQ | `WHERE Region = 'Spain';` |
| ¬=, ~=, ^= | NE | `WHERE Region ~= 'Spain';` |
| > | GT | `WHERE Rainfall > 20;` |
| < | LT | `WHERE Rainfall < AvgRain;` |
| >= | GE | `WHERE Rainfall >= AvgRain + 5;` |
| <= | LE | `WHERE Rainfall <= AvgRain / 1.25;` |
| & | AND | `WHERE Rainfall > 20 AND Temp < 90;` |
| \|,¦,! | OR | `WHERE Rainfall > 20 OR Temp < 90;` |
| | IS NOT MISSING | `WHERE Region IS NOT MISSING;` |
| | BETWEEN AND | `WHERE Region BETWEEN 'Plain' AND 'Spain';` |
| | CONTAINS | `WHERE Region CONTAINS 'ain';` |
| | IN ( *list* ) | `WHERE Region IN ('Rain', 'Spain', 'Plain');` |

---

[1] For more on the WHERE statement, see appendix D. Other ways to subset data include subsetting IF statements (sections 2.13, 3.7, and 6.9), and the WHERE= option (section 6.13).

**Example**  You have a database containing information about well-known painters. A subset of the data appears below. For each artist, the data include the painter's name, primary style, and nation of origin:

```
Mary Cassatt          Impressionism      U
Paul Cezanne          Post-impressionism F
Edgar Degas           Impressionism      F
Paul Gauguin          Post-impressionism F
Claude Monet          Impressionism      F
Pierre Auguste Renoir Impressionism      F
Vincent van Gogh      Post-impressionism N
```

To make this example more realistic, it has two parts: one to create a permanent SAS data set, the other to subset the data. First a DATA step reads the data from a file named Artists.dat, and uses direct referencing (you could use a LIBNAME statement instead) to create a permanent SAS data set named STYLE in a directory named MySASLib (Windows).

```
DATA 'c:\MySASLib\style';
   INFILE 'c:\MyRawData\Artists.dat';
   INPUT Name $ 1-21 Genre $ 23-40 Origin $ 42;
RUN;
```

Suppose a day later you wanted to print a list of just the impressionist painters. The quick-and-easy way to do this is with a WHERE statement and PROC PRINT. The quotation marks around the data set name tell SAS that this is a permanent SAS data set.

```
PROC PRINT DATA = 'c:\MySASLib\style';
   WHERE Genre = 'Impressionism';
   TITLE 'Major Impressionist Painters';
   FOOTNOTE 'F = France N = Netherlands U = US';
RUN;
```

The output looks like this:

```
                  Major Impressionist Painters            1


     Obs    Name                    Genre          Origin

      1     Mary Cassatt            Impressionism  U
      3     Edgar Degas             Impressionism  F
      5     Claude Monet            Impressionism  F
      6     Pierre Auguste Renoir   Impressionism  F


          F = France N = Netherlands U = US
```

## 4.3    Sorting Your Data with PROC SORT

There are many reasons for sorting your data: to organize data for a report, before combining data sets, or before using a BY statement in another PROC or DATA step. Fortunately, PROC SORT is quite simple. The basic form of this procedure is

```
PROC SORT;
    BY variable-1 ... variable-n;
```

The variables named in the BY statement are called BY variables. You can specify as many BY variables as you wish. With one BY variable, SAS sorts the data based on the values of that variable. With more than one variable, SAS sorts observations by the first variable, then by the second variable within categories of the first, and so on. A BY group is all the observations that have the same values of BY variables. If, for example, your BY variable is State then all the observations for North Dakota form one BY group.

The DATA= and OUT= options specify the input and output data sets. If you don't specify the DATA= option, then SAS will use the most recently created data set. If you don't specify the OUT= option, then SAS will replace the original data set with the newly sorted version. This sample statement tells SAS to sort the data set named MESSY, and then put the sorted data into a data set named NEAT:

```
PROC SORT DATA = messy OUT = neat;
```

The NODUPKEY option tells SAS to eliminate any duplicate observations that have the same values for the BY variables. If you specify the DUPOUT= option, then SAS will put the deleted observations in that data set. To use these options, just add them to the PROC SORT statement:

```
PROC SORT DATA = messy OUT = neat   NODUPKEY   DUPOUT = extraobs;
```

The order in which SAS sorts character data values is called the collating sequence. The collating sequence for the z/OS operating environment is EBCDIC. The collating sequence for all other operating environments is ASCII. ASCII sorts data values in this order: blanks, numerals, uppercase letters, then lowercase letters. With EBCDIC, the order is blanks, lowercase letters, uppercase letters, numerals. Since both ASCII and EBCDIC sort upper- and lowercase letters separately, you may want to specify the SORTSEQ=LINGUISTIC option (new in SAS 9.2).

```
PROC SORT DATA = messy OUT = neat SORTSEQ=LINGUISTIC;
```

With this option, upper- and lowercase letters are interleaved so the data values ALASKA and alaska will be together. Note that ALASKA and alaska will still be separate BY groups. Numeric data values are sorted in this order: missing values, then negative values, zero, and positive values.

By default SAS sorts data in ascending order, from lowest to highest. To have your data sorted in the opposite order, add the keyword DESCENDING to the BY statement before each variable that should be sorted in reverse order. This statement tells SAS to sort first by State (from A to Z) and then by City (from Z to A) within State:

```
BY State DESCENDING City;
```

**Example** The following data show the average length in feet of selected whales and sharks.
Notice that each line includes data for more than one shark.

```
beluga    whale 15    dwarf       shark .5    sperm    whale 60
basking   shark 30    humpback      .  50     whale    shark 40
gray      whale 50    blue        whale 100   killer   whale 30
mako      shark 12    whale       shark 40
```

This program reads and sorts the data:

```
DATA marine;
    INFILE 'c:\MyRawData\Lengths.dat';
    INPUT Name $ Family $ Length @@;
RUN;
* Sort the data;
PROC SORT DATA = marine OUT = seasort NODUPKEY;
    BY Family DESCENDING Length;
PROC PRINT DATA = seasort;
    TITLE 'Whales and Sharks';
RUN;
```

The DATA step reads the raw data from a file called Lengths.dat and creates a SAS data set named
MARINE. Then PROC SORT rearranges the observations by family in ascending order, and by
length in descending order. The NODUPKEY option of PROC SORT eliminates any duplicates,
while the OUT= option writes the sorted data into a new data set named SEASORT. The output
from PROC PRINT looks like this:

```
              Whales and Sharks            1

       Obs   Name        Family    Length

        1    humpback              50.0
        2    whale       shark     40.0
        3    basking     shark     30.0
        4    mako        shark     12.0
        5    dwarf       shark      0.5
        6    blue        whale    100.0
        7    sperm       whale     60.0
        8    gray        whale     50.0
        9    killer      whale     30.0
       10    beluga      whale     15.0
```

Notice that the humpback with a missing value for Family became observation 1. That is because
missing values are always low for both numeric and character variables. Also, the NODUPKEY
option eliminated a duplicate observation for the whale shark. The log contains these notes
showing that the sorted data set has one fewer observation than the original data set.

```
NOTE: The data set WORK.MARINE has 11 observations and 3 variables.
NOTE: 1 observations with duplicate key values were deleted.
NOTE: The data set WORK.SEASORT has 10 observations and 3 variables.
```

## 4.4   Printing Your Data with PROC PRINT

The PRINT procedure is perhaps the most widely used SAS procedure. You have seen this procedure used many times in this book to print the contents of a SAS data set. In its simplest form, PROC PRINT prints all variables for all observations in the SAS data set. SAS decides the best way to format the output, so you don't have to worry about things like how many variables will fit on a page. But there are a few more features of PROC PRINT that you might want to use.

The PRINT procedure requires just one statement:

```
PROC PRINT;
```

By default, SAS uses the SAS data set created most recently. If you do not want to print the most recent data set, then use the DATA= option to specify the data set. We recommend always using the DATA= option for clarity in your programs as it is not always easy to quickly determine which data set was created last.

```
PROC PRINT DATA = data-set;
```

Also, SAS prints the observation numbers along with the variables' values. If you don't want observation numbers, use the NOOBS option in the PROC PRINT statement. If you define variable labels with a LABEL statement, and you want to print the labels instead of the variable names, then add the LABEL option as well. The following statement shows all of these options together:

```
PROC PRINT DATA = data-set NOOBS LABEL;
```

The following are optional statements that sometimes come in handy:

| | |
|---|---|
| BY *variable-list*; | The BY statement starts a new section in the output for each new value of the BY variables and prints the values of the BY variables at the top of each section. The data must be presorted by the BY variables. |
| ID *variable-list*; | When you use the ID statement, the observation numbers are not printed. Instead, the variables in the ID variable list appear on the left-hand side of the page. |
| SUM *variable-list*; | The SUM statement prints sums for the variables in the list. |
| VAR *variable-list*; | The VAR statement specifies which variables to print and the order. Without a VAR statement, all variables in the SAS data set are printed in the order that they occur in the data set. |

**Example**   Students from two fourth-grade classes are selling candy to earn money for a special field trip. The class earning more money gets a free box of candy. The following are the data for the results of the candy sale. The students' names are followed by their classroom number, the date they turned in their money, the type of candy: mint patties or chocolate dinosaurs, and the number of boxes sold:

```
Adriana     21  3/21/2008 MP   7
Nathan      14  3/21/2008 CD  19
Matthew     14  3/21/2008 CD  14
Claire      14  3/22/2008 CD  11
Caitlin     21  3/24/2008 CD   9
Ian         21  3/24/2008 MP  18
Chris       14  3/25/2008 CD   6
Anthony     21  3/25/2008 MP  13
Stephen     14  3/25/2008 CD  10
Erika       21  3/25/2008 MP  17
```

The class earns $1.25 for each box of candy sold. The teachers want a report giving the money earned for each classroom, the money earned by each student, the type of candy sold, and the date the students returned their money. The following program reads the data, computes money earned (Profit), and sorts the data by classroom using PROC SORT. Then, the PROC PRINT step uses a BY statement to print the data by Class and a SUM statement to give the totals for Profit. The VAR statement lists the variables to be printed:

```
DATA sales;
   INFILE 'c:\MyRawData\Candy.dat';
   INPUT Name $ 1-11 Class @15 DateReturned MMDDYY10. CandyType $
      Quantity;
   Profit = Quantity * 1.25;
PROC SORT DATA = sales;
   BY Class;
PROC PRINT DATA = sales;
   BY Class;
   SUM Profit;
   VAR Name DateReturned CandyType Profit;
   TITLE 'Candy Sales for Field Trip by Class';
RUN;
```

Here are the results. Notice that the values for the variable DateReturned are printed as their SAS date values. You can use formats, covered in the next section, to print dates in readable forms.

```
                    Candy Sales for Field Trip by Class                    1
------------------------------- Class=14 --------------------------------
                         Date      Candy
       Obs     Name     Returned   Type     Profit

         1   Nathan      17612      CD       23.75
         2   Matthew     17612      CD       17.50
         3   Claire      17613      CD       13.75
         4   Chris       17616      CD        7.50
         5   Stephen     17616      CD       12.50
        -----                               ------
       Class                                 75.00
------------------------------- Class=21 --------------------------------
                         Date      Candy
       Obs     Name     Returned   Type     Profit

         6   Adriana     17612      MP        8.75
         7   Caitlin     17615      CD       11.25
         8   Ian         17615      MP       22.50
         9   Anthony     17616      MP       16.25
        10   Erika       17616      MP       21.25
        -----                               ------
       Class                                 80.00
                                            ======
                                            155.00
```

# 4.5   Changing the Appearance of Printed Values with Formats

| 0  | 1002 |
|----|------|
| 2  | 2012 |
| 31 | 4336 |

➡

| Obs | Date     | Sales |
|-----|----------|-------|
| 1   | 01/01/60 | 1,002 |
| 2   | 01/03/60 | 2,012 |
| 3   | 02/01/60 | 4,336 |

When SAS prints your data, it decides which format is best—how many decimal places to print, how much space to allow for each value, and so on. This is very convenient and makes your job much easier, but SAS doesn't always do what you want. Fortunately you're not stuck with the format SAS thinks is best. You can change the appearance of printed values using SAS formats.

SAS has many formats for character, numeric, and date values. For example, you can use the COMMA*w.d* format to print numbers with embedded commas, the $*w.* format to control the number of characters printed, and the MMDDYY*w.* format to print SAS date values (the number of days since January 1, 1960) in a readable form like 12/03/2003. You can even print your data in more obscure formats like hexadecimal, zoned decimal, and packed decimal, if you like.[1]

The general forms of a SAS format are

| **Character** | **Numeric** | **Date** |
|---------------|-------------|----------|
| $format*w.*   | format*w.d* | format*w.* |

where the $ indicates character formats, *format* is the name of the format, *w* is the total width including any decimal point, and *d* is the number of decimal places. The period in the format is very important because it distinguishes a format from a variable name, which cannot, by default, contain any special characters except the underscore.

**FORMAT statement**   You can associate formats with variables in a FORMAT statement. The FORMAT statement starts with the keyword FORMAT, followed by the variable name (or names if more than one variable is to be associated with the same format), followed by the format. For example, the following FORMAT statement associates the DOLLAR8.2 format with the variables Profit and Loss and associates the MMDDYY8. format with the variable SaleDate:

```
FORMAT Profit Loss DOLLAR8.2 SaleDate MMDDYY8.;
```

FORMAT statements can go in either DATA steps or PROC steps. If the FORMAT statement is in a DATA step, then the format association is permanent and is stored with the SAS data set. If the FORMAT statement is in a PROC step, then it is temporary—affecting only the results from that procedure.

**PUT statement**   You can also use formats in PUT statements when writing raw data files or reports. Place a format after each variable name, as in the following example:

```
PUT Profit DOLLAR8.2 Loss DOLLAR8.2 SaleDate MMDDYY8.;
```

**Example**   In the previous section, results from the fourth-grade candy sale were printed using the PRINT procedure. The names of the students were printed along with the date they turned in their money, the type of candy sold, and the profit. You may have noticed that the dates printed

---

[1] You can also create your own formats using the FORMAT procedure covered in section 4.7.

were numbers like 17612 and 17615. Using the FORMAT statement in the PRINT procedure, we can print the dates in a readable form. At the same time, we can print the variable Profit using the DOLLAR6.2 format so dollar signs appear before the numbers.

Here are the data, where the students' names are followed by their classroom, the date they turned in their money, the type of candy sold: mint patties or chocolate dinosaurs, and the number of boxes sold:

```
Adriana    21   3/21/2008 MP   7
Nathan     14   3/21/2008 CD  19
Matthew    14   3/21/2008 CD  14
Claire     14   3/22/2008 CD  11
Caitlin    21   3/24/2008 CD   9
Ian        21   3/24/2008 MP  18
Chris      14   3/25/2008 CD   6
Anthony    21   3/25/2008 MP  13
Stephen    14   3/25/2008 CD  10
Erika      21   3/25/2008 MP  17
```

The following program reads the raw data and computes Profit. The FORMAT statement in the PRINT procedure associates the DATE9. format with the variable DateReturned and the DOLLAR6.2 format with the variable Profit:

```
DATA sales;
    INFILE 'c:\MyRawData\Candy.dat';
    INPUT Name $ 1-11 Class @15 DateReturned MMDDYY10. CandyType $
        Quantity;
    Profit = Quantity * 1.25;
PROC PRINT DATA = sales;
    VAR Name DateReturned CandyType Profit;
    FORMAT DateReturned DATE9. Profit DOLLAR6.2;
    TITLE 'Candy Sale Data Using Formats';
RUN;
```

Here are the results:

```
                 Candy Sale Data Using Formats                1

                         Date      Candy
        Obs    Name      Returned   Type      Profit

         1     Adriana   21MAR2008   MP       $8.75
         2     Nathan    21MAR2008   CD      $23.75
         3     Matthew   21MAR2008   CD      $17.50
         4     Claire    22MAR2008   CD      $13.75
         5     Caitlin   24MAR2008   CD      $11.25
         6     Ian       24MAR2008   MP      $22.50
         7     Chris     25MAR2008   CD       $7.50
         8     Anthony   25MAR2008   MP      $16.25
         9     Stephen   25MAR2008   CD      $12.50
        10     Erika     25MAR2008   MP      $21.25
```

## 4.6    Selected Standard Formats

| Format | Definition | Width range | Default width |
|---|---|---|---|
| **Character** | | | |
| $HEX*w*. | Converts character data to hexidecimal (specify *w* twice the length of the variable) | 1–32767 | 4 |
| $*w*. | Writes standard character data—does not trim leading blanks (same as $CHAR*w*.) | 1–32767 | Length of variable or 1 |
| **Date, Time, and Datetime**[1] | | | |
| DATE*w*. | Writes SAS date values in form *ddmmmyy* or *ddmmmyyyy* | 5–9 | 7 |
| DATETIME*w.d* | Writes SAS datetime values in form *ddmmmyy:hh:mm:ss.ss* | 7–40 | 16 |
| DAY*w*. | Writes day of month from a SAS date value | 2–32 | 2 |
| EURDFDD*w*. | Writes a SAS date value in form: *dd.mm.yy* | 2–10 | 8 |
| JULIAN*w*. | Writes a Julian date from a SAS date value in form *yyddd* or *yyyyddd* | 5–7 | 5 |
| MMDDYY*w*. | Writes SAS date values in form *mmddyy* or *mmddyyyy* | 2–10 | 8 |
| TIME*w.d* | Writes SAS time values in form *hh:mm:ss.ss* | 2–20 | 8 |
| WEEKDATE*w*. | Writes SAS date values in form *day-of-week, month-name dd, yy* or *yyyy* | 3–37 | 29 |
| WORDDATE*w*. | Writes SAS date values in form *month-name dd, yyyy* | 3–32 | 18 |
| **Numeric** | | | |
| BEST*w*. | SAS chooses best format—this is the default format for writing numeric data | 1–32 | 12 |
| COMMA*w.d* | Writes numbers with commas separating every three digits | 2–32 | 6 |
| DOLLAR*w.d* | Writes numbers with a leading $ and commas separating every three digits | 2–32 | 6 |
| E*w*. | Writes numbers in scientific notation | 7–32 | 12 |
| PD*w.d* | Writes numbers in packed decimal—*w* specifies the number of bytes | 1–16 | 1 |
| *w.d* | Writes standard numeric data | 1–32 | None |

[1] SAS date values are the number of days since January 1, 1960. SAS time values are the number of seconds past midnight, and datetime values are the number of seconds since midnight January 1

| Format | Input data | PUT statement | Results |
|---|---|---|---|
| **Character** | | | |
| $HEX*w*. | AB | PUT Name $HEX4.; | C1C2 (EBCDIC)[2]<br>4142 (ASCII) |
| $*w*. | my cat<br>my snake | PUT Animal $8. '*'; | my cat  *<br>my snak* |
| **Date, Time, and Datetime** | | | |
| DATE*w*. | 8966 | PUT Birth DATE7.;<br>PUT Birth DATE9.; | 19JUL84<br>19JUL1984 |
| DATETIME*w*. | 12182 | PUT Start DATETIME13.;<br>PUT Start DATETIME18.1; | 01JAN60:03:23<br>01JAN60:03:23:02.0 |
| DAY*w*. | 8966 | PUT Birth DAY2.;<br>PUT Birth DAY7.; | 19<br>19 |
| EURDFDD*w*. | 8966 | PUT Birth EURDFDD8.; | 19.07.84 |
| JULIAN*w*. | 8966 | PUT Birth JULIAN5.;<br>PUT Birth JULIAN7.; | 84201<br>1984201 |
| MMDDYY*w*. | 8966 | PUT Birth MMDDYY8.;<br>PUT Birth MMDDYY6.; | 7/19/84<br>071984 |
| TIME*w.d* | 12182 | PUT Start TIME8.;<br>PUT Start TIME11.2; | 3:23:02<br>3:23:02.00 |
| WEEKDATE*w*. | 8966 | PUT Birth WEEKDATE15.;<br>PUT Birth WEEKDATE29.; | Thu, Jul 19, 84<br>Thursday, July 19, 1984 |
| WORDDATE*w*. | 8966 | PUT Birth WORDDATE12.;<br>PUT Birth WORDDATE18.; | Jul 19, 1984<br>July 19, 1984 |
| **Numeric** | | | |
| BEST*w*. | 1200001 | PUT Value BEST6.;<br>PUT Value BEST8.; | 1.20E6<br>1200001 |
| COMMA*w.d* | 1200001 | PUT Value COMMA9.;<br>PUT Value COMMA12.2; | 1,200,001<br>1,200,001.00 |
| DOLLAR*w.d* | 1200001 | PUT Value DOLLAR10.;<br>PUT Value DOLLAR13.2; | $1,200,001<br>$1,200,001.00 |
| E*w*. | 1200001 | PUT Value E7.; | 1.2E+06 |
| PD*w.d* | 128 | PUT Value PD4.; | [3] |
| *w.d* | 23.635 | PUT Value 6.3;<br>PUT Value 5.2; | 23.635<br>23.64 |

[2] The EBCDIC character set is used on most IBM mainframe computers while the ASCII character set is used on most other computers. So, depending on the computer you are using, you will get one or the other.

[3] These values cannot be printed.

## 4.7   Creating Your Own Formats Using PROC FORMAT

| m 2 |
|-----|
| f 1 |
| m 3 |

➡

| Obs | Sex | AgeGroup |
|-----|-----|----------|
| 1 | Male | Adult |
| 2 | Female | Teen |
| 3 | Male | Senior |

At some time you will probably want to create your own custom formats—especially if you use a lot of coded data. Imagine that you have just completed a survey for your company and to save disk space and time, all the responses to the survey questions are coded. For example, the age categories teen, adult, and senior are coded as numbers 1, 2, and 3. This is convenient for data entry and analysis but bothersome when it comes time to interpret the results. You could present your results along with a code book, and your company directors could look up the codes as they read the results. But this will probably not get you that promotion you've been looking for. A better solution is to create user-defined formats using PROC FORMAT and print the formatted values instead of the coded values.

The FORMAT procedure creates formats that will later be associated with variables in a FORMAT statement. The procedure starts with the statement PROC FORMAT and continues with one or more VALUE statements (other optional statements are available):

```
PROC FORMAT;
     VALUE name range-1 = 'formatted-text-1'
                range-2 = 'formatted-text-2'
                          .
                          .
                          .
                range-n = 'formatted-text-n';
```

The *name* in the VALUE statement is the name of the format you are creating. If the format is for character data, the *name* must start with a $. The *name* can't be longer than 32 characters (including the $ for character data), it must not start or end with a number, and cannot contain any special characters except the underscore. In addition, the *name* can't be the name of an existing format. Each *range* is the value of a variable that is assigned to the text given in quotation marks on the right side of the equal sign. The text can be up to 32,767 characters long, but some procedures print only the first 8 or 16 characters. The following are examples of valid range specifications:

```
            'A' = 'Asia'
  1, 3, 5, 7, 9 = 'Odd'
  500000 - HIGH = 'Not Affordable'
       13 -< 20 = 'Teenager'
     0 <- HIGH = 'Positive Non Zero'
         OTHER = 'Bad Data'
```

Character values must be enclosed in quotation marks ('A' for example). If there is more than one value in the range, then separate the values with a comma or use the hyphen (-) for a continuous range. The keywords LOW and HIGH can be used in ranges to indicate the lowest and the highest non-missing value for the variable. You can also use the less than symbol (<) in ranges to exclude either end point of the range. The OTHER keyword can be used to assign a format to any values not listed in the VALUE statement.

**Example**  Universe Cars is surveying its customers as to their preferences for car colors. They have information about the customer's age, sex (coded as 1 for male and 2 for female), annual income, and preferred car color (yellow, gray, blue, or white). Here are the data:

```
19 1 14000 Y
45 1 65000 G
72 2 35000 B
31 1 44000 Y
58 2 83000 W
```

The following program reads the data; creates formats for age, sex, and car color using the FORMAT procedure; then prints the data using the new formats:

```
DATA carsurvey;
    INFILE 'c:\MyRawData\Cars.dat';
    INPUT Age Sex Income Color $;
PROC FORMAT;
    VALUE gender 1 = 'Male'
                 2 = 'Female';
    VALUE agegroup 13 -< 20 = 'Teen'
                   20 -< 65 = 'Adult'
                   65 - HIGH = 'Senior';
    VALUE $col  'W' = 'Moon White'
                'B' = 'Sky Blue'
                'Y' = 'Sunburst Yellow'
                'G' = 'Rain Cloud Gray';
* Print data using user-defined and standard (DOLLAR8.) formats;
PROC PRINT DATA = carsurvey;
    FORMAT Sex gender. Age agegroup. Color $col. Income DOLLAR8.;
    TITLE 'Survey Results Printed with User-Defined Formats';
RUN;
```

This program creates two numeric formats: GENDER. for the variable Sex and AGEGROUP. for the variable Age. The program creates a character format, $COL., for the variable Color. Notice that the format names do not end with periods in the VALUE statement, but they do in the FORMAT statement.

Here is the output:

```
              Survey Results Printed with User-Defined Formats        1

     Obs    Age      Sex       Income    Color

      1     Teen     Male      $14,000   Sunburst Yellow
      2     Adult    Male      $65,000   Rain Cloud Gray
      3     Senior   Female    $35,000   Sky Blue
      4     Adult    Male      $44,000   Sunburst Yellow
      5     Adult    Female    $83,000   Moon White
```

This example creates temporary formats that exist only for the current job or session. Creating and using permanent formats is discussed under the FORMAT Procedure in the SAS Help and Documentation.

# 4.8 Writing Simple Custom Reports

PROC PRINT is flexible and easy to use. Still, there are times when PROC PRINT just won't do: when your report to a state agency has to be spaced just like their fill-in-the-blank form, or when your client insists that the report contain complete sentences, or when you want one page per observation. At those times you can use the flexibility of the DATA step, and format to your heart's content.

You can write data in a DATA step the same way you read data—but in reverse. Instead of using an INFILE statement, you use a FILE statement; instead of INPUT statements, you use PUT statements. This is similar to writing a raw data file in a DATA step (section 9.5), but to write a report you use the PRINT option telling SAS to include the carriage returns and page breaks needed for printing. Here is the general form of a FILE statement for creating a report:

```
FILE 'file-specification' PRINT;
```

Like INPUT statements, PUT statements can be in list, column, or formatted style, but since SAS already knows whether a variable is numeric or character, you don't have to put a $ after character variables. If you use list format, SAS will automatically put a space between each variable. If you use column or formatted styles of PUT statements, SAS will put the variables wherever you specify. You can control spacing with the same pointer controls that INPUT statements use: @*n* to move to column *n*, +*n* to move *n* columns, / to skip to the next line, #*n* to skip to line *n*, and the trailing @ to hold the current line. In addition to printing variables, you can insert a text string by simply enclosing it in quotation marks.

**Example**  To show how this differs from PROC PRINT, we'll use the candy sales data again. Two fourth-grade classes have sold candy to raise money for a field trip. Here are the data with each student's name, classroom number, the date they turned in their money, the type of candy: mint patties or chocolate dinosaurs, and the number of boxes sold:

```
Adriana    21 3/21/2008 MP   7
Nathan     14 3/21/2008 CD  19
Matthew    14 3/21/2008 CD  14
Claire     14 3/22/2008 CD  11
Caitlin    21 3/24/2008 CD   9
Ian        21 3/24/2008 MP  18
Chris      14 3/25/2008 CD   6
Anthony    21 3/25/2008 MP  13
Stephen    14 3/25/2008 CD  10
Erika      21 3/25/2008 MP  17
```

The teachers want a report for each student showing how much money that student earned. They want each student's report on a separate page so it is easy to hand out. Lastly, they want it to be easy for fourth graders to understand, with complete sentences. Here is the program:

```
* Write a report with FILE and PUT statements;
DATA _NULL_;
   INFILE 'c:\MyRawData\Candy.dat';
   INPUT Name $ 1-11 Class @15 DateReturned MMDDYY10.
      CandyType $ Quantity;
   Profit = Quantity * 1.25;
   FILE 'c:\MyRawData\Student.txt' PRINT;
   TITLE;
```

```
   PUT @5 'Candy sales report for ' Name 'from classroom ' Class
      // @5 'Congratulations!  You sold ' Quantity 'boxes of candy'
      / @5 'and earned ' Profit DOLLAR6.2 ' for our field trip.';
   PUT _PAGE_;
RUN;
```

Notice that the keyword _NULL_ appears in the DATA statement instead of a data set name. _NULL_ tells SAS not to bother writing a SAS data set (since the goal is to create a report not a data set), and makes the program run slightly faster. The FILE statement creates the output file for the report, and the PRINT option tells SAS to include carriage returns and page breaks. The null TITLE statement tells SAS to eliminate all automatic titles.

The first PUT statement in this program starts with a pointer, @5, telling SAS to go to column 5. Then it tells SAS to print the words Candy sales report for followed by the current value of the variable Name. The variables Name, Class, and Quantity are printed in list style whereas Profit is printed using formatted style and the DOLLAR6.2 format. A slash line pointer tells SAS to skip to the next line; two slashes skips two lines. You could use multiple PUT statements instead of slashes to skip lines because SAS goes to a new line every time there is a new PUT statement. The statement PUT _PAGE_ inserts a page break after each student's report. When the program is run, the log will contain these notes:

```
NOTE: 10 records were read from the infile 'c:\MyRawData\Candy.dat'.

NOTE: 30 records were written to the file 'c:\MyRawData\Student.txt'.
```

The first three pages of the report look like this:

```
   Candy sales report for Adriana from classroom 21

   Congratulations!  You sold 7 boxes of candy
   and earned  $8.75 for our field trip.
```

```
   Candy sales report for Nathan from classroom 14

   Congratulations!  You sold 19 boxes of candy
   and earned $23.75 for our field trip.
```

```
   Candy sales report for Matthew from classroom 14

   Congratulations!  You sold 14 boxes of candy
   and earned $17.50 for our field trip.
```

# 4.9 Summarizing Your Data Using PROC MEANS

One of the first things people usually want to do with their data, after reading it and making sure it is correct, is look at some simple statistics. Statistics such as the mean value, standard deviation, and minimum and maximum values give you a feel for your data. These types of information can also alert you to errors in your data (a score of 980 in a basketball game, for example, is suspect). The MEANS procedure provides simple statistics on numeric variables.

The MEANS procedure starts with the keywords PROC MEANS, followed by options listing the statistics you want printed:

```
PROC MEANS options;
```

If you do not specify any options, MEANS will print the number of non-missing values, the mean, the standard deviation, and the minimum and maximum values for each variable. There are over 30 different statistics you can request with the MEANS procedure. The following is a list of some of the simple statistics. More options for PROC MEANS are listed in section 8.7.

| | |
|---|---|
| MAX | the maximum value |
| MIN | the minimum value |
| MEAN | the mean |
| MEDIAN | the median |
| MODE | the mode (new in SAS 9.2) |
| N | number of non-missing values |
| NMISS | number of missing values |
| RANGE | the range |
| STDDEV | the standard deviation |
| SUM | the sum |

If you use the PROC MEANS statement with no other statements, then you will get statistics for all observations and all numeric variables in your data set. Here are some of the optional statements you may want to use:

| | |
|---|---|
| BY *variable-list*; | The BY statement performs separate analyses for each level of the variables in the list.[1] The data must first be sorted in the same order as the *variable-list*. (You can use PROC SORT to do this.) |
| CLASS *variable-list*; | The CLASS statement also performs separate analyses for each level of the variables in the list,[1] but its output is more compact than with the BY statement, and the data do not have to be sorted first. |
| VAR *variable-list*; | The VAR statement specifies which numeric variables to use in the analysis. If it is absent then SAS uses all numeric variables. |

---

[1] By default, observations are excluded if they have missing values for BY or CLASS variables. If you want to include missing values, add the MISSING option to the PROC MEANS statement.

**Example**  A wholesale nursery is selling garden flowers, and they want to summarize their sales figures by month. The data file which follows contains the customer ID, date of sale, and number of petunias, snapdragons, and marigolds sold:

```
756-01  05/04/2008 120  80 110
834-01  05/12/2008  90 160  60
901-02  05/18/2008  50 100  75
834-01  06/01/2008  80  60 100
756-01  06/11/2008 100 160  75
901-02  06/19/2008  60  60  60
756-01  06/25/2008  85 110 100
```

The following program reads the data; computes a new variable, Month, which is the month of the sale; sorts the data by Month using PROC SORT; then summarizes the data by Month using PROC MEANS with a BY statement:

```
DATA sales;
   INFILE 'c:\MyRawData\Flowers.dat';
   INPUT CustomerID $ @9 SaleDate MMDDYY10. Petunia SnapDragon
         Marigold;
   Month = MONTH(SaleDate);
PROC SORT DATA = sales;
   BY Month;
* Calculate means by Month for flower sales;
PROC MEANS DATA = sales;
   BY Month;
   VAR Petunia SnapDragon Marigold;
   TITLE 'Summary of Flower Sales by Month';
RUN;
```

Here are the results of the PROC MEANS:

```
                Summary of Flower Sales by Month                    1

- - - - - - - - - - - - - - - - - - - - -  Month=5  - - - - - - - - - - - - - - - - - - - - - - - - -
                         The MEANS Procedure
Variable      N          Mean         Std Dev        Minimum         Maximum

Petunia       3    86.6666667      35.1188458     50.0000000     120.0000000
SnapDragon    3   113.3333333      41.6333200     80.0000000     160.0000000
Marigold      3    81.6666667      25.6580072     60.0000000     110.0000000


- - - - - - - - - - - - - - - - - - - - -  Month=6  - - - - - - - - - - - - - - - - - - - - - - - - -
Variable      N          Mean         Std Dev        Minimum         Maximum

Petunia       4    81.2500000      16.5201897     60.0000000     100.0000000
SnapDragon    4    97.5000000      47.8713554     60.0000000     160.0000000
Marigold      4    83.7500000      19.7378655     60.0000000     100.0000000
```

## 4.10   Writing Summary Statistics to a SAS Data Set

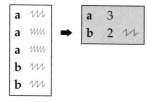

Sometimes you want to save summary statistics to a SAS data set for further analysis, or to merge with other data. For example, you might want to plot the hourly temperature in your office to show how it heats up every afternoon causing you to fall asleep, but the instrument you have records data for every minute. The MEANS procedure can condense the data by computing the mean temperature for each hour and then save the results in a SAS data set so it can be plotted.

There are two methods in PROC MEANS for saving summary statistics in a SAS data set. You can use the OUTPUT destination, which is covered in section 5.3, or you can use the OUTPUT statement. The OUTPUT statement has the following form:

```
OUTPUT OUT = data-set output-statistic-list;
```

Here, *data-set* is the name of the SAS data set which will contain the results (this can be either temporary or permanent), and *output-statistic-list* defines which statistics you want and the associated variable names. You can have more than one OUTPUT statement and multiple output statistic lists. The following is one of the possible forms for *output-statistic-list*:

```
statistic(variable-list) = name-list
```

Here, *statistic* can be any of the statistics available in PROC MEANS (SUM, N, MEAN, for example), *variable-list* defines which of the variables in the VAR statement you want to output, and *name-list* defines the new variable names for the statistics. The new variable names must be in the same order as their corresponding variables in *variable-list*. For example, the following PROC MEANS statements produce a new data set called ZOOSUM, which contains one observation with the variables LionWeight, the mean of the lions' weights, and BearWeight, the mean of the bears' weights:

```
PROC MEANS DATA = zoo NOPRINT;
   VAR Lions Tigers Bears;
   OUTPUT OUT = zoosum MEAN(Lions Bears) = LionWeight BearWeight;
RUN;
```

The NOPRINT option in the PROC MEANS statement tells SAS there is no need to produce any printed results since we are saving the results in a SAS data set.[1]

The SAS data set created in the OUTPUT statement will contain all the variables defined in the *output-statistic-list*; any variables listed in a BY or CLASS statement; plus two new variables, _TYPE_ and _FREQ_. If there is no BY or CLASS statement, then the data set will have just one observation. If there is a BY statement, then the data set will have one observation for each level of the BY group. CLASS statements produce one observation for each level of interaction of the class variables. The value of the _TYPE_ variable depends on the level of interaction. The observation where _TYPE_ has a value of zero is the grand total.[2]

---

[1] Using PROC MEANS with a NOPRINT option is the same as using PROC SUMMARY.

[2] For a more detailed explanation of the _TYPE_ variable, see the SAS Help and Documentation.

**Example**   The following are sales data for a wholesale nursery with the customer ID; date of sale; and the number of petunias, snapdragons, and marigolds sold:

```
756-01   05/04/2008 120  80 110
834-01   05/12/2008  90 160  60
901-02   05/18/2008  50 100  75
834-01   06/01/2008  80  60 100
756-01   06/11/2008 100 160  75
901-02   06/19/2008  60  60  60
756-01   06/25/2008  85 110 100
```

You want to summarize the data so that you have only one observation per customer containing the sum and mean of the number of plant sets sold, and you want to save the results in a SAS data set for further analysis. The following program reads the data from the file; sorts by the variable, CustomerID; and then uses the MEANS procedure with the NOPRINT option to calculate the sums and means by CustomerID. The results are saved in a SAS data set named TOTALS in the OUTPUT statement. The sums are given the original variable names Petunia, SnapDragon, and Marigold, and the means are given new variable names MeanPetunia, MeanSnapDragon, and MeanMarigold. A PROC PRINT is used to show the TOTALS data set:

```
DATA sales;
    INFILE 'c:\MyRawData\Flowers.dat';
    INPUT CustomerID $ @9 SaleDate MMDDYY10. Petunia SnapDragon Marigold;
PROC SORT DATA = sales;
    BY CustomerID;
* Calculate means by CustomerID, output sum and mean to new data set;
PROC MEANS NOPRINT DATA = sales;
    BY CustomerID;
    VAR Petunia SnapDragon Marigold;
    OUTPUT OUT = totals  MEAN(Petunia SnapDragon Marigold) =
        MeanPetunia MeanSnapDragon MeanMarigold
      SUM(Petunia SnapDragon Marigold) = Petunia SnapDragon Marigold;
PROC PRINT DATA = totals;
    TITLE 'Sum of Flower Data over Customer ID';
    FORMAT MeanPetunia MeanSnapDragon MeanMarigold 3.;
RUN;
```

Here are the results:

```
                Sum of Flower Data over Customer ID                    1


                                        Mean
        Customer           Mean    Snap    Mean          Snap
  Obs      ID    _TYPE_ _FREQ_ Petunia Dragon Marigold Petunia Dragon Marigold

   1    756-01     0      3      102    117     95      305    350    285
   2    834-01     0      2       85    110     80      170    220    160
   3    901-02     0      2       55     80     68      110    160    135
```

# 4.11   Counting Your Data with PROC FREQ

A frequency table is a simple list of counts answering the question "How many?" When you have counts for one variable, they are called one-way frequencies. When you combine two or more variables, the counts are called two-way, three-way, and so on up to *n*-way frequencies; or simply cross-tabulations.

The most obvious reason for using PROC FREQ is to create tables showing the distribution of categorical data values, but PROC FREQ can also reveal irregularities in your data. You could get dizzy proofreading a large data set, but data entry errors are often glaringly obvious in a frequency table. The basic form of PROC FREQ is

```
PROC FREQ;
   TABLES variable-combinations;
```

To produce a one-way frequency table, just list the variable name. This statement produces a frequency table listing the number of observations for each value of YearsEducation:

```
TABLES YearsEducation;
```

To produce a cross-tabulation, list the variables separated by an asterisk. This statement produces a cross-tabulation showing the number of observations for each combination of Sex by YearsEducation:

```
TABLES Sex * YearsEducation;
```

You can specify any number of table requests in a single TABLES statement, and you can have as many TABLES statements as you wish. Be careful though; reading cross-tabulations of three or more levels is like playing three-dimensional tic-tac-toe without the benefit of a three-dimensional board.

Options, if any, appear after a slash in the TABLES statement. For a list of statistical options for PROC FREQ see section 8.10. Options for controlling the output of PROC FREQ include

```
LIST           prints cross-tabulations in list format rather than grid
MISSING        includes missing values in frequency statistics
NOCOL          suppresses printing of column percentages in cross-tabulations
NOPERCENT      suppresses printing of percentages
NOROW          suppresses printing of row percentages in cross-tabulations
OUT = data-set writes a data set containing frequencies
```

The statement below, for instance, tells SAS to include missing values in the frequencies:

```
TABLES Sex * YearsEducation / MISSING;
```

**Example**   The proprietor of a coffee shop keeps a record of sales. For each drink sold, she records the type of coffee (cappuccino, espresso, kona, or iced coffee), and whether the customer walked in or came to the drive-up window. Here are the data with ten observations per line:

```
esp w cap d cap w kon w ice w kon d esp d kon w ice d esp d
cap w esp d cap d Kon d  .    d kon w esp d cap w ice w kon w
kon w kon w ice d esp d kon w esp d esp w kon w cap w kon w
```

The following program reads the data and produces one-way and two-way frequencies:

```
DATA orders;
   INFILE 'c:\MyRawData\Coffee.dat';
   INPUT Coffee $ Window $ @@;
* Print tables for Window and Window by Coffee;
PROC FREQ DATA = orders;
   TABLES Window  Window * Coffee;
   RUN;
```

The output contains two tables. The first is a one-way frequency table for the variable Window. You can see that 13 customers came to the drive-up window while 17 walked into the restaurant.

```
                       The FREQ Procedure                              1

                                        Cumulative     Cumulative
     Window      Frequency      Percent   Frequency      Percent
     ─────────────────────────────────────────────────────────────
     d                  13       43.33          13        43.33
     w                  17       56.67          30       100.00

                    Table of Window by Coffee

     Window      Coffee

     Frequency│
     Percent  │
     Row Pct  │
     Col Pct  │ Kon    │ cap    │ esp    │ ice    │ kon    │  Total
     ─────────┼────────┼────────┼────────┼────────┼────────┤
     d        │     1  │     2  │     6  │     2  │     1  │    12
              │  3.45  │  6.90  │ 20.69  │  6.90  │  3.45  │ 41.38
              │  8.33  │ 16.67  │ 50.00  │ 16.67  │  8.33  │
              │100.00  │ 33.33  │ 75.00  │ 50.00  │ 10.00  │
     ─────────┼────────┼────────┼────────┼────────┼────────┤
     w        │     0  │     4  │     2  │     2  │     9  │    17
              │  0.00  │ 13.79  │  6.90  │  6.90  │ 31.03  │ 58.62
              │  0.00  │ 23.53  │ 11.76  │ 11.76  │ 52.94  │
              │  0.00  │ 66.67  │ 25.00  │ 50.00  │ 90.00  │
     ─────────┼────────┼────────┼────────┼────────┼────────┤
     Total          1        6        8        4       10       29
                 3.45    20.69    27.59    13.79    34.48   100.00
                    Frequency Missing = 1
```

The second table is a two-way cross-tabulation of Window by Coffee. Inside each cell, SAS prints the frequency, percentage, percentage for that row, and percentage for that column; while cumulative frequencies and percents appear along the right side and bottom. Notice that the missing value is mentioned but not included in the statistics. (Use the MISSING option if you want missing values to be included in the table.) Also, there is one observation with a value of Kon for Coffee. This data entry error should be kon.

# 4.12  Producing Tabular Reports with PROC TABULATE

Every summary statistic the TABULATE procedure computes can also be produced by other procedures such as PRINT, MEANS, and FREQ, but PROC TABULATE is popular because its reports are pretty. If TABULATE were a box, it would be gift-wrapped.

PROC TABULATE is so powerful that entire books have been written about it, but it is also so concise that you may feel like you're reading hieroglyphics. If you find the syntax of PROC TABULATE a little hard to get used to, that may be because it has roots outside of SAS. PROC TABULATE is based in part on the Table Producing Language, a complex and sophisticated language developed by the U.S. Department of Labor.

The general form of PROC TABULATE is

```
PROC TABULATE;
   CLASS classification-variable-list;
   TABLE page-dimension, row-dimension, column-dimension;
```

The CLASS statement tells SAS which variables contain categorical data to be used for dividing observations into groups, while the TABLE statement tells SAS how to organize your table and what numbers to compute. Each TABLE statement defines only one table, but you may have multiple TABLE statements. If a variable is listed in a CLASS statement, then, by default, PROC TABULATE produces simple counts of the number of observations in each category of that variable. PROC TABULATE offers many other statistics too, and the next section describes how to request those.

**Dimensions**  Each TABLE statement can specify up to three dimensions. Those dimensions, separated by commas, tell SAS which variables to use for the pages, rows, and columns in the report. If you specify only one dimension, then that becomes, by default, the column dimension. If you specify two dimensions, then you get rows and columns, but no page dimension. If you specify three dimensions, then you get pages, rows, and columns.

When you write a TABLE statement, start with the column dimension. Once you have that debugged, add the rows. Once you are happy with your rows and columns, then you are ready to add a page dimension, if you need one. Notice that the order of dimensions in the TABLE statement is page, then row, then column. So, to avoid scrambling your table when you add dimensions, insert the page and row specifications *in front* of the column dimension.

**Missing data**  By default, observations are excluded from tables if they have missing values for variables listed in a CLASS statement. If you want to keep these observations, then simply add the MISSING option to your PROC statement like this:

```
PROC TABULATE MISSING;
```

**Example**  Here are data about pleasure boats including the name of each boat, its home port, whether it is a sailing or power vessel, the type of boat (schooner, catamaran, or yacht), and the price of an excursion.

```
Silent Lady   Maalea   sail   sch 75.00
America II    Maalea   sail   yac 32.95
Aloha Anai    Lahaina  sail   cat 62.00
Ocean Spirit  Maalea   power  cat 22.00
Anuenue       Maalea   sail   sch 47.50
Hana Lei      Maalea   power  cat 28.99
Leilani       Maalea   power  yac 19.99
Kalakaua      Maalea   power  cat 29.50
Reef Runner   Lahaina  power  yac 29.95
Blue Dolphin  Maalea   sail   cat 42.95
```

Suppose you want a report showing the number of boats of each type that are sailing or power vessels in each port. The following DATA step reads the data from a raw data file named Boats.dat. Then PROC TABULATE creates a three-dimensional report with the values of Port for the pages, Locomotion for the rows, and Type for the columns.

```
DATA boats;
   INFILE 'c:\MyRawData\Boats.dat';
   INPUT Name $ 1-12 Port $ 14-20 Locomotion $ 22-26 Type $ 28-30
      Price 32-36;
RUN;
* Tabulations with three dimensions;
PROC TABULATE DATA = boats;
   CLASS Port Locomotion Type;
   TABLE Port, Locomotion, Type;
   TITLE 'Number of Boats by Port, Locomotion, and Type';
RUN;
```

This report has two pages, one for each value of the page dimension. Here is one page:

```
         Number of Boats by Port, Locomotion, and Type              1

    Port Maalea
```

|  | Type | | |
|---|---|---|---|
|  | cat | sch | yac |
|  | N | N | N |
| **Locomotion** | | | |
| power | 3.00 | . | 1.00 |
| sail | 1.00 | 2.00 | 1.00 |

The value of the page dimension appears in the top, left corner of the output. You can see that this is the page for the port of Maalea. The heading N tells you that the numbers in this table are simple counts, the number of boats in each group.

## 4.13    Adding Statistics to PROC TABULATE Output

By default, PROC TABULATE produces simple counts for variables listed in a CLASS statement, but you can request many other statistics in a TABLE statement. You can also concatenate or cross variables within dimensions. In fact, you can write TABLE statements so complicated that even *you* won't know what the report is going to look like until you run it.

While the CLASS statement lists categorical variables, the VAR statement tells SAS which variables contain continuous data. Here is the general form:

```
PROC TABULATE;
   VAR analysis-variable-list;
   CLASS classification-variable-list;
   TABLE page-dimension, row-dimension, column-dimension;
```

You may have both a CLASS statement and a VAR statement, or just one, but all variables listed in a TABLE statement must also appear in either a CLASS or a VAR statement.

**Keywords**    In addition to variable names, each dimension can contain keywords. These are a few of the values TABULATE can compute.

| | |
|---|---|
| ALL | adds a row, column, or page showing the total |
| MAX | highest value |
| MIN | lowest value |
| MEAN | the arithmetic mean |
| MEDIAN | the median |
| MODE | the mode (new in SAS 9.2) |
| N | number of non-missing values |
| NMISS | number of missing values |
| PCTN | the percentage of observations for that group |
| PCTSUM | the percentage of a total sum represented by that group |
| STDDEV | the standard deviation |
| SUM | the sum |

**Concatenating, crossing, and grouping**    Within a dimension, variables and keywords can be concatenated, crossed, or grouped. To concatenate variables or keywords simply list them separated by a space, to cross variables or keywords separate then with an asterisk (*), and to group them enclose the variables or keywords in parentheses. The keyword ALL is generally concatenated. To request other statistics, however, cross that keyword with the variable name.

| | |
|---|---|
| Concatenating: | `TABLE Locomotion Type ALL;` |
| Crossing: | `TABLE MEAN * Price;` |
| Crossing, grouping, and concatenating: | `TABLE PCTN *(Locomotion Type);` |

**Example**    Here again are the boat data containing the name of each boat, its home port, whether it is a sailing or power vessel, the type of boat (schooner, catamaran, or yacht), and the price of an excursion.

```
Silent Lady   Maalea    sail   sch 75.00
America II    Maalea    sail   yac 32.95
Aloha Anai    Lahaina   sail   cat 62.00
Ocean Spirit  Maalea    power  cat 22.00
Anuenue       Maalea    sail   sch 47.50
Hana Lei      Maalea    power  cat 28.99
```

```
Leilani      Maalea   power yac 19.99
Kalakaua     Maalea   power cat 29.50
Reef Runner  Lahaina  power yac 29.95
Blue Dolphin Maalea   sail  cat 42.95
```

The following program is similar to the one in the previous section. However, this PROC
TABULATE includes a VAR statement. The TABLE statement in this program contains only two
dimensions; but it also concatenates, crosses, and groups variables and statistics.

```
DATA boats;
   INFILE 'c:\MyRawData\Boats.dat';
   INPUT Name $ 1-12 Port $ 14-20 Locomotion $ 22-26 Type $ 28-30
      Price 32-36;
RUN;
* Tabulations with two dimensions and statistics;
PROC TABULATE DATA = boats;
   CLASS Locomotion Type;
   VAR Price;
   TABLE Locomotion ALL, MEAN*Price*(Type ALL);
   TITLE 'Mean Price by Locomotion and Type';
RUN;
```

The row dimension of this table concatenates the classification variable Locomotion with ALL to
produce totals. The column dimension, on the other hand, crosses MEAN with the analysis
variable Price and with the classification variable Type (which happens to be concatenated and
grouped with ALL). Here are the results:

```
           Mean Price by Locomotion and Type                    1

                     ┌─────────────────────────────────────────┐
                     │                 Mean                     │
                     ├─────────────────────────────────────────┤
                     │                 Price                    │
                     ├───────────────────────────────┬─────────┤
                     │              Type              │         │
                     ├─────────┬─────────┬───────────┤   All   │
                     │   cat   │   sch   │    yac    │         │
┌──────────────────┬─┴─────────┴─────────┴───────────┴─────────┤
│ Locomotion       │                                           │
├──────────────────┼───────────┬───────────┬──────────┬────────┤
│ power            │     26.83 │         . │    24.97 │  26.09 │
├──────────────────┼───────────┼───────────┼──────────┼────────┤
│ sail             │     52.48 │     61.25 │    32.95 │  52.08 │
├──────────────────┼───────────┼───────────┼──────────┼────────┤
│ All              │     37.09 │     61.25 │    27.63 │  39.08 │
└──────────────────┴───────────┴───────────┴──────────┴────────┘
```

# 4.14 Enhancing the Appearance of PROC TABULATE Output

When you use PROC TABULATE, SAS wraps your data in tidy little boxes, but there may be times when they just don't look right. Using three simple options, you can enhance the appearance of your output. Think of it as changing the wrapping paper.

**FORMAT= option** To change the format of all the data cells in your table, use the FORMAT= option in your PROC statement. For example, if you needed the numbers in your table to have commas and no decimal places, you could use this PROC statement

```
PROC TABULATE FORMAT=COMMA10.0;
```

telling SAS to use the COMMA10.0 format for all the data cells in your table.

**BOX= and MISSTEXT= options** While the FORMAT= option must be used in your PROC statement, the BOX= and MISSTEXT= options go in TABLE statements. The BOX= option allows you to write a brief phrase in the normally empty box that appears in the upper left corner of every TABULATE report. Using this empty space can give your reports a nicely polished look. The MISSTEXT= option, on the other hand, specifies a value for SAS to print in empty data cells. The period that SAS prints, by default, for missing values can seem downright mysterious to someone, perhaps your CEO, who is not familiar with SAS output. You can give them something more meaningful with the MISSTEXT= option. This statement

```
TABLE Region, MEAN*Sales / BOX='Mean Sales by Region' MISSTEXT='No Sales';
```

tells SAS to print the title "Mean Sales by Region" in the upper left corner of the table, and to print the words "No Sales" in any cells of the table that have no data. The BOX= and MISSTEXT= options must be separated from the dimensions of the TABLE statement by a slash.

**Example** Here again are the boat data containing the name of each boat, its home port, whether it is a sailing or power vessel, the type of boat (schooner, catamaran, or yacht), and the price of an excursion.

```
Silent Lady   Maalea   sail   sch 75.00
America II    Maalea   sail   yac 32.95
Aloha Anai    Lahaina  sail   cat 62.00
Ocean Spirit  Maalea   power  cat 22.00
Anuenue       Maalea   sail   sch 47.50
Hana Lei      Maalea   power  cat 28.99
Leilani       Maalea   power  yac 19.99
Kalakaua      Maalea   power  cat 29.50
Reef Runner   Lahaina  power  yac 29.95
Blue Dolphin  Maalea   sail   cat 42.95
```

The following program is the same as the one in the previous section except that the FORMAT=, BOX=, and MISSTEXT= options have been added. Notice that the FORMAT= option goes in the PROC statement, while the BOX= and MISSTEXT= options go in the TABLE statement following a slash. Because the BOX= option serves as a title, a null TITLE statement is used to remove the usual title.

```
DATA boats;
   INFILE 'c:\MyRawData\Boats.dat';
   INPUT Name $ 1-12 Port $ 14-20 Locomotion $ 22-26 Type $ 28-30
      Price 32-36;
RUN;
* PROC TABULATE report with options;
PROC TABULATE DATA = boats FORMAT=DOLLAR9.2;
   CLASS Locomotion Type;
   VAR Price;
   TABLE Locomotion ALL, MEAN*Price*(Type ALL)
      /BOX='Full Day Excursions' MISSTEXT='none';
   TITLE;
RUN;
```

Here is the enhanced output:

1

| Full Day Excursions | Mean | | | |
| --- | --- | --- | --- | --- |
| | Price | | | |
| | Type | | | All |
| | cat | sch | yac | |
| **Locomotion** | | | | |
| power | $26.83 | none | $24.97 | $26.09 |
| sail | $52.48 | $61.25 | $32.95 | $52.08 |
| All | $37.09 | $61.25 | $27.63 | $39.08 |

Notice that all the data cells now use the DOLLAR9.2 format as specified in the FORMAT= option. The text "Full Day Excursions" now appears in the upper left corner which was empty in the previous section. In addition, the one data cell with no data now shows the word "none" instead of a period.

## 4.15   Changing Headers in PROC TABULATE Output

The TABULATE procedure produces reports with a lot of headers. Sometimes there are so many headers that your reports look cluttered; at other times you may simply feel that a different header would be more meaningful. Before you can change a header, though, you need to understand what type of header it is. TABULATE reports have two basic types of headers: headers that are the values of variables listed in a CLASS statement, and headers that are the names of variables and keywords. You use different methods to change different types of headers.

**CLASS variable values**   To change headers which are the values of variables listed in a CLASS statement, use the FORMAT procedure to create a user-defined format. Then assign the format to the variable in a FORMAT statement (section 4.7).

**Variable names and keywords**   To change headers which are the names of variables or keywords, put an equal sign after the variable or keyword followed by the new header enclosed in quotation marks.[1] You can eliminate a header entirely by setting it equal to blank (two quotation marks with nothing in between), and SAS will remove the box for that header. This TABLE statement

```
TABLE Region='', MEAN=''*Sales='Mean Sales by Region';
```

tells SAS to remove the headers for Region and MEAN, and to change the header for the variable Sales to "Mean Sales by Region".

In some cases SAS leaves the empty box when a row header is set to blank. This happens for statistics and analysis variables (but not class variables). To force SAS to remove the empty box, add the ROW=FLOAT option to the end of your TABLE statement like this:

```
TABLE MEAN=''*Sales='Mean Sales by Region', Region='' / ROW=FLOAT;
```

**Example**   Here again are the boat data containing the name of each boat, its home port, whether it is a sailing or power vessel, the type of boat (schooner, catamaran, or yacht), and the price of an excursion.

```
Silent Lady   Maalea    sail   sch 75.00
America II    Maalea    sail   yac 32.95
Aloha Anai    Lahaina sail   cat 62.00
Ocean Spirit Maalea    power cat 22.00
Anuenue       Maalea    sail   sch 47.50
Hana Lei      Maalea    power cat 28.99
Leilani       Maalea    power yac 19.99
Kalakaua      Maalea    power cat 29.50
Reef Runner   Lahaina power yac 29.95
Blue Dolphin Maalea    sail   cat 42.95
```

The following program is the same as the one in the previous section except that the headers have been changed. To start with, a FORMAT procedure creates a user-defined format named $typ.

---

[1] You can also change variable headers with a LABEL statement (section 4.1), and keyword headers with a KEYLABEL statement. However, the TABLE statement method used in this section is the only way that you can remove a variable header without leaving a blank box behind.

Then the $typ. format is assigned to the variable Type using a FORMAT statement. In the TABLE statement, more headers are changed. The headers for Locomotion, MEAN, and Type are all set to blank, while the header for Price is set to "Mean Price by Type of Boat".

```
DATA boats;
   INFILE 'c:\MyRawData\Boats.dat';
   INPUT Name $ 1-12 Port $ 14-20 Locomotion $ 22-26 Type $ 28-30
      Price 32-36;
RUN;
* Changing headers;
PROC FORMAT;
   VALUE $typ  'cat' = 'catamaran'
               'sch' = 'schooner'
               'yac' = 'yacht';
RUN;
PROC TABULATE DATA = boats FORMAT=DOLLAR9.2;
   CLASS Locomotion Type;
   VAR Price;
   FORMAT Type $typ.;
   TABLE Locomotion='' ALL,
      MEAN=''*Price='Mean Price by Type of Boat'*(Type='' ALL)
      /BOX='Full Day Excursions' MISSTEXT='none';
   TITLE;
RUN;
```

This program does not require the ROW=FLOAT option because the only variable being set to blank in the row dimension is a class variable. If you put an analysis variable or statistics keyword in the row dimension and set it equal to blank, then you would need to add the ROW=FLOAT option to remove empty boxes. Here is the output:

| Full Day Excursions | Mean Price by Type of Boat | | | |
|---|---|---|---|---|
| | catamaran | schooner | yacht | All |
| power | $26.83 | none | $24.97 | $26.09 |
| sail | $52.48 | $61.25 | $32.95 | $52.08 |
| All | $37.09 | $61.25 | $27.63 | $39.08 |

This output is the same as the output in the preceding section, except for the new headers. Notice how much cleaner and more compact this report is.

## 4.16 Specifying Multiple Formats for Data Cells in PROC TABULATE Output

Using the FORMAT= option in a PROC TABULATE statement, you can easily specify a format for the data cells; but you can only specify one format, and it must apply to all the data cells. If you want to use more than one format in your table, you can do that by putting the FORMAT= option in your TABLE statement.

To apply a format to an individual variable, cross it with the variable name. The general form of this is

```
variable-name*FORMAT=formatw.d
```

Then you insert this rather convoluted construction in your TABLE statement.

```
TABLE Region, MEAN*(Sales*FORMAT=COMMA8.0 Profit*FORMAT=DOLLAR10.2);
```

This TABLE statement applies the COMMA8.0 format to a variable named Sales, and the DOLLAR10.2 format to Profit.

**Example**   Here again are the boat data containing the name of each boat, its home port, whether it is a sailing or power vessel, the type of boat (schooner, catamaran, or yacht), and the price of an excursion. A new variable has been added showing the length of each boat in feet.

```
Silent Lady  Maalea   sail   sch 75.00   64
America II    Maalea   sail   yac 32.95   65
Aloha Anai   Lahaina  sail   cat 62.00   60
Ocean Spirit Maalea   power  cat 22.00   65
Anuenue      Maalea   sail   sch 47.50   52
Hana Lei     Maalea   power  cat 28.99  110
Leilani      Maalea   power  yac 19.99   45
Kalakaua     Maalea   power  cat 29.50   70
Reef Runner  Lahaina  power  yac 29.95   50
Blue Dolphin Maalea   sail   cat 42.95   65
```

Suppose you want to show the mean price and mean length of boats side-by-side in the same report. Using dollar signs makes sense for price, but not for length. In the program below, the format DOLLAR6.2 is applied to the variable Price, while the format 6.0 is applied to Length. Notice that the FORMAT= options are crossed with the variables using an asterisk.

```
DATA boats;
   INFILE 'c:\MyRawData\Boats.dat';
   INPUT Name $ 1-12 Port $ 14-20 Locomotion $ 22-26 Type $ 28-30
      Price 32-36 Length 38-40;
RUN;
* Using the FORMAT= option in the TABLE statement;
PROC TABULATE DATA = boats;
   CLASS Locomotion Type;
   VAR Price Length;
   TABLE Locomotion ALL,
      MEAN * (Price*FORMAT=DOLLAR6.2 Length*FORMAT=6.0) * (Type ALL);
   TITLE 'Price and Length by Type of Boat';
RUN;
```

Here is the resulting output:

| | Mean | | | | | | | |
|---|---|---|---|---|---|---|---|---|
| | Price | | | | Length | | | |
| | Type | | | | Type | | | |
| | cat | sch | yac | All | cat | sch | yac | All |
| Locomotion | | | | | | | | |
| power | $26.83 | . | $24.97 | $26.09 | 82 | . | 48 | 68 |
| sail | $52.48 | $61.25 | $32.95 | $52.08 | 63 | 58 | 65 | 61 |
| All | $37.09 | $61.25 | $27.63 | $39.08 | 74 | 58 | 53 | 65 |

Price and Length by Type of Boat     1

Notice that the values for Price and Length are printed using different formats.

# 4.17   Producing Simple Output with PROC REPORT

**REPORT**

The REPORT procedure shares features with the PRINT, MEANS, TABULATE, and SORT procedures and the DATA step. With all those features rolled into one procedure, it's not surprising that PROC REPORT can be complex—in fact entire books have been written about it—but with all those features comes power.

Here is the general form of a basic REPORT procedure:

```
PROC REPORT NOWINDOWS;
   COLUMN variable-list;
```

In its simplest form, the COLUMN statement is similar to a VAR statement in PROC PRINT, telling SAS which variables to include and in what order. If you leave out the COLUMN statement, SAS will, by default, include all the variables in your data set. If you leave out the NOWINDOWS option, SAS will open the interactive Report window.[1]

By default, PROC REPORT prints your data immediately beneath the column headers. To visually separate the headers and data, use the HEADLINE or HEADSKIP options like this:

```
PROC REPORT NOWINDOWS HEADLINE HEADSKIP;
```

HEADLINE draws a line under the column headers while HEADSKIP puts a blank line beneath the column headers.[2]

**Numeric versus character data** The type of report you get from PROC REPORT depends, in part, on the type of data you use. If you have at least one character variable in your report, then, by default, you will get a detail report with one row per observation. If, on the other hand, your report includes only numeric variables, then, by default, PROC REPORT will sum those variables. Even dates will be summed, by default, because they are numeric.[3]

**Example** Here are data about national parks and monuments in the USA. The variables are name, type (NP for national park or NM for national monument), region (East or West), number of museums (including visitor centers), and number of campgrounds.

```
Dinosaur               NM West 2  6
Ellis Island           NM East 1  0
Everglades             NP East 5  2
Grand Canyon           NP West 5  3
Great Smoky Mountains  NP East 3 10
Hawaii Volcanoes       NP West 2  2
Lava Beds              NM West 1  1
Statue of Liberty      NM East 1  0
Theodore Roosevelt     NP  .   2  2
Yellowstone            NP West 9 11
Yosemite               NP West 2 13
```

---

[1] The Report window is a non-programming approach to using PROC REPORT. For more information see the SAS Help and Documentation.

[2] The HEADLINE and HEADSKIP options work only for the LISTING destination. If you send your output to another destination such as HTML, SAS will ignore these options. See chapter 5 for an explanation of destinations.

[3] You can override this default by assigning one of your numeric variables a usage type of DISPLAY in a DEFINE statement. See the next section.

The following program reads the data in a DATA step, and then runs two reports. The first report has no COLUMN statement so SAS will use all the variables, while the second uses a COLUMN statement to select just the numeric variables.

```
DATA natparks;
   INFILE 'c:\MyRawData\Parks.dat';
   INPUT Name $ 1-21 Type $ Region $ Museums Camping;
RUN;
PROC REPORT DATA = natparks NOWINDOWS HEADLINE;
   TITLE 'Report with Character and Numeric Variables';
RUN;
PROC REPORT DATA = natparks NOWINDOWS HEADLINE;
   COLUMN Museums Camping;
   TITLE 'Report with Only Numeric Variables';
RUN;
```

While the two PROC steps are only slightly different, the reports they produced differ dramatically. The first report is almost identical to the output you would get from a PROC PRINT except for the absence of the OBS column. The second report, since it contained only numeric variables, was summed.

```
             Report with Character and Numeric Variables            1

    Name                   Type     Region     Museums    Camping
    ─────────────────────────────────────────────────────────────

    Dinosaur               NM       West          2          6
    Ellis Island           NM       East          1          0
    Everglades             NP       East          5          2
    Grand Canyon           NP       West          5          3
    Great Smoky Mountains  NP       East          3         10
    Hawaii Volcanoes       NP       West          2          2
    Lava Beds              NM       West          1          1
    Statue of Liberty      NM       East          1          0
    Theodore Roosevelt     NP                     2          2
    Yellowstone            NP       West          9         11
    Yosemite               NP       West          2         13




             Report with Only Numeric Variables                     2

                     Museums      Camping
                     ─────────────────────

                        33           50
```

# 4.18   Using DEFINE Statements in PROC REPORT

The DEFINE statement is a general purpose statement that specifies options for an individual variable. You can have a DEFINE statement for every variable, but you only need to have a DEFINE statement if you want to specify an option for that particular variable. The general form of a DEFINE statement is

```
DEFINE variable / options 'column-header';
```

In a DEFINE statement, you specify the variable name followed by a slash and any options for that particular variable.

**Usage Options**   The most important option is a usage option that tells SAS how that variable is to be used. Possible values of usage options include:

ACROSS      creates a column for each unique value of the variable.
ANALYSIS    calculates statistics for the variable. This is the default usage for numeric variables, and the default statistic is sum.
COMPUTED    creates a new variable whose value you calculate in a compute block. See section 4.22 for a discussion of compute blocks.
DISPLAY     creates one row for each observation in the data set. This is the default usage for character variables.
GROUP       creates one row for each unique value of the variable.
ORDER       creates one row for each observation with rows arranged according to the values of the order variable.

**Changing column headers**   There are several ways to change column headers in PROC REPORT including using a LABEL statement as described in section 4.1, or specifying a column header in a DEFINE statement. The following statement tells SAS to arrange a report by the values of the variable Age, and use the words "Age at Admission" as the column header for that variable. Putting a slash in a column header tells SAS to split the header at that point.[1]

```
DEFINE Age / ORDER 'Age at/Admission' WIDTH = 9;
```

You may need to specify the WIDTH= option[2] to make your column header fit. The width of a column depends, in part, on the length of that variable and may be too short for the header. In this example, the word Admission is nine characters long so the width must be at least nine.

**Missing data**   By default, observations are excluded from reports if they have missing values for order, group, or across variables. If you want to keep these observations, then simply add the MISSING option to your PROC statement like this:

```
PROC REPORT NOWINDOWS MISSING;
```

**Example**   Here again are the data about national parks and monuments. The variables are name, type (NP for national park or NM for national monument), region (East or West), number of museums (including visitor centers), and number of campgrounds.

---

[1] At the time this book was written, PROC REPORT did not automatically split mixed-case variable names the way most procedures do.

[2] The WIDTH= option affects output only in the ODS LISTING destination. See chapter 5 for more information about ODS.

```
Dinosaur                NM West 2   6
Ellis Island            NM East 1   0
Everglades              NP East 5   2
Grand Canyon            NP West 5   3
Great Smoky Mountains   NP East 3  10
Hawaii Volcanoes        NP West 2   2
Lava Beds               NM West 1   1
Statue of Liberty       NM East 1   0
Theodore Roosevelt      NP  .   2   2
Yellowstone             NP West 9  11
Yosemite                NP West 2  13
```

The following PROC REPORT contains two DEFINE statements. The first defines Region as having a usage type of ORDER. The second specifies a column header for the variable Camping. Camping is a numeric variable and has a default usage of ANALYSIS, so the DEFINE statement does not change its usage. Since the MISSING option appears in the PROC statement, observations with missing values of Region will be included in the report.

```
DATA natparks;
    INFILE 'c:\MyRawData\Parks.dat';
    INPUT Name $ 1-21 Type $ Region $ Museums Camping;
RUN;
* PROC REPORT with ORDER variable, MISSING option, and column header;
PROC REPORT DATA = natparks NOWINDOWS HEADLINE MISSING;
    COLUMN Region Name Museums Camping;
    DEFINE Region / ORDER;
    DEFINE Camping / ANALYSIS 'Camp/Grounds';
    TITLE 'National Parks and Monuments Arranged by Region';
RUN;
```

Here is the resulting output:

```
   National Parks and Monuments Arranged by Region         1


                                                       Camp
    Region    Name                      Museums       Grounds

              Theodore Roosevelt           2             2
    East      Ellis Island                 1             0
              Everglades                   5             2
              Great Smoky Mountains        3            10
              Statue of Liberty            1             0
    West      Dinosaur                     2             6
              Grand Canyon                 5             3
              Hawaii Volcanoes             2             2
              Lava Beds                    1             1
              Yellowstone                  9            11
              Yosemite                     2            13
```

Notice that there are three values of Region: missing, East, and West. If you have more than one order variable, then the data will be arranged according to the values of the one that comes first in the COLUMN statement, then by the one that comes second, and so on.

# 4.19  Creating Summary Reports with PROC REPORT

Two different usage types cause the REPORT procedure to "roll up" data into summary groups based on the values of a variable. While the GROUP usage type produces summary rows, the ACROSS usage type produces summary columns.[1]

**Group variables**  Defining a group variable is fairly simple. Just specify the GROUP usage option in a DEFINE statement. By default, analysis variables will be summed.[2] The following PROC REPORT tells SAS to produce a report showing the sum of Salary and of Bonus with a row for each value of Department.

| Department | Salary | Bonus |
|------------|--------|-------|
| A          | ~~~    | ~~    |
| B          | ~~     | ~     |

```
PROC REPORT DATA = employees NOWINDOWS;
   COLUMN Department Salary Bonus;
   DEFINE Department / GROUP;
```

**Across variables**  To define an across variable, you also use a DEFINE statement. However, by default SAS produces counts rather than sums. To obtain sums[2] for across variables, you must tell SAS which variables to summarize. You do that by putting a comma between the across variable and analysis variable (or variables if you enclose them in parentheses). The following PROC REPORT tells SAS to produce a report showing the sum of Salary and of Bonus with one column for each value of Department.

| Department | | | |
|------------|--|--|--|
| A | | B | |
| Salary | Bonus | Salary | Bonus |
| ~~~ | ~~ | ~~ | ~ |

```
PROC REPORT DATA = employees NOWINDOWS;
   COLUMN Department , (Salary Bonus);
   DEFINE Department / ACROSS;
```

**Example**  Here again are the data about national parks and monuments. The variables are name, type (NP for national park or NM for national monument), region (East or West), number of museums (including visitor centers), and number of campgrounds.

```
Dinosaur               NM West 2   6
Ellis Island           NM East 1   0
Everglades             NP East 5   2
Grand Canyon           NP West 5   3
Great Smoky Mountains  NP East 3  10
Hawaii Volcanoes       NP West 2   2
Lava Beds              NM West 1   1
Statue of Liberty      NM East 1   0
Theodore Roosevelt     NP  .   2   2
Yellowstone            NP West 9  11
Yosemite               NP West 2  13
```

---

[1] If you have any display or order variables in the COLUMN statement, SAS will produce a detail report instead of consolidating data into summary groups.

[2] To request other statistics, see section 4.21.

The following program contains two PROC REPORTs. In the first, Region and Type are both defined as group variables. In the second, Region is still a group variable, but Type is an across variable. Notice that the two COLUMN statements are the same except for punctuation added to the second procedure to cross the across variable with the analysis variables.

```
DATA natparks;
   INFILE 'c:\MyRawData\Parks.dat';
   INPUT Name $ 1-21 Type $ Region $ Museums Camping;
RUN;

* Region and Type as GROUP variables;
PROC REPORT DATA = natparks NOWINDOWS HEADLINE;
   COLUMN Region Type Museums Camping;
   DEFINE Region / GROUP;
   DEFINE Type / GROUP;
   TITLE 'Summary Report with Two Group Variables';
RUN;
* Region as GROUP and Type as ACROSS with sums;
PROC REPORT DATA = natparks NOWINDOWS HEADLINE;
   COLUMN Region Type, (Museums Camping);
   DEFINE Region / GROUP;
   DEFINE Type / ACROSS;
   TITLE 'Summary Report with a Group and an Across Variable';
RUN;
```

Here is the resulting output:

```
          Summary Report with Two Group Variables          1


          Region    Type       Museums    Camping
          _____

          East      NM            2          0
                    NP            8         12
          West      NM            3          7
                    NP           18         29




       Summary Report with a Group and an Across Variable    2

                               Type
                       NM                    NP
          Region    Museums   Camping    Museums   Camping
          _____

          East         2         0          8        12
          West         3         7         18        29
```

# 4.20   Adding Summary Breaks to PROC REPORT Output

Two kinds of statements allow you to insert breaks into a report. The BREAK statement adds a break for each unique value of the variable you specify, while the RBREAK statement does the same for the entire report (or BY-group if you are using a BY statement). The general forms of these statements are

```
BREAK   location variable / options;
RBREAK location / options;
```

where *location* has two possible values—BEFORE or AFTER—depending on whether you want the break to precede or follow that particular section of the report. The options that come after the slash tell SAS what kind of break to insert. Some of the possible options[1] are

| | |
|---|---|
| OL | draws a line over the break |
| PAGE | starts a new page |
| SKIP | inserts a blank line |
| SUMMARIZE | inserts sums of numeric variables |
| UL | draws a line under the break |

Notice that the BREAK statement requires you to specify a variable, but the RBREAK statement does not. That's because the RBREAK statement produces only one break (at the beginning or end), while the BREAK statement produces one break for every unique value of the variable you specify. That variable must be either a group or order variable and therefore must also be listed in a DEFINE statement with either the GROUP or ORDER usage option. You can use an RBREAK statement in any report, but you can use BREAK only if you have at least one group or order variable.

**Example**   Here again are the data about national parks and monuments. The variables are name, type (NP for national park or NM for national monument), region (East or West), number of museums (including visitor centers), and number of campgrounds.

```
Dinosaur                NM West 2   6
Ellis Island            NM East 1   0
Everglades              NP East 5   2
Grand Canyon            NP West 5   3
Great Smoky Mountains   NP East 3  10
Hawaii Volcanoes        NP West 2   2
Lava Beds               NM West 1   1
Statue of Liberty       NM East 1   0
Theodore Roosevelt      NP  .   2   2
Yellowstone             NP West 9  11
Yosemite                NP West 2  13
```

The following program defines Region as an order variable, and then uses both BREAK and RBREAK statements with the AFTER location. The SUMMARIZE option tells SAS to print totals for numeric variables, while the OL and SKIP options tell SAS to draw a line above the totals and skip a line under the totals.

---

[1] The OL, UL, and SKIP options work only for the LISTING destination.

```
DATA natparks;
   INFILE 'c:\MyRawData\Parks.dat';
   INPUT Name $ 1-21 Type $ Region $ Museums Camping;
RUN;

* PROC REPORT with breaks;
PROC REPORT DATA = natparks NOWINDOWS HEADLINE;
   COLUMN Name Region Museums Camping;
   DEFINE Region / ORDER;
   BREAK AFTER Region / SUMMARIZE OL SKIP;
   RBREAK AFTER / SUMMARIZE OL SKIP;
   TITLE 'Detail Report with Summary Breaks';
RUN;
```

Here is the resulting output:

```
            Detail Report with Summary Breaks              1


      Name                  Region    Museums    Camping
      ─────────────────────────────────────────────────

      Ellis Island          East          1          0
      Everglades                          5          2
      Great Smoky Mountains               3         10
      Statue of Liberty                   1          0
                                     ─────────  ─────────

                            East         10         12


      Dinosaur              West          2          6
      Grand Canyon                        5          3
      Hawaii Volcanoes                    2          2
      Lava Beds                           1          1
      Yellowstone                         9         11
      Yosemite                            2         13
                                     ─────────  ─────────

                            West         21         36


                                     ─────────  ─────────

                                         31         48
```

## 4.21 Adding Statistics to PROC REPORT Output

There are several ways to request statistics in the REPORT procedure. An easy method is to insert statistics keywords directly into the COLUMN statement along with the variable names. This is a little like requesting statistics in a TABLE statement in PROC TABULATE, except that instead of using an asterisk to cross a statistics keyword with a variable, you use a comma. In fact, PROC REPORT can produce all the same statistics as PROC TABULATE and PROC MEANS because it uses the same internal engine to compute those statistics. These are a few of the statistics PROC REPORT can compute:

| | |
|---|---|
| MAX | highest value |
| MIN | lowest value |
| MEAN | the arithmetic mean |
| MEDIAN | the median |
| MODE | the mode (new in SAS 9.2) |
| N | number of non-missing values |
| NMISS | number of missing values |
| PCTN | the percentage of observations for that group |
| PCTSUM | the percentage of a total sum represented by that group |
| STD | the standard deviation |
| SUM | the sum |

**Applying statistics to variables** To request a statistic for a particular variable, insert a comma between the statistic and variable in the COLUMN statement. One statistic, N, does not require a comma because it does not apply to a particular variable. If you insert N in a COLUMN statement, then SAS will print the number of observations that contributed to that row of the report. This statement tells SAS to print two columns of data: the median of a variable named Age, and the number of observations in that row.

```
COLUMN  Age,MEDIAN  N;
```

To request multiple statistics or statistics for multiple variables, put parentheses around the statistics or variables. This statement uses parentheses to request two statistics for the variable Age, and then requests one statistic for two variables, Height and Weight.

```
COLUMN Age,(MIN MAX) (Height Weight),MEAN;
```

**Example** Here again are the data about national parks and monuments. The variables are name, type (NP for national park or NM for national monument), region (East or West), number of museums (including visitor centers), and number of campgrounds.

```
Dinosaur               NM West 2   6
Ellis Island           NM East 1   0
Everglades             NP East 5   2
Grand Canyon           NP West 5   3
Great Smoky Mountains  NP East 3  10
Hawaii Volcanoes       NP West 2   2
Lava Beds              NM West 1   1
Statue of Liberty      NM East 1   0
Theodore Roosevelt     NP  .   2   2
Yellowstone            NP West 9  11
Yosemite               NP West 2  13
```

The following program contains two PROC REPORTs. Both procedures request the statistics N and MEAN, but the first report defines Type as a group variable, while the second defines Type as an across variable.

```
DATA natparks;
    INFILE 'c:\MyRawData\Parks.dat';
    INPUT Name $ 1-21 Type $ Region $ Museums Camping;
RUN;
*Statistics in COLUMN statement with two group variables;
PROC REPORT DATA = natparks NOWINDOWS HEADLINE;
    COLUMN Region Type N (Museums Camping),MEAN;
    DEFINE Region / GROUP;
    DEFINE Type / GROUP;
    TITLE 'Statistics with Two Group Variables';
RUN;
*Statistics in COLUMN statement with group and across variables;
PROC REPORT DATA = natparks NOWINDOWS HEADLINE;
    COLUMN Region N Type,(Museums Camping),MEAN;
    DEFINE Region / GROUP;
    DEFINE Type / ACROSS;
    TITLE 'Statistics with a Group and Across Variable';
RUN;
```

Here is the resulting output:

```
               Statistics with Two Group Variables                    1

                                              Museums    Camping
        Region    Type                 N        MEAN       MEAN
        _____

        East      NM                   2          1          0
                  NP                   2          4          6
        West      NM                   2        1.5        3.5
                  NP                   4        4.5       7.25


            Statistics with a Group and Across Variable               2

                                              Type
                              NM                        NP
                      Museums    Camping       Museums    Camping
        Region    N     MEAN       MEAN          MEAN       MEAN
        _____

        East      4       1          0            4          6
        West      6     1.5        3.5          4.5       7.25
```

Notice that these reports are similar to the reports in section 4.19 except that these contain counts and means instead of sums.

## 4.22    Adding Computed Variables to PROC REPORT Output

Unlike most procedures, the REPORT procedure has the ability to compute not only statistics (like sums and means) but also new variables. You do this using a compute block. Compute blocks start with a COMPUTE statement and end with an ENDCOMP statement. In between, you put the programming statements to calculate your new variable. PROC REPORT uses a limited set of programming statements including assignment statements, IF-THEN/ELSE statements, and DO loops. You do not have to specify a DEFINE statement for the new variable, but if you do, then give it a usage type of COMPUTED. The general form of these statements is

```
DEFINE new-variable-name / COMPUTED;

COMPUTE new-variable-name / options;

    programming statements

ENDCOMP;
```

**Computing a numeric variable**    For a numeric variable, simply name the new variable in the COMPUTE statement. If you use any variables with a type of analysis in the compute block, you must append the variable name with its statistic. The default statistic for an analysis variable is SUM. The following statements compute a variable named Income by adding Salary and Bonus.

```
DEFINE Income / COMPUTED;
COMPUTE  Income;
    Income = Salary.SUM + Bonus.SUM;
ENDCOMP;
```

**Computing a character variable**    For a character variable, add the CHAR option to the COMPUTE statement. You will probably also want the LENGTH option. Lengths for computed character variables range from 1 to 200, with a default of 8. The following statements compute a variable named JobType using IF-THEN/ELSE statements.

```
DEFINE JobType / COMPUTED;
COMPUTE  JobType / CHAR LENGTH = 10;
    IF Title = 'Programmer' THEN JobType = 'Technical';
    ELSE JobType = 'Other';
ENDCOMP;
```

**Example**    Here again are the data about national parks and monuments. The variables are name, type (NP for national park or NM for national monument), region (East or West), number of museums (including visitor centers), and number of campgrounds.

```
Dinosaur                NM West 2  6
Ellis Island            NM East 1  0
Everglades              NP East 5  2
Grand Canyon            NP West 5  3
Great Smoky Mountains   NP East 3 10
Hawaii Volcanoes        NP West 2  2
Lava Beds               NM West 1  1
Statue of Liberty       NM East 1  0
Theodore Roosevelt      NP  .   2  2
Yellowstone             NP West 9 11
Yosemite                NP West 2 13
```

The following PROC REPORT computes two variables named Facilities and Note. Facilities is a numeric variable equal to the number of museums plus the number of campgrounds. Note is a character variable which is equal to "No Camping" for parks that have no campgrounds. Notice that the variables Museums and Camping must be listed in the COLUMN statement because they are used to compute the new variables. In order to exclude them from the results, the program uses the NOPRINT option in DEFINE statements.

```
DATA natparks;
   INFILE 'c:\MyRawData\Parks.dat';
   INPUT Name $ 1-21 Type $ Region $ Museums Camping;
RUN;

* COMPUTE new variables that are numeric and character;
PROC REPORT DATA = natparks NOWINDOWS HEADLINE;
   COLUMN Name Region Museums Camping Facilities Note;
   DEFINE Museums / ANALYSIS SUM NOPRINT;
   DEFINE Camping / ANALYSIS SUM NOPRINT;
   DEFINE Facilities / COMPUTED 'Camping/and/Museums';
   DEFINE Note / COMPUTED;
   COMPUTE Facilities;
      Facilities = Museums.SUM + Camping.SUM;
   ENDCOMP;
   COMPUTE Note / CHAR LENGTH = 10;
      IF Camping.SUM = 0 THEN Note = 'No Camping';
   ENDCOMP;
   TITLE 'Report with Two Computed Variables';
RUN;
```

Here is the resulting output:

```
            Report with Two Computed Variables              1


                                          Camping
                                            and
    Name                     Region       Museums   Note
    _____

    Dinosaur                 West            8
    Ellis Island             East            1      No Camping
    Everglades               East            7
    Grand Canyon             West            8
    Great Smoky Mountains    East           13
    Hawaii Volcanoes         West            4
    Lava Beds                West            2
    Statue of Liberty        East            1      No Camping
    Theodore Roosevelt                       4
    Yellowstone              West           20
    Yosemite                 West           15
```

# 4.23　Grouping Data in Procedures with User-Defined Formats

With user-defined formats you can group data in procedure output without creating a new variable. This is handy for cases where you have a lot of data, and it takes a long time to run a DATA step. Also, using this method it is easy to change the groupings by simply creating a new format. This method works for procedures that group data such as PROC FREQ, PROC TABULATE, PROC MEANS with a CLASS statement, and PROC REPORT with GROUP or ACROSS variables.

Grouping data this way is a two-step process. First, use the FORMAT procedure to define a format that assigns all the values that you want to group together to a text string. Second, use the FORMAT statement in the procedure to assign the format to the variable to be grouped.

**Example**　The staff of the local library want to see the type of books people check out by age group. They have the age of the patron in years and the book type: fiction, mystery, science fiction, biography, non-fiction, and reference. Here are the data with nine observations per line:

```
17 sci   9 bio 28 fic 50 mys 13 fic 32 fic 67 fic 81 non 38 non
53 non 16 sci 15 bio 61 fic 52 ref 22 mys 76 bio 37 fic 86 fic
49 mys 78 non 45 sci 64 bio  8 fic 11 non 41 fic 46 ref 69 fic
34 fic 26 mys 23 sci 74 ref 15 sci 27 fic 23 mys 63 fic 78 non
40 bio 12 fic 29 fic 54 mys 67 fic 60 fic 38 sci 42 fic 80 fic
```

Here is the program that reads the data and creates two user-defined formats to group the age data, and one for the book type data. The FREQ procedures count the number of books by age group and book type. The Age variable is grouped into four categories using the AGEGPA. user-defined format in the first PROC FREQ while the second PROC FREQ groups age into two categories using the AGEGPB. format. In both PROC FREQs, BookType is grouped into two categories using the $TYP. user-defined format.

```
DATA books;
   INFILE 'c:\MyRawData\LibraryBooks.dat';
   INPUT Age BookType $ @@;
RUN;
*Define formats to group the data;
PROC FORMAT;
   VALUE agegpa
         0-18     = '0 to 18'
         19-25    = '19 to 25'
         26-49    = '26 to 49'
         50-HIGH = '  50+ ';
   VALUE agegpb
         0-25     = '0 to 25'
         26-HIGH = '  26+ ';
   VALUE $typ
         'bio','non','ref' = 'Non-Fiction'
         'fic','mys','sci' = 'Fiction';
RUN;
```

```
*Create two way table with Age grouped into four categories;
PROC FREQ DATA = books;
    TITLE 'Patron Age by Book Type: Four Age Groups';
    TABLES BookType * Age / NOPERCENT NOROW NOCOL;
    FORMAT Age agegpa. BookType $typ.;
RUN;
*Create two way table with Age grouped into two categories;
PROC FREQ DATA = books;
    TITLE 'Patron Age by Book Type: Two Age Groups';
    TABLES BookType * Age / NOPERCENT NOROW NOCOL;
    FORMAT Age agegpb. BookType $typ.;
RUN;
```

Because the NOPERCENT, NOROW, and NOCOL options were added to the TABLES statements, only frequencies appear in the results.

```
              Patron Age by Book Type: Four Age Groups              1

                         The FREQ Procedure

                      Table of BookType by Age


      BookType       Age

      Frequency   | 0 to 18 | 19 to 25 | 26 to 49 |  50+   |  Total

      Non-Fiction       3         0          3        8        14

      Fiction           6         3         12       10        31

      Total             9         3         15       18        45


              Patron Age by Book Type: Two Age Groups               2

                         The FREQ Procedure

                      Table of BookType by Age


        BookType       Age

        Frequency   | 0 to 25 |   26+   |  Total

        Non-Fiction      3        11        14

        Fiction          9        22        31

        Total           12        33        45
```

**5**

"Some men see things as they are and say, 'Why.' I dream things that never were and say, 'Why not.'"

ROBERT F. KENNEDY

CHAPTER 5

# Enhancing Your Output with ODS

# 5.1    Concepts of the Output Delivery System

You might think that procedures produce output. They don't. Technically, procedures produce only data. Then they send that data to the Output Delivery System (ODS) which determines where the output should go and what it should look like when it gets there. That means the question to ask yourself is not whether you want to use ODS—you always use ODS. The question is whether to accept default output or choose something else.

ODS is like a busy airport. Passengers arrive by car and bus. Once at the airport, passengers check baggage, pass security, eventually board a plane, and fly out to their destinations. In ODS, data are like passengers arriving from various procedures.[1] ODS processes each set of data and sends it off to its proper destination. In fact, different types of ODS output are called destinations. What your data look like when they get to their destination is determined by templates. A template is a set of instructions telling ODS how to format your data. These two concepts—destinations and templates—are fundamental for understanding what you can do with ODS.

**Destinations** Whenever you don't specify a destination, your output will be sent, by default, to the listing. The LISTING destination is what you see in the Output window if you use the SAS windowing environment, or in the listing or output file if you use batch mode. Here are the major destinations:

| | |
|---|---|
| LISTING | standard SAS output |
| HTML | Hypertext Markup Language |
| RTF | Rich Text Format |
| PRINTER | high-resolution printer output[2] |
| PS | PostScript |
| PCL | Printer Control Language |
| PDF | Portable Document Format |
| OUTPUT | SAS output data set |
| MARKUP | markup languages including XML |
| DOCUMENT | output document |

Most of these destinations are designed to create output for viewing on a screen or for printing. The OUTPUT destination creates SAS data sets. The MARKUP destination is a general purpose tool for creating output in formats defined by tagsets. This includes XML (eXtensible Markup Language), EXCELXP, LaTeX, CSV (comma-separated values), and many other formats where data can be thought of as separated by tags. The DOCUMENT destination, on the other hand, allows you to create a reusable output "document" that you can rerender for any destination. So, if your boss decides he really wants that report in PDF, not RTF, you can replay the output document without having to rerun the entire SAS program that created the data. With an output document, you can also rearrange, duplicate, or delete tables to further customize your output.

---

[1] It is also possible to send output to ODS from a DATA step by using a special FILE statement. See the SAS Help and Documentaion for more information.

[2] The PS, PCL, and PDF destinations are part of the PRINTER destination, and are discussed in section 5.4.

**Style and table templates**  Templates tell ODS how to format and present your data. The two most common types of templates are table templates and style templates (also called table definitions and style definitions). A table template specifies the basic structure of your output (which variable will be in the first column?); while a style template specifies how the output will look (will the headers be blue or red?). ODS combines the data produced by a procedure with a table template and together they are called an output object. The output object is then combined with a style template and sent to a destination to create your final output.[3]

**data from**  ·  **table**  ·  **style**  ·  **output**
**procedure**  ·  **template**  ·  **template**

You can create your own table and style templates using the TEMPLATE procedure. However, PROC TEMPLATE's syntax is rather arcane. Fortunately, there are other, easier, ways to control and modify output. The quickest and easiest way to change the look of your output is to use one of the many built-in style templates. To view a list of the style templates available on your system, submit the following PROC TEMPLATE statements, and look in the output window for the list:

```
PROC TEMPLATE;
   LIST STYLES;
RUN;
```

A few of the built-in style templates are

| | | | |
|---|---|---|---|
| ANALYSIS | D3D | MINIMAL | SASWEB |
| BARETTSBLUE | DEFAULT | PRINTER | SANSPRINTER |
| BRICK | JOURNAL | RTF | STATISTICAL |

Notice that RTF and PRINTER are names of both destinations and styles. Some styles work better with certain destinations than with others. DEFAULT is the default style for HTML output, RTF is the default style for RTF output, and PRINTER is the default style for output sent to the PRINTER destination.

A few procedures, most notably PRINT, REPORT, and TABULATE, don't have ready-made table templates. Instead, the syntax for these procedures acts like a custom table template. While all procedures that produce printable output allow you to use style templates to control the overall look of that output, these three procedures also allow you to do something special. With PRINT, REPORT, and TABULATE, you can use the STYLE= option directly in the procedure code to control individual features of your output without having to create a whole new style template.

---

[3] For the LISTING destination, style templates apply to graphical output but not tabular output because tabular output is rendered as plain text.

## 5.2  Tracing and Selecting Procedure Output

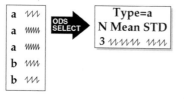

When ODS receives data from a procedure, it combines that data with a table template. Together the data and corresponding table template are called an output object. For many procedures ODS produces just one output object, while for others it produces several. In addition, for most procedures when you use a BY statement, SAS produces one output object for each BY group. Every output object has a name. You can find the names of output objects using the ODS TRACE statement, and then use an ODS SELECT (or ODS EXCLUDE) statement to choose just the output objects you want.

**The ODS TRACE statement**  The ODS TRACE statement tells SAS to print information about output objects in your SAS log. There are two ODS TRACE statements: one to turn on the trace, and one to turn it off. Here is how to use these statements in a program:

```
ODS TRACE ON;
the PROC steps you want to trace go here
RUN;
ODS TRACE OFF;
```

Notice that the RUN statement comes before the ODS TRACE OFF statement. Unlike most other SAS statements, the ODS statement executes immediately—without waiting for a RUN, PROC, or DATA statement. If you put the ODS TRACE OFF statement before the RUN statement, then the trace would turn off before the procedure completes.

**Example**  Here are data about varieties of giant tomatoes. Each line of data includes the name of the variety, its color (red or yellow), the number of days from planting to harvest, and the weight (in pounds) of a typical tomato.

```
Big Zac, red, 80, 5
Delicious, red, 80, 3
Dinner Plate, red, 90, 2
Goliath, red, 85, 1.5
Mega Tom, red, 80, 2
Big Rainbow, yellow, 90, 1.5
Pineapple, yellow, 85, 2
```

The following program creates a data set named GIANT, and then traces PROC MEANS using ODS TRACE ON and ODS TRACE OFF statements:

```
DATA giant;
   INFILE 'c:\MyRawData\Tomatoes.dat' DSD;
   INPUT Name :$15. Color $ Days Weight;
* Trace PROC MEANS;
ODS TRACE ON;
PROC MEANS DATA = giant;
   BY Color;
RUN;
ODS TRACE OFF;
```

If you run this program, you will see the following trace in your SAS log. Because it contains a BY statement, the MEANS procedure produces one output object for each BY group (red and yellow). Notice that these two output objects have the same name, label, and template, but different paths.

```
Output Added:
-------------
Name:       Summary
Label:      Summary statistics
Template:   base.summary
Path:       Means.ByGroup1.Summary
-------------
NOTE: The above message was for the following by-group: Color=red

Output Added:
-------------
Name:       Summary
Label:      Summary statistics
Template:   base.summary
Path:       Means.ByGroup2.Summary
-------------
NOTE: The above message was for the following by-group: Color=yellow
```

**The ODS SELECT statement**  Once you know the names of the output objects, you can use an ODS SELECT (or EXCLUDE) statement to choose just the output objects you want. The general form of an ODS SELECT statement is

```
The PROC step with the output objects you want to select
ODS SELECT output-object-list;
RUN;
```

where *output-object-list* is the name, label, or path of one or more output objects separated by spaces. By default, an ODS SELECT statement lasts for only one PROC step,[1] so by placing the SELECT statement after the PROC statement and before the RUN, you are sure to capture the correct output. ODS EXCLUDE statements work the same way except you list output objects that you want to eliminate.

**Example**  This program runs PROC MEANS again using the Giant data set and an ODS SELECT statement to select just the first output object: Means.ByGroup1.Summary.

```
PROC MEANS DATA = giant;
   BY Color;
   TITLE 'Red Tomatoes';
ODS SELECT Means.ByGroup1.Summary;
RUN;
```

Here are the results containing just the first BY group.

```
                             Red Tomatoes                               1

- - - - - - - - - - - - - - - - - -  Color=red  - - - - - - - - - - - - - - - - - -

                          The MEANS Procedure

    Variable  N        Mean        Std Dev       Minimum       Maximum

    Days      5    83.0000000     4.4721360    80.0000000    90.0000000
    Weight    5     2.7000000     1.3964240     1.5000000     5.0000000
```

---

[1] To make your selection last longer, use the PERSIST option. See the SAS Help and Documentation for more information.

## 5.3  Creating SAS Data Sets from Procedure Output

Sometimes you may want to put the results from a procedure into a SAS data set. Once the results are in a data set, you can merge them with another data set, create new variables based on the results, or use the results as input for other procedures. Some procedures have OUTPUT statements, or OUT= options, allowing you to save the results as a SAS data set. But with ODS you can save almost any part of procedure output as a SAS data set by sending it to the OUTPUT destination. First you use an ODS TRACE statement (discussed in the previous section) to determine the name of the output object you want. Then you use an ODS OUTPUT statement to send that object to the OUTPUT destination.

**The ODS OUTPUT statement**  Here is the general form of a basic ODS OUTPUT statement:

```
ODS OUTPUT output-object = new-data-set;
```

where *output-object* is the name, label or path of the piece of output you want to save, and *new-data-set* is the name of the SAS data set you want to create.

The ODS OUTPUT statement does not belong to either a DATA or PROC step, but you need to be careful where you put it in your program. The ODS OUTPUT statement opens a SAS data set and waits for the correct procedure output. The data set remains open until the next encounter with the end of a PROC step. Because the ODS OUTPUT statement executes immediately, it will apply to whatever PROC is currently being processed, or it will apply to the next PROC if there is not a current PROC. To ensure that you get the correct output, we recommend that you put the ODS OUTPUT statement after your PROC statement, and before the next PROC, DATA, or RUN statement.

**Example**  Here again are data about varieties of giant tomatoes. Each line of data includes the name of the variety, its color (red or yellow), the number of days from planting to harvest, and the weight (in pounds) of a typical tomato.

```
Big Zac, red, 80, 5
Delicious, red, 80, 3
Dinner Plate, red, 90, 2
Goliath, red, 85, 1.5
Mega Tom, red, 80, 2
Big Rainbow, yellow, 90, 1.5
Pineapple, yellow, 85, 2
```

Here is an excerpt from a SAS log showing the trace produced by PROC TABULATE. TABULATE produces one output object named Table.

```
Output Added:
-------------
Name:        Table
Label:       Table 1
Data Name:   Report
Path:        Tabulate.Report.Table
-------------
```

The following program reads the data, and uses an ODS OUTPUT statement to create a SAS data set named TABOUT from the Table output object. Then PROC PRINT prints the new data set.

```
DATA giant;
    INFILE 'c:\MyRawData\Tomatoes.dat' DSD;
    INPUT Name :$15. Color $ Days Weight;
PROC TABULATE DATA = giant;
    CLASS Color;
    VAR Days Weight;
    TABLE Color ALL, (Days Weight) * MEAN;
    TITLE 'Standard TABULATE Output';
ODS OUTPUT Table = tabout;
RUN;
PROC PRINT DATA = tabout;
    TITLE 'OUTPUT SAS Data Set from TABULATE';
RUN;
```

Here are the results showing two pieces of output. The first is the standard tabular result produced by PROC TABULATE. Below that is the TABOUT data set created by the ODS OUTPUT statement and printed by PROC PRINT.

```
                  Standard TABULATE Output                    1

                         ┌─────────────┬─────────────┐
                         │    Days     │   Weight    │
                         ├─────────────┼─────────────┤
                         │    Mean     │    Mean     │
        ┌────────────────┼─────────────┼─────────────┤
        │ Color          │             │             │
        ├────────────────┤             │             │
        │ red            │       83.00 │        2.70 │
        ├────────────────┼─────────────┼─────────────┤
        │ yellow         │       87.50 │        1.75 │
        ├────────────────┼─────────────┼─────────────┤
        │ All            │       84.29 │        2.43 │
        └────────────────┴─────────────┴─────────────┘
```

```
              Output Data Set from TABULATE                   2

                                              Days_    Weight_
                                              Mean      Mean
    Obs    Color     _TYPE_    _PAGE_  _TABLE_

     1     red         1         1        1   83.0000   2.70000
     2     yellow      1         1        1   87.5000   1.75000
     3                 0         1        1   84.2857   2.42857
```

# 5.4    Using ODS Statements to Create HTML Output

When you send output to the HTML destination, you get files in Hypertext Markup Language (HTML) format. These files are ready to be posted on a Web site for viewing by your boss or colleagues, but HTML output has other uses too. It can be read into spreadsheets, and even printed or imported into word processors (though some formatting may change). To generate HTML files, all you need are two statements—one to open the HTML file, and one to close it.

**The ODS statement**    To send output to the HTML destination, use the ODS HTML statement. The general form of this statement is

```
ODS HTML FILE = 'body-filename.html' options;
```

The body file contains your results. The options FILE= and BODY= are synonymous. Other options available for this destination include

| | |
|---|---|
| CONTENTS = 'filename' | creates a table of contents with links to the body file. |
| PAGE = 'filename' | creates a table of contents with links by page number. |
| FRAME = 'filename' | creates a frame that allows you to view the body file and the contents or the page file at the same time. If you do not want either the contents or the page file, then you don't need to create a frame file. |
| STYLE = style-name | specifies a style template. The default style is named DEFAULT. |

You always want to create a body file, but the other files are optional. The following statement tells SAS to send output to the HTML destination, save the results in a file named AnnualReport.html, and use the D3D style.

```
ODS HTML FILE = 'AnnualReport.html' STYLE = D3D;
```

ODS statements are global, and do not belong to either DATA steps or PROC steps. However, if you put them in the wrong place, they won't capture the output that you want. A good place to put the first ODS statement is just before the step (or steps) whose output you wish to capture.

Here is the ODS statement which closes the HTML file.

```
ODS HTML CLOSE;
```

Put this statement after the step (or steps) whose output you wish to capture, and following a RUN statement.

Some procedures (such as PROC MEANS and PROC FREQ) include the name of the procedure in your output. You can remove procedure names using the ODS NOPROCTITLE statement.

```
ODS NOPROCTITLE;
```

**Example**    This example uses data about average lengths, in feet, of selected whales and sharks.

```
beluga    whale 15   dwarf     shark  .5   sperm    whale 60
basking   shark 30   humpback  whale 50   whale    shark 40
gray      whale 50   blue      whale 100  killer    whale 30
mako      shark 12
```

The following program produces two pieces of output: one from the MEANS procedure, and one from the PRINT procedure. There are three ODS statements in the program. The first ODS statement opens an HTML body file, the second ODS statement turns off procedure titles, and the third closes the HTML file.

```
* Create the HTML files and remove procedure name;
ODS HTML FILE = 'c:\MyHTMLFiles\Marine.html';
ODS NOPROCTITLE;
DATA marine;
    INFILE 'c:\MyRawData\Sealife.dat';
    INPUT Name $ Family $ Length @@;
RUN;
PROC MEANS DATA = marine MEAN MIN MAX;
    CLASS Family;
    TITLE 'Whales and Sharks';
RUN;
PROC PRINT DATA = marine;
RUN;
* Close the HTML files;
ODS HTML CLOSE;
```

Here is what the Marine.html file looks like when viewed with a browser. Since no style was specified, SAS used the DEFAULT style.

### Whales and Sharks

| Analysis Variable : Length | | | | |
|---|---|---|---|---|
| Family | N Obs | Mean | Minimum | Maximum |
| shark | 4 | 20.6250000 | 0.5000000 | 40.0000000 |
| whale | 6 | 50.8333333 | 15.0000000 | 100.0000000 |

### Whales and Sharks

| Obs | Name | Family | Length |
|---|---|---|---|
| 1 | beluga | whale | 15.0 |
| 2 | dwarf | shark | 0.5 |
| 3 | sperm | whale | 60.0 |
| 4 | basking | shark | 30.0 |
| 5 | humpback | whale | 50.0 |
| 6 | whale | shark | 40.0 |
| 7 | gray | whale | 50.0 |
| 8 | blue | whale | 100.0 |
| 9 | killer | whale | 30.0 |
| 10 | mako | shark | 12.0 |

## 5.5 Using ODS Statements to Create RTF Output

Rich Text Format (RTF) was developed by Microsoft for document interchange. When you create RTF output, you can copy it into a Word document and edit or resize it like other Word tables. Sending output to the RTF destination is similar to sending it to the HTML destination except you use the ODS RTF statement.

**The ODS statement** The general form of the ODS statement to open RTF files is

```
ODS RTF  FILE = 'filename.rtf' options;
```

Unlike HTML, there is only one kind of RTF file, a file containing output. FILE= and BODY= are synonymous. Here are some of the most commonly used options for this destination:

| | |
|---|---|
| BODYTITLE | puts titles and footnotes in the main part of the RTF document instead of in Word headers or footers. |
| COLUMNS=*n* | requests columnar output where n is the number of columns. |
| SASDATE | by default, the date and time that appear at the top of RTF output indicate when the file was last opened or printed in Word. This option tells SAS to use the date and time when the current SAS session or job started running.[1] |
| STARTPAGE = *value* | controls page breaks. The default value, YES, inserts a break between procedures. A value of NO turns off breaks. A value of NOW inserts a break at that point. |
| STYLE = *style-name* | specifies a style template. The default style is named RTF. |

The following statement tells SAS to send output to the RTF destination, save the results in a file named AnnualReport.rtf, and use the SANSPRINTER style:

```
ODS RTF  FILE = 'AnnualReport.rtf' STYLE = SANSPRINTER;
```

ODS statements are global, and do not belong to either DATA steps or PROC steps. However, if you put them in the wrong place, they won't capture the output that you want. A good place to put the first ODS statement is just before the step (or steps) whose output you wish to capture.

Here is the ODS statement which closes the RTF file.

```
ODS RTF CLOSE;
```

Put this statement after the step (or steps) whose output you wish to capture, and following a RUN statement.

Some procedures (such as PROC MEANS and PROC FREQ) include the name of the procedure in your output. You can remove procedure names using the ODS NOPROCTITLE statement.

```
ODS NOPROCTITLE;
```

---

[1] If you have the system option DTRESET turned on, and you use the SASDATE option, then SAS will use the date and time when the current job ran instead of when SAS started.

**Example** Here again are the data about average lengths, in feet, of selected whales and sharks.

```
beluga    whale 15    dwarf     shark .5    sperm   whale 60
basking   shark 30    humpback  whale 50    whale   shark 40
gray      whale 50    blue      whale 100   killer  whale 30
mako      shark 12
```

The following program produces output with the MEANS and PRINT procedures. There are three ODS statements in the program: one to open an RTF file, one to turn off procedure titles, and one to close the RTF file.

```
* Create an RTF file;
ODS RTF FILE = 'c:\MyRTFFiles\Marine.rtf' BODYTITLE COLUMNS=2;
ODS NOPROCTITLE;
DATA marine;
    INFILE 'c:\MyRawData\Sealife.dat';
    INPUT Name $ Family $ Length @@;
RUN;
PROC MEANS DATA = marine MEAN MIN MAX;
    CLASS Family;
    TITLE 'Whales and Sharks';
RUN;
PROC PRINT DATA = marine;
RUN;
* Close the RTF file;
ODS RTF CLOSE;
```

Here is what the Marine.rtf file looks like when viewed in Microsoft Word. Notice that the output appears in two columns because the option COLUMNS=2 was specified. Because the BODYTITLE option was specified, the titles appear with the tables instead of in a Word header. Since no style was specified, SAS used the default style, RTF.

1

**Whales and Sharks**

| Analysis Variable : Length | | | | |
|---|---|---|---|---|
| Family | N Obs | Mean | Minimum | Maximum |
| shark | 4 | 20.6250000 | 0.5000000 | 40.0000000 |
| whale | 6 | 50.8333333 | 15.0000000 | 100.0000000 |

**Whales and Sharks**

| Obs | Name | Family | Length |
|---|---|---|---|
| 1 | beluga | whale | 15.0 |
| 2 | dwarf | shark | 0.5 |
| 3 | sperm | whale | 60.0 |
| 4 | basking | shark | 30.0 |
| 5 | humpback | whale | 50.0 |
| 6 | whale | shark | 40.0 |
| 7 | gray | whale | 50.0 |
| 8 | blue | whale | 100.0 |
| 9 | killer | whale | 30.0 |
| 10 | mako | shark | 12.0 |

## 5.6 Using ODS Statements to Create PRINTER Output

The PRINTER destination produces output for high-resolution printers, and it has some unique properties. By default, it sends output automatically to your printer, but it can also write files in PostScript, PCL, and PDF formats. Like other destinations, you need two statements to generate PRINTER output—one to open the destination and one to close it.

**The ODS statement** The most basic form of the ODS statement to open the PRINTER destination is

```
ODS PRINTER;
```

If you use this simple statement, SAS will create whatever type of output your default system printer wants, and automatically print the output instead of saving it in a file. To save your output, add the FILE= option. FILE= and BODY= are synonymous. Like the RTF destination, the PRINTER destination produces only one kind of file. Here are the general forms of statements to create specific kinds of output.

| | |
|---|---|
| Default printer: | `ODS PRINTER FILE = 'filename.extension' options;` |
| PCL: | `ODS PCL FILE = 'filename.pcl' options;` |
| PDF: | `ODS PDF FILE = 'filename.pdf' options;` |
| PostScript: | `ODS PS  FILE = 'filename.ps'  options;` |

The options available for this destination include

| | |
|---|---|
| `COLUMNS = n` | requests columnar output where n is the number of columns. |
| `STARTPAGE = value` | controls page breaks. The default value, YES, inserts a break between procedures. A value of NO turns off breaks. A value of NOW inserts a break at that point. |
| `STYLE = style-name` | specifies a style template. The default style is named PRINTER. |

The following statement tells SAS to create PostScript output, save the results in a file named AnnualReport.ps, and use the SANSPRINTER style.

```
ODS PS FILE = 'AnnualReport.ps' STYLE = SANSPRINTER;
```

ODS statements are global, and do not belong to either DATA steps or PROC steps. However, if you put them in the wrong place, they won't capture the output that you want. A good place to put the first ODS statement is just before the step (or steps) whose output you wish to capture.

The general form of the ODS statement to close a PRINTER file is

```
ODS destination-name CLOSE;
```

where destination-name is either PRINTER, PCL, PDF, or PS matching the destination name in your opening statement. Put this statement after the step (or steps) whose output you wish to capture, and following a RUN statement.

Some procedures (such as PROC MEANS and PROC FREQ) include the name of the procedure in your output. You can remove procedure names using the ODS NOPROCTITLE statement.

```
ODS NOPROCTITLE;
```

**Example** Here again are the data about average lengths, in feet, of selected whales and sharks.

```
beluga    whale 15   dwarf     shark .5    sperm    whale 60
basking   shark 30   humpback  whale 50    whale    shark 40
gray      whale 50   blue      whale 100   killer   whale 30
mako      shark 12
```

The following program produces output with the MEANS and PRINT procedures. There are three ODS statements in the program: one to open the PDF file, one to turn off procedure titles, and one to close the PDF file.

```
* Create the PDF file;
ODS PDF FILE = 'c:\MyPDFFiles\Marine.pdf' STARTPAGE = NO;
ODS NOPROCTITLE;
DATA marine;
    INFILE 'c:\MyRawData\Sealife.dat';
    INPUT Name $ Family $ Length @@;
RUN;
PROC MEANS DATA = marine MEAN MIN MAX;
    CLASS Family;
    TITLE 'Whales and Sharks';
RUN;
PROC PRINT DATA = marine;
RUN;
* Close the PDF file;
ODS PDF CLOSE;
```

Here is what the report looks like when viewed in Adobe Acrobat. Because the option STARTPAGE=NO was specified, the output from both procedures appears on the same page. Since no style was specified, SAS used the default style, PRINTER.

*Whales and Sharks*                                                          1

| Analysis Variable : Length | | | | |
|--------|-------|-----------|-----------|-------------|
| Family | N Obs | Mean | Minimum | Maximum |
| shark | 4 | 20.6250000 | 0.5000000 | 40.0000000 |
| whale | 6 | 50.8333333 | 15.0000000 | 100.0000000 |

| Obs | Name | Family | Length |
|-----|----------|--------|--------|
| 1 | beluga | whale | 15.0 |
| 2 | dwarf | shark | 0.5 |
| 3 | sperm | whale | 60.0 |
| 4 | basking | shark | 30.0 |
| 5 | humpback | whale | 50.0 |
| 6 | whale | shark | 40.0 |
| 7 | gray | whale | 50.0 |
| 8 | blue | whale | 100.0 |
| 9 | killer | whale | 30.0 |
| 10 | mako | shark | 12.0 |

## 5.7 Customizing Titles and Footnotes

In ODS output, your style template tells SAS how titles and footnotes should look. However, you can easily change the appearance of titles and footnotes by inserting a few simple options in your TITLE and FOOTNOTE statements.

The general form for a TITLE or FOOTNOTE statement is

```
TITLE options 'text-string-1' options 'text-string-2' … options 'text-string-n';

FOOTNOTE options 'text-string-1' options 'text-string-2' … options 'text-string-n';
```

Text can be broken into pieces with different options applying to each piece. SAS will concatenate text strings just the way you type them, so be sure to include any necessary blanks. Each option applies to the text string that follows, and stays in effect until another value is specified for that option, or until the end of the statement. Here are the main options that you can choose:

| | |
|---|---|
| COLOR= | specifies a color for the text |
| BCOLOR= | specifies a color for the background of the text |
| HEIGHT= | specifies the height of the text |
| JUSTIFY= | requests justification |
| FONT= | specifies a font for the text |
| BOLD | makes text bold |
| ITALIC | makes text italic |

**Color** The COLOR= option specifies the color of the text. This statement

```
TITLE COLOR=BLACK 'Black  ' COLOR=GRAY 'Gray  ' COLOR=LTGRAY 'Light Gray';
```

would produce this title:

### ***Black*** *Gray* *Light Gray*

SAS supports hundreds of colors ranging from primary colors—red—to more esoteric colors—LIGRPR (light grayish purplish red). These colors can be specified by name—BLUE—or by hexadecimal code—#0000FF. In fact, SAS recognizes at least a half-dozen naming schemes for specifying color.[1] Names of colors need quotation marks if the name is longer than 8 characters or contains embedded spaces. RGB hexadecimal codes beginning with a pound sign also require quotation marks. If you want to specify colors by name, here is a list of basic colors you can start with: AQUA, BLACK, BLUE, FUCHSIA, GREEN, GRAY, LIME, MAROON, NAVY, OLIVE, PURPLE, RED, SILVER, TEAL, WHITE, YELLOW.

**Background color** The BCOLOR= option specifies a background color. This statement uses an RGB hexadecimal code:

```
TITLE BCOLOR='#C0C0C0' 'This Title Has a Gray Background';
```

---

[1] See "Color-Naming Schemes" in the SAS/GRAPH section of the SAS Help and Documentation for details about how to specify colors. To see a list of Web-safe colors in the SAS windowing environment, type REGEDIT in the command box on the tool bar to open the Registry Editor. Double-click COLORNAMES. Then double-click HTML.

and produces this title:

### This Title Has a Gray Background

You can choose among the same colors as with the COLOR= option.

**Height**   To change the height of the text, use the HEIGHT= option where the value of HEIGHT is a number expressed in points, inches, or centimeters. This statement

```
TITLE HEIGHT=12pt 'Small  ' HEIGHT=.25in 'Medium  ' HEIGHT=1cm 'Large';
```

would produce this title:

*Small* *Medium* **Large**

**Justification**   You can control justification of text using the JUSTIFY= option which can have the values LEFT, CENTER, or RIGHT. You can even mix these options within a single statement. This statement

```
TITLE JUSTIFY=LEFT 'Left ' JUSTIFY=CENTER 'vs. ' JUSTIFY=RIGHT 'Right';
```

would produce this title:

*Left*                              *vs.*                              *Right*

**Font**   Use the FONT= option to specify a font. This statement

```
TITLE 'Default  ' FONT=Arial 'Arial    '
   FONT='Times New Roman' 'Times New Roman   ' FONT=Courier 'Courier';
```

would produce this title:

*Default*   Arial   Times New Roman   Courier

The particular fonts available to you depend on your operating environment and hardware. Courier, Arial, Times, and Helvetica work in most situations.

**Bold and italic**   By default, titles and footnotes are both bold and italic. When you change the font, you also turn off the bold and italic features. You can turn them on by using the BOLD and ITALIC options. There is no option to turn off boldness and italics, so if you wish to turn them off, use the FONT= option. Here are the three options together:

```
TITLE FONT=Courier 'Courier  '
   BOLD 'Bold ' BOLD ITALIC 'Bold and Italic';
```

This statement produces this title:

Courier   **Bold**   ***Bold and Italic***

## 5.8 ▸ Customizing PROC PRINT Output with the STYLE= Option

If you want to change the overall look of any output, you can use a different style template by specifying it in a STYLE= option in your ODS statement. But what if you want to change the appearance of just the headers, or just one column of your output? Well, you're in luck! The reporting procedures, PRINT, REPORT, and TABULATE, allow you to change the style of various parts of the table that these procedures produce using the STYLE= option in the procedures' statements.[1]

The general form of the STYLE= option in the PROC PRINT statement is

```
PROC PRINT STYLE(location-list) = {style-attribute = value};
```

The *location-list* indicates which parts of the table should take on the style, the *style-attribute* indicates the attribute you want to change, and the *value* is the value of the attribute. (See section 5.12 for a table of attributes and possible values.)  For example, the following statement says that the DATA location should have the BACKGROUND style attribute set to the value PINK.

```
PROC PRINT STYLE(DATA) = {BACKGROUND = pink};
```

You can have several STYLE= options on one PROC PRINT statement, and you can have the same style apply to several locations. The following shows some of the locations you can specify and which parts of the table they represent.

| Location | Table region affected |
|---|---|
| DATA | all the data cells |
| HEADER | the column headers (variable names) |
| OBS | the data in the OBS column, or ID column if using an ID statement |
| OBSHEADER | the header for the OBS or ID column |
| TOTAL | the data in the totals row produced by a SUM statement |
| GRANDTOTAL | the data for the grand total produced by a SUM statement |

If you place the STYLE= option in the PROC PRINT statement, the entire table is affected. For example, if you specify HEADER as the location, then all of the column headers will have the new style. But what if you just want to change the header of just one column?  Then you can put the STYLE= option in the VAR statement as follows:

```
VAR variable-list / STYLE(location-list) = {style-attribute = value};
```

Only the variables listed in the VAR statement will have the specified style. If you want different variables to have different styles, then use multiple VAR statements. Only the DATA and HEADER locations are valid on the VAR statement. If you leave out the location, then both the data and the header will have the style. (You cannot leave out the location on the PROC PRINT statement.)

**Example** The following data are the Olympic gold medal winners for the women's 5000 meter speed skating event. The Olympic year is followed by the skater's name, country, time, and record (WR is world record) if any.

---

[1] To change the style of output from other procedures, you need to create a new style template using PROC TEMPLATE, then apply the new style by using a STYLE= option in your ODS statement. See the SAS Help and Documentation for more information on the TEMPLATE procedure.

```
1992,Gunda Niemann,GER,7:31.57
1994,Claudia Pechstein,GER,7:14.37
1998,Claudia Pechstein,GER,6:59.61,WR
2002,Claudia Pechstein,GER,6:46.91,WR
2006,Clara Hughes,CAN,6:59.07
```

The following program reads the data and uses PROC PRINT to create an HTML file using the DEFAULT style template. The resulting output is shown on the right.

```
ODS HTML FILE='c:\MyHTML\results.htm';
DATA skating;
   INFILE 'c:\MyData\Women.csv' DSD MISSOVER;
   INPUT Year Name :$20. Country $
         Time $ Record $;
RUN;
PROC PRINT DATA=skating;
   TITLE 'Women''s 5000 Meter Speed Skating';
   ID Year;
RUN;
ODS HTML CLOSE;
```

### Women's 5000 Meter Speed Skating

| Year | Name | Country | Time | Record |
|------|------|---------|------|--------|
| 1992 | Gunda Niemann | GER | 7:31.57 | |
| 1994 | Claudia Pechstein | GER | 7:14.37 | |
| 1998 | Claudia Pechstein | GER | 6:59.61 | WR |
| 2002 | Claudia Pechstein | GER | 6:46.91 | WR |
| 2006 | Clara Hughes | CAN | 6:59.07 | |

The next program also uses the DEFAULT style template, but the STYLE= option on the PROC PRINT statement changes the background of the data cells in the table to white.

```
ODS HTML FILE='c:\MyHTML\results2.htm';
PROC PRINT DATA=skating
      STYLE(DATA)={BACKGROUND=white};
   TITLE 'Women''s 5000 Meter Speed Skating';
   ID Year;
RUN;
ODS HTML CLOSE;
```

### Women's 5000 Meter Speed Skating

| Year | Name | Country | Time | Record |
|------|------|---------|------|--------|
| 1992 | Gunda Niemann | GER | 7:31.57 | |
| 1994 | Claudia Pechstein | GER | 7:14.37 | |
| 1998 | Claudia Pechstein | GER | 6:59.61 | WR |
| 2002 | Claudia Pechstein | GER | 6:46.91 | WR |
| 2006 | Clara Hughes | CAN | 6:59.07 | |

This program adds VAR statements to change the font style and the font weight of just the Record column to italic and bold.

```
ODS HTML FILE='c:\MyHTML\results3.htm';
PROC PRINT DATA=skating
      STYLE(DATA)={BACKGROUND=white};
   TITLE 'Women''s 5000 Meter Speed Skating';
   VAR Name Country Time;
   VAR Record/STYLE(DATA)=
      {FONT_STYLE=italic FONT_WEIGHT=bold};
   ID Year;
RUN;
ODS HTML CLOSE;
```

### Women's 5000 Meter Speed Skating

| Year | Name | Country | Time | Record |
|------|------|---------|------|--------|
| 1992 | Gunda Niemann | GER | 7:31.57 | |
| 1994 | Claudia Pechstein | GER | 7:14.37 | |
| 1998 | Claudia Pechstein | GER | 6:59.61 | *WR* |
| 2002 | Claudia Pechstein | GER | 6:46.91 | *WR* |
| 2006 | Clara Hughes | CAN | 6:59.07 | |

## 5.9    Customizing PROC REPORT Output with the STYLE= Option

Using the STYLE= option in PROC REPORT is similar to the PRINT procedure because you have to specify a location. The general form of the STYLE= option in the PROC REPORT statement is

```
PROC REPORT STYLE(location-list) = {style-attribute = value};
```

where *location-list* specifies the parts of the table that should take on the style, *style-attribute* is the characteristic you wish to change, and *value* is the way you want the style attribute to look. (See section 5.12 for a table of attributes and possible values.) For example, to give column headers a green background, you could use this statement:

```
PROC REPORT DATA = mysales STYLE(HEADER) = {BACKGROUND = green};
```

You can specify more than one location in a single STYLE= option, and you can have several STYLE= options in one PROC REPORT statement. Here are some of the locations whose appearance you can control in PROC REPORT:

| Location | Table region affected |
|----------|----------------------|
| HEADER | column headings |
| COLUMN | data cells |
| SUMMARY | totals created by SUMMARIZE option in BREAK or RBREAK statements |

If you put a STYLE= option in a PROC REPORT statement, then it will affect the whole table, for example, all the column headings, all the data cells, or all the summary breaks. You can change part of a report by using the STYLE= option in other statements. To specify a style for a particular variable, put the STYLE= option in a DEFINE statement. If you use a GROUP variable, you may want to add the SPANROWS option (new in SAS 9.2) to the PROC statement. The SPANROWS option combines cells in the same group into a single cell. These statements tell SAS to use Month as a group variable, and make the background BLUE for both the data and header:

```
PROC REPORT DATA = mysales SPANROWS;
   DEFINE Month / GROUP STYLE(HEADER COLUMN) = {BACKGROUND = blue};
```

To specify a style for particular summary breaks, use the STYLE= option in a BREAK or RBREAK statement. These statements tell SAS to use a red background for summary breaks for each value of Month.

```
BREAK AFTER Month / SUMMARIZE STYLE(SUMMARY) = {BACKGROUND = red};
```

**Example**  The following data show women who have won gold medals in Olympic speed skating in more than one year. The variables are name, country, the number of years in which gold medals were won, and the total number of gold medals. Each line contains two records.

```
Lydia Skoblikova, URS, 2, 6, Karin Enke, GDR, 2, 3
Christa Rothenburger, GDR, 2, 2, Bonnie Blair, USA, 3, 5
Gunda Nieman, GDR, 2, 3, Claudia Pechstein, GER, 4, 5
Catriona LeMay, CAN, 2, 2, Marianne Timmer, NED, 2, 3
```

The following program reads the data and uses PROC REPORT to create an HTML file using the DEFAULT style template. The resulting output is shown on the right.

```
DATA skating;
    INFILE 'c:\MyRawData\Speed.dat' DSD;
    INPUT Name :$20. Country $
        NumYears NumGold @@;
RUN;
ODS HTML FILE='c:\MyHTML\speed.htm';
PROC REPORT DATA = skating NOWINDOWS;
    COLUMN Country Name NumGold;
    DEFINE Country / GROUP;
    TITLE 'Olympic Women''s '
        'Speed Skating';
RUN;
ODS HTML CLOSE;
```

### Olympic Women's Speed Skating

| Country | Name | NumGold |
|---------|------|---------|
| CAN | Catriona LeMay | 2 |
| GDR | Karin Enke | 3 |
|  | Christa Rothenburger | 2 |
|  | Gunda Nieman | 3 |
| GER | Claudia Pechstein | 5 |
| NED | Marianne Timmer | 3 |
| URS | Lydia Skoblikova | 6 |
| USA | Bonnie Blair | 5 |

The next program also uses the DEFAULT style template, but adds a STYLE= option in the PROC REPORT statement to change the font weight of all the data cells to bold and to center the data. The SPANROWS option combines the three lines for GDR into one cell.

```
* STYLE= option in PROC statement;
ODS HTML FILE='c:\MyHTML\speed2.htm';
PROC REPORT DATA = skating NOWINDOWS
    SPANROWS  STYLE(COLUMN) =
    {FONT_WEIGHT = bold JUST = center};
    COLUMN Country Name NumGold;
    DEFINE Country / GROUP;
    TITLE 'Olympic Women''s '
        'Speed Skating';
RUN;
ODS HTML CLOSE;
```

### Olympic Women's Speed Skating

| Country | Name | NumGold |
|---------|------|---------|
| CAN | Catriona LeMay | 2 |
| GDR | Karin Enke | 3 |
|  | Christa Rothenburger | 2 |
|  | Gunda Nieman | 3 |
| GER | Claudia Pechstein | 5 |
| NED | Marianne Timmer | 3 |
| URS | Lydia Skoblikova | 6 |
| USA | Bonnie Blair | 5 |

Now the STYLE= option has been moved to a DEFINE statement so that just the values of Country are bold and centered.

```
* STYLE= option in DEFINE statement;
ODS HTML FILE='c:\MyHTML\speed3.htm';
PROC REPORT DATA = skating NOWINDOWS
    SPANROWS;
    COLUMN Country Name NumGold;
    DEFINE Country / GROUP STYLE(COLUMN) =
        {FONT_WEIGHT = bold JUST = center};
    TITLE 'Olympic Women''s '
        'Speed Skating';
RUN;
ODS HTML CLOSE;
```

### Olympic Women's Speed Skating

| Country | Name | NumGold |
|---------|------|---------|
| CAN | Catriona LeMay | 2 |
| GDR | Karin Enke | 3 |
|  | Christa Rothenburger | 2 |
|  | Gunda Nieman | 3 |
| GER | Claudia Pechstein | 5 |
| NED | Marianne Timmer | 3 |
| URS | Lydia Skoblikova | 6 |
| USA | Bonnie Blair | 5 |

## 5.10  Customizing PROC TABULATE Output with the STYLE= Option

Using the STYLE= option in the TABULATE procedure, you can customize the look of the table that TABULATE produces. There are a number of different style attributes you can change, affecting things like color and font of text. (See section 5.12 for a table of style attributes and their possible values.) The part of the table affected depends on where you place the STYLE= option. The following shows some of the TABULATE statements that accept the STYLE= option and which parts of the table are affected:

| Statement | Table region affected |
|---|---|
| PROC TABULATE | all the data cells |
| CLASS | class variable name headings |
| CLASSLEV | class level value headings |
| TABLE (crossed with elements)[1] | element's data cell |
| VAR | analysis variable name headings |

**PROC TABULATE statement**  If you place the STYLE= option on the PROC TABULATE statement, all the table's data cells will have the style. For example, if you wanted all the data cells in your table created from the MYSALES SAS data set to have a yellow background, then you would use the following statement:

```
PROC TABULATE DATA = mysales STYLE = {BACKGROUND = yellow};
```

**TABLE statement**  If you want some of the data cells to have a different style from the rest, then you need to add the STYLE= option to the TABLE statement and cross the style with the variable or keyword you want to change (similar to having different formats for different parts of the table as discussed in section 4.16). Any style assigned in a TABLE statement will override styles assigned in the PROC TABULATE statement. For example the following TABLE statement produces a table where the data cells in the ALL column have a red background:

```
TABLE City, Month ALL*{STYLE = {BACKGROUND = red}};
```

**CLASSLEV, VAR, and CLASS statements**  The CLASSLEV, VAR, and CLASS statements all require that you place the STYLE= option after a slash (/). Any variable that appears in a CLASSLEV statement must also appear in a CLASS statement. For example, suppose you had a table with a class variable MONTH, and you wanted all the values of MONTH to have a foreground color of green, then you would use the CLASSLEV statement as follows:

```
CLASSLEV Month / STYLE = {FOREGROUND = green};
```

**Example**  The following data are for men's speed skating events in the winter Olympics. The Olympic year is followed by the event and the record for that event. OR is an Olympic record, WR is a world record, and None indicates that neither an Olympic nor world record was set that year. Note that there are four observations per line of data.

---

[1] You can also use STYLE= as an option on the TABLE statement and then it affects the structural parts of the table (such as borders and cell widths). See the SAS Help and Documentation for more information.

```
1994 m500 OR 1998 m500 OR 2002 m500 OR 2006 m500 None
1994 m1000 WR 1998 m1000 OR 2002 m1000 WR 2006 m1000 None
1994 m1500 WR 1998 m1500 WR 2002 m1500 WR 2006 m1500 None
1994 m5000 WR 1998 m5000 WR 2002 m5000 WR 2006 m5000 None
1994 m10000 WR 1998 m10000 WR 2002 m10000 WR 2006 m10000 None
```

The following program reads the data into a SAS data set named SKATING. The TABLE statement in the TABULATE procedure sets up a table which has the Olympic year as rows and the record (None, OR, or WR) as columns. The Year and N headings are eliminated by setting them equal to a null string (='') in the TABLE statement. The ODS statements create an HTML file using the DEFAULT style. The resulting output is shown on the right.

```
ODS HTML FILE='c:\MyHTML\table.htm';
DATA skating;
   INFILE 'c:\MyData\Records.dat';
   INPUT Year  Event $ Record $ @@;
RUN;
PROC TABULATE DATA=skating;
   CLASS Year Record;
   TABLE Year='',Record*N='';
   TITLE 'Men''s Speed Skating';
   TITLE2 'Records Set at Olympics';
RUN;
ODS HTML CLOSE;
```

**Men's Speed Skating Records Set at Olympics**

| | Record | | |
|---|---|---|---|
| | None | OR | WR |
| 1994 | . | 1 | 4 |
| 1998 | . | 2 | 3 |
| 2002 | . | 1 | 4 |
| 2006 | 5 | . | . |

Now, suppose we decide that the numbers in the data cells just don't stand out enough, and it would be nice to have the numbers centered in the cells. We can do this by using the STYLE= option in the PROC TABULATE statement and setting the JUST attribute to center and the BACKGROUND attribute to white as follows:

```
ODS HTML FILE='c:\MyHTML\table2.htm';
PROC TABULATE DATA=skating
     STYLE={JUST=center BACKGROUND=white};
   CLASS Year Record;
   TABLE Year='',Record*N='';
   TITLE 'Men''s Speed Skating';
   TITLE2 'Records Set at Olympics';
RUN;
ODS HTML CLOSE;
```

This table still uses the DEFAULT style template, but the style of the data cells has been changed.

**Men's Speed Skating Records Set at Olympics**

| | Record | | |
|---|---|---|---|
| | None | OR | WR |
| 1994 | . | 1 | 4 |
| 1998 | . | 2 | 3 |
| 2002 | . | 1 | 4 |
| 2006 | 5 | . | . |

## 5.11   Adding Traffic-Lighting to Your Output

Traffic-lighting is a feature that allows you to control the style of cells in the table based on the value of the cell. This way you can draw attention to important values in your report, or highlight relationships between values. Traffic-lighting can be used in any of the three reporting procedures: PRINT, REPORT, and TABULATE.

To implement traffic-lighting you need to do two things. First, create a user-defined format specifying different values for the style attribute you want to change over the range in data values. (See the next section for a table of style attributes and possible values.)  Then set the style attribute equal to the format you defined in the STYLE= option. For example, if you had a FORMAT procedure that created a format as follows:

```
PROC FORMAT;
   VALUE posneg
      LOW -< 0 = 'red'
      0-HIGH = 'black';
```

Then in a VAR statement in a PRINT procedure, you could set the value of the attribute equal to the format in the STYLE= option as follows:

```
VAR Balance / STYLE = {FOREGROUND = posneg.};
```

Then all the data cells for the variable Balance would have red numbers if they are negative and black numbers if they are positive.

**Example**   The following data are the top five finishers in the men's 5000 meter speed skating event at the 2002 Winter Olympics. The skater's place is followed by his name, country, and time in seconds.

```
1,Jochem Uytdehaage, Netherlands,374.66
2,Derek Parra, United States,377.98
3,Jens Boden, Germany,381.73
4,Dmitry Shepel, Russia,381.85
5,KC Boutiette, United States,382.97
```

The following program reads and prints the data using PROC PRINT. The resulting HTML file using the DEFAULT style is shown on the right.

```
ODS HTML FILE='c:\MyHTML\mens.html';
DATA results;
   INFILE
      'c:\MyRawData\Mens5000.dat' DSD;
   INPUT Place Name :$20.
         Country :$15. Time ;
RUN;
PROC PRINT DATA=results;
   ID Place;
   TITLE 'Men''s 5000m Speed Skating';
   TITLE2 '2002 Olympic Results';
RUN;
ODS HTML CLOSE;
```

### Men's 5000m Speed Skating 2002 Olympic Results

| Place | Name | Country | Time |
|---|---|---|---|
| 1 | Jochem Uytdehaage | Netherlands | 374.66 |
| 2 | Derek Parra | United States | 377.98 |
| 3 | Jens Boden | Germany | 381.73 |
| 4 | Dmitry Shepel | Russia | 381.85 |
| 5 | KC Boutiette | United States | 382.97 |

To give an idea of how these times compare with previous times skaters set for this event, we can use traffic lighting. Prior to the 2002 Olympics, the world record for the 5000 meter speed skating was 378.72 seconds and the Olympic record was 382.20 seconds. To show which skaters skated faster than these records, we first create a user-defined format, REC, where the color red is assigned to times less than the world record, orange is assigned to times less than the Olympic record, and the other times are assigned white. Next, we add two VAR statements to the PROC PRINT. The second VAR statement uses the STYLE= option to assign a style to the Time variable. Now instead of setting the BACKGOUND attribute equal to a constant value, we set it equal to the format we just defined, REC.

```
ODS HTML FILE='c:\MyHTML\mens2.html';
PROC FORMAT;
   VALUE rec 0 -< 378.72 ='red'
            378.72 -< 382.20 = 'orange'
            382.20 - HIGH = 'white';
RUN;
PROC PRINT DATA=results;
   ID Place;
   VAR Name Country;
   VAR Time/STYLE={BACKGROUND=rec.};
   TITLE 'Men''s 5000m Speed Skating';
   TITLE2 '2002 Olympic Results';
RUN;
ODS HTML CLOSE;
```

Here is the output showing the different color backgrounds based on the value of the Time variable. Those skaters who broke the previous world record have red backgrounds, those who broke the Olympic record show an orange background, and the fifth skater who didn't break any records shows a white background. (The colors appear here as shades of gray.)

### Men's 5000m Speed Skating 2002 Olympic Results

| Place | Name | Country | Time |
|-------|------|---------|------|
| 1 | Jochem Uytdehaage | Netherlands | 374.66 |
| 2 | Derek Parra | United States | 377.98 |
| 3 | Jens Boden | Germany | 381.73 |
| 4 | Dmitry Shepel | Russia | 381.85 |
| 5 | KC Boutiette | United States | 382.97 |

## 5.12 Selected Style Attributes

| Attribute | Description | Possible Values |
|---|---|---|
| BACKGROUND | Specifies the background color of the table or cell. | Any valid color[1] |
| BACKGROUNDIMAGE | Specifies a background image to be used for the table or cell. Not valid for RTF. | Any GIF, JPEG, or PNG image file[2] |
| FLYOVER | Specifies the pop-up text displayed when the cursor is held over the text (HTML) or if you double-click on the text (PDF). | Any text string enclosed in quotation marks |
| FONT_FACE | Specifies the font to use for the text in the cells. | Any valid font (Most devices support Times, Courier, Arial, and Helvetica) |
| FONT_SIZE | Specifies the relative size of the font for the text in cells.[3] | 1 to 7 |
| FONT_STYLE | Specifies the style of the font used in the cells. | ITALIC, ROMAN, or SLANT (Italic and slant may map to the same font) |
| FONT_WEIGHT | Specifies the weight of the font used in the cells. | BOLD, MEDIUM, or LIGHT |
| FOREGROUND | Specifies the color of the text in the cells. | Any valid color[1] |
| JUST | Specifies the justification of the text in the cells. | R \| RIGHT, C \| CENTER, L \| LEFT, or D (decimal) |
| PRETEXT or POSTTEXT | Specifies text that goes either before (PRETEXT) or after (POSTTEXT) the text in the cells. | Any text string enclosed in quotation marks |
| PREIMAGE or POSTIMAGE | Specifies an image that will be inserted either before (PREIMAGE) or after (POSTIMAGE) the text in the cells. | Any GIF, JPEG or PNG image file (JPEG and PNG only for RTF)[2] |
| URL | Specifies the URL to link to from the text in the cell. HTML, PDF, and RTF only. | Any URL |

[1] There are several ways that you can specify color and these are discussed in the SAS/GRAPH documentation. If you want an exact color, you may use the RGB notation (e.g. #00FF00 is green), or if you want to use colors by name, then the following are some colors you may choose: AQUA, BLACK, BLUE, FUCHSIA, GREEN, GRAY, LIME, MAROON, NAVY, OLIVE, PURPLE, RED, SILVER, TEAL, WHITE, YELLOW.

| Attribute | STYLE= code | Result |
|---|---|---|
| BACKGROUND | `STYLE(DATA)=`<br>`    {BACKGROUND=white};` | speed skating |
| BACKGROUNDIMAGE | `STYLE(DATA)=`<br>`    {BACKGROUNDIMAGE=`<br>`'c:\MyImages\snow.gif'};` | speed skating |
| FLYOVER | `STYLE(DATA)=`<br>`    {FLYOVER='Try it!'};` | speed skating<br>Try it! |
| FONT_FACE | `STYLE(DATA)=`<br>`    {FONT_FACE=courier};` | speed skating |
| FONT_SIZE | `STYLE(DATA)=`<br>`    {FONT_SIZE=2};` | speed skating |
| FONT_STYLE | `STYLE(DATA)=`<br>`    {FONT_STYLE=italic};` | *speed skating* |
| FONT_WEIGHT | `STYLE(DATA)=`<br>`    {FONT_WEIGHT=bold};` | **speed skating** |
| FOREGROUND | `STYLE(DATA)=`<br>`    {FOREGROUND=white};` | speed skating |
| JUST | `STYLE(DATA)=`<br>`    {JUST=right};` | speed skating |
| PRETEXT or POSTTEXT | `STYLE(DATA)=`<br>`    {POST_TEXT=' is fun'};` | speed skating is fun |
| PREIMAGE or POSTIMAGE | `STYLE(DATA)=`<br>`    {PREIMAGE='SS2.gif'};` | speed skating |
| URL | `STYLE(DATA)=`<br>`    {URL='http://skating.org'};` | speed skating |

[2] For HTML, if you use a simple file name, then the SAS internal browser may not be able to find the file. If you use a complete path, then edit the HTML file to reflect any changes if you move the files to a new location.

[3] For some destinations, you can specify size in units of measure: cm, in, mm, pt, px (pixels). For example, if you want text that is 24 points, then you would specify FONT_SIZE=24pt.

**6**

> " I usually say, 'The computer is the dumbest thing on campus. It does exactly what you tell it to; not necessarily what you want. Logic is up to you.' "

NECIA A. BLACK, R.N., PH.D.

From the SAS L Listserv, May 6, 1994. Reprinted by permission of the author.

# CHAPTER 6

## Modifying and Combining SAS Data Sets

# 6.1 ▸ Modifying a Data Set Using the SET Statement

The SET statement in the DATA step allows you to read a SAS data set so you can add new variables, create a subset, or otherwise modify the data set. If you were short on disk space, for example, you might not want to store your computed variables in a permanent SAS data set. Instead, you might want to calculate them as needed for analysis. Likewise, to save processing time, you might want to create a subset of a SAS data set when you only want to look at a small portion of a large data set. The SET statement brings a SAS data set, one observation at a time, into the DATA step for processing.[1]

To read a SAS data set, start with the DATA statement specifying the name of the new data set. Then follow with the SET statement specifying the name of the old data set you want to read. If you don't want to create a new data set, you can specify the same name in the DATA and SET statements. Then the results of the DATA step will overwrite the old data set named in the SET statement.[2] The following shows the general form of the DATA and SET statements:

```
DATA new-data-set;
   SET data-set;
```

Any assignment, subsetting IF, or other DATA step statements usually follow the SET statement. For example, the following creates a new data set, FRIDAY, which is a replica of the SALES data set, except FRIDAY has only the observations for Fridays, and it has an additional variable, Total:

```
DATA friday;
   SET sales;
   IF Day = 'F';
   Total = Popcorn + Peanuts;
RUN;
```

**Example**  The Fun Times Amusement Park is collecting data about their train ride. They can add more cars on the train during peak hours to shorten the wait, or take them off when they're not needed to save fuel costs. The raw data file contains data for the time of day, the number of cars on the train, and the total number of people on the train:

```
10:10   6 21
12:15  10 56
15:30  10 25
11:30   8 34
13:15   8 12
10:45   6 13
20:30   6 32
23:15   6 12
```

---

[1] The MODIFY statement also allows you to modify a single data set. See the SAS Help and Documentation for more information.

[2] By default, SAS will not overwrite a data set in a DATA step that has errors.

The data are read into a permanent SAS data set, TRAINS, stored in the MySASLib directory on the park's central computer by means of the following program:

```
* Create permanent SAS data set trains;
DATA 'c:\MySASLib\trains';
    INFILE 'c:\MyRawData\Train.dat';
    INPUT Time TIME5. Cars People;
RUN;
```

This example uses direct referencing to tell SAS where to store the permanent SAS data set, but you could use a LIBNAME statement instead.

Each train car holds a maximum of six people. After collecting the data, the Fun Times management decides they want to know the average number of people per car on each ride. This number was not calculated in the original DATA step which created the permanent SAS data set, but can be calculated by the following program:

```
* Read the SAS data set trains with a SET statement;
DATA averagetrain;
    SET 'c:\MySASLib\trains';
    PeoplePerCar = People / Cars;
RUN;
PROC PRINT DATA = averagetrain;
    TITLE 'Average Number of People per Train Car';
    FORMAT Time TIME5.;
RUN;
```

The DATA statement defines a new temporary SAS data set named AVERAGETRAIN. Then the SET statement reads the permanent SAS data set TRAINS, and an assignment statement creates the new variable PeoplePerCar. Here are the results of the PROC PRINT:

```
            Average Number of People per Train Car              1


                                           People
        Obs     Time    Cars    People     PerCar


         1     10:10     6       21       3.50000
         2     12:15    10       56       5.60000
         3     15:30    10       25       2.50000
         4     11:30     8       34       4.25000
         5     13:15     8       12       1.50000
         6     10:45     6       13       2.16667
         7     20:30     6       32       5.33333
         8     23:15     6       12       2.00000
```

## 6.2    Stacking Data Sets Using the SET Statement

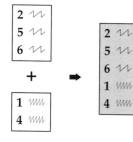

The SET statement with one SAS data set allows you to read and modify the data. With two or more data sets, in addition to reading and modifying the data, the SET statement concatenates or stacks the data sets one on top of the other. This is useful when you want to combine data sets with all or most of the same variables but different observations. You might, for example, have data from two different locations or data taken at two separate times, but you need the data together for analysis.

In a DATA step, first specify the name of the new SAS data set in the DATA statement, then list the names of the old data sets you want to combine in the SET statement:[1]

```
DATA new-data-set;
   SET data-set-1 data-set-n;
```

The number of observations in the new data set will equal the sum of the number of observations in the old data sets. The order of observations is determined by the order of the list of old data sets. If one of the data sets has a variable not contained in the other data sets, then the observations from the other data sets will have missing values for that variable.

**Example**    The Fun Times Amusement Park has two entrances where they collect data about their customers. The data file for the south entrance has an S (for south) followed by the customers' Fun Times pass numbers, the sizes of their parties, and their ages. The file for the north entrance has an N (for north), the same data as the south entrance, plus one more column for the parking lot where they left their cars (the south entrance has only one lot). The following shows samples of the two data files:

| Data for South Entrance | Data for North Entrance |
|---|---|
| S 43 3 27 | N 21 5 41 1 |
| S 44 3 24 | N 87 4 33 3 |
| S 45 3  2 | N 65 2 67 1 |
|  | N 66 2  7 1 |

The first two parts of the following program read the raw data for the south and north entrances into SAS data sets and print them to make sure they are correct. The third part combines the two SAS data sets using a SET statement. The same DATA step creates a new variable, AmountPaid, which tells how much each customer paid based on their age. This final data set is printed using PROC PRINT:

```
DATA southentrance;
   INFILE 'c:\MyRawData\South.dat';
   INPUT Entrance $ PassNumber PartySize Age;
PROC PRINT DATA = southentrance;
   TITLE 'South Entrance Data';
RUN;
DATA northentrance;
   INFILE 'c:\MyRawData\North.dat';
   INPUT Entrance $ PassNumber PartySize Age Lot;
PROC PRINT DATA = northentrance;
   TITLE 'North Entrance Data';
RUN;
```

---

[1] Starting with SAS 9.2, you can also use numbered range lists and name prefix lists for data set lists in SET statements. This is similar to the variable name lists covered in section 3.12. See the SAS Help and Documentation for details.

```
* Create a data set, both, combining northentrance and southentrance;
* Create a variable, AmountPaid, based on value of variable Age;
DATA both;
   SET southentrance northentrance;
   IF Age = . THEN AmountPaid = .;
      ELSE IF Age < 3  THEN AmountPaid = 0;
      ELSE IF Age < 65 THEN AmountPaid = 35;
      ELSE AmountPaid = 27;
PROC PRINT DATA = both;
   TITLE 'Both Entrances';
RUN;
```

The following are the results of the three PRINT procedures in the program. Notice that the final data set has missing values for the variable Lot for all the observations which came from the south entrance. Because the variable Lot was not in the SOUTHENTRANCE data set, SAS assigned missing values to those observations.

South Entrance Data                                1

| Obs | Entrance | Pass Number | Party Size | Age |
|-----|----------|-------------|------------|-----|
| 1 | S | 43 | 3 | 27 |
| 2 | S | 44 | 3 | 24 |
| 3 | S | 45 | 3 | 2 |

North Entrance Data                                2

| Obs | Entrance | Pass Number | Party Size | Age | Lot |
|-----|----------|-------------|------------|-----|-----|
| 1 | N | 21 | 5 | 41 | 1 |
| 2 | N | 87 | 4 | 33 | 3 |
| 3 | N | 65 | 2 | 67 | 1 |
| 4 | N | 66 | 2 | 7 | 1 |

Both Entrances                                3

| Obs | Entrance | Pass Number | Party Size | Age | Lot | Amount Paid |
|-----|----------|-------------|------------|-----|-----|-------------|
| 1 | S | 43 | 3 | 27 | . | 35 |
| 2 | S | 44 | 3 | 24 | . | 35 |
| 3 | S | 45 | 3 | 2 | . | 0 |
| 4 | N | 21 | 5 | 41 | 1 | 35 |
| 5 | N | 87 | 4 | 33 | 3 | 35 |
| 6 | N | 65 | 2 | 67 | 1 | 27 |
| 7 | N | 66 | 2 | 7 | 1 | 35 |

## 6.3    Interleaving Data Sets Using the SET Statement

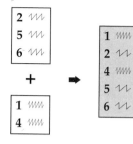

The previous section explained how to stack data sets that have all or most of the same variables but different observations. However, if you have data sets that are already sorted by some important variable, then simply stacking the data sets may unsort the data sets. You could stack the two data sets and then re-sort them using PROC SORT. But if your data sets are already sorted, it is more efficient to preserve that order, than to stack and re-sort. All you need to do is use a BY statement with your SET statement. Here's the general form:

```
DATA new-data-set;
    SET data-set-1 data-set-n;
    BY variable-list;
```

In a DATA statement, you specify the name of the new SAS data set you want to create. In a SET statement, you list the data sets to be interleaved. Then in a BY statement, you list one or more variables that SAS should use for ordering the observations. The number of observations in the new data set will be equal to the sum of the number of observations in the old data sets. If one of the data sets has a variable not contained in the other data sets, then values of that variable will be set to missing for observations from the other data sets.

Before you can interleave observations, the data sets must be sorted by the BY variables. If one or the other of your data sets is not already sorted, then use PROC SORT to do the job.

**Example**  To show how this is different from stacking data sets, we'll use the amusement park data again. There are two data sets, one for the south entrance and one for the north. For every customer, the park collects the following data: the entrance (S or N), the customer's Fun Times pass number, size of that customer's party, and age. For customers entering from the north, the data set also includes parking lot number. Here is a sample of the data:

| Data for South Entrance | Data for North Entrance |
|---|---|
| S 43 3 27 | N 21 5 41 1 |
| S 44 3 24 | N 87 4 33 3 |
| S 45 3  2 | N 65 2 67 1 |
|  | N 66 2  7 1 |

Notice that the data for the south entrance are already sorted by pass number, but the data for the north entrance are not.

Instead of stacking the two data sets, this program interleaves the data sets by pass number. This program first reads the data for the south entrance and prints them to make sure they are correct. Then the program reads the data for the north entrance, sorts them, and prints them. Then in the final DATA step, SAS combines the two data sets, NORHTENTRANCE and SOUTHENTRANCE, creating a new data set named INTERLEAVE. The BY statement tells SAS to combine the data sets by PassNumber:

```
DATA southentrance;
    INFILE 'c:\MyRawData\South.dat';
    INPUT Entrance $ PassNumber PartySize Age;
PROC PRINT DATA = southentrance;
    TITLE 'South Entrance Data';
RUN;
```

```
DATA northentrance;
    INFILE 'c:\MyRawData\North.dat';
    INPUT Entrance $ PassNumber PartySize Age Lot;
PROC SORT DATA = northentrance;
    BY PassNumber;
PROC PRINT DATA = northentrance;
    TITLE 'North Entrance Data';
RUN;
* Interleave observations by PassNumber;
DATA interleave;
    SET northentrance southentrance;
    BY PassNumber;
PROC PRINT DATA = interleave;
    TITLE 'Both Entrances, By Pass Number';
RUN;
```

Here are the results of the three PRINT procedures. Notice how the observations have been interleaved so that the new data set is sorted by PassNumber:

### South Entrance Data  1

| Obs | Entrance | Pass Number | Party Size | Age |
|-----|----------|-------------|------------|-----|
| 1 | S | 43 | 3 | 27 |
| 2 | S | 44 | 3 | 24 |
| 3 | S | 45 | 3 | 2 |

### North Entrance Data  2

| Obs | Entrance | Pass Number | Party Size | Age | Lot |
|-----|----------|-------------|------------|-----|-----|
| 1 | N | 21 | 5 | 41 | 1 |
| 2 | N | 65 | 2 | 67 | 1 |
| 3 | N | 66 | 2 | 7 | 1 |
| 4 | N | 87 | 4 | 33 | 3 |

### Both Entrances, By Pass Number  3

| Obs | Entrance | Pass Number | Party Size | Age | Lot |
|-----|----------|-------------|------------|-----|-----|
| 1 | N | 21 | 5 | 41 | 1 |
| 2 | S | 43 | 3 | 27 | . |
| 3 | S | 44 | 3 | 24 | . |
| 4 | S | 45 | 3 | 2 | . |
| 5 | N | 65 | 2 | 67 | 1 |
| 6 | N | 66 | 2 | 7 | 1 |
| 7 | N | 87 | 4 | 33 | 3 |

# 6.4 Combining Data Sets Using a One-to-One Match Merge

When you want to match observations from one data set with observations from another, use the MERGE statement in the DATA step. If you know the two data sets are in EXACTLY the same order, you don't have to have any common variables between the data sets. Typically, however, you will want to have, for matching purposes, a common variable or several variables which taken together uniquely identify each observation. This is important. Having a common variable to merge by ensures that the observations are properly matched. For example, to merge patient data with billing data, you would use the patient ID as a matching variable. Otherwise you risk getting Mary Smith's visit to the obstetrician mixed up with Matthew Smith's visit to the optometrist.

Merging SAS data sets is a simple process. First, if the data are not already sorted, use the SORT procedure to sort all data sets by the common variables. Then, in the DATA statement, name the new SAS data set to hold the results and follow with a MERGE statement listing the data sets to be combined.[1] Use a BY statement to indicate the common variables:

```
DATA new-data-set;
   MERGE data-set-1 data-set-n;
   BY variable-list;
```

If you merge two data sets, and they have variables with the same names—besides the BY variables—then variables from the second data set will overwrite any variables having the same name in the first data set.

**Example**  A Belgian chocolatier keeps track of the number of each type of chocolate sold each day. The code number for each chocolate and the number of pieces sold that day are kept in a file. In a separate file she keeps the names and descriptions of each chocolate as well as the code number. In order to print the day's sales along with the descriptions of the chocolates, the two files must be merged together using the code number as the common variable. Here is a sample of the data:

**Sales data**
```
C865 15
K086  9
A536 21
S163 34
K014  1
A206 12
B713 29
```

**Descriptions**
```
A206 Mokka      Coffee buttercream in dark chocolate
A536 Walnoot    Walnut halves in bed of dark chocolate
B713 Frambozen  Raspberry marzipan covered in milk chocolate
C865 Vanille    Vanilla-flavored rolled in ground hazelnuts
K014 Kroon      Milk chocolate with a mint cream center
K086 Koning     Hazelnut paste in dark chocolate
M315 Pyramide   White with dark chocolate trimming
S163 Orbais     Chocolate cream in dark chocolate
```

---

[1] Starting with SAS 9.2, you can use numbered range lists and prefix name lists for data set lists in MERGE statements. This is similar to the variable name lists covered in section 3.12. See the SAS Help and Documentation for details.

The first two parts of the following program read the descriptions and sales data. The descriptions data are already sorted by CodeNum, so we don't need to use PROC SORT. The sales data are not sorted, so a PROC SORT follows the DATA step. (If you attempt to merge data which are not sorted, SAS will refuse and give you this error message: ERROR: BY variables are not properly sorted.)

```
DATA descriptions;
    INFILE 'c:\MyRawData\chocolate.dat' TRUNCOVER;
    INPUT CodeNum $ 1-4 Name $ 6-14 Description $ 15-60;
RUN;
DATA sales;
    INFILE 'c:\MyRawData\chocsales.dat';
    INPUT CodeNum $ 1-4 PiecesSold 6-7;
PROC SORT DATA = sales;
    BY CodeNum;
RUN;
* Merge data sets by CodeNum;
DATA chocolates;
    MERGE sales descriptions;
    BY CodeNum;
PROC PRINT DATA = chocolates;
    TITLE "Today's Chocolate Sales";
RUN;
```

The final part of the program creates a data set named CHOCOLATES by merging the SALES data set and the DESCRIPTIONS data set. The common variable CodeNum in the BY statement is used for matching purposes. The following output shows the final data set after merging:

```
                    Today's Chocolate Sales                        1

       Code  Pieces
Obs    Num    Sold   Name        Description

  1    A206    12    Mokka       Coffee buttercream in dark chocolate
  2    A536    21    Walnoot     Walnut halves in bed of dark chocolate
  3    B713    29    Frambozen   Raspberry marzipan covered in milk chocolate
  4    C865    15    Vanille     Vanilla-flavored rolled in ground hazelnuts
  5    K014     1    Kroon       Milk chocolate with a mint cream center
  6    K086     9    Koning      Hazelnut paste in dark chocolate
  7    M315     .    Pyramide    White with dark chocolate trimming
  8    S163    34    Orbais      Chocolate cream in dark chocolate
```

Notice that the final data set has a missing value for PiecesSold in the seventh observation. This is because there were no sales for the Pyramide chocolate. All observations from both data sets were included in the final data set whether they had a match or not.

## 6.5 ▶ Combining Data Sets Using a One-to-Many Match Merge

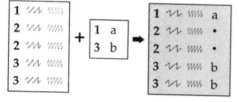

Sometimes you need to combine two data sets by matching one observation from one data set with more than one observation in another. Suppose you had data for every state in the U.S. and wanted to combine it with data for every county. This would be a one-to-many match merge because each state observation matches with many county observations.

The statements for a one-to-many match merge are identical to the statements for a one-to-one match merge:

```
DATA new-data-set;
   MERGE data-set-1 data-set-2;
   BY variable-list;
```

The order of the data sets in the MERGE statement does not affect the matching. In other words, a one-to-many merge will match the same observations as a many-to-one merge.

Before you merge two data sets, they must be sorted by one or more common variables. If your data sets are not already sorted in the proper order, then use PROC SORT to do the job.

You cannot do a one-to-many merge without a BY statement. SAS uses the variables listed in the BY statement to decide which observations belong together. Without a BY statement, SAS simply joins together the first observation from each data set, then the second observation from each data set, and so on. In other words, SAS performs a one-to-one unmatched merge, which is probably not what you want.

If you merge two data sets, and they contain variables with the same name—besides the BY variables—then you should either rename the variables or drop one of the duplicate variables. Otherwise variables from the second data set may overwrite variables having the same name in the first data set. For example, if you merge two data sets that each contain a variable named BirthDate, then you could rename the variables (perhaps as BirthDate1 and BirthDate2), or you could simply drop BirthDate from one data set. Then the values of BirthDate will not overwrite each other. You can use the RENAME= and DROP= data set options (discussed in section 6.11) to prevent the overwriting of data values.

**Example**  A distributor of athletic shoes is putting all its shoes on sale at 20 to 30% off the regular price. The distributor has two data files, one with information about each type of shoe and one with the discount factors. The first file contains one record for each shoe with values for style, type of exercise (running, walking, or cross-training), and regular price. The second file contains one record for each type of exercise and its discount. Here are the two raw data files:

**Shoes data**

```
Max Flight       running 142.99
Zip Fit Leather  walking  83.99
Zoom Airborne    running 112.99
Light Step       walking  73.99
Max Step Woven   walking  75.99
Zip Sneak        c-train  92.99
```

**Discount data**

```
c-train .25
running .30
walking .20
```

To find the sale price, the following program combines the two data files:

```
DATA regular;
   INFILE 'c:\MyRawData\Shoe.dat';
   INPUT Style $ 1-15 ExerciseType $ RegularPrice;
PROC SORT DATA = regular;
   BY ExerciseType;
RUN;
DATA discount;
   INFILE 'c:\MyRawData\Disc.dat';
   INPUT ExerciseType $ Adjustment;
RUN;
* Perform many-to-one match merge;
DATA prices;
   MERGE regular discount;
   BY ExerciseType;
   NewPrice = ROUND(RegularPrice - (RegularPrice * Adjustment), .01);
PROC PRINT DATA = prices;
   TITLE 'Price List for May';
RUN;
```

The first DATA step reads the regular prices, creating a data set named REGULAR. That data set is then sorted by ExerciseType using PROC SORT. The second DATA step reads the price adjustments, creating a data set named DISCOUNT. This data set is already arranged by ExerciseType, so it doesn't have to be sorted. The third DATA step creates a data set named PRICES, merging the first two data sets by ExerciseType, and computes a variable called NewPrice. The output looks like this:

```
                       Price List for May                    1

                    Exercise      Regular                New
   Obs   Style         Type        Price    Adjustment   Price

    1    Zip Sneak     c-train      92.99      0.25       69.74
    2    Max Flight    running     142.99      0.30      100.09
    3    Zoom Airborne running     112.99      0.30       79.09
    4    Zip Fit Leather walking    83.99      0.20       67.19
    5    Light Step    walking      73.99      0.20       59.19
    6    Max Step Woven walking     75.99      0.20       60.79
```

Notice that the values for Adjustment from the DISCOUNT data set are repeated for every observation in the REGULAR data set with the same value of ExerciseType.

## 6.6 Merging Summary Statistics with the Original Data

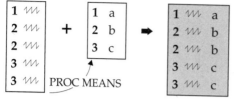

Once in a while you need to combine summary statistics with your data, such as when you want to compare each observation to the group mean, or when you want to calculate a percentage using the group total. To do this, summarize your data using PROC MEANS, and put the results in a new data set. Then merge the summarized data back with the original data using a one-to-many match merge.

**Example**   A distributor of athletic shoes is considering doing a special promotion for the top selling styles. The vice-president of marketing has asked you to produce a report. The report should be divided by type of exercise (running, walking, or cross-training) and show the percentage of sales for each style within its type. For each shoe, the raw data file contains the style name, type of exercise, and total sales for the last quarter:

```
Max Flight        running 1930
Zip Fit Leather   walking 2250
Zoom Airborne     running 4150
Light Step        walking 1130
Max Step Woven    walking 2230
Zip Sneak         c-train 1190
```

Here is the program:

```
DATA shoes;
   INFILE 'c:\MyRawData\Shoesales.dat';
   INPUT Style $ 1-15 ExerciseType $ Sales;
PROC SORT DATA = shoes;
   BY ExerciseType;
RUN;
* Summarize sales by ExerciseType and print;
PROC MEANS NOPRINT DATA = shoes;
   VAR Sales;
   BY ExerciseType;
   OUTPUT OUT = summarydata SUM(Sales) = Total;
PROC PRINT DATA = summarydata;
   TITLE 'Summary Data Set';
RUN;
* Merge totals with the original data set;
DATA shoesummary;
   MERGE shoes summarydata;
   BY ExerciseType;
   Percent = Sales / Total * 100;
PROC PRINT DATA = shoesummary;
   BY ExerciseType;
   ID ExerciseType;
   VAR Style Sales Total Percent;
   TITLE 'Sales Share by Type of Exercise';
RUN;
```

This program is long but straightforward. It starts by reading the raw data in a DATA step and sorting them with PROC SORT. Then it summarizes the data with PROC MEANS by the variable ExerciseType. The OUTPUT statement tells SAS to create a new data set named SUMMARYDATA, containing a variable named Total, which equals the sum of the variable Sales. The NOPRINT option tells SAS not to print the standard PROC MEANS report. Instead, the summary data set is printed by PROC PRINT:

```
                     Summary Data Set                              1

             Exercise
   Obs         Type      _TYPE_     _FREQ_      Total

    1        c-train        0          1        1190
    2        running        0          2        6080
    3        walking        0          3        5610
```

In the last part of the program, the original data set, SHOES, is merged with SUMMARYDATA to make a new data set, SHOESUMMARY. This DATA step computes a new variable called Percent. Then the last PROC PRINT writes the final report with percentage of sales by ExerciseType for each title. Using a BY and an ID statement together gives this report a little different look:

```
                Sales Share by Type of Exercise                    2

   Exercise
     Type      Style              Sales    Total    Percent

   c-train     Zip Sneak           1190     1190    100.000

   running     Max Flight          1930     6080     31.743
               Zoom Airborne       4150     6080     68.257

   walking     Zip Fit Leather     2250     5610     40.107
               Light Step          1130     5610     20.143
               Max Step Woven      2230     5610     39.750
```

# 6.7 Combining a Grand Total with the Original Data

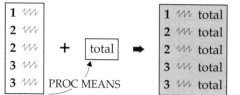

You can use the MEANS procedure to create a data set containing a grand total rather than BY group totals. But you cannot use a MERGE statement to combine a grand total with the original data because there is no common variable to merge by. Luckily, there is another way. You can use two SET statements like this:

```
DATA new-data-set;
   IF _N_ = 1 THEN SET summary-data-set;
   SET original-data-set;
```

In this DATA step, *original-data-set* is the data set with more than one observation (the original data) and *summary-data-set* is the data set with a single observation (the grand total). SAS reads *original-data-set* in a normal SET statement, simply reading the observations in a straightforward way. SAS also reads *summary-data-set* with a SET statement but only in the first iteration of the DATA step (when _N_ equals 1).[1] SAS then retains the values of variables from *summary-data-set* for all observations in *new-data-set*.

This works because variables read with a SET statement are automatically retained. Normally you don't notice this because the retained values are overwritten by the next observation. But in this case the variables from *summary-data-set* are read once at the first iteration of the DATA step and then retained for all other observations. The effect is similar to a RETAIN statement (discussed in section 3.10). This technique can be used any time you want to combine a single observation with many observations, without a common variable.

**Example** To show how this is different from merging BY group summary statistics with original data, we'll use the same data as in the previous section. A distributor of athletic shoes is considering doing a special promotion for the top-selling styles. The vice-president of marketing asks you to produce a report showing the percentage of total sales for each style. For each style of shoe the raw data file contains the style name, type of exercise, and sales for the last quarter:

```
Max Flight       running 1930
Zip Fit Leather  walking 2250
Zoom Airborne    running 4150
Light Step       walking 1130
Max Step Woven   walking 2230
Zip Sneak        c-train 1190
```

---

[1] See section 6.15 for an explanation of _N_.

Here is the program:

```
DATA shoes;
   INFILE 'c:\MyRawData\Shoesales.dat';
   INPUT Style $ 1-15 ExerciseType $ Sales;
RUN;
* Output grand total of sales to a data set and print;
PROC MEANS NOPRINT DATA = shoes;
   VAR Sales;
   OUTPUT OUT = summarydata SUM(Sales) = GrandTotal;
PROC PRINT DATA = summarydata;
   TITLE 'Summary Data Set';
RUN;
* Combine the grand total with the original data;
DATA shoesummary;
   IF _N_ = 1 THEN SET summarydata;
   SET shoes;
   Percent = Sales / GrandTotal * 100;
PROC PRINT DATA = shoesummary;
   VAR Style ExerciseType Sales GrandTotal Percent;
   TITLE 'Overall Sales Share';
RUN;
```

This program starts with a DATA step to input the raw data. Then PROC MEANS creates an output data set named SUMMARYDATA with one observation containing a variable named GrandTotal, which is equal to the sum of Sales. This will be a grand total because there is no BY or CLASS statement. The second DATA step combines the original data with the grand total using two SET statements and then computes the variable Percent using the grand total data.

The output looks like this:

```
                       Summary Data Set                          1

                                        Grand
            Obs     _TYPE_     _FREQ_    Total

             1        0          6       12880



                     Overall Sales Share                         2

                        Exercise          Grand
       Obs    Style       Type     Sales  Total    Percent

        1    Max Flight    running   1930  12880    14.9845
        2    Zip Fit Leather walking 2250  12880    17.4689
        3    Zoom Airborne  running  4150  12880    32.2205
        4    Light Step     walking  1130  12880     8.7733
        5    Max Step Woven walking  2230  12880    17.3137
        6    Zip Sneak      c-train  1190  12880     9.2391
```

## 6.8  Updating a Master Data Set with Transactions

The UPDATE statement is used far less than the MERGE statement, but it is just right for those times when you have a master data set that must be updated with bits of new information. A bank account is a good example of this type of transaction-oriented data, since it is regularly updated with credits and debits.

The UPDATE statement is similar to the MERGE statement, because both combine data sets by matching observations on common variables.[1] However, there are critical differences:

♦ First, with UPDATE the resulting master data set always has just one observation for each unique value of the common variables. That way, you don't get a new observation for your bank account every time you deposit a paycheck.

♦ Second, missing values in the transaction data set do not overwrite existing values in the master data set. That way, you are not obliged to enter your address and tax ID number every time you make a withdrawal.

The basic form of the UPDATE statement is

```
DATA master-data-set;
   UPDATE master-data-set transaction-data-set;
   BY variable-list;
```

Here are a few points to remember about the UPDATE statement. You can specify only two data sets: one master and one transaction. Both data sets must be sorted by their common variables. Also, the values of those BY variables must be unique in the master data set. Using the bank example, you could have many transactions for a single account, but only one observation per account in the master data set.

**Example**  A hospital maintains a master database with information about patients. A sample appears below. Each record contains the patient's account number, last name, address, date of birth, sex, insurance code, and the date that patient's information was last updated.

```
620135 Smith    234 Aspen St.     12-21-1975 m CBC 02-16-1998
645722 Miyamoto 65 3rd Ave.       04-03-1936 f MCR 05-30-1999
645739 Jensvold 505 Glendale Ave. 06-15-1960 f HLT 09-23-2006
874329 Kazoyan  76-C La Vista         .       . MCD 01-15-2008
```

Whenever a patient is admitted to the hospital, the admissions staff check the data for that patient. They create a transaction record for every new patient and for any returning patients whose status has changed. Here are three transactions:

```
620135 .          .                  .       . HLT 06-15-2008
874329 .          .          04-24-1954 m .       06-15-2008
235777 Harman    5656 Land Way 01-18-2000 f MCD 06-15-2008
```

---

[1] The MODIFY statement is another way to update a master data set. See the SAS Help and Documentation for more information.

The first transaction is for a returning patient whose insurance has changed. The second transaction fills in missing information for a returning patient. The last transaction is for a new patient who must be added to the database.

Since master data sets are updated frequently, they are usually saved as permanent SAS data sets. To make this example more realistic, this program puts the master data into a permanent data set named PATIENTMASTER in the MySASLib directory on the C drive (Windows).

```
LIBNAME perm 'c:\MySASLib';
DATA perm.patientmaster;
   INFILE 'c:\MyRawData\Admit.dat';
   INPUT Account LastName $ 8-16 Address $ 17-34
      BirthDate MMDDYY10. Sex $ InsCode $ 48-50 @52 LastUpdate MMDDYY10.;
RUN;
```

The next program reads the transaction data and sorts them with PROC SORT. Then it adds the transactions to PATIENTMASTER with an UPDATE statement. The master data set is already sorted by Account and, therefore, doesn't need to be sorted again:

```
LIBNAME perm 'c:\MySASLib';
DATA transactions;
   INFILE 'c:\MyRawData\NewAdmit.dat';
   INPUT Account LastName $ 8-16 Address $ 17-34 BirthDate MMDDYY10.
      Sex $ InsCode $ 48-50 @52 LastUpdate MMDDYY10.;
PROC SORT DATA = transactions;
   BY Account;
RUN;
* Update patient data with transactions;
DATA perm.patientmaster;
   UPDATE perm.patientmaster transactions;
   BY Account;
PROC PRINT DATA = perm.patientmaster;
   FORMAT BirthDate LastUpdate MMDDYY10.;
   TITLE 'Admissions Data';
RUN;
```

The results of the PROC PRINT look like this:

```
                            Admissions Data                            1

                                                     Ins
      Obs Account LastName Address          BirthDate Sex Code LastUpdate

       1   235777 Harman   5656 Land Way    01/18/2000  f  MCD  06/15/2008
       2   620135 Smith    234 Aspen St.    12/21/1975  m  HLT  06/15/2008
       3   645722 Miyamoto 65 3rd Ave.      04/03/1936  f  MCR  05/30/1999
       4   645739 Jensvold 505 Glendale Ave.06/15/1960  f  HLT  09/23/2006
       5   874329 Kazoyan  76-C La Vista    04/24/1954  m  MCD  06/15/2008
```

## 6.9  Writing Multiple Data Sets Using the OUTPUT Statement

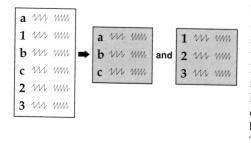

Up to this point, all the DATA steps in this book have created a single data set, except for DATA _NULL_ statements which produce no data set at all. Normally you want to make only one data set in each DATA step. However, there may be times when it is more efficient or more convenient to create multiple data sets in a single DATA step. You can do this by simply putting more than one data set name in your DATA statement. The statement below tells SAS to create three data sets named LIONS, TIGERS, and BEARS:

```
DATA lions tigers bears;
```

If that is all you do, then SAS will write all the observations to all the data sets, and you will have three identical data sets. Normally, of course, you want to create different data sets. You can do that with an OUTPUT statement.

Every DATA step has an implied OUTPUT statement at the end which tells SAS to write the current observation to the output data set before returning to the beginning of the DATA step to process the next observation. You can override this implicit OUTPUT statement with your own OUTPUT statement. The basic form of the OUTPUT statement is

```
OUTPUT data-set-name;
```

If you leave out the data set name then the observation will be written to all data sets named in the DATA statement. OUTPUT statements can be used alone or in IF-THEN or DO-loop processing.

```
IF family = 'Ursidae' THEN OUTPUT bears;
```

**Example**  A local zoo maintains a database about the feeding of the animals. A portion of the data appears below. For each group of animals the data include the scientific class, the enclosure those animals live in, and whether they get fed in the morning, afternoon, or both:

```
bears      Mammalia E2 both
elephants  Mammalia W3 am
flamingos  Aves     W1 pm
frogs      Amphibia S2 pm
kangaroos  Mammalia N4 am
lions      Mammalia W6 pm
snakes     Reptilia S1 pm
tigers     Mammalia W9 both
zebras     Mammalia W2 am
```

To help with feeding the animals, the following program creates two lists, one for morning feedings and one for afternoon feedings.

```
DATA morning afternoon;
   INFILE 'c:\MyRawData\Zoo.dat';
   INPUT Animal $ 1-9 Class $ 11-18 Enclosure $ FeedTime $;
   IF FeedTime = 'am' THEN OUTPUT morning;
      ELSE IF FeedTime = 'pm' THEN OUTPUT afternoon;
      ELSE IF FeedTime = 'both' THEN OUTPUT;
RUN;
PROC PRINT DATA = morning;
   TITLE 'Animals with Morning Feedings';
PROC PRINT DATA = afternoon;
   TITLE 'Animals with Afternoon Feedings';
RUN;
```

This DATA step creates two data sets named MORNING and AFTERNOON. Then the IF-THEN/ELSE statements tell SAS which observations to put in each data set. Because the final OUTPUT statement does not specify a data set, SAS adds those observations to both data sets. The log contains these notes saying that SAS read one input file and wrote two data sets:

```
NOTE: 9 records were read from the infile 'c:\MyRawData\Zoo.dat'.

NOTE: The data set WORK.MORNING has 5 observations and 4 variables.

NOTE: The data set WORK.AFTERNOON has 6 observations and 4 variables.
```

Here are the two reports, one for each data set:

```
                      Animals with Morning Feedings                    1


                                                        Feed
       Obs    Animal        Class        Enclosure      Time

        1     bears         Mammalia        E2          both
        2     elephants     Mammalia        W3          am
        3     kangaroos     Mammalia        N4          am
        4     tigers        Mammalia        W9          both
        5     zebras        Mammalia        W2          am

                     Animals with Afternoon Feedings                   2


                                                        Feed
       Obs    Animal        Class        Enclosure      Time

        1     bears         Mammalia        E2          both
        2     flamingos     Aves            W1          pm
        3     frogs         Amphibia        S2          pm
        4     lions         Mammalia        W6          pm
        5     snakes        Reptilia        S1          pm
        6     tigers        Mammalia        W9          both
```

OUTPUT statements have other uses besides writing multiple data sets in a single DATA step and can be used any time you want to explicitly control when SAS writes observations to a data set.

## 6.10    Making Several Observations from One Using the OUTPUT Statement

Usually SAS writes an observation to a data set at the end of the DATA step, but you can override this default using the OUTPUT statement. If you want to write several observations for each pass through the DATA step, you can put an OUTPUT statement in a DO loop or just use several OUTPUT statements. The OUTPUT statement gives you control over when an observation is written to a SAS data set. If your DATA step doesn't have an OUTPUT statement, then it is implied at the end of the step. Once you put an OUTPUT statement in your DATA step, it is no longer implied, and SAS writes an observation only when it encounters an OUTPUT statement.

**Example**  The following program demonstrates how you can use an OUTPUT statement in a DO loop to generate data. Here we have a mathematical equation ($y = x^2$) and we want to generate data points for later plotting:

```
* Create data for variables x and y;
DATA generate;
   DO x = 1 TO 6;
      y = x ** 2;
      OUTPUT;
   END;
PROC PRINT DATA = generate;
   TITLE 'Generated Data';
RUN;
```

This program has no INPUT or SET statement—so there is only one iteration of the entire DATA step—but it has a DO loop with six iterations. Because the OUTPUT statement is inside the DO loop, an observation is created each time through the loop. Without the OUTPUT statement, SAS would have written only one observation at the end of the DATA step when it reached the implied OUTPUT. The following are the results of the PROC PRINT:

```
                          Generated Data                          1

                       Obs    x     y

                        1     1     1
                        2     2     4
                        3     3     9
                        4     4    16
                        5     5    25
                        6     6    36
```

**Example** Here's how you can use OUTPUT statements to create several observations from a single pass through the DATA step. The following data are for ticket sales at three movie theaters. After the month are the theaters' names and sales for all three theaters:

```
Jan Varsity 56723 Downtown 69831 Super-6 70025
Feb Varsity 62137 Downtown 43901 Super-6 81534
Mar Varsity 49982 Downtown 55783 Super-6 69800
```

For the analysis you want to do, you need to have the theater name as one variable and the ticket sales as another variable. The month should be repeated three times, once for each theater.

The following program has three INPUT statements all reading from the same raw data file. The first INPUT statement reads values for Month, Location, and Tickets, and then holds the data line using the trailing at sign (@). The OUTPUT statement that follows writes an observation. The next INPUT statement reads the second set of data for Location and Tickets and again holds the data line. Another OUTPUT statement writes another observation. Month still has the same value because it isn't in the second INPUT statement. The last INPUT statement reads the last values for Location and Tickets, this time releasing the data line for the next iteration through the DATA step. The final OUTPUT statement writes the third observation for that iteration of the DATA step. The program has three OUTPUT statements for the three observations created in each iteration of the DATA step:

```
* Create three observations for each data line read
*    using three OUTPUT statements;
DATA theaters;
    INFILE 'c:\MyRawData\Movies.dat';
    INPUT Month $ Location $ Tickets @;
    OUTPUT;
    INPUT Location $ Tickets @;
    OUTPUT;
    INPUT Location $ Tickets;
    OUTPUT;
RUN;
PROC PRINT DATA = theaters;
    TITLE 'Ticket Sales';
RUN;
```

The following are the results of the PROC PRINT. Notice that there are three observations in the data set for each line in the raw data file and that the value for Month is repeated:

```
                       Ticket Sales                          1

        Obs    Month    Location     Tickets

         1      Jan     Varsity       56723
         2      Jan     Downtown      69831
         3      Jan     Super-6       70025
         4      Feb     Varsity       62137
         5      Feb     Downtown      43901
         6      Feb     Super-6       81534
         7      Mar     Varsity       49982
         8      Mar     Downtown      55783
         9      Mar     Super-6       69800
```

## 6.11 Using SAS Data Set Options

In this book, you have already seen a lot of options. It may help to keep them straight if you realize that the SAS language has three basic types of options: system options, statement options, and data set options. System options have the most global influence, followed by statement options, with data set options having the most limited effect.

System options are those that stay in effect for the duration of your job or session. These options affect how SAS operates, and are usually issued when you invoke SAS or via an OPTIONS statement. System options include the CENTER option, which tells SAS to center all output, and the LINESIZE= option setting the maximum line length for output.[1]

Statement options appear in individual statements and influence how SAS runs that particular DATA or PROC step. The NOPRINT option in PROC MEANS, for example, tells SAS not to produce a printed report. DATA= is a statement option that tells SAS which data set to use for a procedure. You can use DATA= in any procedure that reads a SAS data set. Without it, SAS defaults to the most recently created data set.

In contrast, data set options affect only how SAS reads or writes an individual data set. You can use data set options in DATA steps (in DATA, SET, MERGE, or UPDATE statements) or in PROC steps (in conjuction with a DATA= statement option). To use a data set option, you simply put it between parentheses directly following the data set name. These are the most frequently used data set options:

|  |  |
|---|---|
| KEEP = *variable-list* | tells SAS which variables to keep. |
| DROP = *variable-list* | tells SAS which variables to drop. |
| RENAME = (*oldvar* = *newvar*) | tells SAS to rename certain variables. |
| FIRSTOBS = *n* | tells SAS to start reading at observation *n*. |
| OBS = *n* | tells SAS to stop reading at observation *n*. |
| LABEL = '*data-set-label*' | specifies a descriptive label for a SAS data set. |
| IN = *new-var-name* | creates a temporary variable for tracking whether that data set contributed to the current observation (discussed in section 6.12). |
| WHERE = *conditon* | selects observations that meet a specified condition (discussed in section 6.13). |

**Selecting and renaming variables** Here are examples of the KEEP=, DROP=, and RENAME= data set options:

```
DATA selectedvars;
   SET animals (KEEP = Class Species Status);

PROC PRINT DATA = animals (DROP = Habitat);

DATA animals (RENAME = (Class = Type Habitat = Home));
   SET animals;
```

---

[1] Other system options are discussed in section 1.14.

```
PROC PRINT DATA = animals (RENAME =(Class = Type Habitat = Home));
```

You could probably get by without these options, but they play an important role in fine tuning SAS programs. Data sets, for example, have a way of accumulating unwanted variables. Dropping unwanted variables will make your program run faster and use less disk space. Likewise, when you read a large data set, you often need only a few variables. By using the KEEP= option, you can avoid reading a lot of variables you don't intend to use.

The DROP=, KEEP=, and RENAME= options are similar to the DROP, KEEP, and RENAME statements. However, the statements apply to all data sets named in the DATA statement while the options apply only to the particular data set whose name they follow. Also, the statements are more limited than the options since they can be used only in DATA steps, and apply only to the data set being created. In contrast, the data set options can be used in DATA or PROC steps and can apply to input or output data sets. Please note that these options do not change input data sets; they change only what is read from input data sets.

### Selecting observations by observation number
You can use the FIRSTOBS= and OBS= data set options together to tell SAS which observations to read from a data set. The options in the following statements tell SAS to read just 20 observations:

```
DATA animals;
    SET animals (FIRSTOBS = 101 OBS = 120);

PROC PRINT DATA = animals (FIRSTOBS = 101 OBS = 120);
```

If you use large data sets, you can save development time by testing your programs with a subset of your data with the FIRSTOBS= and OBS= options.

The FIRSTOBS= and OBS= data set options are similar to statement and system options with the same name. The statement options apply only to raw data files being read with an INFILE statement, whereas the data set options apply only to existing SAS data sets that you read in a DATA or PROC step. The system options apply to all files and data sets. If you use similar system and data set options, the data set option will override the system option for that particular data set.

### Labeling SAS data sets
The LABEL= option is somewhat different from other options covered here. All the other options affect your data, but not LABEL=. Instead, LABEL= adds a text string to the descriptor portion of your data set. In this example, SAS creates a data set named RARE, and gives it the label "Endangered Species Data":

```
DATA rare (LABEL = 'Endangered Species Data');
    SET animals;
    IF Status = 'Endangered';
```

The LABEL= data set option is similar to the LABEL statement used in DATA and PROC steps. However, the LABEL statement applies labels to individual variables while the LABEL= data set option applies a label to an entire data set. Using data set labels is a good habit because it helps to document your work. Data set labels are displayed in the output of PROC CONTENTS and at the top of the Viewtable window.

## 6.12 Tracking and Selecting Observations with the IN= Option

Select matching observations

OR

Select non-matching observations

When you combine two data sets, you can use IN= options to track which of the original data sets contributed to each observation in the new data set. You can think of the IN= option as a sort of tag. Instead of saying "Product of Canada," the tag says something like "Product of data set one." Once you have that information, you can use it in many ways including selecting matching or non-matching observations during a merge.

The IN= data set option can be used any time you read a SAS data set in a DATA step—with SET, MERGE, or UPDATE—but is most often used with MERGE. To use the IN= option, you simply put the option in parentheses directly following the data set you want to track, and specify a name for the IN= variable. The names of IN= variables must follow standard SAS naming conventions—start with a letter or underscore; be 32 characters or fewer in length; and contain only letters, numerals, or underscores.

The DATA step below creates a data set named BOTH by merging two data sets named STATE and COUNTY. Then the IN= options create two variables named InState and InCounty:

```
DATA both;
   MERGE state (IN = InState) county (IN = InCounty);
   BY StateName;
```

Unlike most variables, IN= variables are temporary, existing only during the current DATA step. SAS gives the IN= variables a value of 0 or 1. A value of 1 means that data set did contribute to the current observation, and a value of 0 means the data set did not contribute. Suppose the COUNTY data set above contained no data for Louisiana. (Louisiana has parishes, not counties.) In that case, the BOTH data set would contain one observation for Louisiana which would have a value of 1 for the variable InState and a value of 0 for InCounty because the STATE data set contributed to that observation, but the COUNTY data set did not.

You can use this variable like any other variable in the current DATA step, but it is most often used in subsetting IF or IF-THEN statements such as these:

```
Subsetting IF:    IF InState = 1;
                  IF InCounty = 0;
                  IF InState = 1 AND InCounty = 1;
IF-THEN:          IF InCounty = 1 THEN Origin = 1;
                  IF InState = 1 THEN State = 'Yes';
```

**Example**  A sporting goods manufacturer wants to send a sales rep to contact all customers who did not place any orders during the third quarter of the year. The company has two data files, one that contains all customers and one that contains all orders placed during the third quarter. To compile a list of customers without orders, you merge the two data sets using the IN= option, and then select customers who had no observations in the orders data set. The customer data file contains the customer number, name, and address. The orders data file contains the customer number and total price, with one observation for every order placed during the third quarter. Here are samples of the two raw data files:

| Customer data | | Orders data |
|---|---|---|
| 101 Murphy's Sports | 115 Main St. | 102 562.01 |
| 102 Sun N Ski | 2106 Newberry Ave. | 104 254.98 |
| 103 Sports Outfitters | 19 Cary Way | 104 1642.00 |
| 104 Cramer & Johnson | 4106 Arlington Blvd. | 101 3497.56 |
| 105 Sports Savers | 2708 Broadway | 102 385.30 |

Here is the program that finds customers who did not place any orders:

```
DATA customer;
    INFILE 'c:\MyRawData\CustAddress.dat' TRUNCOVER;
    INPUT CustomerNumber Name $ 5-21 Address $ 23-42;
DATA orders;
    INFILE 'c:\MyRawData\OrdersQ3.dat';
    INPUT CustomerNumber Total;
PROC SORT DATA = orders;
    BY CustomerNumber;
RUN;
* Combine the data sets using the IN= option;
DATA noorders;
    MERGE customer orders (IN = Recent);
    BY CustomerNumber;
    IF Recent = 0;
PROC PRINT DATA = noorders;
    TITLE 'Customers with No Orders in the Third Quarter';
RUN;
```

The customer data are already sorted by customer number and so do not need to be sorted with PROC SORT. The orders data, however, are in the order received and must be sorted by customer number before merging. In the final DATA step, the IN= option creates a variable named Recent, which equals 1 if the ORDERS data set contributed to that observation and 0 if it did not. Then a subsetting IF statement keeps only the observations where Recent is equal to 0—those observations with no orders data. Notice that there is no IN= option on the CUSTOMER data set. Only one IN= option was needed to identify customers who did not place any orders. Here is the list that can be given to sales reps:

```
          Customers with No Orders in the Third Quarter              1


           Customer
   Obs      Number          Name             Address          Total

    1        103       Sports Outfitters   19 Cary Way          .
    2        105       Sports Savers       2708 Broadway        .
```

The values for the variable Total are missing because these customers did not have observations in the ORDERS data set. The variable Recent does not appear in the output because, as a temporary variable, it was not added to the NOORDERS data set.

# 6.13  Selecting Observations with the WHERE= Option

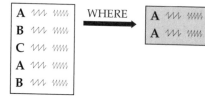

By this point, you've probably realized that with SAS programing there is usually more than one way to perform any particular task. Of all the things you can do with SAS, subsetting your data probably presents you with the most choices. The idea is simple: you have a data set, but you want to use only part of it. Maybe you have census data for all 50 states, but you want data only for Arkansas, or for males, or for households with more than 10 people. In any particular case, the best way to subset your data depends on the type of data file you have, and what you want to do after you subset the data. That's why SAS offers you so many ways to do this.

This book has already covered several ways to subset a data set. If your data are in a raw data file, then you can read part of the file using multiple INPUT statements (section 2.13). If your data are in a SAS data set, you can use a subsetting IF statement in a DATA step (section 3.7). If you are using a procedure, you can subset your data using a WHERE statement (section 4.2). WHERE statements can also be used in DATA steps (appendix D). You can use OUTPUT statements to control which observations are written to a data set (section 6.9). Even with all these ways to subset your data, there is another way worth knowing: the WHERE= data set option.

The WHERE= data set option is the most flexible of all ways to subset data. You can use it in DATA steps or PROC steps, when you read existing data sets and when you write new data sets. The basic form of a WHERE= data set option is

```
WHERE = (condition)
```

Only observations satisfying the condition will be used by SAS. The WHERE= data set option is, not surprisingly, similar to the WHERE statement, and uses the same symbolic and mnemonic operators listed in section 4.2. To use the WHERE= data set option in a DATA step, you simply put it between parentheses following the name of the data set to which it applies. If used in a SET, MERGE, or UPDATE statement, the WHERE= option will be applied to the data set that is being read. If used in a DATA statement, the WHERE= option will be applied to the data set that is being written.

```
DATA gone;
   SET animals (WHERE = (Status = 'Extinct'));

DATA uncommon (WHERE = (Status IN ('Endangered', 'Threatened')));
   SET animals;
```

The following procedures will use only observations that satisfy the WHERE= condition.

```
PROC IMPORT DATAFILE = 'c:\MyRawData\Wildlife.csv'
   OUT = animals (WHERE = (Class = 'Mammalia')) REPLACE;

PROC PRINT DATA = animals (WHERE = (Habitat='Riparian'));

PROC EXPORT DATA = animals (WHERE = (Status='Threatened'))
   OUTFILE = 'c:\MyRawData\Wildlife.xls';
```

Note that in order to use a WHERE= option with a PROC IMPORT you must know—ahead of time—the name that SAS will give your variables. See sections 2.16 and 2.17 for more information about the IMPORT procedure and sections 9.3 and 9.4 for the EXPORT procedure.

**Example** The following data contain information about the Seven Summits, the highest mountains on each continent. Each line of data includes the name of a mountain, its continent, and height in meters.

```
Kilimanjaro    Africa          5895
Vinson Massif  Antarctica      4897
Everest        Asia            8848
Elbrus         Europe          5642
McKinley       North America   6194
Aconcagua      South America   6962
Kosciuszko     Australia       2228
```

This program reads the data with an INPUT statement, and creates two data sets named TALLPEAKS and AMERICAN. The WHERE= data set options control which observations are included in each data set.

```
*Input the data and create two subsets;
DATA tallpeaks (WHERE = (Height > 6000))
     american (WHERE = (Continent CONTAINS ('America')));
   INFILE 'c:\MyRawData\Mountains.dat';
   INPUT Name $1-14 Continent $15-28 Height;
RUN;
PROC PRINT DATA = tallpeaks;
   TITLE 'Members of the Seven Summits above 6,000 Meters';
PROC PRINT DATA = american;
   TITLE 'Members of the Seven Summits in the Americas';
RUN;
```

Here are the results:

```
                 Members of the Seven Summits above 6,000 Meters              1


        Obs      Name         Continent          Height


         1       Everest      Asia                8848
         2       McKinley     North America       6194
         3       Aconcagua    South America       6962


                 Members of the Seven Summits in the Americas                 2


        Obs      Name         Continent          Height


         1       McKinley     North America       6194
         2       Aconcagua    South America       6962
```

# 6.14  Changing Observations to Variables Using PROC TRANSPOSE

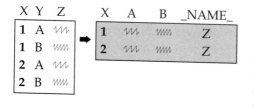

We have already seen ways to combine data sets, create new variables, and sort data. Now, using PROC TRANSPOSE, we will flip data—so get your spatulas ready.

The TRANSPOSE procedure transposes SAS data sets, turning observations into variables or variables into observations. In most cases, to convert observations into variables, you can use the following statements:

```
PROC TRANSPOSE DATA = old-data-set OUT = new-data-set;
   BY variable-list;
   ID variable;
   VAR variable-list;
```

In the PROC TRANSPOSE statement, *old-data-set* refers to the SAS data set you want to transpose, and *new-data-set* is the name of the newly transposed data set.

**BY statement**  You can use the BY statement if you have any grouping variables that you want to keep as variables. These variables are included in the transposed data set, but they are not themselves transposed. The transposed data set will have one observation for each BY level per variable transposed. For example, in the figure above, the variable X is the BY variable. The data set must be sorted by these variables before transposing.

**ID statement**  The ID statement names the variable whose formatted values will become the new variable names. The ID values must occur only once in the data set; or if a BY statement is present, then the values must be unique within BY-groups. If the ID variable is numeric, then the new variable names have an underscore for a prefix (_1 or _2, for example). If you don't use an ID statement, then the new variables will be named COL1, COL2, and so on. In the figure above, the variable Y is the ID variable. Notice how its values are the new variable's names in the transposed data set.

**VAR statement**  The VAR statement names the variables whose values you want to transpose. In the figure above, the variable Z is the VAR variable. SAS creates a new variable, _NAME_, which has as values the names of the variables in the VAR statement. If there is more than one VAR variable, then _NAME_ will have more than one value.

**Example**  Suppose you have the following data about players for minor league baseball teams. You have the team name, player's number, the type of data (salary or batting average), and the entry:

```
Garlics 10 salary 43000
Peaches  8 salary 38000
Garlics 21 salary 51000
Peaches 10 salary 47500
Garlics 10 batavg .281
Peaches  8 batavg .252
Garlics 21 batavg .265
Peaches 10 batavg .301
```

You want to look at the relationship between batting average and salary. To do this, salary and batting average must be variables. The following program reads the raw data into a SAS data set and sorts the data by team and player. Then the data are transposed using PROC TRANSPOSE.

```
DATA baseball;
    INFILE 'c:\MyRawData\Transpos.dat';
    INPUT Team $ Player Type $ Entry;
PROC SORT DATA = baseball;
    BY Team Player;
PROC PRINT DATA = baseball;
    TITLE 'Baseball Data After Sorting and Before Transposing';
RUN;
* Transpose data so salary and batavg are variables;
PROC TRANSPOSE DATA = baseball OUT = flipped;
    BY Team Player;
    ID Type;
    VAR Entry;
PROC PRINT DATA = flipped;
    TITLE 'Baseball Data After Transposing';
RUN;
```

In the PROC TRANSPOSE step, the BY variables are Team and Player. You want those variables to remain in the data set, and they define the new observations (you want only one observation for each team and player combination). The ID variable is Type, whose values (salary and batavg) will be the new variable names. The variable to be transposed, Entry, is specified in the VAR statement. Notice that its name, Entry, now appears as a value under the variable _NAME_. The TRANSPOSE procedure automatically generates the _NAME_ variable, but in this application it is not very meaningful and could be dropped.

Here are the results:

```
              Baseball Data After Sorting and Before Transposing        1

        Obs      Team      Player      Type        Entry

         1      Garlics       10       salary     43000.00
         2      Garlics       10       batavg         0.28
         3      Garlics       21       salary     51000.00
         4      Garlics       21       batavg         0.27
         5      Peaches        8       salary     38000.00
         6      Peaches        8       batavg         0.25
         7      Peaches       10       salary     47500.00
         8      Peaches       10       batavg         0.30

                   Baseball Data After Transposing                      2

        Obs      Team      Player     _NAME_      salary     batavg

         1      Garlics      10       Entry        43000      0.281
         2      Garlics      21       Entry        51000      0.265
         3      Peaches       8       Entry        38000      0.252
         4      Peaches      10       Entry        47500      0.301
```

# 6.15   Using SAS Automatic Variables

In addition to the variables you create in your SAS data set, SAS creates a few more called automatic variables. You don't ordinarily see these variables because they are temporary and are not saved with your data. But they are available in the DATA step, and you can use them just like you use any variable that you create yourself.

**_N_ and _ERROR_**   The _N_ and _ERROR_ variables are always available to you in the DATA step. _N_ indicates the number of times SAS has looped through the DATA step. This is not necessarily equal to the observation number, since a simple subsetting IF statement can change the relationship between observation number and the number of iterations of the DATA step. The _ERROR_ variable has a value of 1 if there is a data error for that observation and 0 if there isn't. Things that can cause data errors include invalid data (such as characters in a numeric field), conversion errors (like division by zero), and illegal arguments in functions (including log of zero).

**FIRST.*variable* and LAST.*variable***   Other automatic variables are available only in special circumstances. The FIRST.*variable* and LAST.*variable* automatic variables are available when you are using a BY statement in a DATA step. The FIRST.*variable* will have a value of 1 when SAS is processing an observation with the first occurrence of a new value for that variable and a value of 0 for the other observations. The LAST.*variable* will have a value of 1 for an observation with the last occurrence of a value for that variable and the value 0 for the other observations.

**Example**   Your hometown is having a walk around the town square to raise money for the library. You have the following data: entry number, age group, and finishing time. (Notice that there is more than one observation per line of data.)

```
54 youth  35.5 21 adult   21.6  6 adult   25.8 13 senior 29.0
38 senior 40.3 19 youth   39.6  3 adult   19.0 25 youth  47.3
11 adult  21.9  8 senior  54.3 41 adult   43.0 32 youth  38.6
```

The first thing you want to do is create a new variable for overall finishing place and print the results. The first part of the following program reads the raw data, and sorts the data by finishing time (Time). Then another DATA step creates the new Place variable and gives it the current value of _N_. The PRINT procedure produces the list of finishers:

```
DATA walkers;
   INFILE 'c:\MyRawData\Walk.dat';
   INPUT Entry AgeGroup $ Time @@;
PROC SORT DATA = walkers;
   BY Time;
* Create a new variable, Place;
DATA ordered;
   SET walkers;
   Place = _N_;
PROC PRINT DATA = ordered;
   TITLE 'Results of Walk';
```

```
PROC SORT DATA = ordered;
    BY AgeGroup Time;
* Keep the first observation in each age group;
DATA winners;
    SET ordered;
    BY AgeGroup;
    IF FIRST.AgeGroup = 1;
PROC PRINT DATA = winners;
    TITLE 'Winners in Each Age Group';
RUN;
```

The second part of this program produces a list of the top finishers in each age category. The ORDERED data set containing the new Place variable is sorted by AgeGroup and Time. In the DATA step, the SET statement reads the ORDERED data set. The BY statement in the DATA step generates the FIRST.AgeGroup and LAST.AgeGroup temporary variables. The subsetting IF statement, IF FIRST.AgeGroup = 1, keeps only the first observation in the BY group. Since the Winners data set is sorted by AgeGroup and Time, the first observation in each BY group is the top finisher of that group.

Here are the results of the two PRINT procedures. The first page shows the data after sorting by Time and including the new variable Place. Notice that the _N_ temporary variable does not appear in the printout. The second page shows the results of the second part of the program—the winners for each age category and their overall place:

```
                                Results of Walk                         1


                              Age
          Obs     Entry       Group       Time     Place

           1        3         adult       19.0       1
           2       21         adult       21.6       2
           3       11         adult       21.9       3
           4        6         adult       25.8       4
           5       13         senior      29.0       5
           6       54         youth       35.5       6
           7       32         youth       38.6       7
           8       19         youth       39.6       8
           9       38         senior      40.3       9
          10       41         adult       43.0      10
          11       25         youth       4₹.3      11
          12        8         senior      54.3      12


                        Winners in Each Age Group                       2
                              Age
          Obs     Entry       Group       Time     Place

           1        3         adult       19.0       1
           2       13         senior      29.0       5
           3       54         youth       35.5       6
```

**7** "Nobody is too old to learn—but a lot of people keep putting it off."

WILLIAM O'NEILL

# CHAPTER 7

# Writing Flexible Code with the SAS Macro Facility

## 7.1    Macro Concepts

Not so long ago the SAS macro facility was considered an advanced topic relevant only to experienced SAS users. Over time, however, macros have become more prevalent so that now even new SAS users would do well to know a little about the SAS macro facility. Fortunately, the basic macro concepts are not difficult to understand. This chapter introduces the most commonly used features of the SAS macro language.

Because macros take longer to write and debug than standard SAS code, you generally won't want macros in programs that will be run only a few times. But used properly, macros can make the development and maintenance of production programs much easier. They do this in several ways. First, with macros you can make one small change in your program and have SAS echo that change throughout your program. Second, macros allow you to write a piece of code once and use it over and over, in the same program or in different programs. You can even store programs in a central location—an autocall library—and share them between programs and between programmers. Third, you can make your programs data driven, letting SAS decide what to do based on actual data values.

**The macro processor**    When you submit a standard SAS program, SAS compiles and then immediately executes it. But when you write a macro, there is an additional step. Before SAS can compile and execute your program, SAS must pass your macro statements to the macro processor which "resolves" your macros, generating standard SAS code. Because you are writing a program that writes a program, this is sometimes called meta-programming.

**Macros and macro variables**    SAS macro code consists of two basic parts: macros and macro variables. The names of macro variables are prefixed with an ampersand (&) while the names of macros are prefixed with a percent sign (%).[1] A macro variable is like a standard data variable except that, having only a single value, it does not belong to a data set, and its value is always character. This value could be a variable name, a numeral, or any text that you want substituted into your program. A macro, on the other hand, is a larger piece of a program that may contain complex logic including complete DATA and PROC steps and macro statements such as %DO, %END, and %IF-%THEN/%ELSE.

When SAS users talk about "macros" they sometimes mean macros, and sometimes mean macro processing in general. Macro variables are usually called *macro variables*.

---

[1] There are exceptions. Macro names prefixed with a % are called name-style macros. Two other types of macros do not start with a %: command-style and statement-style. In general, macros starting with a prefix are superior both because they are more efficient (the macro processor recognizes them more quickly) and because they are less easily confused with SAS keywords.

Also the %INCLUDE, %LIST, and %RUN statements are NOT part of the macro facility despite their % prefix.

**Local versus global**    Macro variables can have two kinds of "scope"—either local or global. Generally, a macro variable is local if it is defined inside a macro. A macro variable is generally global if it is defined in "open code" which is everything outside a macro. You can use a global macro variable anywhere in your program, but you can use a local macro variable only inside its own macro. [2] If you keep this in mind as you write your programs, you will avoid two common errors: trying to use a local macro variable outside its macro and accidentally creating local and global macro variables with the same name.

**Turning on the macro processor**    Before you can use macros you must have the MACRO system option turned on. This option is usually turned on by default, but may be turned off, especially on mainframes, because SAS runs slightly faster when it doesn't have to bother with checking for macros. If you are not sure whether the MACRO option is on, you can find out by submitting these statements:

```
PROC OPTIONS OPTION = MACRO;
RUN;
```

Check your SAS log. If you see the option MACRO, then the macro processor is turned on, and you can use it. If you see NOMACRO there, you need to specify the MACRO option at invocation or in a configuration file. Specifying this type of option is system dependent. For details about how to do this, see the SAS Help and Documentation for your operating environment.

**Avoiding macro errors**    There's no question about it, macros can make your head hurt. You can avoid the macro migraine by developing your program in a piecewise fashion. First, write your program in standard SAS code. Then, when it's bug-free, convert it to macro logic adding one feature at a time. This modular approach to programming is always a good idea, but it's critical with macros.

---

[2] There are ways to force a local macro variable to become global and vice versa. See the SAS Help and Documentation for the SAS Macro Language if you need to change the scope of your macro variables.

## 7.2    Substituting Text with Macro Variables

Macro variables may be the most straightforward and easy-to-use part of the macro facility, yet if you master only this one feature of macro programming you will have greatly increased your flexibility as a SAS programmer. Suppose you have a SAS program that you run once a week. Each time you run it you have to edit the program so it will select data for the correct range of dates and print the correct dates in the title. This process is time-consuming and prone to errors. (What if you accidentally delete a semicolon?!) Instead, you can use a macro variable to insert the correct date. Then you can have another cup of coffee while someone else, someone who knows very little about SAS, runs this program for you.

When SAS encounters the name of a macro variable, the macro processor simply replaces the name with the value of that macro variable. That value is a character constant that you specify.

**Creating a macro variable with %LET**   The simplest way to assign a value to a macro variable is with the %LET statement. The general form of this statement is

```
%LET macro-variable-name = value;
```

where *macro-variable-name* must follow the rules for SAS variable names (32 characters or fewer in length; start with a letter or underscore; and contain only letters, numerals, and underscores). *Value* is the text to be substituted for the macro variable name, and can be longer than you are ever likely to need—almost 64,000 characters long. The following statements each create a macro variable.

```
%LET iterations = 10;

%LET country = New Zealand;
```

Notice that unlike an ordinary assignment statement, *value* does not require quotation marks even when it contains characters. Except for blanks at the beginning and end, which are trimmed, everything between the equals sign and the semicolon becomes part of the value for that macro variable.

**Using a macro variable**   To use a macro variable you simply add the ampersand prefix (&) and stick the macro variable name wherever you want its value to be substituted. Keep in mind that the macro processor doesn't look for macros inside *single* quotation marks. To get around this, simply use double quotation marks. The following statements show possible ways to use the macro variables defined above.

```
DO i = 1 to &iterations;

TITLE "Addresses in &country";
```

After being resolved by the macro processor, these statements would become

```
DO i = 1 to 10;

TITLE "Addresses in New Zealand";
```

**Example**  A grower of tropical flowers records information about each sale in a raw data file. The data include customer ID, date of sale, variety of flower, and quantity.

```
240W 02-07-2008 Ginger     120
240W 02-07-2008 Protea     180
356W 02-08-2008 Heliconia   60
356W 02-08-2008 Anthurium 300
188R 02-11-2008 Ginger      24
188R 02-11-2008 Anthurium   24
240W 02-12-2008 Heliconia   48
240W 02-12-2008 Protea       48
356W 02-12-2008 Ginger     240
```

Periodically, the grower needs a report about sales of a single variety. The macro variable in this program allows the grower to choose one variety without editing the DATA or PROC step. Instead, he just types the name of the variety once, in the %LET statement.

```
%LET flowertype = Ginger;

* Read the data and subset with a macro variable;
DATA flowersales;
    INFILE 'c:\MyRawData\TropicalSales.dat';
    INPUT CustomerID $4. @6 SaleDate MMDDYY10. @17 Variety $9. Quantity;
    IF Variety = "&flowertype";
RUN;
* Print the report using a macro variable;
PROC PRINT DATA = flowersales;
    FORMAT SaleDate WORDDATE18.;
    TITLE "Sales of &flowertype";
RUN;
```

The program starts with a %LET statement that creates a macro variable named &FLOWERTYPE, assigning to it a value of Ginger. Because the variable &FLOWERTYPE is defined outside a macro, it is a global macro variable and can be used anywhere in this program. In this case, the value Ginger is substituted for &FLOWERTYPE in a subsetting IF statement and a TITLE statement. Here are the results:

```
                        Sales of Ginger                         1

              Customer
    Obs          ID            SaleDate      Variety    Quantity

     1          240W      February 7, 2008   Ginger        120
     2          188R      February 11, 2008  Ginger         24
     3          356W      February 12, 2008  Ginger        240
```

This is a short program, so using a macro variable didn't save much trouble. However, if you had a program 100 or even 1,000 lines long, a macro variable could be a blessing.

## 7.3  Creating Modular Code with Macros

Anytime you find yourself writing the same or similar SAS statements over and over, you should consider using a macro. A macro lets you package a piece of bug-free code and use it repeatedly within a single SAS program or in many SAS programs.

You can think of a macro as a kind of sandwich. The %MACRO and %MEND statements are like two slices of bread. Between those slices you can put any statements you want. The general form of a macro is

```
%MACRO macro-name;
   macro-text
%MEND macro-name;
```

The %MACRO statement tells SAS that this is the beginning of a macro, while %MEND marks the end. *Macro-name* is a name you make up, and can be up to 32 characters in length, start with a letter or underscore, and contain only letters, numerals, and underscores. The *macro-name* in the MEND statement is optional, but your macros will be easier to debug and maintain if you include it. That way there's no question which %MACRO statement goes with which %MEND. *Macro-text* (also called a macro definition) is a set of SAS statements.

**Invoking a macro**  After you have defined a macro you can invoke it by adding the percent sign prefix to its name like this:

```
%macro-name
```

A semicolon is not required when invoking a macro, though adding one generally does no harm.

**Example**  Using the data from the previous section, this example creates a simple macro. The data include customer ID, date of sale, variety of flower, and quantity.

```
240W 02-07-2008 Ginger     120
240W 02-07-2008 Protea     180
356W 02-08-2008 Heliconia   60
356W 02-08-2008 Anthurium  300
188R 02-11-2008 Ginger      24
188R 02-11-2008 Anthurium   24
240W 02-12-2008 Heliconia   48
240W 02-12-2008 Protea      48
356W 02-12-2008 Ginger     240
```

The following program creates a macro named %SAMPLE to sort the data by Quantity and print the five observations with the largest sales. Then the program reads the data in a standard DATA step, and invokes the macro.

```
* Macro to print 5 largest sales;
%MACRO sample;
   PROC SORT DATA = flowersales;
      BY DESCENDING Quantity;
   RUN;
   PROC PRINT DATA = flowersales (OBS = 5);
      FORMAT SaleDate WORDDATE18.;
      TITLE 'Five Largest Sales';
   RUN;
%MEND sample;

* Read the flower sales data;
DATA flowersales;
   INFILE 'c:\MyRawData\TropicalSales.dat';
   INPUT CustomerID $4. @6 SaleDate MMDDYY10. @17 Variety $9. Quantity;
RUN;

* Invoke the macro;
%sample
```

Here is the output:

```
                        Five Largest Sales                    1

              Customer
    Obs          ID              SaleDate      Variety      Quantity

     1          356W        February 8, 2008   Anthurium      300
     2          356W        February 12, 2008  Ginger         240
     3          240W        February 7, 2008   Protea         180
     4          240W        February 7, 2008   Ginger         120
     5          356W        February 8, 2008   Heliconia       60
```

This macro is fairly limited because it does the same thing every time. To increase the flexibility of macros, combine them with %LET statements or add parameters as described in the next section.

**Macro autocall libraries** The macros in this book are defined and invoked inside a single program, but you can also store macros in a central location, called an autocall library. Macros in a library can be shared by programs and programmers. Basically you save your macros as files in a directory or as members of a partitioned data set (depending on your operating environment), and use the MAUTOSOURCE and SASAUTOS= system options to tell SAS where to look for macros. Then you can invoke a macro even though the original macro does not appear in your program. For more information see the SAS Help and Documentation.

## 7.4    Adding Parameters to Macros

Macros can save you a lot of trouble, allowing you to write a set of statements once and then use them over and over. However, you usually don't want to repeat exactly the same statements. You may want the same report, but for a different data set, or product, or patient. Parameters allow you to do this.

Parameters are macro variables whose value you set when you invoke a macro. The simplest macros, like the macro in the previous section, have no parameters. To add parameters to a macro, you simply list the macro-variable names between parentheses in the %MACRO statement. Here is one of the possible forms of the parameter-list.

```
%MACRO macro-name (parameter-1= ,parameter-2= , . . . parameter-n=);
   macro-text
%MEND macro-name;
```

For example, a macro named %QUARTERLYREPORT might start like this:

```
%MACRO quarterlyreport(quarter=,salesrep=);
```

This macro has two parameters: &QUARTER and &SALESREP. You could invoke the macro with this statement:

```
%quarterlyreport(quarter=3,salesrep=Smith)
```

The SAS macro processor would replace each occurrence of the macro variable &QUARTER with the value 3, and would substitute Smith for &SALESREP.

**Example**   Using the tropical flower data again, suppose the grower often needs a report showing sales to an individual customer. The following program defines a macro that lets the grower select sales for a single customer and then sort the results. As before, the data contain the customer ID, date of sale, variety of flower, and quantity.

```
240W 02-07-2008 Ginger    120
240W 02-07-2008 Protea    180
356W 02-08-2008 Heliconia  60
356W 02-08-2008 Anthurium 300
188R 02-11-2008 Ginger     24
188R 02-11-2008 Anthurium  24
240W 02-12-2008 Heliconia  48
240W 02-12-2008 Protea     48
356W 02-12-2008 Ginger    240
```

The following program defines a macro named %SELECT and then invokes the macro twice. This macro sorts and prints the FlowerSales data, using parameters to create two macro variables named &CUSTOMER and &SORTVAR.

```
* Macro with parameters;
%MACRO select(customer=,sortvar=);
    PROC SORT DATA = flowersales OUT = salesout;
        BY &sortvar;
        WHERE CustomerID = "&customer";
    RUN;
    PROC PRINT DATA = salesout;
        FORMAT SaleDate WORDDATE18.;
        TITLE1 "Orders for Customer Number &customer";
        TITLE2 "Sorted by &sortvar";
    RUN;
%MEND select;

* Read all the flower sales data;
DATA flowersales;
    INFILE 'c:\MyRawData\TropicalSales.dat';
    INPUT CustomerID $4. @6 SaleDate MMDDYY10. @17 Variety $9. Quantity;
RUN;

*Invoke the macro;
%select(customer = 356W, sortvar = Quantity)
%select(customer = 240W, sortvar = Variety)
```

Here is the output:

```
                    Orders for Customer Number 356W                    1
                         Sorted by Quantity


            Customer
     Obs      ID            SaleDate      Variety      Quantity

      1      356W       February 8, 2008  Heliconia       60
      2      356W       February 12, 2008 Ginger         240
      3      356W       February 8, 2008  Anthurium      300

                    Orders for Customer Number 240W                    2
                         Sorted by Variety


            Customer
     Obs      ID            SaleDate      Variety      Quantity

      1      240W       February 7, 2008  Ginger         120
      2      240W       February 12, 2008 Heliconia       48
      3      240W       February 7, 2008  Protea         180
      4      240W       February 12, 2008 Protea          48
```

# 7.5   Writing Macros with Conditional Logic

Combining macros and macro variables gives you a lot of flexibility, but you can increase that flexibility even more by adding macro statements such as %IF. Fortunately, many macro statements have parallel statements in standard SAS code so they should feel familiar. Here are the general forms of the statements used for conditional logic in macros:

```
%IF condition %THEN action;
   %ELSE %IF condition %THEN action;
   %ELSE action;

%IF condition %THEN %DO;
   SAS statements
%END;
```

These macro statements can be used only inside a macro.

You may be wondering why anyone needs these statements. Why not just use the standard IF-THEN? You may indeed use standard IF-THEN statements in your macros, but you will use them for different actions. %IF statements can contain actions that standard IF statements can't contain, such as complete DATA or PROC steps and even other macro statements. The %IF-%THEN statements don't appear in the standard SAS code generated by your macro. Remember you are writing a program that writes a program.

**Automatic macro variables** . Every time you invoke SAS, the macro processor automatically creates certain macro variables. You can use these variables in your programs. The most common automatic macro variables are

| Variable name | Example | Description |
|---|---|---|
| &SYSDATE | 28MAY08 | the character value of the date that job or session began |
| &SYSDAY | Wednesday | the day of the week that job or session began |

For example, you could combine conditional logic and an automatic variable like this:

```
%IF &SYSDAY = Tuesday %THEN %LET country = Belgium;
   %ELSE %LET country = France;
```

**Example** Using the tropical flower data again, this example shows a macro with conditional logic. The grower wants to print one report on Monday and a different report on Tuesday. You can write one program that will run either report. The raw data contain the customer ID, date of sale, variety of flower, and quantity.

```
240W 02-07-2008 Ginger     120
240W 02-07-2008 Protea     180
356W 02-08-2008 Heliconia   60
356W 02-08-2008 Anthurium  300
188R 02-11-2008 Ginger      24
188R 02-11-2008 Anthurium   24
240W 02-12-2008 Heliconia   48
240W 02-12-2008 Protea      48
356W 02-12-2008 Ginger     240
```

Here is the program:

```
%MACRO dailyreports;
   %IF &SYSDAY = Monday %THEN %DO;
      PROC PRINT DATA = flowersales;
         FORMAT SaleDate WORDDATE18.;
         TITLE 'Monday Report: Current Flower Sales';
      RUN;
   %END;
   %ELSE %IF &SYSDAY = Tuesday %THEN %DO;
      PROC MEANS DATA = flowersales MEAN MIN MAX;
         CLASS Variety;
         VAR Quantity;
         TITLE 'Tuesday Report: Summary of Flower Sales';
      RUN;
   %END;
%MEND dailyreports;

DATA flowersales;
   INFILE 'c:\MyRawData\TropicalSales.dat';
   INPUT CustomerID $4. @6 SaleDate MMDDYY10. @17 Variety $9. Quantity;
RUN;

%dailyreports
```

When the program is submitted on Tuesday, the macro processor will write this program:

```
DATA flowersales;
   INFILE 'c:\MyRawData\TropicalSales.dat';
   INPUT CustomerID $ @6 SaleDate MMDDYY10. @17 Variety $9. Quantity;
RUN;

PROC MEANS DATA = flowersales MEAN MIN MAX;
   CLASS Variety;
   VAR Quantity;
   TITLE 'Tuesday Report: Summary of Flower Sales';
RUN;
```

If you run this program on Tuesday the output will look like this:

```
            Tuesday Report: Summary of Flower Sales            1

                        The MEANS Procedure
                     Analysis Variable : Quantity

                        N
         Variety       Obs        Mean       Minimum       Maximum
        ─────────────────────────────────────────────────────────
         Anthurium      2     162.0000000    24.0000000   300.0000000
         Ginger         3     128.0000000    24.0000000   240.0000000
         Heliconia      2      54.0000000    48.0000000    60.0000000
         Protea         2     114.0000000    48.0000000   180.0000000
        ─────────────────────────────────────────────────────────
```

## 7.6  Writing Data-Driven Programs with CALL SYMPUT

When you submit a SAS program containing macros it goes first to the macro processor which generates standard SAS code from the macro references. Then SAS compiles and executes your program. Not until execution—the final stage—does SAS see any actual data values. This is the tricky part of writing data-driven programs: SAS doesn't know the values of your data until the execution phase, and by that time it is ordinarily too late. However, there is a way to have your digital cake and eat it too—CALL SYMPUT.

CALL SYMPUT takes a value from a DATA step and assigns it to a macro variable. You can then use this macro variable in later steps. To assign a value to a single macro variable, you use CALL SYMPUT with this general form:

```
CALL SYMPUT("macro-variable-name",value);
```

where *macro-variable-name*, enclosed in quotation marks, is the name of a macro variable, either new or old, and *value* is the value you want to assign to that macro variable. *Value* can be the name of a variable whose value SAS will use, or it can be a constant value enclosed in quotation marks.

CALL SYMPUT is often used in IF-THEN statements such as this:

```
IF Age >= 18 THEN CALL SYMPUT("status", "Adult");
   ELSE CALL SYMPUT("status", "Minor");
```

These statements create a macro variable named &STATUS and assign to it a value of either Adult or Minor depending on the variable Age. The following CALL SYMPUT uses a variable as its *value*:

```
IF TotalSales > 1000000 THEN CALL SYMPUT("bestseller", BookTitle);
```

This statement tells SAS to create a macro variable named &BESTSELLER which is equal to the value of the variable BookTitle when TotalSales exceed 1,000,000.

**Caution**  You cannot create a macro variable with CALL SYMPUT and use it in the same DATA step because SAS does not assign a value to the macro variable until the DATA step executes. DATA steps execute when SAS encounters a step boundary such as a subsequent DATA, PROC, or RUN statement.

**Example**  Here are the flower sales data consisting of customer ID, date of sale, variety of flower, and quantity.

```
240W 02-07-2008 Ginger     120
240W 02-07-2008 Protea     180
356W 02-08-2008 Heliconia   60
356W 02-08-2008 Anthurium  300
188R 02-11-2008 Ginger      24
188R 02-11-2008 Anthurium   24
240W 02-12-2008 Heliconia   48
240W 02-12-2008 Protea      48
356W 02-12-2008 Ginger     240
```

In this example, the grower wants a program that will find the customer with the single largest order, and print all the orders for that customer.

```
* Read the raw data;
DATA flowersales;
    INFILE 'c:\MySASLib\TropicalSales.dat';
    INPUT CustomerID $4. @6 SaleDate MMDDYY10. @17 Variety $9. Quantity;
PROC SORT DATA = flowersales;
    BY DESCENDING Quantity;
RUN;
* Find biggest order and pass the customer id to a macro variable;
DATA _NULL_;
    SET flowersales;
    IF _N_ = 1 THEN CALL SYMPUT("selectedcustomer",CustomerID);
    ELSE STOP;
RUN;
PROC PRINT DATA = flowersales;
    WHERE CustomerID = "&selectedcustomer";
    FORMAT SaleDate WORDDATE18.;
    TITLE "Customer &selectedcustomer Had the Single Largest Order";
RUN;
```

This program has a lot of steps, but each step is fairly simple. The first DATA step reads the data from the raw data file. Then PROC SORT sorts the data by descending Quantity. That way, the largest single order will be the first observation in the newly sorted data set.

The second DATA step then uses CALL SYMPUT to assign the value of the variable CustomerID to the macro variable &SELECTEDCUSTOMER when _N_ equals 1 (the first iteration of the DATA step). Since that is all we need from this DATA step, we can use the STOP statement to tell SAS to end this DATA step. The STOP statement is not necessary, but it is efficient because it prevents SAS from reading the remaining observations for no reason.

When SAS reaches the RUN statement, SAS knows that the DATA step has ended so SAS executes the DATA step. At this point the macro variable &SELECTEDCUSTOMER has the value 356W (the customer ID with the largest single order) and can be used in the PROC PRINT. The output looks like this:

```
         Customer 356W Had the Single Largest Order                1

              Customer
    Obs         ID                SaleDate    Variety      Quantity

     1          356W          February 8, 2008   Anthurium       300
     2          356W          February 12, 2008  Ginger          240
     5          356W          February 8, 2008   Heliconia        60
```

For more information on CALL routines, see the SAS Help and Documentation.

## 7.7  Debugging Macro Errors

Many people find that writing macros is not that hard. Debugging them, however, is another matter. This section covers techniques to ease the debugging process.

**Avoiding macro errors**  As much as possible, develop your program in standard SAS code first. Then, when it is bug-free, add the macro logic one feature at a time. Add your %MACRO and %MEND statements. When that's working, add your macro variables, one at a time, and so on, until your macro is complete and bug-free.

**Quoting problems**  The macro processor doesn't resolve macros inside single quotation marks. To get around this, use double quotation marks whenever you refer to a macro or macro variable and you want SAS to resolve it. For example, below are two TITLE statements containing a macro variable named &MONTH. If the value of &MONTH is January, then SAS will substitute January in the title with the double quotation marks, but not the title with single quotation marks.

| Original statement | Statement after resolution |
|---|---|
| TITLE 'Report for &month'; | TITLE 'Report for &month'; |
| TITLE "Report for &month"; | TITLE "Report for January"; |

**System options for debugging macros**  These five system options affect the kinds of messages SAS writes in your log. The default settings appear in bold.

| | |
|---|---|
| **MERROR** \| NOMERROR | when this option is on, SAS will issue a warning if you invoke a macro that SAS cannot find. |
| **SERROR** \| NOSERROR | when this option is on, SAS will issue a warning if you use a macro variable that SAS cannot find. |
| MLOGIC \| **NOMLOGIC** | when this option is on, SAS prints in your log details about the execution of macros. |
| MPRINT \| **NOMPRINT** | when this option is on, SAS prints in your log the standard SAS code generated by macros. |
| SYMBOLGEN \| **NOSYMBOLGEN** | when this option is on, SAS prints in your log the values of macro variables. |

While you want the MERROR and SERROR options to be on at all times, you will probably want to turn on MLOGIC, MPRINT, and SYMBOLGEN one at a time and only while you are debugging since they tend to make your log hard to read. To turn them on (or off), use the OPTIONS statement, for example:

```
OPTIONS MPRINT NOSYMBOLGEN NOMLOGIC;
```

**MERROR message**   If SAS has trouble finding a macro, and the MERROR option is on, then SAS will print this message:

```
WARNING: Apparent invocation of macro SAMPL not resolved.
```

Check for a misspelled macro name.

**SERROR message**   If SAS has trouble resolving a macro variable in open code, and the SERROR option is on, then SAS will print this message:

```
WARNING: Apparent symbolic reference FLOWER not resolved.
```

Check for a misspelled macro variable name. If the name is spelled right, then the scope may be wrong. Check to see if you are using a local variable outside of its macro. See section 7.1 for definitions of local and global macro variables.

**MLOGIC messages**   When the MLOGIC option is on, SAS prints messages in your log describing the actions of the macro processor. Here is a macro named %SAMPLE:

```
%MACRO sample(flowertype=);
    PROC PRINT DATA = flowersales;
       WHERE Variety = "&flowertype";
    RUN;
%MEND sample;
```

If you run %SAMPLE with the MLOGIC option, your log will look like this:

```
24    OPTIONS MLOGIC;
25    %sample(flowertype=Anthurium)
MLOGIC(SAMPLE):  Beginning execution.
MLOGIC(SAMPLE):  Parameter FLOWERTYPE has value Anthurium
MLOGIC(SAMPLE):  Ending execution.
```

**MPRINT messages**   When the MPRINT option is on, SAS prints messages in your log showing the SAS statements generated by your macro. If you run %SAMPLE with the MPRINT option, your log will look like this:

```
36    OPTIONS MPRINT;
37    %sample(flowertype=Anthurium)
MPRINT(SAMPLE):   PROC PRINT DATA = flowersales;
MPRINT(SAMPLE):   WHERE Variety = "Anthurium";
MPRINT(SAMPLE):   RUN;
```

**SYMBOLGEN messages**   When the SYMBOLGEN option is on, SAS prints messages in your log showing the value of each macro variable after resolution. If you run %SAMPLE with the SYMBOLGEN option, your log will look like this:

```
30    OPTIONS SYMBOLGEN;
31    %sample(flowertype=Anthurium)
SYMBOLGEN:  Macro variable FLOWERTYPE resolves to Anthurium
```

# 8

"33⅓% of the mice used in the experiment were cured by the test drug; 33⅓% of the test population were unaffected by the drug and remained in a moribund condition; the third mouse got away."

ERWIN NETER

From "How to Write a Scientific Paper" by Robert A. Day, ASM News, vol. 41, no. 7, pp 486-494, July 1975. Reprinted by permission of publisher and author. Also appears in *How to Write and Publish a Scientific Paper* 4th edition by Robert A. Day, copyright 1994 by Oryx Press.

# CHAPTER 8

# Using Basic Graphical and Statistical Procedures

# 8.1 ► Concepts of ODS Graphics

ODS Graphics, which is new with SAS 9.2, is designed to give you high-quality graphs with a minimum of effort. ODS Graphics is an extension of the Output Delivery System.[1] Instead of creating tabular output, ODS Graphics creates graphs, and it produces them using the same destinations and styles as ODS tabular output.

To use ODS Graphics you must have SAS/GRAPH software which is licensed separately from Base SAS, but there are some differences between the graphs produced by ODS Graphics and graphs produced by traditional SAS/GRAPH procedures. Traditional graphs are saved in SAS graphics catalogs, viewed in the Graph window, and controlled by GOPTIONS statements. ODS Graphics, on the other hand, produces graphs in standard image file formats (such as PNG and JPEG), displays graphs using standard viewers (such as a Web browser for HTML output), and uses ODS styles to control the appearance of graphs. Graphs produced using ODS Graphics can be edited with the ODS Graphics Editor (see the SAS Help and Documentation for more information).

**Using ODS Graphics in statistical procedures**   In SAS 9.2 over 60 statistical procedures have the ability to produce graphs using ODS Graphics. Included are procedures from Base SAS, SAS/STAT, SAS/ETS, and SAS/QC. To turn on this feature, include this statement before your statistical procedure statements:

```
ODS GRAPHICS ON;
```

Statistical procedures that support ODS Graphics then create graphs that are appropriate for their analyses, either by default or when you specify procedure options to request specific graphs. ODS Graphics will remain in effect for all procedures that follow. You do not need to turn it off, but if you wish to turn it off (to save resources, for example) use this statement:

```
ODS GRAPHICS OFF;
```

**Using ODS Graphics for stand-alone graphs**   ODS Graphics includes a new family of procedures designed to create stand-alone graphs (graphs that are not embedded in the output of a statistical procedure). The SGPLOT procedure is one of these. PROC SGPLOT produces a wide variety of graphs ranging from simple bar charts to scatter plots overlaid with loess curves. The next five sections cover PROC SGPLOT in more detail.

Because these procedures always produce graphs, you do not need to specify the ODS GRAPHICS ON statement. However, you may still want to use this statement so that you can specify graphics options.

**ODS destinations**   Using standard ODS statements, you can send graphical output to ODS destinations. For most destinations (including RTF and PDF), graphs will be integrated with tabular output into a single file. The LISTING and HTML destinations, however, are different. When you use the LISTING destination, graphs are saved in individual files separate from tabular output. When you use the HTML destination, graphs are saved in individual files, but then linked to tabular output so they appear integrated when viewed in a Web browser.

**Styles for graphical output**   ODS style templates control the overall appearance of your output. You can use the same style templates for graphs as you use for tabular output. However, some styles are better suited to statistical graphics than others. The following table lists styles that are recommended for statistical results.

---

[1] See section 5.1 for a more general discussion of the Output Delivery System.

| Desired Output | Style Name | Default for Destination |
| --- | --- | --- |
| Color | ANALYSIS | |
| | DEFAULT | HTML |
| | LISTING | LISTING (graphs only) |
| | PRINTER | PRINTER, PDF, PS |
| | RTF | RTF |
| | STATISTICAL | |
| Gray scale | JOURNAL | |
| Black and white | JOURNAL2 | |

You can specify a style for your graphs using the STYLE= option in the ODS statement for a destination. For example, to produce gray-scale graphics in the LISTING destination you would use this statement:

```
ODS LISTING STYLE = JOURNAL;
```

For the LISTING destination, the STYLE= option applies only to graphical output; tabular output is still rendered as text. Also keep in mind that every destination has a default style associated with it, so if you change the destination for a graph, its appearance may change too.

## Viewing ODS Graphics

When you produce ODS Graphics in the SAS windowing environment, the Results Viewer window generally opens displaying your results. However, when you use the LISTING destination, graphs are not automatically displayed. You can view your graphs by double-clicking their graph icons in the Results window.

### Accessing individual graphs

If you are writing a paper or creating a presentation, you may need to access individual graphs. For the HTML, PDF, and RTF destinations in the Windows operating environment, you can copy and paste images when you view them in SAS.

If you are using a destination—such as PDF or RTF—where images and tabular output are saved together in the same file, you can use the FILE= option to tell SAS where to save your output.[2] This statement would create PDF output and save it in a file named Report.pdf in a folder named MyPDFFiles on the C drive (Windows):

```
ODS PDF FILE = 'c:\MyPDFFiles\Report.pdf';
```

For the LISTING and HTML destinations, the FILE= option will apply to tabular output only—not images.[3] For these two destinations, you can use the GPATH= option to tell SAS where to save the individual graphics image files. This statement would save all ODS Graphics images in a folder named MyGraphics on the C drive (Windows):

```
ODS LISTING GPATH = 'c:\MyGraphics';
```

You can use the IMAGEFMT= option to control the format of your images. LISTING is the best destination for this since it offers the most file types and saves images in separate files. Image file types supported for LISTING include PNG (the default), BMP, GIF, JPEG, PS, and many others. To create a graph in JPEG format you would use this statement:

```
ODS GRAPHICS ON / IMAGEFMT = JPEG;
```

---

[2] By default, ODS output, including graphics, is saved in the current SAS working directory. If you are using the SAS windowing environment, the path of your current working directory appears in the lower right corner of the SAS window.

[3] If you specify the FILE= option for the LISTING destination, tabular output will be saved in a text file, and images will be saved in separate files, but no output will appear in either the Output window or the Results window.

## 8.2  Creating Bar Charts with PROC SGPLOT

The SGPLOT procedure creates an impressive array of graphs: bar charts, histograms, box plots, series plots, step plots, needle plots, and scatter plots with or without ellipses or regression curves and confidence limits. The SGPLOT procedure produces individual graphs, but you can overlay multiple graphs of the same or different type as long as combining them makes sense.[1] Additional statements and options allow you to control the axes and legends, and add reference lines. The ODS GRAPHICS ON statement is not required when you use PROC SGPLOT. However, you may want to use that statement so you can specify options on it.

The basic form of PROC SGPLOT for a bar chart with vertical bars is

```
PROC SGPLOT;
   VBAR variable-name / options;
```

For horizontal bars, specify the keyword HBAR instead of VBAR. Possible options include

| | |
|---|---|
| RESPONSE = *variable-name* | specifies a numeric variable to be summarized. |
| STAT = *statistic* | specifies a statistic, either FREQ, MEAN, or SUM. FREQ is the default if there is no response variable. SUM is the default when you specify a response variable. |
| GROUP = *variable-name* | specifies a variable used to group the data in a stacked bar chart. |
| BARWIDTH = *n* | sets the width of bars. Values range from 0.1 to 1 with a default of 0.8. |
| TRANSPARENCY = *n* | sets the transparency of graph features such as bars, lines, or markers. Values range from 0 to 1 with a default of 0. |

When you overlay graphs, the order of statements is important because the second graph may hide parts of the first. To make both graphs visible at the same time, you may need to use the TRANSPARENCY= option on the second graph. With bar charts, you can also solve this problem by making the second set of bars narrower than the first set of bars using the BARWIDTH= option.

You can specify options for axes using the XAXIS and YAXIS statements (discussed section 8.4), and you can add horizontal or vertical reference lines to charts using the REFLINE statement (see section 8.5).

**Example**  A chocolate manufacturer is considering whether to add four new varieties of chocolate (80% cacao, Earl Grey, ginger, and pear) to its line of products. The company asked 12 adults and 12 children to taste the new flavors and choose a favorite. Each person also rated the uniqueness of that favorite flavor (from 1 for not unique to 5 for very unique). The data contain each person's age group, followed by their favorite flavor, and its uniqueness score. Notice that each line of data contains six responses.

```
A Pear 4 A 80%Cacao 1 A EarlGrey 4 C 80%Cacao 2 A Ginger 5 C Pear 5
C 80%Cacao 3 C Pear 2 C Pear 2 A EarlGrey 3 A 80%Cacao 1 C 80%Cacao 2
A Ginger 5 A Pear 3 C EarlGrey 3 C 80%Cacao 1 A 80%Cacao 2 A EarlGrey 5
A 80%Cacao 2 C Pear 1 C Pear 3 A 80%Cacao 2 C Pear 3 C 80%Cacao 3
```

---

[1] To produce graphs that are side-by-side or in a grid, use the SGSCATTER or SGPANEL procedures.

The DATA step below reads the raw data from a file called Choc.dat. Then two PROC SGPLOTs graph the data. The first SGPLOT procedure requests a vertical bar chart for the variable FavoriteFlavor grouped by the variable AgeGroup. The second SGPLOT procedure requests a bar chart using the variable Uniqueness in the RESPONSE= option. The statistic for Uniqueness is set to MEAN.

```
DATA chocolate;
    INFILE 'c:\MyRawData\Choc.dat';
    INPUT AgeGroup $ FavoriteFlavor $ Uniqueness @@;
RUN;

* Bar charts for favorite flavor;
PROC SGPLOT DATA = chocolate;
   VBAR FavoriteFlavor / GROUP = AgeGroup;
   LABEL FavoriteFlavor = 'Flavor of Chocolate';
   TITLE 'Favorite Chocolate Flavors by Age Group';
RUN;

PROC SGPLOT DATA = chocolate;
   VBAR FavoriteFlavor / RESPONSE = Uniqueness STAT = MEAN;
   LABEL FavoriteFlavor = 'Flavor of Chocolate';
   TITLE 'Uniqueness Ratings for Chocolate Flavors';
RUN;
```

Because no destination was specified, the charts will be sent to the default destination, LISTING, and saved as PNG files. To view these charts, double-click their icons in the Results window.

Here are the results:

## 8.3 ▶ Creating Histograms and Box Plots with PROC SGPLOT

The bar charts in the preceding section are designed to show the distribution of categorical data. For continuous data, PROC SGPLOT offers two kinds of distribution plots: histograms and box-and-whisker plots.

**Histograms**   The basic form of PROC SGPLOT for a histogram is

```
PROC SGPLOT;
   HISTOGRAM variable-name / options;
```

Options you may want to use include

SCALE=*scaling-type*         specifies the scale for the vertical axis, either PERCENT (the default), COUNT, or PROPORTION.

SHOWBINS                          places tick marks at the midpoints of the bins. By default, tick marks are placed at regular intervals based on minimum and maximum values.

You can overlay a density curve on a histogram using the DENSITY statement. The basic form of a DENSITY statement is

```
PROC SGPLOT;
   DENSITY variable-name / options;
```

One option you may want to use is

TYPE=*distribution-type*   specifies the type of distribution curve, either NORMAL (the default) or KERNEL.

The HISTOGRAM and DENSITY statements can be used together, but not with other types of graphs. Keep in mind that when you overlay graphs, the order of statements is important because the second graph will be drawn on top of the first and could hide it.

**Box plots**   The basic form of PROC SGPLOT for a vertical box plot is

```
PROC SGPLOT;
   VBOX variable-name / options;
```

For a horizontal box plot, specify the keyword HBOX instead of VBOX. One option you may want to use is

CATEGORY=*variable*         specifies a categorical variable. One box plot will be created for each value of the categorical variable.

The VBOX and HBOX statements cannot be used with statements that create other types of plots.

You can use the REFLINE statement (described in section 8.5) to add horizontal or vertical reference lines to either histograms or box plots.

**Example**  A small town sponsors an annual bicycle criterium. That's a race where bicyclists go round and round a loop. The racers compete in three divisions: Youth, Adult, and Masters. The data include each bicyclist's division and the number of laps they completed in one hour.

```
Adult    44 Adult    33 Youth    33 Masters 38 Adult    40
Masters 32 Youth    32 Youth    38 Youth    33 Adult    47
Masters 37 Masters 46 Youth    34 Adult    42 Youth    24
Masters 33 Adult    44 Youth    35 Adult    49 Adult    38
Adult    39 Adult    42 Adult    32 Youth    42 Youth    31
Masters 33 Adult    33 Masters 32 Youth    37 Masters 40
```

The DATA step below reads the raw data from a file named Criterium.dat. Then two PROC SGPLOTs graph the data. The first SGPLOT procedure creates a histogram for the number of laps. Two density distributions will be overlaid on the histogram: the normal distribution and the kernel density estimate. The second SGPLOT procedure requests box plots of the number of laps. The CATEGORY= option tells SAS to create a separate box plot for each division.

```
DATA bikerace;
    INFILE 'c:\MyRawData\Criterium.dat';
    INPUT Division $ NumberLaps @@;
RUN;
* Create histogram;
PROC SGPLOT DATA = bikerace;
    HISTOGRAM NumberLaps / SHOWBINS;
    DENSITY NumberLaps;
    DENSITY NumberLaps / TYPE = KERNEL;
    TITLE 'Bicycle Criterium Results';
RUN;
* Create box plot;
PROC SGPLOT DATA = bikerace;
    VBOX NumberLaps / CATEGORY = Division;
    TITLE 'Bicycle Criterium Results';
RUN;
```

Because no destination was specified, the graphs will be sent to the default destination, LISTING, and saved as PNG files. To view these graphs, double-click their icons in the Results window.

Here are the results:

## 8.4 Creating Scatter Plots with PROC SGPLOT

Scatter plots are an effective way to show the relationship between two continuous variables. To create scatter plots, use the SCATTER statement like this:

```
PROC SGPLOT;
   SCATTER X=horizontal-variable Y=vertical-variable / options;
```

One option you may want to add to the SCATTER statement is

GROUP = *variable-name*   specifies a third variable to be used for grouping the data.

XAXIS and YAXIS statements can be added as needed to specify options for the axes. These two statements can be used with all types of graphs, not just scatter plots, and have this general form:

```
XAXIS options;

YAXIS options;
```

Options that you may want to add to an XAXIS or YAXIS statement include

LABEL = '*label*'   specifies a text string enclosed in quotes to be used as the label for an axis in place of the variable name or variable label. The default is the variable label, or if there is no variable label, then the variable name.

TYPE = *axis-type*   specifies the type of axis. DISCRETE is the default for character variables. LINEAR is the default for numeric variables. TIME is the default for variables that have date, time, or datetime formats associated with them. LOG specifies a logarithmic scale and is not a default.

VALUES = *(values-list)* specifies values for tick marks on axes. Values must be enclosed in parentheses and can be specified either as a list (0 5 10 15 20) or a range (0 TO 20 BY 5).

You can also add horizontal or vertical reference lines to plots using the REFLINE statement (discussed in the next section).

**Example**   To illustrate the use of scatter plots, here are data about the Walla Walla Sweets, a local minor league baseball team. For each home game, the data contain the name of the visiting team, onion ring sales at concession stands and in the bleachers, number of hits for the home team, hits for the visiting team, runs for the home team, and runs for the visiting team:

```
Columbia Peaches      102  67  1 10 2 1
Plains Peanuts        210  54  2  5 0 1
Gilroy Garlics         15 335 12 11 7 6
Sacramento Tomatoes   124 185 15  4 9 1
Boise Spuds           162  75  5  6 2 3
Orlando Tangelos      144  86  9  3 4 2
Des Moines Corncobs    73 210 10  5 9 3
```

The ballpark owners suspect that in games with a lot of hits and runs, more onion rings are sold in the bleachers. To investigate this, the DATA step below reads the raw data and adds together all the runs and hits to create a variable named Action. Then PROC SGPLOT creates two plots: one for sales in the bleachers by Action, and one for sales at concession stands by Action. These plots will be overlaid. The XAXIS and YAXIS statements specify the labels for each axis while the LABEL statement specifies variable labels that will appear in the legend. The XAXIS statement also specifies tick marks for the horizontal axis.

```
DATA onionrings;
   INFILE 'c:\MyRawData\Onions.dat';
   INPUT VisTeam $ 1-20 CSales BSales OurHits VisHits OurRuns VisRuns;
   Action = OurHits + VisHits + OurRuns + VisRuns;
RUN;

* Plot Bleacher Sales by Action;
PROC SGPLOT DATA = onionrings;
   SCATTER X = Action Y = BSales;
   SCATTER X = Action Y = CSales;
   XAXIS LABEL = 'Hits + Runs' VALUES = (0 TO 40 BY 10);
   YAXIS LABEL = 'Number Sold';
   LABEL BSales = 'Sales in Bleachers'
         CSales = 'Sales at Stands';
   TITLE 'Onion Ring Sales vs. Game Action';
RUN;
```

Because no destination was specified, the graph will be sent to the default destination, LISTING, and saved as a PNG file. To view this graph, double-click its icon in the Results window.

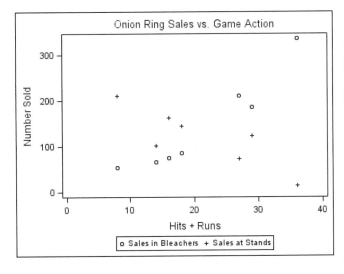

Here is the output. Looking at this plot, it appears that the ballpark owners are right. As Action increases, sales tend to increase in the bleachers but not at the concession stands.

## 8.5 Creating Series Plots with PROC SGPLOT

A series plot is appropriate for data that must be displayed in a specific order. Dates and times of any kind are good candidates for series plots. In a series plot, data points are connected by a line. The general form for a series plot is

```
PROC SGPLOT;
    SERIES X=horizontal-variable Y=vertical-variable / options;
```

When lines are drawn, points are connected in the order in which they appear in the data set. In order to have the points connected properly, your data must be sorted by your horizontal variable. If your data are not already sorted, use PROC SORT before you create your plot.

Options you may want to add to the SERIES statement include

GROUP = *variable-name*     specifies a third variable to be used for grouping the data. A separate line is created for each unique value of the grouping variable.

MARKERS     adds data point markers to the lines.

Adding reference lines to a graph can help to show which points are above or below important levels. You can add reference lines to many types of graphs using the REFLINE statement. The general form of this statement is

```
REFLINE value-list / options;
```

The values can be specified either as a list, 0 5 10 15 20, or a range, 0 TO 20 BY 5. Options that you may want to add to a REFLINE statement include

AXIS = *axis*     specifies the axis that contains the reference line values. The default is Y which produces horizontal lines. For vertical reference lines, specify AXIS=X.

LABEL = ( *label-list* )     specifies one or more text strings (each enclosed in quotes and separated by spaces) to be used as labels for the reference lines.

TRANSPARENCY = *n*     sets the transparency of the line. Values range from 0 to 1 with a default of 0.

PROC SGPLOT draws plot elements in the order they are specified. So if a REFLINE statement comes first, then the reference line will be behind any plot lines or bar charts. If a REFLINE statement comes last, then the reference line will be drawn on top.

**Example**  This example compares average high temperatures in three cities: International Falls, Minnesota; Raleigh, North Carolina; and Yuma, Arizona. The variables are month and high temperature in International Falls, Raleigh, and Yuma. Temperatures are in Fahrenheit, and each line of data contains data for two months.

```
 1  12.2 50.7  68.5   2  20.1 54.5  74.1
 3  32.4 63.7  79.0   4  49.6 72.7  86.7
 5  64.4 79.7  94.1   6  73.0 85.8 103.1
 7  78.1 88.7 106.9   8  75.6 87.4 105.6
 9  64.0 82.6 101.5  10  52.2 72.9  91.0
11  32.5 63.9  77.5  12  17.8 54.1  68.9
```

To compare the three cities, the DATA step below reads the raw data. Then PROC SGPLOT plots three series lines, one for each city. Reference lines will be drawn at 32 and 75 degrees. The X axis is given a type of DISCRETE in an XAXIS statement (discussed in the preceding section). A label is specified for the Y axis in a YAXIS statement. In this data set, the variable Month is simply a number (1–12) rather than a SAS date value. In order to avoid having values of month such as 3.5, the axis type must be set to DISCRETE.

```
DATA temperatures;
   INFILE 'c:\MyRawData\Temps.dat';
   INPUT Month IntFalls Raleigh Yuma @@;
RUN;

* Plot average high and low temperatures by city;
PROC SGPLOT DATA = temperatures;
   SERIES X = Month Y = IntFalls;
   SERIES X = Month Y = Raleigh;
   SERIES X = Month Y = Yuma;
   REFLINE 32 75 / TRANSPARENCY = 0.5 LABEL = ('32 degrees' '75 degrees');
   XAXIS TYPE = DISCRETE;
   YAXIS LABEL = 'Average High Temperature (F)';
   TITLE 'Temperatures by Month for International Falls, '
       'Raleigh, and Yuma';
RUN;
```

Note that the data did not need to be sorted because they were already ordered by the variable Month.

Because no destination was specified, the plot will be sent to the default destination, LISTING, and saved as a PNG file. To view this plot, double-click its icon in the Results window.

The plot looks like this:

## 8.6 ▷ Creating Fitted Curves with PROC SGPLOT

Using the SCATTER statement in SGPLOT (discussed in section 8.4) you can produce simple scatter plots of your data. SGPLOT can also plot regression lines, loess curves, and penalized B-spline curves along with the data points. All you have to do to create a scatter plot with a fit curve, is replace the SCATTER keyword with the keyword for the desired fit. The general form of SGPLOT for fit curves is

```
PROC SGPLOT;
    Fit-type-keyword X=horizontal-variable Y=vertical-variable / options;
```

Where the *fit-type-keyword* can be

| Keyword[1] | Description |
|---|---|
| REG | regression line or curve |
| LOESS | loess curve |
| PBSPLINE | penalized B-spline curve |

Options that apply to all these statements include

| | |
|---|---|
| CLM | confidence limits for mean predicted values. |
| GROUP = *variable-name* | specifies a third variable to be used for grouping the data. A separate line is created for each unique value of the grouping variable. |
| NOLEGCLM | removes legend entry for CLM band. |
| NOLEGFIT | removes legend entry for fit curve. |
| NOMARKERS | removes markers for data points. |

You can also add reference lines to your graphs using the REFLINE statement discussed in the previous section.

**Example**  The following are the winning race times in seconds for the men's 1500 meter run at the Olympics. The Olympic year is followed by the time rounded to the nearest second. There are several observations per line of data.

```
1896 273 1900 246 1904 245 1906 252 1908 243 1912 237 1920 242
1924 234 1928 233 1932 231 1936 228 1948 230 1952 225 1956 221
1960 216 1964 218 1968 215 1972 216 1976 219 1980 218 1984 213
1988 216 1992 220 1996 216 2000 212 2004 214
```

Here is the program that reads the data and produces two plots. The DATA step reads the data into a SAS data set. The first SGPLOT procedure produces two overlaid fit plots for the men's results: a regression plot and a loess plot. The NOMARKERS option on the LOESS statement prevents the data from being plotted twice since the data points are already plotted with the REG statement. The second SGPLOT procedure uses the PBSPLINE statement to fit a penalized B-spline curve. The CLM option generates the confidence limit band for the mean predicted values, while the NOLEGCLM option tells SAS not to include the confidence limit band in the legend.

---

[1] Each of these fit types uses default values for interpolation methods and fit parameters. You can change the default values using additional options. See the SAS Help and Documentation for more information.

```
DATA Olympic1500;
   INFILE 'C:\MyRawData\Olympic1500.dat';
   INPUT Year Men @@;
RUN;
PROC SGPLOT DATA=Olympic1500;
   REG X=Year Y=Men;
   LOESS X=Year Y=Men / NOMARKERS;
   YAXIS LABEL='Time in Seconds';
   TITLE "Olympic Times for Men's 1500 Meter Run";
RUN;
PROC SGPLOT DATA=Olympic1500;
   PBSPLINE X=Year Y=Men/CLM NOLEGCLM;
   YAXIS LABEL='Time in Seconds';
   TITLE "Olympic Times for Men's 1500 Meter Run";
RUN;
```

Because no destination was specified, the plots will be sent to the default destination, LISTING, and saved as a PNG file. To view these plots, double-click the icons in the Results window.

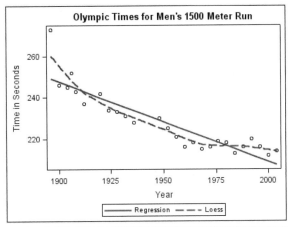

This graph overlays the data points with both a regression line and a loess curve. Because the NOMARKERS option was included on the LOESS statement, the data points are only plotted once.

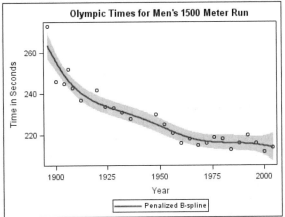

This graph shows a penalized B-spline curve fitted to the same data as the above plot. The resulting curve looks very similar to the loess curve for this example, but there are slight differences. The confidence limits for mean predicted values are shown with the gray band surrounding the fit line.

## 8.7 ▸ Examining the Distribution of Data with PROC UNIVARIATE

When you are doing statistical analysis, you usually have a goal in mind, a question you are trying to answer, or a hypotheses you want to test. But before you jump into statistical tests, it is a good idea to pause and do a little exploration. A good procedure to use at this point is PROC UNIVARIATE.

PROC UNIVARIATE, which is part of Base SAS software, produces statistics and graphs describing the distribution of a single variable. The statistics include the mean, median, mode, standard deviation, skewness, and kurtosis.

Using PROC UNIVARIATE is fairly simple. After the PROC statement, you specify one or more numeric variables in a VAR statement:

```
PROC UNIVARIATE;
    VAR variable-list;
```

Without a VAR statement, SAS will calculate statistics for all numeric variables in your data set. You can specify other options in the PROC statement, if you wish, such as NORMAL which produces tests of normality:

```
PROC UNIVARIATE NORMAL;
```

**Example**  The following data consist of test scores from a statistics class. Each line contains scores for 10 students.

```
56 78 84 73 90 44 76 87 92 75
85 67 90 84 74 64 73 78 69 56
87 73 100 54 81 78 69 64 73 65
```

This program reads the data from a file called Scores.dat and then runs PROC UNIVARIATE:

```
DATA class;
    INFILE 'c:\MyRawData\Scores.dat';
    INPUT Score @@;
RUN;
PROC UNIVARIATE DATA = class;
    VAR Score;
    TITLE;
RUN;
```

The output appears on the next page. The output starts with basic information about your distribution: number of observations (N), mean, and standard deviation. Skewness indicates how asymmetrical the distribution is (whether it is more spread out on one side) while kurtosis indicates how flat or peaked the distribution is. The normal distribution has values of 0 for both skewness and kurtosis.[1] Other sections of the output contain three measures of central tendency: mean, median, and mode; tests of the hypothesis that the population mean is 0; quantiles; and extreme observations (in case you have outliers).

---

[1] There are two formulas for kurtosis. SAS software uses the formula that has a value of 0 for a normal distribution. For details about the formula that SAS uses to compute kurtosis, see the SAS Help and documentation.

```
                    The UNIVARIATE Procedure                    1

                      Variable:  Score

                            Moments
N                           30  Sum Weights                30
Mean                  74.633333  Sum Observations         2239
Std Deviation         12.584839  Variance             158.37816
Skewness              -0.349506  Kurtosis             0.1038576
Uncorrected SS           171697  Corrected SS         4592.9667
Coeff Variation       16.862222  Std Error Mean       2.2976666

                   Basic Statistical Measures

          Location                    Variability

     Mean       74.63333    Std Deviation        12.58484
     Median     74.50000    Variance             158.3782
     Mode       73.00000    Range                56.00000
                            Interquartile Range  17.00000

              Tests for Location: Mu0=0.00
     Test Statistic      Value            p-value

     Student's t  t    32.48223    Pr > |t|    <.0001
     Sign         M          15    Pr >= |M|   <.0001
     Signed Rank  S       232.5    Pr >= |S|   <.0001

                 Quantiles (Definition 5)
                   Quantile    Estimate

                   100% Max      100.0
                   99%           100.0
                   95%            92.0
                   90%            90.0
                   75% Q3         84.0
                   50% Med        74.5
                   25% Q1         67.0
                   10%            56.0
                   5%             54.0
                   1%             44.0
                   0% Min         44.0

                  Extreme Observations
        ------Lowest-----          -----Highest-----
         Value      Obs             Value      Obs

            44        6                87        21
            54       24                90         5
            56       20                90        13
            56        1                92         9
            64       28               100        23
```

**8.8**  Creating Statistical Graphics with PROC UNIVARIATE

The UNIVARIATE procedure can produce several graphs that are useful for data exploration.[1] For example, histograms are a good way to visualize the distribution of a variable while probability and quantile-quantile plots can show how the data compare to theoretical distributions. To produce these graphs using ODS Graphics, you must turn on statistical graphics using the ODS GRAPHICS statement. Here is the general form of PROC UNIVARIATE with ODS Graphics:

```
ODS GRAPHICS ON;
PROC UNIVARIATE;
   VAR variable-list;
   Plot-request variable-list / options;
RUN;
```

**Plot requests**  The following graphs can be created with PROC UNIVARIATE:

| | |
|---|---|
| CDFPLOT | requests a cumulative distribution function plot |
| HISTOGRAM | requests a histogram |
| PPPLOT | requests a probability-probability plot |
| PROBPLOT | requests a probability plot |
| QQPLOT | requests a quantile-quantile plot |

All variables specified in the variable list for the plot must also appear in the variable list on the VAR statement. If no variable list is specified, then plots will be produced for all variables in the VAR statement.

**Plot options**  The CDFPLOT and HISTOGRAM plots show the distribution of the specified variable. To overlay a curve showing a standard distribution, specify the desired distribution with a plot option. Available distributions options include: BETA, EXPONENTIAL, GAMMA, LOGNORMAL, NORMAL, and WEIBULL. All other plots use the normal distribution as the default. If you would like to use a different distribution, specify it with a plot option. For example, to create a probability plot of the variable Score using the exponential distribution, use the following:

```
PROBPLOT Score/EXPONENTIAL;
```

**Example**  This example uses the data from the previous section. The data are test scores from a statistics class. The following program creates a histogram of the Score variable with the normal distribution overlaid and a probability plot using the normal distribution:

---

[1] ODS Graphics is experimental for the UNIVARIATE procedure in SAS 9.2.

```
ODS GRAPHICS ON;
PROC UNIVARIATE DATA = class;
    VAR Score;
    HISTOGRAM Score/NORMAL;
    PROBPLOT Score;
    TITLE;
RUN;
```

Because no ODS destination was specified, results will be sent to the default destination, LISTING. To view the plots, open the Results window and double-click the plot icons labeled Histogram for Score and Probability Plot for Score.

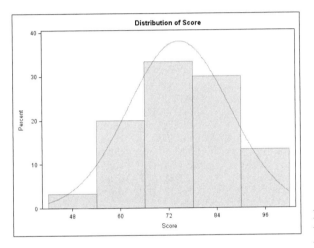

Here are the two plots: a histogram with a normal distribution and a probability plot.

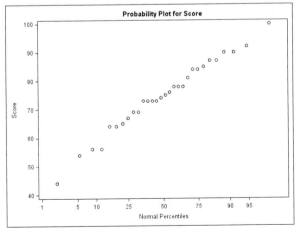

## 8.9 ▶ Producing Statistics with PROC MEANS

Most of the descriptive statistics that you produce with PROC UNIVARIATE you can also produce with PROC MEANS. UNIVARIATE is useful when you want an in-depth statistical analysis of the data distribution. But if you know you want only a few statistics then MEANS is a better way to go. With MEANS you can ask for just the statistics you want. The MEANS procedure does not use ODS Graphics.

The MEANS procedure requires only one statement:

```
PROC MEANS statistic-keywords;
```

If you do not include any statistic keywords, then MEANS will produce the mean, the number of non-missing values, the standard deviation, the minimum value, and the maximum value for each numeric variable. The following table shows statistics you can request. (Some statistics have two names; the alternate name is shown in parentheses.) If you add any statistic keywords in the PROC MEANS statement, then MEANS will no longer produce the default statistics—you must request them.

| | | | |
|---|---|---|---|
| CLM | two-sided confidence limits | RANGE | the range |
| CSS | corrected sum of squares | SKEWNESS | skewness |
| CV | coefficient of variation | STDDEV | standard deviation |
| KURTOSIS | kurtosis | STDERR | standard error of the mean |
| LCLM | lower confidence limit | SUM | the sum |
| MAX | maximum value | SUMWGT | sum of weight variables |
| MEAN | mean | UCLM | upper confidence limit |
| MIN | minimum value | USS | uncorrected sum of squares |
| MODE | mode | VAR | variance |
| N | number of non-missing values | PROBT | probability for Student's $t$ |
| NMISS | number of missing values | T | Student's $t$ |
| MEDIAN (P50) | median | Q3 (P75) | 75% quantile |
| Q1 (P25) | 25% quantile | P5 | 5% quantile |
| P1 | 1% quantile | P90 | 90% quantile |
| P10 | 10% quantile | P99 | 99% quantile |
| P95 | 95% quantile | | |

**Confidence limits**  The default confidence level for the confidence limits is .05 or 95%. If you want a different confidence level, then request it with the ALPHA= option in the PROC MEANS statement. For example, if you want 90% confidence limits, then specify ALPHA=.10 along with the CLM option. Then the PROC MEANS statement would look like this:

```
PROC MEANS ALPHA=.10 CLM;
```

**The VAR statement**  By default MEANS will produce statistics for all numeric variables in your data set. If you do not want all the variables, then specify the ones you want in the VAR statement. Here is the general form of the MEANS procedure with the VAR statement:

```
PROC MEANS options;
   VAR variable-list;
```

**Example**  Your friend is an aspiring author of children's books. To increase her chances of getting her books published, she wants to know how many pages her books should have. At the local library, she counts the number of pages in a random selection of children's picture books. Here are the data:

```
34 30 29 32 52 25 24 27 31 29
24 26 30 30 30 29 21 30 25 28
28 28 29 38 28 29 24 24 29 31
30 27 45 30 22 16 29 14 16 29
32 20 20 15 28 28 29 31 29 36
```

To determine the average number of pages in children's picture books, use the MEANS procedure. PROC MEANS can also produce the median number of pages as well as the 90% confidence limits. Here is the program that will read the data and produce the desired statistics:

```
DATA booklengths;
    INFILE 'c:\MyRawData\Picbooks.dat';
    INPUT NumberOfPages @@;
RUN;
*Produce summary statistics;
PROC MEANS DATA=booklengths N MEAN MEDIAN CLM ALPHA=.10;
    TITLE 'Summary of Picture Book Lengths';
RUN;
```

Here are the results of the MEANS procedure:

```
                    Summary of Picture Book Lengths            1

                         The MEANS Procedure

                    Analysis Variable : NumberOfPages

                                        Lower 90.0%      Upper 90.0%
    N          Mean          Median     CL for Mean      CL for Mean
    ─────────────────────────────────────────────────────────────────
    50      28.0000000    29.0000000     26.4419136       29.5580864
    ─────────────────────────────────────────────────────────────────
```

The average number of pages in the children's books sampled was 28. The median value of 29 says that half the books sampled had 29 pages or fewer. The confidence limits tell us that we are 90% certain that the true population mean (all children's picture books) falls between 26.44 and 29.56 pages. From this analysis your friend concludes that she should make her books between 26 and 30 pages long to maximize her chances of getting published (of course subject matter and writing style might also help).

## 8.10   Testing Categorical Data with PROC FREQ

PROC FREQ, which is part of Base SAS software, produces many statistics for categorical data. The best known of these is chi-square. One of the most common uses of PROC FREQ is to test the hypothesis of no association between the variables. Another use is to compute measures of association, which indicate the strength of the relationship between the variables. The basic form of PROC FREQ is

```
PROC FREQ;
   TABLES variable-combinations / options;
```

**Options**   Here are a few of the statistical options available:

| | |
|---|---|
| AGREE | requests tests and measures of classification agreement including McNemar's test, Bowker's test, Cochran's Q test, and kappa statistics |
| CHISQ | requests chi-square tests of homogeneity and measures of association |
| CL | requests confidence limits for measures of association |
| CMH | requests Cochran-Mantel-Haenszel statistics |
| EXACT | requests Fisher's exact test for tables larger than 2X2 |
| MEASURES | requests measures of association including Pearson and Spearman correlation coefficients, gamma, Kendall's tau-b, Stuart's tau-c, Somer's D, lambda, odds ratios, risk ratios, and confidence intervals |
| PLCORR | requests polychoric correlation coefficient |
| RELRISK | requests relative risk measures for 2X2 tables |
| TREND | requests the Cochran-Armitage test for trend |

**Example**   One day your neighbor, who rides the bus to work, complains that the regular bus is usually late. He says the express bus is usually on time. Realizing that this is categorical data, you decide to test whether there really is a relationship between the type of bus and arriving on time. You collect two variables: type of bus (E for express or R for regular) and promptness (L for late or O for on time). Each line of data contains 10 observations.

```
E O E L E L R O E O E O E O R L R O R L
R O E O R L E O R L R O E O E O R L E L
E O R L E O R L E O R L E O R O E L E O
E O E O E O E L E O E O R L R L R O R L
E L E O R L R O E O E O E O E L R O R L
```

The following program reads the raw data and runs PROC FREQ with the CHISQ option:

```
DATA bus;
   INFILE 'c:\MyRawData\Bus.dat';
   INPUT BusType $ OnTimeOrLate $ @@;
RUN;
PROC FREQ DATA = bus;
   TABLES BusType * OnTimeOrLate / CHISQ;
   TITLE;
RUN;
```

The output appears on the next page. Assuming that bus type and arrival time are independent, the probability of obtaining a chi-square this large or larger by chance alone is 0.0071. So the data do support the idea that there is an association between type of bus and arrival time.

```
                     The FREQ Procedure

          Table of BusType by OnTimeOrLate

             BusType       OnTimeOrLate

             Frequency│
             Percent  │
             Row Pct  │
             Col Pct  │L        │O        │  Total

             E         │       7 │      22 │     29
                       │   14.00 │   44.00 │  58.00
                       │   24.14 │   75.86 │
                       │   35.00 │   73.33 │

             R         │      13 │       8 │     21
                       │   26.00 │   16.00 │  42.00
                       │   61.90 │   38.10 │
                       │   65.00 │   26.67 │

             Total            20        30        50
                           40.00     60.00    100.00
```

Statistics for Table of BusType by OnTimeOrLate

| Statistic | DF | Value | Prob |
|---|---|---|---|
| Chi-Square | 1 | 7.2386 | 0.0071 |
| Likelihood Ratio Chi-Square | 1 | 7.3364 | 0.0068 |
| Continuity Adj. Chi-Square | 1 | 5.7505 | 0.0165 |
| Mantel-Haenszel Chi-Square | 1 | 7.0939 | 0.0077 |
| Phi Coefficient | | -0.3805 | |
| Contingency Coefficient | | 0.3556 | |
| Cramer's V | | -0.3805 | |

Fisher's Exact Test

```
          Cell (1,1) Frequency (F)          7
          Left-sided Pr <= F           0.0081
          Right-sided Pr >= F          0.9987

          Table Probability (P)        0.0067
          Two-sided Pr <= P            0.0097

              Sample Size = 50
```

# 8.11 Creating Statistical Graphics with PROC FREQ

The FREQ procedure uses ODS Graphics to produce several plots that help you visualize your data including: frequency plots, odds ratio plots, deviation plots, and two types of plots with Kappa statistics and confidence limits. Here is the general form of PROC FREQ with ODS Graphics:

```
ODS GRAPHICS ON;
PROC FREQ;
   TABLES variable-combinations / options PLOTS = (plot-list);
RUN;
```

**Plot requests** The plots available to you depend on the type of table you request. For example, the DEVIATIONPLOT is only available for one-way tables when using the CHISQ option on the TABLES statement. Here are the plots you can request along with the required option, if any, and type of table request:

| Plot Name | Table type | Required option on TABLES statement |
|---|---|---|
| CUMFREQPLOT | one-way | |
| DEVIATIONPLOT | one-way | CHISQ |
| FREQPLOT | any request | |
| KAPPAPLOT | three-way | AGREE |
| ODDSRATIOPLOT | hx2x2 | MEASURES or RELRISK |
| WTKAPPAPLOT | hxrxr (r>2) | AGREE |

If you do not specify any plots in the TABLE statement, and you have ODS Graphics turned on, then all plots associated with the table you request will be produced.

**Plot options** Many options are available that control the look of the plots generated. For a complete list of options, see the SAS Help and Documentation. In particular, the FREQPLOT has options for controlling the layout of the plots for two-way tables. By default, the bars are grouped vertically. To group the bars horizontally, use

```
TABLES variable1 * variable2 / PLOTS = FREQPLOT(TWOWAY = GROUPHORIZONTAL);
```

To stack the bars, use the TWOWAY=STACKED option.

**Example** This example uses the same data as the previous section, and also requests two way frequency tables. Because ODS Graphics is turned on, the first table request produces a frequency plot even though no plot is specifically requested. The second table request produces a second frequency plot, but with the bars grouped horizontally instead of vertically:

```
ODS GRAPHICS ON;
PROC FREQ DATA = bus;
   TABLES BusType * OnTimeOrLate;
   TABLES BusType * OnTimeOrLate / PLOTS=FREQPLOT(TWOWAY=GROUPHORIZONTAL);
   TITLE;
RUN;
```

Because no ODS destination was specified, results will be sent to the default destination, LISTING. To view the plots, open the Results window and double-click the plot icons both labeled Frequency Plot.

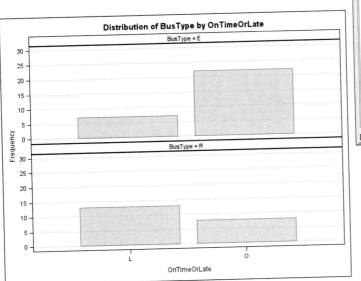

Here are the two plots. They both show the same data, but one plot is grouped vertically and the other plot is grouped horizontally.

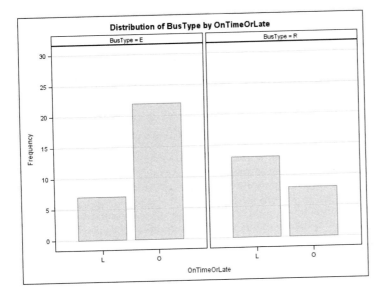

# 8.12   Examining Correlations with PROC CORR

The CORR procedure, which is included with Base SAS software, computes correlations. A correlation coefficient measures the strength of the relationship between two variables, or how co-related they are. If two variables were completely unrelated, they would have a correlation of 0. If two variables were perfectly correlated, they would have a correlation of 1.0 or –1.0. In real life, correlations fall somewhere between these numbers. The basic statement for PROC CORR is rather simple:

```
PROC CORR;
```

These two words tell SAS to compute correlations between all the numeric variables. You can add the VAR and WITH statements to specify variables:

```
VAR variable-list;
WITH variable-list;
```

Variables listed in the VAR statement appear across the top of the table of correlations, while variables listed in the WITH statement appear down the side of the table. If you use a VAR statement but no WITH statement, then the variables appear both across the top and down the side.

By default, PROC CORR computes Pearson product-moment correlation coefficients. You can add options to the PROC statement to request non-parametric correlation coefficients. The SPEARMAN option in the statement below tells SAS to compute Spearman's rank correlations instead of Pearson's correlations:

```
PROC CORR  SPEARMAN;
```

Other options include HOEFFDING (for Hoeffding's D statistic) and KENDALL (for Kendall's tau-b coefficient).

**Example** Each student in a statistics class recorded three values: test score, the number of hours spent watching television in the week prior to the test, and the number of hours spent exercising during the same week. Here are the raw data:

```
56 6 2    78 7 4    84 5 5    73 4 0    90 3 4
44 9 0    76 5 1    87 3 3    92 2 7    75 8 3
85 1 6    67 4 2    90 5 5    84 6 5    74 5 2
64 4 1    73 0 5    78 5 2    69 6 1    56 7 1
87 8 4    73 8 3   100 0 6    54 8 0    81 5 4
78 5 2    69 4 1    64 7 1    73 7 3    65 6 2
```

Notice that each line contains data for five students. The following program reads the raw data from a file called Exercise.dat and then uses PROC CORR to compute the correlations:

```
DATA class;
   INFILE 'c:\MyRawData\Exercise.dat';
   INPUT Score Television Exercise @@;
RUN;
```

```
PROC CORR DATA = class;
   VAR Television Exercise;
   WITH Score;
   TITLE 'Correlations for Test Scores';
   TITLE2 'With Hours of Television and Exercise';
RUN;
```

Here is the report from PROC CORR:

```
                    Correlations for Test Scores                    1
                With Hours of Television and Exercise

                          The CORR Procedure

              1 'WITH' Variables:  Score
              2 'VAR'  Variables:  Television Exercise


                          Simple Statistics

   Variable         N      Mean   Std Dev       Sum   Minimum   Maximum

   Score           30   74.6333   12.5848    2239.0   44.0000     100.0
   Television       30    5.1000    2.3393     153.0         0    9.0000
   Exercise         30    2.8333    1.9491   85.0000         0    7.0000


             ❶ Pearson Correlation Coefficients, N = 30
                 ❷ Prob > |R| under Ho: Rho=0


                    Television            Exercise

        Score      ❶  -0.55390         ❶  0.79733
                   ❷  0.0015           ❷  0.0001
```

This report starts with descriptive statistics for each variable and then lists the correlation matrix which contains: ❶correlation coefficients (in this case, Pearson), and ❷the probability of getting a larger absolute value for each correlation assuming the population correlation is zero.

In this example, both hours of television and hours of exercise are correlated with test score, but exercise is positively correlated while television is negatively correlated. This means students who watched more television tended to have lower scores, while the students who spent more time exercising tended to have higher scores.

## 8.13 Creating Statistical Graphics with PROC CORR

The CORR procedure evaluates the strength of the relationship between pairs of variables. The tabular output gives the correlation coefficients and other simple statistics, and using ODS Graphics you can also visualize the relationship. Here is the general form of PROC CORR with ODS Graphics:

```
ODS GRAPHICS ON;
PROC CORR PLOTS = (plot-list);
   VAR variable-list;
   WITH variable-list;
RUN;
```

**Plot requests** The CORR procedure can produce two types of plots:

SCATTER    creates scatter plots for pairs of variables. Prediction or confidence ellipses are overlaid on the plot.

MATRIX    creates a matrix of scatter plots for all variables.

If you do not specify the PLOTS= option, then a matrix plot will be produced.

**Plot options** By default, the scatter plots have prediction ellipses. If you want confidence ellipses, then specify the ELLIPSE=CONFIDENCE option on the scatter plot:

```
PROC CORR PLOTS = SCATTER(ELLIPSE = CONFIDENCE);
```

If you do not want any ellipses on your scatter plots, then use the ELLIPSE=NONE option.

If you do not have a WITH statement, then matrix plots will show a symmetrical plot with all variable combinations appearing twice. By default the diagonal cells in the matrix will be empty. If you use the HISTOGRAM option for the matrix plot, then a histogram will be produced for each variable and displayed along the diagonal.

```
PROC CORR PLOTS = MATRIX(HISTOGRAM);
```

**Example** Here are the same PROC CORR statements shown in the previous section except the ODS GRAPHICS ON statement has been added, and both the scatter and matrix plots are requested:

```
ODS GRAPHICS ON;
PROC CORR DATA = class PLOTS = (SCATTER MATRIX);
   VAR Television Exercise;
   WITH Score;
   TITLE 'Correlations for Test Scores';
   TITLE2 'With Hours of Television and Exercise';
RUN;
```

Because no ODS destination was specified, results will be sent to the default destination, LISTING. To view the plots, open the Results window and double-click the plot icons which are labeled Score by Television, Score by Exercise, and Scatter Plot Matrix.

Here is the scatter plot for Score by Television and the Scatter Plot Matrix.

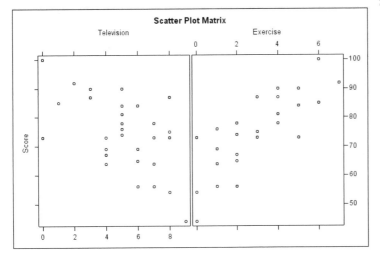

## 8.14 Using PROC REG for Simple Regression Analysis

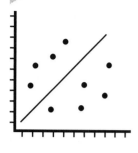

The REG procedure fits linear regression models by least-squares and is one of many SAS procedures which perform regression analysis. PROC REG is part of SAS/STAT, which is licensed separately from Base SAS software. We will show an example of a simple regression analysis using continuous numeric variables with only one regressor variable. However, PROC REG is capable of analyzing models with many regressor variables using a variety of model-selection methods including stepwise regression, forward selection, and backward elimination. Other procedures in SAS/STAT will perform non-linear and logistic regression. In SAS/ETS you will find procedures for time-series analysis. If you are unsure about what type of analysis you need, or are unfamiliar with basic statistical principles, we recommend that you seek advice from a trained statistician, or consult a good statistical textbook.

The REG procedure has only two required statements. It must start with the PROC REG statement and have a MODEL statement specifying the analysis model. The following shows the general form of the REG procedure:

```
PROC REG;
   MODEL dependent = independent;
```

In the MODEL statement, the dependent variable is listed on the left side of the equal sign and the independent, or regressor, variable is listed on the right.

**Example** At your young neighbor's T-ball game (that's where the players hit the ball from the top of a tee instead of having the ball pitched to them), he said to you, "You can tell how far they'll hit the ball by how tall they are." To give him a little practical lesson in statistics, you decide to test his hypothesis. You gather data from 30 players, measuring their height in inches and their longest of three hits in feet. The following are the data. Notice that data for five players are listed on one line:

```
50 110   49 135   48 129   53 150   48 124
50 143   51 126   45 107   53 146   50 154
47 136   52 144   47 124   50 133   50 128
50 118   48 135   47 129   45 126   48 118
45 121   53 142   46 122   47 119   51 134
49 130   46 132   51 144   50 132   50 131
```

The following program reads the data and performs the regression analysis:

```
DATA hits;
   INFILE 'c:\MyRawData\Baseball.dat';
   INPUT Height Distance @@;
RUN;
* Perform regression analysis;
PROC REG DATA = hits;
   MODEL Distance = Height;
   TITLE 'Results of Regression Analysis';
RUN;
```

In the MODEL statement, Distance is the dependent variable, and Height is the independent variable.

The first section of output is the analysis of variance section, which gives information about how well the model fits the data:

```
                    Results of Regression Analysis                    1

                          The REG Procedure
                           Model: MODEL1
                      Dependent Variable: Distance

                        Analysis of Variance

                                    Sum of       ❷ Mean
       Source             ❶ DF      Squares        Square    ❸ F Value ❹Pr > F

       Model                  1    1365.50831    1365.50831     16.86   0.0003
       Error                 28    2268.35836      81.01280
       Corrected Total       29    3633.86667

                   ❺Root MSE            9.00071   R-Square     0.3758
                    Dependent Mean    130.73333   ❼ Adj R-Sq   0.3535
                   ❻Coeff Var           6.88479
```

| ❶ DF | degrees of freedom associated with the source |
|------|-----------------------------------------------|
| ❷ Mean Square | mean square (sum of squares divided by the degrees of freedom) |
| ❸ F value | F value for testing the null hypothesis (all parameters are zero except intercept) |
| ❹ Pr > F | significance probability |
| ❺ Root MSE | root mean square error |
| ❻ Coeff Var | the coefficient of variation |
| ❼ Adj R-sq | the R-square value adjusted for degrees of freedom |

The parameter estimates follow the analysis of variance section and give the parameters for each term in the model, including the intercept:

```
                        Parameter Estimates

                          Parameter      Standard
        Variable    ❶ DF    Estimate        Error   ❷ t Value  ❸ Pr > |t|

        Intercept     1    -11.00859     34.56363    -0.32      0.7525
        Height        1      2.89466      0.70506     4.11      0.0003
```

| ❶ DF | degrees of freedom for the variable |
|------|-------------------------------------|
| ❷ t Value | *t* test for the parameter equal to zero |
| ❸ Pr > \|t\| | two-tailed significance probability |

From the parameter estimates you can construct the regression equation:

```
    Distance = -11.00859 + (2.89466 * Height)
```

In this example, the distance the ball was hit did increase with the player's height. The slope of the model is significant (significance probability = .0003) but the relationship is not very strong (R-square = 0.3758). Perhaps age or years of experience are better predictors of how far the ball will go.

# 8.15   Creating Statistical Graphics with PROC REG

There are many plots that are useful for visualizing the results of regression analysis and for assessing how well the model fits the data. PROC REG uses ODS Graphics to produce many such plots including a diagnostic panel that contains up to nine plots in one figure. Here is the general form of PROC REG with ODS Graphics:

```
ODS GRAPHICS ON;
PROC REG PLOTS(options) = (plot-list);
   MODEL dependent = independent;
RUN;
```

**Plot requests**   Here are some plots you can request for simple linear regression:

| | |
|---|---|
| FITPLOT | scatter plot with regression line and confidence and prediction bands |
| RESIDUALS | residuals plotted against independent variable |
| DIAGNOSTICS | diagnostics panel including all of the following plots |
| COOKSD | Cook's $D$ statistic by observation number |
| OBSERVEDBYPREDICTED | dependent variable by predicted values |
| QQPLOT | normal quantile plot of residuals |
| RESIDUALBYPREDICTED | residuals by predicted values |
| RESIDUALHISTOGRAM | histogram of residuals |
| RFPLOT | residual fit plot |
| RSTUDENTBYLEVERAGE | studentized residuals by leverage |
| RSTUDENTBYPREDICTED | studentized residuals by predicted values |

**Options**   By default the FITPLOT, RESIDUALS and DIAGNOSTICS plots are generated automatically. If you choose specific plots in the plot-list, these default plots will still be created unless you use the ONLY global option:

```
PROC REG PLOTS(ONLY) = (plot-list);
```

**Example**   The following example uses the same program from the previous section except the ODS GRAPHICS ON statement has been added and only the FITPLOT and DIAGNOSTICS plots are requested:

```
ODS GRAPHICS ON;
PROC REG DATA = hits PLOTS(ONLY) = (DIAGNOSTICS FITPLOT);
   MODEL Distance = Height;
   TITLE 'Results of Regression Analysis';
RUN;
```

Because no ODS destination was specified, results will be sent to the default destination, LISTING. To view the plots, open the Results window and double-click the plot icons which are labeled Fit Diagnostics and Fit Plot.

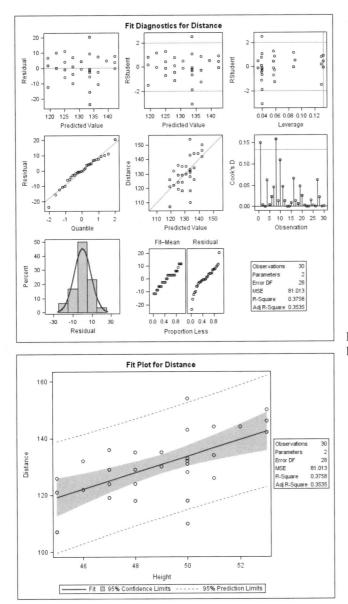

Here are the results for the Fit Diagnostics panel and the Fit Plot.

# 8.16  Using PROC ANOVA for One-Way Analysis of Variance

The ANOVA procedure is one of many in SAS that perform analysis of variance. PROC ANOVA is part of SAS/STAT, which is licensed separately from Base SAS software. PROC ANOVA is specifically designed for balanced data—data where there are equal numbers of observations in each combination of the classification factors. An exception is for one-way analysis of variance where the data do not need to be balanced. If you are not doing one-way analysis of variance and your data are not balanced, then you should use the GLM procedure, whose statements are almost identical to those of PROC ANOVA. Although we are discussing only simple one-way analysis of variance in this section, PROC ANOVA can handle multiple classification variables and models that include nested and crossed effects as well as repeated measures. If you are unsure of the appropriate analysis for your data, or are unfamiliar with basic statistical principles, we recommend that you seek advice from a trained statistician or consult a good statistical textbook.

The ANOVA procedure has two required statements: the CLASS and MODEL statements. The following is the general form of the ANOVA procedure:

```
PROC ANOVA;
   CLASS variable-list;
   MODEL dependent = effects;
```

The CLASS statement must come before the MODEL statement and defines the classification variables. For one-way analysis of variance, only one variable is listed. The MODEL statement defines the dependent variable and the effects. For one-way analysis of variance, the effect is the classification variable.

As you might expect, there are many optional statements for PROC ANOVA. One of the most useful is the MEANS statement, which calculates means of the dependent variable for any of the main effects in the MODEL statement. In addition, the MEANS statement can perform several types of multiple comparison tests including Bonferroni $t$ tests (BON), Duncan's multiple-range test (DUNCAN), Scheffe's multiple-comparison procedure (SCHEFFE), pairwise $t$ tests (T), and Tukey's studentized range test (TUKEY). The MEANS statement has the following general form:

```
MEANS effects / options;
```

The effects can be any main effect in the MODEL statement (no crossed or nested effects), and options include the name of the desired multiple comparison test (DUNCAN for example).

**ODS Graphics**  If you have ODS Graphics turned on, then PROC ANOVA will produce a grouped box plot of the effect variable for one-way analysis of variance and for all effects in a MEANS statement. Turn on ODS Graphics by placing the ODS GRAPHICS ON statement before PROC ANOVA.

**Example**  Your friend says his daughter complains that it seems like the girls on all the other basketball teams are taller than the girls on her team. You decide to test her hypothesis by getting the heights for all the girls and performing one-way analysis of variance to see if there are any differences among teams. You have the team name and each girl's height for players on five different teams. Notice that there are data for six girls on each line:

```
red   55 red   48 red   53 red   47 red   51 red   43
red   45 red   46 red   55 red   54 red   45 red   52
blue  46 blue  56 blue  48 blue  47 blue  54 blue  52
blue  49 blue  51 blue  45 blue  48 blue  55 blue  47
gray  55 gray  45 gray  47 gray  56 gray  49 gray  53
gray  48 gray  53 gray  51 gray  52 gray  48 gray  47
pink  53 pink  53 pink  58 pink  56 pink  50 pink  55
pink  59 pink  57 pink  49 pink  55 pink  56 pink  57
gold  53 gold  55 gold  48 gold  45 gold  47 gold  56
gold  55 gold  46 gold  47 gold  53 gold  51 gold  50
```

You want to know which, if any, teams are taller than the rest, so you use the MEANS statement in your program and choose Scheffe's multiple-comparison procedure to compare the means. Here is the program to read the data and perform the analysis of variance:

```
DATA basket;
    INFILE 'c:\MyRawData\Basketball.dat';
    INPUT Team $ Height @@;
RUN;
* Use ANOVA to run one-way analysis of variance;
ODS GRAPHICS ON;
PROC ANOVA DATA = basket;
   CLASS Team;
   MODEL Height = Team;
   MEANS Team / SCHEFFE;
    TITLE "Girls' Heights on Basketball Teams";
RUN;
```

In this case, Team is the classification variable and also the effect in the MODEL statement. Height is the dependent variable. The MEANS statement will produce means of the girls' heights for each team, and the SCHEFFE option will test which teams are different from the others.

Because no ODS destination was specified, results will be sent to the default destination, LISTING. To view the plot, open the Results window and double-click the plot icon labeled Box Plot. Here is the box plot created from the above program. The tabular output is shown and discussed in the next section.

## 8.17 Reading the Output of PROC ANOVA

The output from PROC ANOVA has at least two parts. First ANOVA produces a table giving information about the classification variables: number of levels, values, and number of observations. Next it produces an analysis of variance table. If you use optional statements like MEANS, then their output will follow.

The example from the previous section, where we wanted to test to see if there are differences in the heights among basketball teams, used the following PROC ANOVA statements:

```
PROC ANOVA DATA = basket;
   CLASS Team;
   MODEL Height = Team;
   MEANS Team / SCHEFFE;
   TITLE "Girls' Heights on Basketball Teams";
RUN;
```

The first page of the output gives information about the classification variable:

```
                    Girls' Heights on Basketball Teams                    1

                           The ANOVA Procedure

                        Class Level Information

          Class          Levels    Values

          Team              5       blue gold gray pink red

                    Number of observations    60
```

Here the CLASS variable is Team. It has five levels with values blue, gold, gray, pink, and red representing the five teams. There are a total of 60 observations in the data set.

The second part of the output is the analysis of variance table:

```
                    Girls' Heights on Basketball Teams                    2
                           The ANOVA Procedure
   Dependent Variable: Height

                                 ❸ Sum of
 ❶ Source                ❷ DF      Squares  ❹ Mean Square  ❺ F Value  ❻ Pr > F
   Model                   4    228.0000000    57.0000000     4.14     0.0053
   Error                  55    758.0000000    13.7818182
   Corrected Total        59    986.0000000

           ❼ R-Square   ❽ Coeff Var   ❾ Root MSE   ❿ Height Mean
             0.231237     7.279190     3.712387      51.00000

   Source                   DF     Anova SS    Mean Square   F Value   Pr > F
   Team                      4    228.0000000    57.0000000     4.14     0.0053
```

Highlights of the output are

❶ `Source`           source of variation
❷ `DF`               degrees of freedom for the model, error, and total
❸ `Sum of Squares`   sum of squares for the portion attributed to the model, error, and total
❹ `Mean Square`      mean square (sum of squares divided by the degrees of freedom)
❺ `F Value`          F value (mean square for model divided by the mean square for error)
❻ `Pr > F`           significance probability associated with the F statistic
❼ `R-Square`         R-square
❽ `Coeff Var`        coefficient of variation
❾ `Root MSE`         root mean square error
❿ `Height Mean`      mean of the dependent variable

Because the effect of Team is significant (significance probability = .0053), we conclude that not all the teams are the same height. The SCHEFFE option in the MEANS statement compares the heights between the teams. Letters are used to group means, and means with the same letters are not significantly different from each other (at the 0.05 level). The following results show that your friend's daughter is partially correct—one team (PINK) is taller than her team (RED) but not all the teams are taller.

```
                 Girls' Heights on Basketball Teams                    3

                         The ANOVA Procedure


                      Scheffe's Test for Height

       NOTE: This test controls the type I experimentwise error rate.


                 Alpha                              0.05
                 Error Degrees of Freedom             55
                 Error Mean Square              13.78182
                 Critical Value of F            2.53969
                 Minimum Significant Difference  4.8306


            Means with the same letter are not significantly different.

          Scheffe Grouping          Mean      N    Team

                           A       54.833     12    pink
                           A
                     B     A       50.500     12    gold
                     B     A
                     B     A       50.333     12    gray
                     B
                     B             49.833     12    blue
                     B
                     B             49.500     12    red
```

**9**

> "When we try to pick out anything by itself, we find it hitched to everything in the Universe."

JOHN MUIR

From *My First Summer in the Sierra* by John Muir. Public domain.

# CHAPTER 9

## Exporting Your Data

## 9.1 Methods for Exporting Your Data

In our ever increasingly complex world, people often need to transfer data from one application to another or from one type of computer to another. Fortunately, SAS gives you many options for doing this.

**Exporting data to other applications** The types of files that you can create and the methods available for creating those files depends on what operating environment you are using and whether you have SAS/ACCESS software. There are three general methods for exporting data to other applications: create delimited or text files that the other software can read; create files in formats like HTML, RTF, or XML that the other software can read; or write the data in the other software's native format.

♦   No matter what your environment, you can always create delimited files and most software has the ability to read these types of data files. The DATA step, discussed in section 9.5, gives you the most control over the format of your files, but requires the most steps. The Export Wizard, discussed in section 9.2, and the EXPORT procedure, discussed in section 9.3, are easy to use, but you have less control over the result and not everyone has access to these tools. The Output Delivery System (ODS), discussed in section 9.6, can create comma-separated values (CSV) files from any procedure output and a simple PROC PRINT will produce a reasonable file for importing into other programs.

♦   Using ODS, discussed in section 9.6, you can create HTML, RTF, and XML files from any procedure output. Many applications can read data in these types of files. Although we do not cover creating RTF and XML files for this purpose, the general method is the same as creating HTML files.

♦   If you have SAS/ACCESS Interface to PC Files, then you can create several different file types that are common for PC applications. Both the Export Wizard, discussed in section 9.2, and the EXPORT procedure, discussed in section 9.4, can produce PC files. By creating the files in the native format of the application, you avoid the extra step of importing the file into the other application. There are also other SAS/ACCESS products for many popular database management systems including ORACLE, DB2, INGRES, and SYBASE. If you don't have SAS/ACCESS Interface to PC Files, and you are using Windows, you can use Dynamic Data Exchange (DDE) or Open Database Connectivity (ODBC) to move data from SAS to PC applications without creating any intermediate files. For more information on using other SAS/ACCESS products, DDE, or ODBC to export SAS data, see the SAS Help and Documentation.

**Exporting SAS data sets to other operating environments** Since not all computers store data using the same representation, sometimes it is necessary to convert data from one type to another if you are moving your data from one operating environment to another. The following are some of the available methods: Cross-Environment Data Access (CEDA), the XPORT engine or the CPORT procedure, the XML engine, and SAS/CONNECT software.

♦ CEDA, covered in section 9.7, is by far the simplest method for moving SAS data sets to other operating environments. However CEDA cannot be used for SAS Version 6 data sets, nor for data stored in z/OS bound libraries.

♦ Both the XPORT engine and the CPORT procedure create transport files which can be moved to other operating environments and then converted back into SAS data sets. Creating transport files can cause loss in numerical precision, but for SAS Version 6 data sets, or data stored in z/OS bound libraries, CEDA is not an option so you may need to use one of these methods. See the SAS Help and Documentation for more information about the XPORT engine and the CPORT procedure.

♦ If you are using SAS 9 or later, then you can use the XML engine on the LIBNAME statement to create XML documents from your SAS data sets. The XML documents can then be transferred to another computer and turned back into SAS data sets using the XML engine for input. See the SAS Help and Documentation for more information.

♦ SAS/CONNECT software (not part of Base SAS software), along with many other capabilities, allows you to transfer SAS data sets to other operating environments without creating intermediate transport files. SAS/CONNECT software can move SAS data sets from an earlier version of SAS to a later version and vice versa. See the SAS Help and Documentation for more information about SAS/CONNECT software.

## 9.2 Writing Files Using the Export Wizard

The Export Wizard[1] provides an easy way to produce files that can be imported into other software.[2] The Export Wizard is a Graphical User Interface (GUI) to the EXPORT procedure (discussed in sections 9.3 and 9.4) and if you need to export data only once in a while, then it's easier than trying to remember the PROC EXPORT statements.

Start the Export Wizard by selecting `Export Data...` from the File menu.

In the first Export Wizard window, choose the library and member name for the SAS data set that you want to export. If you are exporting a temporary SAS data set, then the library is WORK. If you are exporting a permanent SAS data set, then make sure your library is defined before you start the Export Wizard. Then choose the library from the drop-down list. The member name is the name of the SAS data set. In this window you can also choose to use the variable labels instead of the variable names as the column names (available starting with SAS 9.2).

In the next window, choose the type of file you would like to create. Either choose from the pull-down list of standard data sources, or check the box next to `User-defined formats`. The User-defined formats takes you to the External File Interface (EFI) facility which enables you to assign formats to your variables, as well as choose either a delimited file structure, or a file that is arranged into columns. If you select one of the standard data sources, then any formats that you have assigned to variables in the SAS data set

---

[1] The Export Wizard is available for the Windows, UNIX, and OpenVMS operating environments.

[2] The Export Wizard can write data files in many different formats including space-, comma-, and tab-delimited files and files formatted into columns. In addition, if you have SAS/ACCESS Interface to PC Files, under Windows and UNIX you can write dBase files and, starting with SAS 9.2, SPSS, Stata, JMP, and Paradox files. Under Windows you can write Microsoft Excel and Lotus files, and under 32-bit Windows you can also write Microsoft Access files.

will be applied when creating the data file. If you choose either the Microsoft Excel or Microsoft Access file types, then you will be presented with additional windows where you can make choices about table names for Microsoft Excel, and database information for Microsoft Access.

In the next window you choose the location for the exported data. If you are exporting delimited data, then you may also choose the delimiter by clicking the Options button in this window. If any of your data contain the delimiter that you choose, then that value will be enclosed in double quotation marks. For delimited, CSV, and tab-delimited file types, you can choose to write variable names or variable labels in the first row of the file, or write the data only by clicking the Options button.

In the final window you have the option to save the PROC EXPORT statements that are generated through the Export Wizard.

## 9.3 Writing Delimited Files with the EXPORT Procedure

The EXPORT procedure, like the Export Wizard, is available for Windows, UNIX, and OpenVMS operating environments. Since the Export Wizard is an interface to the EXPORT procedure, you can create the same types of files with the EXPORT procedure that you can with the Export Wizard. The advantage of using the procedure over the wizard is that you can incorporate the procedure code into existing SAS programs, and you don't need to step through all the Export Wizard windows every time you want to create a file.

**The EXPORT procedure** The general form of PROC EXPORT is

```
PROC EXPORT DATA = data-set OUTFILE = 'filename';
```

where *data-set* is the SAS data set you want to export, and *filename* is the name you make up for the output data file. The following statement tells SAS to read a temporary SAS data set named HOTELS and write a comma-delimited file named Hotels.csv in a directory named MyRawData on the C drive (Windows):

```
PROC EXPORT DATA = hotels OUTFILE = 'c:\MyRawData\Hotels.csv';
```

SAS uses the last part of the filename, called the file extension, to decide what type of file to create. You can also specify the file type by adding the DBMS= option to the PROC EXPORT statement. The following table shows the filename extensions and DBMS identifiers currently available with Base SAS software. If you specify the DBMS option, then it takes precedence over the file extension.

| Type of file | Extension | DBMS Identifier |
|---|---|---|
| Comma-delimited | .csv | CSV |
| Tab-delimited | .txt | TAB |
| Space-delimited | | DLM |

Notice that for space-delimited files, there is no standard extension so you must use the DBMS= option. The following statement, containing the DBMS= option, tells SAS to create a space-delimited file named Hotels.spc. The REPLACE option tells SAS to replace any file with the same name.

```
PROC EXPORT DATA = hotels OUTFILE = 'c:\MyRawData\Hotels.spc'
      DBMS = DLM REPLACE;
```

If you want to create a file with a delimiter other than a comma, tab, or space, then you can add the DELIMITER statement. If you use the DELIMITER statement, then it does not matter what file extension you use, or what DBMS identifier you specify, the file will have the delimiter that you specify in the DELIMITER statement. For example, the following would produce a file, Hotels.txt, that has the ampersand (&) as the delimiter:

```
PROC EXPORT DATA = hotels OUTFILE = 'c:\MyRawData\Hotels.txt'
      DBMS = DLM REPLACE;
   DELIMITER='&';
```

**Example** A travel company maintains a SAS data set containing information about golf courses. For each golf course the file includes its name, number of holes, par, yardage, and greens fees. Here is a subset of the data:

```
Kapalua Plantation 18 73 7263 125.00
Pukalani           18 72 6945  55.00
Sandlewood         18 72 6469  35.00
Silversword        18 71    .  57.00
Waiehu Municipal   18 72 6330  25.00
Grand Waikapa      18 72 6122 200.00
```

The following program uses INFILE and INPUT statements to read the data and put them in a permanent SAS data set named GOLF in the MySASLib directory on the C drive (Windows). This example uses a LIBNAME statement to tell SAS where to store the permanent SAS data set, but you could use direct referencing instead:

```
LIBNAME travel 'c:\MySASLib';
DATA travel.golf;
   INFILE 'c:\MyRawData\Golf.dat';
   INPUT CourseName $18. NumberOfHoles Par Yardage GreenFees;
RUN;
```

Now, suppose you want to write a letter to a potential customer and insert the golf data. The following program writes a plain text, tab-delimited file that you can read with any text editor or word processor:

```
LIBNAME travel 'c:\MySASLib';
* Create Tab-delimited file;
PROC EXPORT DATA = travel.golf OUTFILE = 'c:\MyRawData\Golf.txt' REPLACE;
RUN;
```

Because the name of the output file ends with .txt and there is no DELIMITER statement, SAS will write a tab-delimited file. If you run this program, your log will contain the following note about the output file:

```
NOTE: 7 records were written to the file 'c:\MyRawData\Golf.txt'.
```

Notice that while the data set contained six observations, SAS wrote seven records. The extra record contains the variable names. If you read this file into a word processor and set the tabs, it will look like this:

```
CourseName          NumberOfHoles  Par  Yardage  GreenFees
Kapalua Plantation  18             73   7263     125
Pukalani            18             72   6945     55
Sandlewood          18             72   6469     35
Silversword         18             71            57
Waiehu Municipal    18             72   6330     25
Grand Waikapa       18             72   6122     200
```

Any format that you have assigned to variables in the SAS data set will be used by PROC EXPORT when creating the delimited file. If you want to change a format, use a FORMAT statement (discussed in section 4.5) in a DATA step before running PROC EXPORT.

## 9.4 Writing PC Files with the EXPORT Procedure

If you are using the Windows or UNIX operating environments, and you have SAS/ACCESS Interface to PC Files, then you can use the EXPORT procedure to create PC file types in addition to delimited files. File types you can write include: Microsoft Excel, Lotus (not on UNIX), dBase, Microsoft Access, and starting with SAS 9.2, JMP, Paradox, SPSS, and Stata.

Here is the general form of PROC EXPORT for writing PC files except Microsoft Access:

```
PROC EXPORT DATA = data-set OUTFILE = 'filename' REPLACE;
```

where *data-set* is the SAS data set you want to export, and *filename* is the name you make up for the output data file. The REPLACE option tells SAS to replace the file if it already exists. SAS uses the last part of the filename, called the file extension, to decide what type of file to create. You can also specify the file type by adding the DBMS= option. The following table shows the filename extensions and DBMS identifiers:

| Type of file | Extension | DBMS Identifier |
| --- | --- | --- |
| Microsoft Excel | .xls | EXCEL |
| | | XLS |
| dBase | .dbf | DBF |
| JMP | .jmp | JMP |
| Lotus | .wk4 | WK4 |
| Paradox | .db | PARADOX |
| SPSS Save file | .sav | SAV |
| Stata | .dta | DTA |

**Microsoft Excel files**  For Excel 97 through Excel 2003 files,[1] you can use the default EXCEL identifier under 32-bit Windows, or the XLS identifier for UNIX and both 32- and 64-bit Windows. By default, the name of the Microsoft Excel sheet will be the same as the name of the SAS data set. If you want the sheet to have a different name, then specify it in the SHEET= statement. Special characters in sheet names will be converted to underscores, and the $ is not allowed at the end of the sheet name. The following statement creates a sheet named Golf_Hotels:

```
SHEET = 'Golf Hotels';
```

**Microsoft Access files**  If you want to create a Microsoft Access database file, then instead of using the OUTFILE= option, you use the OUTTABLE= option and you add the DATABASE= statement. The general form of PROC EXPORT for Microsoft Access files is

```
PROC EXPORT DATA = data-set OUTTABLE = 'filename' DBMS = identifier;
    DATABASE = 'filename';
```

The DATABASE statement specifies which Microsoft Access database you wish to modify or create and the OUTTABLE= option specifies the name of the table in that database. If you need to specify user IDs, passwords, or workgroups for your database, there are optional statements that allow you to do this. See the SAS Help and Documentation for more information. You must specify the DBMS option to create a Microsoft Access table. To write Microsoft Access 97 files,

---

[1] To create files readable by Excel5, use the EXCEL5 identifier (not available under UNIX). Excel 2007 files are supported starting with SAS 9.2 Phase 2.

use the ACCESS97 identifier, for 2000 to 2003 files, use the ACCESS identifier. All Microsoft Access files have the .mdb extension.

| Type of file | Extension | DBMS Identifier |
|---|---|---|
| Microsoft Access | .mdb | ACCESS[2] |
|  |  | ACCESS97 |

**Example**  A travel company maintains a SAS data set containing information about golf courses. For each golf course the file includes its name, number of holes, par, yardage, and greens fees. Here is a subset of the data:

```
Kapalua Plantation 18 73 7263 125.00
Pukalani           18 72 6945  55.00
Sandlewood         18 72 6469  35.00
Silversword        18 71   .   57.00
Waiehu Municipal   18 72 6330  25.00
Grand Waikapa      18 72 6122 200.00
```

The following program uses INFILE and INPUT statements to read the data and put them in a permanent SAS data set named GOLF in the MySASLib directory on the C drive (Windows):

```
LIBNAME travel 'c:\MySASLib';
DATA travel.golf;
    INFILE 'c:\MyRawData\Golf.dat';
    INPUT CourseName $18. NumberOfHoles Par Yardage GreenFees;
RUN;
```

Now suppose your office mate needs that information, but she wants it in a Microsoft Excel file. The following program writes a Microsoft Excel file from the SAS data set GOLF:

```
LIBNAME travel 'c:\MySASLib';
* Create Microsoft Excel file';
PROC EXPORT DATA=travel.golf OUTFILE = 'c:\MyExcel\Golf.xls' REPLACE;
RUN;
```

Here is what the Microsoft Excel file looks like. Notice that the name of the sheet is the same as the name of the SAS data set.

If you have user-defined formats which have been associated with variables, PROC EXPORT will export them to JMP, SPSS, and Stata files, but not to other PC file types.

---

[2] To write Microsoft Access files under the UNIX operating environment, you will need the PC Files Server installed, and you will use the ACCESSCS identifier. Microsoft Access 2007 files are supported starting with SAS 9.2 Phase 2. See the SAS Help and Documentation for more information.

# 9.5  Writing Raw Data Files with the DATA Step

When you need total control over the contents and format of raw data files that you are creating, then the DATA step is the way to go. Using FILE and PUT statements in the DATA step, you can write almost any form of raw data file. This method has, to some extent, been replaced by the easier-to-use PROC EXPORT and Export Wizard,[1] but while PROC EXPORT gives you only a few options in formatting your files, the DATA step gives you flexibility to create raw data files just the way you want.

You can write raw data the same way that you read raw data, with just a few changes. Instead of naming the external file in an INFILE statement, you name it in a FILE statement. Instead of reading variables with an INPUT statement, you write them with a PUT statement. To say it another way, you use INFILE and INPUT statements to get raw data into SAS, and FILE and PUT statements to get raw data out.

PUT statements can be in list, column, or formatted style, just like INPUT statements, but since SAS already knows whether a variable is numeric or character, you don't have to put a $ after character variables. If you use list format, SAS will automatically put one space between each variable, creating a space-delimited file. To write files with other delimiters, use a list-style PUT statement and the DSD= and DLM= options in your FILE statement.[2]

```
FILE 'file-specification' DSD DLM = 'delimiter';
```

If you use column or formatted styles of PUT statements, SAS will put the variables wherever you specify. You can control spacing with the same pointer controls that INPUT statements use: @$n$ to move to column $n$, +$n$ to move $n$ columns, / to skip to the next line, #$n$ to skip to line $n$, and the trailing @ to hold the current line. In addition to printing variables, you can insert a text string by simply enclosing it in quotation marks.

**Example**  To show how much more control you have using the DATA step as opposed to PROC EXPORT, this example uses the same data containing information about golf courses. For each course the file includes the course name, number of holes, par, yardage, and greens fees. Here is a subset of the data:

```
Kapalua Plantation 18 73 7263 125.00
Pukalani           18 72 6945  55.00
Sandlewood         18 72 6469  35.00
Silversword        18 71    .  57.00
Waiehu Municipal   18 72 6330  25.00
Grand Waikapa      18 72 6122 200.00
```

---

[1] In the z/OS operating environment you cannot use EXPORT, but you can use the DATA step to write raw data files.

[2] See section 2.15 for a discussion of the DSD= and DLM= options.

The following program uses INFILE and INPUT statements to read the data from a file called Golf.dat and put it in a permanent SAS data set named GOLF in the MySASLib directory on the C drive (Windows):

```
LIBNAME travel 'c:\MySASLib';
DATA travel.golf;
    INFILE 'c:\MyRawData\Golf.dat';
    INPUT CourseName $18. NumberOfHoles Par Yardage GreenFees;
RUN;
```

Suppose you want to put the data in a raw data file, but with only three variables, in a new order, and with dollar signs added to the variable GreenFees. The following program reads the SAS data set and writes a raw data file using FILE and PUT statements:

```
LIBNAME travel 'c:\MySASLib';
DATA _NULL_;
    SET travel.golf;
    FILE 'c:\MyRawData\Newfile.dat';
    PUT CourseName 'Golf Course' @32 GreenFees DOLLAR7.2 @40 'Par ' Par;
RUN;
```

The word _NULL_ appears in the DATA statement instead of a SAS data set name. You could put a data set name there, but _NULL_ is a special keyword that tells SAS not to bother making a new SAS data set. By not writing a new SAS data set, you save computer resources.

The SET statement simply tells SAS to read the permanent SAS data set GOLF. The FILE statement tells SAS the name of the output file you want to create. Then, the PUT statement tells SAS what to write and where. The PUT statement contains two quoted strings, "Golf Course" and "Par" which SAS inserts in the raw data file. The PUT statement also tells SAS exactly where to place the data values for each variable using the @ column pointer, and to use the DOLLAR7.2 format to write the values for the GreenFees variable. Using the PUT statement you have complete control over the content of your raw data files.

If you run this program, your log will contain the following note telling how many records were written to the output file:

```
NOTE: 6 records were written to the file 'c:\MyRawData\Newfile.dat'.
```

Here is what the output file looks like in the text editor Microsoft Notepad:

## 9.6 Writing Delimited and HTML Files Using ODS

The Output Delivery System (ODS) is a powerful tool for creating all sorts of output formats. Some of the output formats that ODS can create are useful for transferring data from SAS to other applications. Many applications can read data that are in either CSV or HTML format, and the great thing is that you can use this method in any operating environment and it's included in Base SAS software.

Since all procedure output goes to ODS, you can use ODS to export data by choosing the appropriate output destination for your application, and using PROC PRINT to get a listing of your data. By default, SAS will print a period for any missing numeric data. If you would rather have SAS print nothing for missing numeric data, then you can use the MISSING='' system option. Also by default, PROC PRINT includes observation numbers. If you don't want observation numbers in your output file, then use the NOOBS option on the PROC PRINT statement.

**CSV files** CSV files have commas separating all the data values and the values are enclosed in double quotation marks. The double quotation marks allow values to contain commas as part of the value. To create a CSV file containing your data, use the following ODS statements:

```
ODS CSV FILE = 'filename.csv';
  Your PROC PRINT statements go here
RUN;
ODS CSV CLOSE;
```

Where *filename.csv* is the name of the CSV file that you are creating, and you insert the appropriate PROC PRINT statements for your data. The CSV output destination does not include titles or footnotes; if you want titles and footnotes to appear in the CSV file, then use the CSVALL output destination instead of CSV.

**HTML files** Use the following statements to produce an HTML file of your data (and any titles or footnotes) with the default style. You can choose a different style by adding the STYLE= option to the ODS HTML statement. Or, if you do not want any styling, then use the CHTML (compact HTML) output destination instead of HTML.

```
ODS HTML FILE = 'filename.html';
  Your PROC PRINT statements go here
RUN;
ODS HTML CLOSE;
```

**Example** This example uses the permanent SAS data set, GOLF (created in the previous section), which has information about golf courses in Hawaii. The following program uses ODS to create a CSV file, golfinfo.csv, from the results of the PRINT procedure:

```
LIBNAME travel 'c:\MySASLib';
ODS CSV FILE='c:\MyCSVFiles\golfinfo.csv';
PROC PRINT DATA = travel.golf;
  TITLE 'Golf Course Information';
RUN;
ODS CSV CLOSE;
```

This is what the CSV file, golfinfo.csv, looks like if you open it in a simple editor such as Microsoft Notepad:

If you open the same file, golfinfo.csv, using Microsoft Excel, this is what you see:

The following program creates an HTML file, golfinfo.html,[1] of the GOLF data, this time using the NOOBS option on the PROC PRINT statement to eliminate the Obs column:

```
LIBNAME travel 'c:\MySASLib';
ODS HTML FILE='c:\MyHTMLFiles\golfinfo.html';
PROC PRINT DATA = travel.golf NOOBS;
   TITLE 'Golf Course Information';
RUN;
ODS HTML CLOSE;
```

This is what the HTML file looks like when you open it Microsoft Excel. You can see that although the data are the same as in the CSV file, the HTML file also includes the title and the default HTML styling.

---

[1] If you want the HTML file to be automatically recognized as a Microsoft Excel file, then give the file the .xls extension instead of the .html extension.

## 9.7   Sharing SAS Data Sets with Other Types of Computers

When you access a SAS data set,[1] SAS looks at the data set to determine if it is compatible with the operating environment that you are using. If the data set is in a representation of a different operating environment, then SAS will automatically use Cross-Environment Data Access (CEDA) to dynamically translate the data into a form that SAS in your operating environment can understand. Two cases where CEDA cannot be used are: SAS data sets in z/OS bound libraries and SAS Version 6 or earlier data sets. For these types of data sets see "If you can't use CEDA" at the end of this section.

**Determining data representation**  Whenever SAS uses CEDA to access your data, a note will appear in your SAS log[2]. The note informs you that you are using a data set native to another host. Here is an example of the note:

---
```
INFO: Data file TEST.MYUNIX.DATA is in a format that is native to another
host, or the file encoding does not match the session encoding. Cross
Environment Data Access will be used, which might require additional CPU
resources and might reduce performance.
```
---

To find out which foreign host was used to create the data set, run the CONTENTS procedure for the SAS data set.

**Creating SAS data sets for foreign hosts**  If you need to use your SAS data sets on a computer with a different operating environment than the one where they were created, then you might want to create the data sets in the representation of the other computer. This way when the other computer accesses the data, it doesn't have to waste resources translating the data to its own format. You do this by using the OUTREP= option on either the LIBNAME statement, if you want all the data sets in that library to have the specified host representation, or as a data set option if you only want it to apply to one data set. The general form for the LIBNAME statement is:

```
LIBNAME libref 'path' OUTREP = data-representation;
```

The general form for the data set option is:

```
data-set-name(OUTREP = data-representation)
```

There are many possible values for *data-representation*. The data representation is basically the name of the operating environment. For example if you want the data representation for the Microsoft Windows 64-Bit Edition, the value is: WINDOWS_64. If you want the data representation for the Solaris 32-Bit Edition, the value is: SOLARIS_32. See the SAS Help and Documentation for a complete list of possible values.

---

[1] Accessing data sets includes reading the data and performing simple functions such as sorting, setting, or reading the data set in a procedure. Some functions, such as using the MODIFY statement, are not allowed. If you get an error message when trying to access a data set created on a different host, then convert the data set to your operating environment before continuing.

[2] If you are using SAS 8, then you may need to set the MSGLEVEL system option to I for the CEDA note to appear in the SAS log.

**Example** You have data about golf courses in Hawaii stored in a permanent SAS data set named GOLF on your Windows desktop computer. Your friend, who needs to use the golf data, is a LINUX guru and always gives you a hard time for using Windows. You decide to send him the data in LINUX format so you won't get any grief for using Windows. The following program uses the SET statement in a DATA step to read the GOLF data from the SPORTS library, then the OUTREP= data set option on the DATA statement tells SAS to write the data in LINUX format for a 32-bit platform creating a SAS data set named GOLFLINUX.

```
LIBNAME sports 'c:\MySASLib';
DATA sports.golflinux(OUTREP=LINUX_32);
  SET sports.golf;
RUN;
```

The following note is added to the SAS log informing you that CEDA was used to create the GOLFLINUX data set:

```
INFO: Data file SPORTS.GOLFLINUX.DATA is in a format that is native to another
host, or the file encoding does not match the session encoding. Cross
Environment Data Access will be used, which might require additional CPU
resources and might reduce performance.
```

**Moving SAS data sets** If both computers have access to the same file system, then simply point your LIBNAME statement to the directory where the SAS data set is located. Otherwise you can transfer the SAS data set using FTP (File Transfer Protocol) in binary mode, or use external media such as a CD, DVD, or flash drive.

**FAT file systems** Some Windows systems which use FAT (File Allocation Table) file systems can have only files with three-character extensions. For these systems the extension for SAS data sets is .sd7 instead of the usual .sas7bdat. If you receive a SAS data set with a three letter extension, then use the MIGRATE procedure as follows to convert the data.

```
LIBNNAME libref1 'path-for-files-with-short-extension' SHORTFILEEXT;
LIBNNAME libref2 'path-for-new-files';
PROC MIGRATE IN=libref1 OUT=libref2;
RUN;
```

**If you can't use CEDA** If you need to read a SAS Version 6 data set that was created in a different operating environment, or if you are using SAS data sets in bound libraries in the z/OS operating environment, then you will not be able to use CEDA. In these cases, you will either need to create a SAS data set in transport format, create an XML document using the XML engine, or use SAS/CONNECT software to transfer data. You can use either the XPORT engine or PROC CPORT to create transport files. Transport files created using the XPORT engine must be read with the XPORT engine and files created with PROC CPORT must be read with PROC CIMPORT. The drawbacks to using transport files include the following: extra steps are needed to create and read the files, they do not support variable names over 8 characters, and you can lose precision in numeric data. Creating XML documents will preserve your long variable names, but you must have SAS 9 or higher to read the XML documents. SAS/CONNECT software does not create an intermediate file, but it is an add-on product and not every one has it. See the SAS Help and Documentation for more information on moving and accessing SAS files.

# 10

"Problems that go away by themselves come back by themselves."

MARCY E. DAVIS

CHAPTER 10

# Debugging Your SAS Programs

## 10.1 Writing SAS Programs That Work

It's not always easy to write a program that works the first time you run it. Even experienced SAS programmers will tell you it's a delightful surprise when their programs run on the first try. The longer and more complicated the program, the more likely it is to have syntax or logic errors. But don't despair, there are a few guidelines you can follow that can make your programs run correctly sooner and help you discover errors more easily.

**Make programs easy to read**  One simple thing you can do is develop the habit of writing programs in a neat and consistent manner. Programs that are easy to read are easier to debug and will save you time in the long run. The following are suggestions on how to write your programs:

♦ Put only one SAS statement on a line. SAS allows you to put as many statements on a line as you wish, which may save you some space in your program, but the saved space is rarely worth the sacrifice in readability.

♦ Use indention to show the different parts of the program. Indent all statements within the DATA and PROC steps. This way you can tell at a glance how many DATA and PROC steps there are in a program and which statement belongs to which step. It's also helpful to further indent any statements between a DO statement and its END statement.

♦ Use comment statements generously to document your programs. This takes some discipline but is important, especially if anyone else is likely to read or use your program. Everyone has a different programming style, and it is often impossible to figure out what someone else's program is doing and why. Comment statements take the mystery out of the program.

**Test each part of the program**  You can increase your programming efficiency tremendously by making sure each part of your program is working before moving on to write the next part. If you were building a house, you would make sure the foundation was level and square before putting up the walls. You would test the plumbing before finishing the bathroom. You are required to have each stage of the house inspected before moving on to the next. The same should be done for your SAS program. But you don't have to wait for the inspector to come out; you can do it yourself.

If you are reading data from a file, use Viewtable or PROC PRINT to check the SAS data set at least once to make sure it is correct before moving on. Sometimes, even though there are no errors or even suspicious notes in your SAS log, the SAS data set is not correct. This could happen because SAS did not read the data the way you imagined (after all it does what you say, not what you're thinking) or because the data had some peculiarities you did not realize. For example, a researcher who received two data files from Taiwan wanted to merge them together by date. She could not figure out why they refused to merge correctly until she printed both data sets and realized one of the files used Taiwanese dates, which are offset by 11 years.

It's a good habit to look at all the SAS data sets you create in a program at least once to make sure they are correct. As with reading raw data files, sometimes merging and setting data sets can produce the wrong result even though there were no error messages. So when in doubt, use Viewtable or PROC PRINT.

**Test programs with small data sets** Sometimes it's not practical to test your program with your entire data set. If your data files are very large, you may not want to print all the data and it may take a long time for your programs to run. In these cases, you can test your program with a subset of your data.

If you are reading data from a file, you can use the OBS= option in the INFILE statement to tell SAS to stop reading when it gets to that line in the file. This way you can read only the first 50 or 100 lines of data or however many it takes to get a good representation of your data. The following statement will read only the first 100 lines of the raw data file Mydata.dat:

```
INFILE 'Mydata.dat' OBS = 100;
```

You can also use the FIRSTOBS= option to start reading from the middle of the data file. So, if the first 100 data lines are not a good representation of your data but 101 through 200 are, you can use the following statement to read just those lines:

```
INFILE 'Mydata.dat' FIRSTOBS = 101 OBS = 200;
```

Here FIRSTOBS= and OBS= relate to the records of raw data in the file. These do not necessarily correspond to the observations in the SAS data set created. If, for example, you are reading two records for each observation, then you would need to read 200 records to get 100 observations.

If you are reading a SAS data set instead of a raw data file, you can use the OBS= and FIRSTOBS= data set options in the SET, MERGE, or UPDATE statements.[1] This controls which observations are processed in the DATA step. For example, the following DATA step will read the first 50 observations in the CATS data set. Note that when reading SAS data sets, OBS= and FIRSTOBS= truly do correspond to the observations and not to data lines:

```
DATA sampleofcats;
   SET cats (OBS = 50);
```

**Test with representative data** Using OBS= and FIRSTOBS= is an easy way to test your programs, but sometimes it is difficult to get a good representation of your data this way. You may need to create a small test data set by extracting representative parts of the larger data set. Or you may want to make up representative data for testing purposes. Making up data has the advantage that you can simplify the data and make sure you have every possible combination of values to test.

Sometimes you may want to make up data and write a small program just to test one aspect of your larger program. This can be extremely useful for narrowing down possible sources of error in a large, complicated program.

**Syntax sensitive editors** In the Windows operating environment the Enhanced Editor is the default editor; in other operating environments the Program Editor is the default. Both the Enhanced Editor and the Program Editor color code your program as you write it. SAS keywords appear in one color, variables in another. All text within quotation marks appears in the same color, so it is immediately obvious when you forget to close your quotation marks. Similarly, missing semicolons are much easier to discover because the colors in your program are not right. Catching errors as you type them can be a real time saver.

---

[1] Data set options are discussed in section 6.11.

## 10.2   Fixing Programs That Don't Work

In spite of your best efforts, sometimes programs just don't work. More often than not, programs don't run the first time. Even with simple programs it is easy to forget a semicolon or misspell a keyword—everyone does sometime. If your program doesn't work, the source of the problem may be obvious like an error message with the offending part of your program underlined, or not so obvious as when you have no errors but still don't have the expected results. Whatever the problem, here are a few guidelines you can follow to help fix your program.

**Read the SAS log**   The SAS log has a wealth of information about your program. In addition to listing the program statements, it tells you things like how many lines were read from your raw data file and what were the minimum and maximum line lengths. It gives the number of observations and variables in each SAS data set you create. Information like this may seem inconsequential at first but can be very helpful in finding the source of your errors.

The SAS log has three types of messages about your program: errors, warnings, and notes.

**Errors**   These are hard to ignore. Not only do they come up in red on your screen, but your program will not run with errors. Usually errors are some kind of syntax or spelling mistake. The following shows the error message when you accidentally add a slash between the PROC PRINT and DATA= keywords. SAS underlines the problem (the slash) and tells you there is a syntax error. Sometimes SAS will tell you what is expected in the location where the error occurred and often this is very revealing.

```
1     PROC PRINT / DATA=one;
                  -
                  22
                  200
      ERROR 22-322: Syntax error, expecting one of the following: ;, BLANKLINE, DATA,
      DOUBLE, HEADING, LABEL, N, NOOBS, OBS, ROUND, ROWS, SPLIT, STYLE, UNIFORM, WIDTH.
      ERROR 200-322: The symbol is not recognized and will be ignored.
```

The location of the error is easy to find, because it is usually underlined, but the source of the error can sometimes be tricky. Sometimes what is wrong is not what is underlined but something else earlier in the program.

**Warnings**   These are less serious than errors because your program will run with warnings. But beware, a warning may mean that SAS has done something you have not intended. For example, SAS will attempt to correct your spelling of certain keywords. If you misspell INPUT as IMPUT you will get the following message in your log:

```
WARNING 1-322: Assuming the symbol INPUT was misspelled as IMPUT.
```

Usually you would think, "SAS is so smart—it knows what I meant to say," but occasionally that may not be what you meant at all. Make sure that you know what all the warnings are about and that you agree with them.

**Notes**   These are less straightforward than either warnings or errors. Sometimes notes just give you information, like telling you the execution time of each step in your program. But sometimes notes can indicate a problem. Suppose, for example, that you have the following note in your SAS log:

```
NOTE: SAS went to a new line when INPUT statement reached past the end of a line.
```

This could mean that SAS did exactly what you wanted, or it could indicate a problem with either your program or your data. Make sure that you know what each note means and why it is there.

**Start at the beginning**    Whenever you read the SAS log, start at the beginning. This seems like a ridiculous statement—why wouldn't you start at the beginning? Well, if you are using the SAS windowing environment, the SAS log rolls by in the Log window. When the program is finished, you are left looking at the end of the log. If you happen to see an error at the end of the log, it is natural to try to fix that error first—the first one you see. Avoid this temptation. Often errors at the end of the log are caused by earlier ones. If you fix the first error, often most or all of the other errors will disappear. If your lawnmower is out of gas and won't start, it's probably better to add gas before trying to figure out why it won't start. The same logic applies to debugging SAS programs; fixing one problem will often fix others.

**Look for common mistakes first**    More often than not there is a simple reason why your program doesn't work. Look for the simple reason before trying to find something more complicated. The remainder of this chapter consists of sections discussing the most common errors encountered in SAS programming. When you see this little bug in the upper-right corner of a section, you'll know that the material deals with how to debug your program. Some programming errors produce error messages, some just notes. If your SAS log contains an error or a suspicious note, look in this chapter for a section which discusses your error or note.

Sometimes error messages just don't make any sense. For example, you may get an error message saying the INPUT statement is not valid. This doesn't make much sense because you know INPUT is a valid SAS statement. In cases like these, look for missing semicolons in the statements before the error. If SAS has underlined an item, be sure to look not only at the underlined item but also at the previous few statements.

Finally, if you just can't figure out why you are not getting the results you expect, make sure to use Viewtable or PROC PRINT to check any new SAS data sets you create. This can really help you discover errors in your logic, and sometimes uncover surprising details about your data.

**Check your syntax**    If you have large data sets, you may want to check for syntax errors in your program before processing your data. Do this by telling SAS not to process any data when you submit your program. Add the following line to your program and submit it in the usual way:

```
OPTIONS OBS=0 NOREPLACE;
```

The OBS=0 option tells SAS not to process any data, while the NOREPLACE option tells SAS not to replace existing SAS data sets with empty ones. Once you know your syntax is correct, you can resubmit your program without the OPTIONS statement in batch mode, or replace the OPTIONS with the following if you are using the SAS windowing environment.

```
OPTIONS OBS=MAX REPLACE;
```

Remember that this syntax check will not uncover any errors related to your data or logic.

## 10.3   Searching for the Missing Semicolon

Missing semicolons are the most common source of errors in SAS programs. For whatever reason, we humans can't seem to remember to put a semicolon at the end of all our statements. (Maybe we all have rebellious right pinkies—who knows.) This is unfortunate because, while it is easy to forget the semicolon, it is not always easy to find the missing semicolon. The error messages produced are often misleading, making it difficult to find the error.

SAS reads statements from one semicolon to the next without regard to the layout of the program. If you leave off a semicolon, you in effect concatenate two SAS statements. Then SAS gets confused because it seems as though you are missing statements, or it tries to interpret entire statements as options in the previous statement. This can produce some very puzzling messages. So, if you get an error message that just doesn't make sense, look for missing semicolons.

**Example**   The following program is missing a semicolon on the comment statement before the DATA statement:

```
* Read the data file ToadJump.dat using list input
DATA toads;
    INFILE 'c:\MyRawData\ToadJump.dat';
    INPUT ToadName $ Weight Jump1 Jump2 Jump3;
RUN;
```

Here is the SAS log after the program has run:

```
1      * Read the data file ToadJump.dat using list input
2      DATA toads;
3          INFILE 'c:\MyRawData\ToadJump.dat';
       ------                          '
       180

ERROR 180-322: Statement is not valid or it is used out of proper order.

4          INPUT ToadName $ Weight Jump1 Jump2 Jump3;
       -----
       180

ERROR 180-322: Statement is not valid or it is used out of proper order.
5      RUN;
```

In this case, DATA toads becomes part of the comment statement. Because there is now no DATA statement, SAS underlines the INFILE and INPUT keywords and says, "Hey these statements are in the wrong place; they have to be part of a DATA step." This doesn't make much sense to you because you know INFILE and INPUT are valid statements, and you did put them in a DATA step (or so you thought). That's when you should suspect a missing semicolon.

**Example**  The next example shows the same program, but now the semicolon is missing from the DATA statement. The INFILE statement becomes part of the DATA statement, and SAS tries to create a SAS data set named INFILE. SAS also tries to interpret the filename, 'c:\MyRawData\ToadJump.dat' as a SAS data set name, but the .dat extension is not valid for SAS data sets. It also gives you an error saying that there is no DATALINES or INFILE statement. In addition, you get some warnings about data sets being incomplete. This is a good example of how one simple mistake can produce a lot of confusing messages:

```
30    * Read the data file ToadJump.dat using list input;
31    DATA toads
32       INFILE 'C:\MyRawData\ToadJump.dat';
33       INPUT ToadName $ Weight Jump1 Jump2 Jump3;
34    RUN;

ERROR: No DATALINES or INFILE statement.
ERROR: Extension for physical file name "C:\MyRawData\ToadJump.dat" does not
correspond to a valid member type.
NOTE: The SAS System stopped processing this step because of errors.
WARNING: The data set WORK.TOADS may be incomplete.  When this step was stopped
there were 0 observations and 5 variables.
WARNING: Data set WORK.TOADS was not replaced because this step was stopped.
WARNING: The data set WORK.INFILE may be incomplete.  When this step was stopped
there were 0 observations and 5 variables.
```

Missing semicolons can produce a variety of error messages. Usually the messages say that either a statement is not valid, or an option or parameter is not valid or recognized. Sometimes you don't get an error message, but the results are still not right. If you leave off the semicolon from the last RUN statement when submitting programs in the SAS windowing environment, you won't get an error. But SAS won't run the last part of your program either.

**The DATASTMTCHK system option**  Some missing semicolons, such as the one in the last example, are easier to find if you use the DATASTMTCHK system option. This option controls what names you can use for SAS data sets in a DATA statement. By default it is set so that you cannot use the words: MERGE, RETAIN, SET, or UPDATE as a SAS data set name. This prevents you from accidentally overwriting an existing data set just because you forget a semicolon at the end of a DATA statement. You can make all SAS keywords invalid SAS data set names by setting the DATASTMTCHK option to ALLKEYWORDS. The partial log below again shows a missing semicolon at the end of the DATA statement, but this time DATASTMTCHK is set to ALLKEYWORDS:

```
35    OPTIONS DATASTMTCHK=ALLKEYWORDS;
36    * Read the data file ToadJump.dat using list input;
37    DATA toads
38       INFILE 'C:\MyRawData\ToadJump.dat';
         ------
         57
ERROR 57-185: INFILE is not allowed in the DATA statement when option
DATASTMTCHK=ALLKEYWORDS.  Check for a missing semicolon in the DATA statement,
or use DATASTMTCHK=NONE.

39       INPUT ToadName $ Weight Jump1 Jump2 Jump3;
40    RUN;
```

# 10.4   Note: INPUT Statement Reached Past the End of the Line

The note "SAS went to a new line when INPUT statement reached past the end of a line" is rather innocent looking, but its presence can indicate a problem. This note often goes unnoticed. It doesn't come up in red or even green lettering. It doesn't cause your program to stop. But look for it in your SAS log because it is a common note that usually means there is a problem.

This note means that as SAS was reading your data, it got to the end of the data line before it read values for all the variables in your INPUT statement. When this happens, SAS goes by default to the next line of data to get values for the remaining variables. Sometimes this is exactly what you want SAS to do, but if it's not, take a good look at your SAS log and output to be sure you know why this is happening.

Look in your SAS log where it tells you the number of lines it read from the data file and the number of observations in the SAS data set. If you have fewer observations than lines read, and you planned to have one observation per line, then you know you have a problem. Check the SAS data set using PROC PRINT or Viewtable. This can be very helpful in determining the source of the problem.

**Example**   This example shows what can happen if you are using list input, and don't have periods for missing values. The following data come from a toad-jumping contest, where the toad's number is followed by its weight and distances for each of three jumps. When a toad was disqualified from a jump, no entry was made for that jump:

```
13   65 1.9 3.0
25 131 2.5 3.1 .5
10 202 3.8
8   128 3.2 1.9 2.6
3   162
21   99 2.4 1.7 3.0
```

Here is the SAS log from a program that reads the raw data using list input:

```
1    DATA toads;
2       INFILE 'c:\MyRawData\Toadjmp2.dat';
3       INPUT ToadNumber Weight Jump1 Jump2 Jump3;
4    RUN;

NOTE: The infile 'c:\MyRawData\Toadjmp2.dat' is:
      File Name=c:\MyRawData\Toadjmp2.dat,
      RECFM=V,LRECL=256

❶ NOTE:  6 records were read from the infile 'c:\MyRawData\Toadjmp2.dat'.
         The minimum record length was 6.
         The maximum record length was 18.
❸ NOTE:  SAS went to a new line when INPUT statement reached past the end of a line.
❷ NOTE:  The data set WORK.TOADS has 3 observations and 5 variables.
   NOTE:  DATA statement used (Total process time):
          real time           0.37 seconds
```

❶ Notice that there were six records read from the raw data file.

❷ But there are only three observations in the SAS data set.

❸ The note, "…INPUT statement reached…," should alert you that there may be a problem.

If you look at the data set in Viewtable, you can see that there is a problem. The numbers don't look at all correct. (Can a toad jump 128 meters?)

| | ToadNumber | Weight | Jump1 | Jump2 | Jump3 |
|---|---|---|---|---|---|
| 1 | 13 | 65 | 1.9 | 3 | 25 |
| 2 | 10 | 202 | 3.8 | 8 | 128 |
| 3 | 3 | 162 | 21 | 99 | 2.4 |

VIEWTABLE: Work.Toads

Here SAS went to a new line when you didn't want it to. To fix this problem, the simplest thing to do is use the MISSOVER option in the INFILE statement. MISSOVER instructs SAS to assign missing values to any variables for which there were no data instead of going to the next line for data. The INFILE statement would look like this:

```
INFILE 'c:\MyRawData\Toadjmp2.dat' MISSOVER;
```

**Possible causes**  Other reasons for receiving a note informing you that the INPUT statement reached past the end of the line include

♦   You planned for SAS to go to the next data line when it ran out of data.

♦   Blank lines in your data file, usually at the beginning or end, can cause this note. Look at the minimum line length in the SAS log. If it is zero, then you have blank lines. Edit out the blank lines and rerun your program.

♦   If you are using list input and you do not have a space between every value, you can get this note. For example, if you try to read the following data using list input, SAS will run out of data for the Gilroy Garlics because there is no space between the 15 and the 1035. SAS will read it as one number, then read the 12 where it should have been reading the 1035, and so on. To correct this problem, either add a space between the two numbers, or use column or formatted input.

```
Columbia Peaches      35  67  1 10   2   1
Gilroy Garlics        151035 12 11   7   6
Sacramento Tomatoes   124  85 15   4   9   1
```

♦   If you have some data lines which are shorter than the rest, and you are using column or formatted input, this can cause a problem. If you try to read a name, for example, in columns 60 through 70 when some of the names extend only to column 68, and you didn't add spaces at the end of the line to fill it out to column 70, then SAS will go to the next line to read the name. To avoid this problem, use the TRUNCOVER option in the INFILE statement (discussed in section 2.14). For example:

```
INFILE 'c:\MyRawData\Addresses.dat' TRUNCOVER;
```

## 10.5  Note: Lost Card

Lost card? You thought you were writing SAS programs, not playing a card game. This note makes more sense if you remember that computer programs and data used to be punched out on computer cards. A lost card means that SAS was expecting another line (or card) of data and didn't find it.

If you are reading multiple lines of data for each observation, then a lost card could mean you have missing or duplicate lines of data. If you are reading two data lines for each observation, then SAS will expect an even number of lines in the data file. If you have an odd number, then you will get the lost-card message. It can often be difficult to locate the missing or duplicate lines, especially with large data files. Printing the SAS data set as well as careful proofreading of the data file can be helpful in identifying problem areas.

**Example** The following example shows what can happen if you have a missing data line. The raw data show the normal high and low temperatures and the record high and low for the month of July for each city. The last city is missing the last data line:

```
Nome AK
55 44
88 29
Miami FL
90 75
97 65
Raleigh NC
88 68
```

The following shows the SAS log from a program which reads the data, three lines per observation:

```
1    DATA highlow;
2       INFILE 'c:\MyRawData\Temps1.dat';
3       INPUT City $ State $ / NormalHigh NormalLow / RecordHigh RecordLow;

NOTE: The infile 'c:\MyRawData\Temps1.dat' is:
      File Name=c:\MyRawData\Temps1.dat,
      RECFM=V,LRECL=256

NOTE: LOST CARD.
City=Raleigh State=NC NormalHigh=88 NormalLow=68 RecordHigh=. RecordLow=.
_ERROR_=1 _N_=3
NOTE: 8 records were read from the infile 'c:\MyRawData\Temps1.dat'.
      The minimum record length was 5.
      The maximum record length was 10.
NOTE: The data set WORK.HIGHLOW has 2 observations and 6 variables.
NOTE: DATA statement used (Total process time):
      real time           0.03 seconds
      cpu time            0.03 seconds
```

In this case, you get the lost-card note, and SAS prints the values of the variables it read for the observation with the lost card. The observation is not included in the SAS data set. You can see from the log that SAS read eight records from the file (it should have been a multiple of three) but the SAS data set has only two observations. The last partial observation was not included.

**Example** It is very common to get other messages along with the lost-card note. The invalid-data note is a common byproduct of the lost card. If the second line were missing from the temperature data, then you would get invalid data as well as a lost card because SAS will try to read Miami FL as the record high and low. The following shows the invalid-data note from the SAS log:

```
Nome AK
88 29
Miami FL
90 75
97 65
Raleigh NC
88 68
105 50
```

```
NOTE: Invalid data for RecordHigh in line 3 1-5.
NOTE: Invalid data for RecordLow in line 3 7-8.
RULE:      ----+----1----+----2----+----3----+----4----+----5----+----6----+
3          Miami FL
City=Nome State=AK NormalHigh=88 NormalLow=29 RecordHigh=. RecordLow=.
_ERROR_=1 _N_=1
```

**Example** In addition to getting the lost-card note, it is also common to get a note indicating that the INPUT statement reached past the end of a line. If you forgot the last number in the file, as in the following example, then you would get these two notes together:

```
Nome AK
55 44
88 29
Miami FL
90 75
97 65
Raleigh NC
88 68
105
```

Because the program uses list input, SAS will try to go to the next line to get the data for the last variable. Since there isn't another line of data, you get the lost-card note. The following is part of the SAS log showing these two messages together:

```
NOTE: LOST CARD.
City=Raleigh State=NC NormalHigh=88 NormalLow=68 RecordHigh=105 RecordLow=.
_ERROR_=1 _N_=3
NOTE: 9 records were read from the infile
      'c:\MyRawData\Temps3.dat'.
      The minimum record length was 3.
      The maximum record length was 10.
NOTE: SAS went to a new line when INPUT statement reached past the end of a line.
NOTE: The data set WORK.HIGHLOW has 2 observations and 6 variables.
```

For this example, the solution is to add the missing data to the raw data file and rerun the program.

## 10.6  Note: Invalid Data

The typical new SAS user, upon seeing the invalid-data note, will ignore it, hoping perhaps that it will simply go away by itself. That's rather ironic considering that the message is explicit and easy to interpret once you know how to read it.

**Interpreting the message**   The invalid-data note appears when SAS is unable to read from a raw data file because the data are inconsistent with the INPUT statement. This note almost always indicates a problem. For example, one common mistake is typing in the letter O instead of the number 0. If the variable is numeric, then SAS is unable to interpret the letter O. In response, SAS does two things; it sets the value of this variable to missing and prints out a message like this for the problematic observation:

```
❶ NOTE: Invalid data for IDNumber in line 8 1-5.
❷ RULE:----+----1----+----2----+----3----+----4----+----5----+----6----+
❷ 8     007  James Bond     SA341

❸ IDNumber=. Name=James Bond Class=SA Q1=3 Q2=4 Q3=1 _ERROR_=1 _N_=8
```

❶   The first line tells you where the problem occurred. Specifically, it states the name of the variable SAS got stuck on and the line number and columns of the raw data file that SAS was trying to read. In this example, the error occurred while SAS was trying to read a variable named IDNumber from columns 1 through 5 in line 8 of the input file.

❷   The next line is a type of ruler with columns as the increments. The numeral 1 marks the tenth column, 2 marks the twentieth, and so on. Below the ruler, SAS dumps the actual line of raw data so you can see the little troublemaker for yourself. Using the ruler as a guide, you can count over to the column in question. At this point you can compare the actual raw data to your INPUT statement, and the error is usually obvious. The value of IDNumber should be zero-zero-seven, but looking at the line of actual data you can see that a careless typist has typed zero-letter O-seven. Such an error may seem minor to you, but you'll soon learn that computers are hopelessly persnickety.

❸   As if this weren't enough, SAS prints one more piece of information: the values of each variable for that observation as SAS read it. In this case, you can see that IDNumber equals missing, Name equals James Bond, and so on. Two automatic variables appear at the end of the line: _ERROR_ and _N_. The _ERROR_ variable has a value of 1 if there is a data error for that observation, and 0 if there is not. In an invalid-data note, _ERROR_ always equals 1. The automatic variable _N_ is the number of times SAS has looped through the DATA step.

**Unprintable characters**  Occasionally invalid data contain unprintable characters. In these cases, SAS shows you the raw data in hexadecimal format.

```
NOTE: Invalid data for IDNumber in line 10 1-5.
    RULE: ----+----1----+----2----+----3----+----4----+----5----+----6----+
❶   CHAR  ..   Indiana Jones PI83.
❷   ZONE  20222466666624666725433222222222222222222222222222222222222222222
❷   NUMR  E90009E491E10AFE5300983E0000000000000000000000000000000000000000000
IdNumber=. Name=Indiana Jones Class=PI Q1=8 Q2=3 Q3=. _ERROR_=1 _N_=10
```

❶  As before, SAS prints the line of raw data that contains the invalid data.

❷  Directly below the line of raw data, SAS prints two lines containing the hexadecimal equivalent of the data. You needn't understand hexadecimal values to be able to read this. SAS prints the data this way because the normal 10 numerals and 26 letters don't provide enough values to represent all computer symbols uniquely. Hexadecimal uses two characters to represent each symbol. To read hexadecimal, take a digit from the first line (labeled ZONE) together with the corresponding digit from the second line (labeled NUMR). In this case, a tab slipped into column 2 and appears as a harmless-looking period in the line of data. In hexadecimal, however, the tab appears as 09, while a real period in column 1 is 2E in hex.[1]

**Possible causes**  Common reasons for receiving the invalid-data note include

♦  character values in a field that should be numeric (including using the letter O instead of the numeral zero)

♦  forgetting to specify that a variable is character (SAS assumes it is numeric)

♦  incorrect column specifications producing embedded spaces in numeric data

♦  list-style input with two periods in a row and no space in between

♦  missing data not marked with a period for list-style input causing SAS to read the next data value

♦  special characters such as tab, carriage-return-line-feed, or form-feed in numeric data

♦  using the wrong informat such as MMDDYY. instead of DDMMYY.

♦  invalid dates (such as September 31) read with a date informat.

**Double question mark format modifier**  Sometimes you have invalid data, and there is nothing you can do about it. You know the data are bad, and you just want SAS to go ahead and set those values to missing without filling your log with notes. At those times, you can use the ?? format modifier. The ?? format modifier supresses the invalid-data note, and prevents the automatic variable _ERROR_ from being set to 1. Just insert the two question marks after the name of the problematic variable and before any informat or column specifications. For example, to prevent the preceding invalid-data notes for the variable IdNumber, you would add ?? to the INPUT statement like this:

```
INPUT IdNumber ?? 1-5 Name $ 6-18 Class $ 20-21 Q1 22 Q2 23 Q3 24;
```

---

[1] In z/OS the hexadecimal representation of a tab is 05.

## 10.7  Note: Missing Values Were Generated

The missing-values note appears when SAS is unable to compute the value of a variable because of preexisting missing values in your data. This is not necessarily a problem. It is possible that your data contain legitimate missing values and that setting a new variable to missing is a desirable response. But it is also possible that the missing values result from an error and that you need to fix your program or your data. A good rule is to think of the missing-values note as a flag telling you to check for an error.

**Example**  Here again are the data from the toad-jumping contest including the toad's name and the distance jumped in each of three trials:

```
Lucky  1.9  .   3.0
Spot   2.5 3.1 0.5
Tubs   .    .   3.8
Hop    3.2 1.9 2.6
Noisy  1.3 1.8 1.5
Winner .    .   .
```

Notice that several of the toads have missing values for one or more jumps. To compute the average distance jumped, the program in the following SAS log reads the raw data, adds together the values for the three jumps, and divides by three:

```
1     DATA toads;
2        INFILE 'c:\MyRawData\Jump.dat';
3        INPUT ToadName $ Jump1 Jump2 Jump3;
4        AverageJump = (Jump1 + Jump2 + Jump3) / 3;
5     RUN;

NOTE: The infile 'c:\MyRawData\Jump.dat' is:
      FILE NAME=c:\MyRawData\Jump.dat,
      RECFM=V,LRECL=132

NOTE: 6 records were read from the infile 'c:\MyRawData\Jump.dat'.
      The minimum record length was 17.
      The maximum record length was 18.

NOTE: ❶Missing values were generated as a result of performing an
      operation on missing values.
      ❷Each place is given by: (Number of times) at (Line):(Column)
      3 at 4:25

NOTE: The data set WORK.TOADS has 6 observations and 5 variables.
```

Because of missing values in the data, SAS was unable to compute AverageJump for some of the toads. In response, SAS printed the missing-values note which has two parts:

❶    The first part of the note says that SAS was forced to set some values to missing.

❷    The second part is a bit more cryptic. SAS lists the number of times values were set to missing. This generally corresponds to the number of observations that generated missing values, unless the problem occurs within a DO-loop. Next SAS states where in the program it encountered the problem. In the preceding example, SAS set three values to missing: at line 4, column 25. Looking at the program, you can see that line 4 is the line which calculates AverageJump, and column 25 contains the first plus sign. Looking at the raw data, you can see that three observations have missing values for Jump1, Jump2, or Jump3. Those observations are the three times mentioned in the missing-values note.

**Finding the missing values** In this case it was easy to find the observations with missing values. But if you had a data set with hundreds, or millions, of observations, then you couldn't just glance at the data. In that case, you could subset the problematic observations with a subsetting IF statement like this:

```
DATA missing;
   INFILE 'c:\MyRawData\Jump.dat';
   INPUT ToadName $ Jump1 Jump2 Jump3;
   AverageJump = (Jump1 + Jump2 + Jump3) / 3;
   IF AverageJump = .;
RUN;
```

Once you have selected just the observations that have missing values, you can use Viewtable or PROC PRINT to examine them. Here is Viewtable showing the observations with missing values for AverageJump:

| | ToadName | Jump1 | Jump2 | Jump3 | AverageJump |
|---|---|---|---|---|---|
| 1 | Lucky | 1.9 | . | 3 | . |
| 2 | Tubs | . | . | 3.8 | . |
| 3 | Winner | . | . | . | . |

**Using the SUM and MEAN functions** You may be able to circumvent this problem when you are computing a sum or mean by using the SUM or MEAN function instead of an arithmetic expression. In the preceding program, you could remove this line:

```
AverageJump = (Jump1 + Jump2 + Jump3) / 3;
```

And substitute this line:

```
AverageJump = MEAN(Jump1, Jump2, Jump3);
```

The SUM and MEAN functions use only non-missing values for the computation. In this example, you would still get the missing-values note for one toad, Winner, because it had missing values for all three jumps.

## 10.8   Note: Numeric Values Have Been Converted to Character (or Vice Versa)

Even with only two data types, numeric and character, SAS programmers sometimes get their variables mixed up. When you accidentally mix numeric and character variables, SAS tries to fix your program by converting variables from numeric to character or vice versa, as needed. Programmers sometimes ignore this problem, but that is not a good idea. If you ignore this message, it may come back to haunt you as you find new incompatibilities resulting from the fix. If, indeed, a variable needs to be converted, you should do it yourself, explicitly, so you know what your variables are doing.

**Example**  To show how SAS handles this kind of incompatibility, here are data about a class. Each line of data contains a student's ID number, name, and scores on two tests.

```
110 Linda    53 60
203 Derek    72 64
105 Kathy    98 82
224 Michael  80 55
```

The instructor runs the following program to read the data and create a permanent SAS data set named SCORES.

```
LIBNAME students 'c:\MySASLib';
DATA students.scores;
   INFILE 'c:\MyRawData\TestScores.dat';
   INPUT StudentID Name $ Score1 Score2 $;
RUN;
```

After creating the permanent SAS data set, the instructor runs a program to compute the total score and substring the first digit of StudentID. (Students in section 1 of the class have IDs starting with 1 while students in section 2 have IDs starting with 2.) Here is the log from the program:

```
2    DATA grades;
3       SET students.scores;
4       TotalScore = Score1 + Score2;
5       Class = SUBSTR(StudentID,2,1);
6    Run;

NOTE: Character values have been converted to numeric values at the places
      given by:(Line):(Column).
      4:26
NOTE: Numeric values have been converted to character values at the places
      given by:(Line):(Column).
      5:19
NOTE: There were 4 observations read from the data set STUDENTS.SCORES.
NOTE: The data set WORK.GRADES has 4 observations and 6 variables.
NOTE: DATA statement used (Total process time):
      real time            0.04 seconds
      cpu time             0.04 seconds
```

This program produces two values-have-been-converted notes. The first conversion occurred in line 4, column 26. Looking at the log you can see that the variable Score2 appears in column 26 of line 4. Score2 was accidentally input as a character variable, so SAS had to convert it to numeric before adding it to Score1 to compute TotalScore.

The second conversion occurred in line 5, column 19. Looking at the log you can see that the variable StudentID appears in column 19 of line 5. StudentID was input as a numeric variable, but the SUBSTR function requires character variables, so SAS was forced to convert StudentID to character.

**Converting variables**  You could go back and input the raw data with the correct types, but sometimes that's just not practical. Instead you can convert the variables from one type to another. To convert variables from character to numeric, you use the INPUT function. To convert from numeric to character, you use the PUT function. Most often, you would use these functions in an assignment statement with the following syntax:

<table>
<tr><td align="center">**Character to Numeric**</td><td align="center">**Numeric to Character**</td></tr>
<tr><td align="center">*newvar* = INPUT(*oldvar, informat*);</td><td align="center">*newvar* = PUT(*oldvar, format*);</td></tr>
</table>

These two slightly eccentric functions are first cousins of the PUT and INPUT statements. Just as an INPUT statement uses informats, the INPUT function uses informats; and just as PUT statements use formats, the PUT function uses formats. These functions can be confusing because they are similar but different. In the case of the INPUT function, the informat must be the type you are converting to—numeric. In contrast, the format for the PUT function must be the type you are converting from—numeric.[1] To convert the troublesome variables in the preceding program, you would use these statements:

<table>
<tr><td align="center">**Character to Numeric**</td><td align="center">**Numeric to Character**</td></tr>
<tr><td align="center">NewScore2 = INPUT(Score2, 2.);</td><td align="center">NewID = PUT(StudentID, 3.);</td></tr>
</table>

Here is a log showing the program with the statements to convert Score2 and StudentID:

```
7      DATA grades;
8         SET students.scores;
9         NewScore2 = INPUT(Score2, 2.);
10        TotalScore = Score1 + NewScore2;
11        NewID = PUT(StudentID,3.);
12        Class = SUBSTR(NewID,2,1);
13    Run;

NOTE: There were 4 observations read from the data set STUDENTS.SCORES.
NOTE: The data set WORK.GRADES has 4 observations and 8 variables.
NOTE: DATA statement used (Total process time):
      real time           0.03 seconds
      cpu time            0.03 seconds
```

Notice that this version of the program runs without any suspicious messages.

---

[1] In this discussion, we are talking about converting variables from numeric to character or vice versa, but you can also use the PUT function to change one character value to another character value. When you do this, *oldvar* and *newvar* would be character variables, and the format would be a character format.

## 10.9   DATA Step Produces Wrong Results but No Error Message

Some of the hardest errors to debug aren't errors at all, at least not to SAS. If you do complex programming, you may write a DATA step that runs just fine—with no errors or suspicious notes—but produces the wrong results. The more complex your programs are, the more likely you are to get this kind of error. Sometimes it seems like a DATA step is a black box. You know what goes in, and you know what comes out, but what happens in the middle is a mystery. This problem is actually a logic error; somewhere along the way SAS got the wrong instruction.

**Example**  Here is a program that illustrates this problem and how to debug it. The raw data file below contains information from a class. For each student there are three scores from tests, and one score from homework:

```
Linda     53 60   66 42
Derek     72 64   56 32
Kathy     98 82 100 48
Michael 80 55   95 50
```

This program is supposed to select students whose average score is below 70, but it doesn't work. Here is the log from the wayward program:

```
1    * Keep only students with mean below 70;
2    DATA lowscore;
3        INFILE 'c:\MyRawData\Class.dat';
4        INPUT Name $ Score1 Score2 Score3 Homework;
5        Homework = Homework * 2;
6        AverageScore = MEAN(Score1 + Score2 + Score3 + Homework);
7        IF AverageScore < 70;
8    RUN;

NOTE: The infile 'c:\MyRawData\Class.dat' is:
      File Name=c:\MyRawData\Class.dat,
      RECFM=V,LRECL=256

NOTE: 4 records were read from the infile 'c:\MyRawData\Class.dat'.
      The minimum record length was 20.
      The maximum record length was 20.
NOTE: The data set WORK.LOWSCORE has 0 observations and 6 variables.
```

First, the DATA step reads the raw data from a file called Class.dat. The highest possible score on homework is 50. To make the homework count the same as a test, the program doubles the value of Homework. Then the program computes the mean of the three test scores and Homework, and subsets the data by selecting only observations with a mean score below 70. Unfortunately, something went wrong. The LOWSCORE data set contains no observations. A glance at the raw data confirms that there should be students whose mean scores are below 70.

**Using the PUT and PUTLOG statements to debug**  To debug a problem like this, you have to figure out exactly what is happening inside the DATA step. A good way to do this is with PUT or PUTLOG statements. Elsewhere in this book, PUT statements are used along with FILE statements to write raw data files and custom reports. If you use a PUT statement without a FILE statement, then SAS writes in the SAS log. PUTLOG statements are the same except that they always write to the log even when you have a FILE statement. PUT and PUTLOG statements can take many forms, but for debugging, a handy style is

```
PUTLOG _ALL_;
```

SAS will print all the variables in your data set: first the variable name, then the actual data value, with an equal sign in between. If you have a lot of variables, you can print just the relevant ones this way:

```
PUTLOG variable-1=   variable-2=   . . .   variable-n=;
```

Without the equal signs, SAS would print just the data values. Adding the equal signs tells SAS to label the data so that you know which data values are which.

The DATA step below is identical to the one shown earlier except that a PUTLOG statement was added. In a longer DATA step, you might choose to have PUTLOG statements at several points. In this case, one will suffice. This PUTLOG statement is placed before the subsetting IF, since in this particular program the subsetting IF eliminates all observations:

```
9      * Keep only students with mean below 70;
10     DATA lowscore;
11        INFILE 'c:\MyRawData\Class.dat';
12        INPUT Name $ Score1 Score2 Score3 Homework;
13        Homework = Homework * 2;
14        AverageScore = MEAN(Score1 + Score2 + Score3 + Homework);
15        PUTLOG Name= Score1= Score2= Score3= Homework= AverageScore=;
16        IF AverageScore < 70;
17     RUN;

NOTE: The infile 'c:\MyRawData\Class.dat' is:
      FILE NAME=c:\MyRawData\Class.dat,
      RECFM=V,LRECL=256

Name=Linda Score1=53 Score2=60 Score3=66 Homework=84 AverageScore=263
Name=Derek Score1=72 Score2=64 Score3=56 Homework=64 AverageScore=256
Name=Kathy Score1=98 Score2=82 Score3=100 Homework=96 AverageScore=376
Name=Michael Score1=80 Score2=55 Score3=95 Homework=100 AverageScore=330

NOTE: 4 records were read from the infile 'c:\MyRawData\Class.dat'.
      The minimum record length was 20.
      The maximum record length was 20.
NOTE: The data set WORK.LOWSCORE has 0 observations and 6
      variables.
```

Looking at the the log, you can see the result of the PUTLOG statement. The data listed in the middle of the log show that the variables are being input properly, and the variable Homework is being adjusted properly. However, something is wrong with the values of AverageScore; they are much too high. There is a syntax error in the line that computes AverageScore. Instead of commas separating the three score variables in the MEAN function, there are plus signs. Since functions can contain arithmetic expressions, SAS simply added the four variables together, as instructed, and computed the mean of a single number. That's why no observations had values of AverageScore below 70.

# 10.10 The DATA Step Debugger

If you use the SAS windowing environment, then you have another option when it comes to debugging logic errors. Instead of the PUT and PUTLOG statements discussed in the previous section, you can use the DATA step debugger.

To understand the DATA step debugger, you have to know that SAS runs every program in two phases. When you run the program, it looks like one action, but in reality SAS first compiles your program, then SAS executes your program. Errors can occur during either phase, but they are different types of errors. Syntax errors and some data errors (such as numeric-to-character-conversion) occur at compile time. Other errors such as logic errors and some data errors (such as missing-values-were-generated) compile just fine, but cause problems at execution.

The DATA step debugger does its work at execution time. That means you can't use the DATA step debugger to find compile-time errors such as missing semicolons. (You don't really need it for these errors since they always generate messages in your log.) However, if you have an execution-time error, then the DATA step debugger may be a big help.

**Example**  To show how the DATA step debugger compares to using PUT statements to debug logic errors, this example uses the same program as the previous section. The raw data file below contains five variables—student's name, scores from three tests, and score from homework:

```
Linda     53 60   66 42
Derek     72 64   56 32
Kathy     98 82 100 48
Michael 80 55   95 50
```

**Starting the debugger**  The following program is supposed to select students whose average score is below 70, but it doesn't work. To invoke the debugger, simply add the DEBUG option to the end of your DATA statement, and submit the DATA step from the SAS windowing environment.

```
* Keep only students with mean below 70;
DATA lowscore / DEBUG;
    INFILE 'c:\MyRawData\Class.dat';
    INPUT Name $ Score1 Score2 Score3 Homework;
    Homework = Homework * 2;
    AverageScore = MEAN(Score1 + Score2 + Score3 + Homework);
    IF AverageScore < 70;
RUN;
```

**The debugger windows**  After you submit the DATA step, two windows will appear: the DEBUGGER LOG window and the DEBUGGER SOURCE window. The DEBUGGER LOG window contains messages from the debugger and a command line. The DEBUGGER SOURCE window contains your DATA step statements with the current line highlighted.

One nice bonus of the DATA step debugger is the ability to watch SAS executing a DATA step line-by-line and observation-by-observation. Since the highlighting in the DEBUGGER SOURCE window marks each line as SAS executes it, the debugger provides a graphic illustration of the structure of a DATA step. For a beginner, this alone could be very enlightening. You may even want to take a DATA step that works just fine, and run it through the DATA step debugger just to see this.

**Executing debugger commands** You can control the debugger in two ways—using pull-down menus or typing commands at a command line. Once you invoke the DATA step debugger, you will see some new menu options. The View, Run, and Breakpoint menus contain debugger commands. If you prefer to type commands, you can type them next to the arrow at the bottom of the DEBUGGER LOG window. In the DEBUGGER LOG window to the right, the STEP command has been typed at the command line. The following table shows the most common commands:

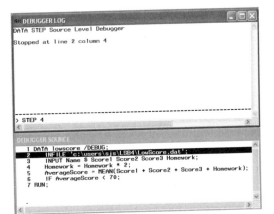

| Menu Selection | Command | Result |
|---|---|---|
| Run-Step | `<return>` | executes one statement |
| | `STEP n` | executes *n* statements, where *n* is a numeral |
| View-Examine values | `EXAMINE variable-list` | prints the values of variables |
| View-Set values | `SET variable = expression` | assigns a value to a specified variable for the current observation |
| Run-Go | `GO` | finishes executing the DATA step |
| Run-Quit debugger | `QUIT` | closes the debugger |

In this DEBUGGER LOG window you can see the programmer has used the STEP command to move to line 6 of the program. Then the programmer typed EXAMINE _ALL_, and SAS listed all the variables and their values. Looking at the data values, you can see the value of AverageScore is much too high. There is a logic error in the line that computes AverageScore. The plus signs should be commas. Once you find the error, quit the debugger, and correct the error, remembering to remove the DEBUG option.

## 10.11 Error: Invalid Option, Error: The Option Is Not Recognized, or Error: Statement Is Not Valid

If SAS cannot make sense out of one of your statements, it stops executing the current DATA or PROC step and prints one of these messages:

```
ERROR 22-7: Invalid option name.

ERROR 202-322: The option or parameter is not recognized and will be
    ignored.

ERROR 180-322: Statement is not valid or it is used out of proper order.
```

The invalid-option message and its cousin, the option-is-not-recognized message, tell you that you have a valid statement, but SAS can't make sense out of an apparent option. The statement-is-not-valid message, on the other hand, means that SAS can't understand the statement at all. Thankfully, with all three messages SAS underlines the point at which it got confused so you know where to look for the problem.

**Example**  The SAS log below contains an invalid option:

```
1      DATA class (ROP = Score1);
                    ---
                    22
ERROR 22-7: Invalid option name ROP.

2          INFILE 'c:\MyRawData\Scores.dat';
3          INPUT  Name $ Score1 Score2 Score3 Homework;
4      RUN;

NOTE: The SAS System stopped processing this step because of errors.
NOTE: DATA statement used (Total process time):
      real time          0.03 seconds
      cpu time           0.00 seconds
```

In this DATA step, the word DROP was misspelled as ROP. Since SAS cannot interpret this, it underlines the word ROP, prints the invalid-option message, and stops processing the DATA step.

**Example**  The following log contains an option-is-not-recognized message:

```
5      PROC PRINT
6          VAR Score2;
           ---
           22
           202
ERROR 22-322:  Syntax error, expecting one of the following: ;, BLANKLINE,
      DATA, DOUBLE, HEADING, LABEL, N, NOOBS, OBS, ROUND, ROWS, SPLIT, STYLE,
      UNIFORM, WIDTH.
ERROR 202-322: The option or parameter is not recognized and will be ignored.
7      RUN;

NOTE: The SAS System stopped processing this step because of errors.
NOTE: PROCEDURE PRINT used (Total process time):
      real time          0.25 seconds
      cpu time           0.09 seconds
```

SAS underlined the VAR statement. This message may seem puzzling since VAR is not an option, but a statement, and a valid statement at that. But if you look at the previous statement, you will see that the PROC statement is missing one of those pesky semicolons. As a result, SAS tried to interpret the words VAR and Score2 as options in the PROC statement. Since no options exist with those names, SAS stopped processing the step and printed the option-is-not-recognized message. SAS also printed the syntax-error message listing all the valid options for a PROC statement.

**Example**  Here is a log with the statement-is-not-valid message:

```
8     PROC PRINT;
9        SET class;
         ---
         180
ERROR 180-322: Statement is not valid or it is used out of proper order.
10    RUN;

NOTE: The SAS System stopped processing this step because of errors.
NOTE: PROCEDURE PRINT used (Total process time):
      real time            0.01 seconds
      cpu time             0.01 seconds
```

In this case, a SET statement was used in a PROC step. Since SET statements can be used only in DATA steps, SAS underlines the word SET and prints the statement-is-not-valid message.

**Possible causes**  Generally, with these error messages, the cause of the problem is easy to detect. You should check the underlined item and the previous statement for possible errors. Possible causes include

- ◆ a misspelled keyword

- ◆ a missing semicolon

- ◆ a DATA step statement in a PROC step (or vice versa)

- ◆ a RUN statement in the middle of a DATA or PROC step (this does not cause errors for some procedures)

- ◆ the correct option with the wrong statement

- ◆ an unmatched quotation mark

- ◆ an unmatched comment.

## 10.12  Note: Variable Is Uninitialized or Error: Variable Not Found

If you find one of these messages in your SAS log, then SAS is telling you that the variable named in the message does not exist:

```
NOTE: Variable X is uninitialized.
WARNING: Variable X not found.
ERROR: Variable X not found.
```

Generally, the first time you get one of these messages, it is quite a shock. You may be sure that the variable does exist. After all, you remember creating it. Fortunately, the problem is usually easy to fix once you understand what SAS is telling you.

If the problem happens in a DATA step, then SAS prints the variable-is-uninitialized note, initializes the variable, and continues to execute your program. Normally variables are initialized when they are read (via an INPUT, SET, MERGE, or UPDATE statement) or when they are created via an assignment statement. If you use a variable for the first time in a way that does not assign a value to the variable (such as on the right side of an assignment statement, in the condition of an IF statement, or in a DROP or KEEP option) then SAS tries to fix the problem by assigning a value of missing to the variable for all observations. This is very generous of SAS, but it almost never fixes the problem, since you probably don't want the variable to have missing values for all observations.

When the problem happens in a PROC step, the results are more grave. If the error occurs in a critical statement such as a VAR statement, then SAS prints the variable-not-found error and does not execute the step. If the error occurs in a less critical statement such as a LABEL statement, then SAS prints the variable-not-found warning message, and attempts to run the step.

**Example**  Here is the log from a program with missing-variable problems in both a DATA and a PROC step:

```
1     DATA highscore (KEEP = Name Total);
2         INPUT Name $ Score1 Score2;
3         IF Scor1 > 5;
4         Total = Score1 + Score2;
5         DATALINES;

NOTE: Variable Scor1 is uninitialized.
NOTE: The data set WORK.HIGHSCORE has 0 observations and 2 variables.
NOTE: DATA statement used (Total process time):
      real time           0.04 seconds
      cpu time            0.03 seconds
8        ;
9
10    PROC PRINT DATA = highscore;
11        VAR Name Score2 Total;
ERROR: Variable SCORE2 not found.
12    RUN;

NOTE: The SAS System stopped processing this step because of errors.
NOTE: PROCEDURE PRINT used (Total process time):
      real time           0.03 seconds
      cpu time            0.01 seconds
```

In this DATA step, the INPUT statement reads three variables: Name, Score1, and Score2. But a misspelling in the subsetting IF statement causes SAS to initialize a new variable named Scor1. Because Scor1 has missing values, none of the observations satisfies the subsetting IF, and the data set HIGHSCORE is left with zero observations.

In the PROC PRINT, the VAR statement requests three variables: Name, Score2, and Total. Score2 did exist but was dropped from the data set by the KEEP= option in the DATA statement. That KEEP= option kept only two variables, Name and Total. As a result, SAS prints the variable-not-found error message, and does not execute the PROC PRINT.

**Possible causes**  Common ways to "lose" variables include

- misspelling a variable name
- using a variable that was dropped at some earlier time
- using the wrong data set
- committing a logic error, such as using a variable before it is created.

If the source of the problem is not immediately obvious, PROC CONTENTS can often help you figure out what is going on. PROC CONTENTS, which is discussed in section 2.22, gives you information about what is in a SAS data set including variable names.

# 10.13 SAS Truncates a Character Variable

Sometimes you may notice that some, or all, of the values of a character variable are truncated. You may be expecting "peanut butter" and get "peanut b" or "chocolate ice cream" and get "chocolate ice." This usually happens when you use IF statements to create a new character variable, or when you are using list-style input and you have values longer than eight characters.

All character variables have a fixed length determined by one of the following methods.

**INPUT statement**  If a variable's values are read from a raw data file, then the length is determined by the INPUT statement. If you are using list-style input, then the length defaults to 8. If you are using column or formatted input, then the length is determined by the number of columns, or informat. The following shows examples of INPUT statements that read values for the variable Food and the resulting lengths of Food:

| INPUT statement | Length of Food |
|---|---|
| INPUT Food $; | 8 |
| INPUT Food $ 1-10; | 10 |
| INPUT Food $15.; | 15 |

**Assignment statement**  If you are creating the variable in an assignment statement, then the length is determined by the first occurrence of the new variable name. For example, the following program creates a variable, Status, whose values are determined by the Temperature variable:

```
DATA summer;
   SET temps;
   IF Temperature > 100 THEN Status = 'Hot';
      ELSE Status = 'Cold';
RUN;
```

Because the word Hot has three characters and that is the first statement which uses the variable, Status has a length of 3. Any other values for that variable would be truncated to three characters (Col instead of Cold, for example).

**LENGTH statement**  The LENGTH statement in a DATA step defines variable lengths and, if it comes before the INPUT or assignment statement, will override either of the previous two methods of determining length. The following LENGTH statement sets the length of the Status variable to 4 and the Food variable to 15:

```
LENGTH Status $4 Food $15;
```

**ATTRIB statement**  You can also assign variable lengths in an ATTRIB statement in a DATA step where you can associate formats, informats, labels, and lengths to variables in a single statement. Always place the LENGTH option before a FORMAT option in an ATTRIB statement to ensure that the variables are assigned proper lengths. For example, the following statement assigns the character variable Status a length of 4 and the label Hot or Cold:

```
ATTRIB Status LENGTH = $4 LABEL = 'Hot or Cold';
```

**Example** The following example shows what can happen if you let SAS determine the length of a character variable (in this case, using the assignment statement method). You have the following data for a consumer survey of car color preferences. Age is followed by sex (coded as 1 for male and 2 for female), annual income, and preferred car color (yellow, gray, blue, or white):

```
19 1 14000 Y
45 1 65000 G
72 2 35000 B
31 1 44000 Y
58 2 83000 W
```

You want to create a new variable, AgeGroup, which has these values: Teen for customers under 20, Adult for ages 20 through 64, and Senior for those 65 and over. In the following program, a series of IF-THEN/ELSE statements create AgeGroup:

```
DATA carsurvey;
    INFILE 'c:\MyRawData\Cars.dat';
    INPUT Age Sex Income Color $;
    IF Age < 20 THEN AgeGroup = 'Teen';
        ELSE IF Age < 65 THEN AgeGroup = 'Adult ';
        ELSE AgeGroup = 'Senior';
PROC PRINT DATA = carsurvey;
    TITLE 'Car Color Survey Results';
RUN;
```

The following results of the PROC PRINT show how the values of AgeGroup are truncated to four characters—the number of characters in Teen.

```
                     Car Color Survey Results                        1


                                                    Age
        Obs    Age    Sex    Income    Color     Group

         1     19      1     14000       Y        Teen
         2     45      1     65000       G        Adul
         3     72      2     35000       B        Seni
         4     31      1     44000       Y        Adul
         5     58      2     83000       W        Adul
```

The addition of a LENGTH statement in the DATA step, as follows, would eliminate the truncation problem:

```
DATA carsurvey;
    INFILE 'c:\MyRawData\Cars.dat';
    INPUT Age Sex Income Color $;
    LENGTH AgeGroup $6;
    IF Age < 20 THEN AgeGroup = 'Teen';
        ELSE IF Age < 65 THEN AgeGroup = 'Adult';
        ELSE AgeGroup = 'Senior';
RUN;
```

# 10.14 SAS Stops in the Middle of a Job

One of the most disconcerting errors encountered by SAS users is having SAS stop in the middle of a job. It's as if your program has suddenly dropped dead without so much as an error message to act as a smoking gun. Without an error message, you are left to sleuth this problem on your own. Often the problem has nothing to do with SAS. Instead the operating environment may have stopped your program in its tracks. Other times the problem results from programming errors that prevent SAS from seeing the entire job.

A number of completely unrelated reasons can cause SAS to stop in the middle of a job. They are listed below, starting with the most general problems and ending with the ones that are specific to certain execution modes or operating environments.

**An unmatched quotation mark**   Unmatched quotation marks wreak havoc on SAS programs, including making SAS stop in the middle of a job. In this case, SAS stops because, in effect, it thinks the remainder of the job is part of a quote. In batch or noninteractive mode, the solution is simple enough. Insert the missing quotation mark and resubmit the program. In the SAS windowing environment you can't just resubmit the program because SAS is still waiting for the other quotation mark. The solution is to submit a sacrificial quotation mark like this:

```
';
RUN;
```

Then edit your program, correct the problem (remembering to delete the extra quotation mark and RUN statement at the end), and rerun the program. Some prefer to exit SAS and start over. If you do, just remember to save your program before exiting.

**An unmatched comment**   Unmatched comments can cause SAS to stop in the middle of a program, much like unmatched quotation marks. The problem is that SAS can't read the entire program because part of it is accidentally stuck in a comment. This isn't so likely to happen if you use the kind of comment that starts with an asterisk and ends with a semicolon since programs contain many semicolons, and any semicolon will do to end a comment. But if you use the style of comment that starts with /* and ends with */, and you forget to include the last */, then SAS will assume that the remainder of your job is one long comment. The solution, in batch or noninteractive mode is to insert the missing end-of-comment and resubmit the program. In the SAS windowing environment, the solution is to submit a lone end-of-comment like this:

```
*/;
RUN;
```

Then edit your program, correct the problem (remembering to delete the extra end-of-comment and RUN statement at the end), and rerun the program. Some prefer to exit SAS and start over. If you do, just remember to save your program before exiting.

**No RUN statement at the end of a program**  This problem occurs only in interactive SAS. In noninteractive or in batch mode there is an implicit RUN statement at the end of every SAS job. The problem is that in interactive mode SAS has no way of knowing when it is time to execute your last step unless you tell it with a RUN statement. The solution is to submit the wayward statement:

```
RUN;
```

**Not sure what the problem is?**  If you are working in the SAS windowing environment, and you think you have an unmatched quotation mark, unmatched comment, or missing RUN statement, but you're not sure, you may want to submit the following set of statements:

```
* ';
* ";
* /;
RUN;
```

Together these statements form a sort of universal terminator for SAS programs. If the program has no problems, these statements do nothing since the first three would then be comments, and an extra RUN statement between steps does nothing. That means you can submit these without fear of causing any harm.

**Out of time**  Batch systems may have time limits, measured in CPU seconds, for computer jobs. These limits are set locally by your systems programmers. And these limits are helpful because they allow small jobs to be submitted to a special queue with a higher priority. That way your short job doesn't have to wait for some mega-job to finish processing. Time limits may also be set to stop jobs that accidentally get into an infinite loop. If your job stops in the middle, and you are running in batch mode, and you can find no unmatched quotation marks or comments, then you should consider whether your job might have stopped because it ran into a time limit. To find out how to fix this problem, talk to a systems programmer or to other SAS users at your site.

**/\* in the first column**  Under z/OS there is a unique hazard. Recall that one style of SAS comment starts with a slash-asterisk (/*). Batch jobs under z/OS use Job Control Language (JCL). In JCL a /* starting in column one signals the end of your program file. So if SAS programmers start a comment with a /* in column one, they inadvertently instruct the computer to stop right then and there. SAS never even sees the remainder of the job. The solution, of course, is to move the comment out of column one or to change to a comment starting with an asterisk (*) and ending with a semicolon (;).

# 10.15 SAS Runs Out of Memory or Disk Space

What do you do when you finally get your program running, and you get a message that your computer is out of memory or disk space? Well, you could petition to buy a more powerful computer, which isn't really such a bad idea, but there are a few things you can try before resorting to spending money. Because this issue is very system dependent, it is not possible to cover everything you might be able to do in this section. However, this section describes a few universal actions you can take to remedy the situation.

It is helpful, in trying to solve the problem, to know why it happens. Usually when you run out of memory, it's when you are doing some pretty intensive computations or sorting data sets with lots of variables. The GLM procedure (General Linear Models), for example, can use lots of memory when your model is complicated and there are many levels for each classification variable. You run out of disk space because SAS uses disk space to store all its temporary working files, including temporary SAS data sets, and the SAS log and output. If you are creating many large temporary SAS data sets during the course of a SAS session, this can quickly fill up your disk space.

**Memory and disk space** One thing you can do to help decrease disk storage is decrease the number of bytes needed to store data. This can also help memory problems that arise when sorting data sets with character data. Since all numbers are expanded to the fullest precision while SAS is processing data, changing storage requirements for numeric data will not help memory problems. Both character (if you are using list input), and numeric variables have a default storage requirement of eight bytes. This works for most situations. But if memory or disk space is at a premium, you can usually find some variables which require fewer bytes.

For character data, each character requires one byte of storage. The length of a character variable is determined by one of the following: the INPUT statement, the LENGTH or ATTRIB statement, or, if it is created in an assignment statement, the length of the first value. If you are using list input, then variables are given a length of eight. If your data are only one character long, Y or N for example, then you are using eight times the storage space you actually need. You can use the LENGTH statement before the INPUT statement to change the default length. For example, the following gives the character variable Answer a length of one byte:

```
LENGTH Answer $1;
```

If you are using column input, then the length is equal to the number of columns you are reading; if you are using formatted input, then the length is equal to the width of the informat. You can change the lengths of variables in existing SAS data sets by using a LENGTH statement between a DATA statement and a SET, MERGE, or UPDATE statement.

**Disk space** If you are running out of disk space, in addition to shortening the lengths of character variables, you may also be able to decrease the lengths of numeric variables. Numeric data are a little trickier than character when it comes to length. All numbers can be safely stored in eight bytes, and that's why eight is the default. Some numbers can be safely stored in fewer bytes, but which numbers depends on your operating environment. Look in the SAS Help and Documentation for your operating environment to determine the length and precision of numeric variables. For example, under Windows and UNIX, you can safely store integers up to 8,192 in three bytes. In general, if your numbers contain decimal values, then you must use eight bytes. If you have small integer values, then you can use four bytes (in some operating environments two or three bytes). Use the LENGTH statement to change the lengths of numeric data:

```
LENGTH Tigers 4;
```

This statement changes the length of the numeric variable Tigers to four bytes. If your numbers are categorical, like 1 for male and 2 for female, then you can read them as character data with a length of 1 and save even more space.

Another thing you can try if you are running out of disk space is to decrease the number and size of SAS data sets created during a SAS session. If you are going to use only a fraction of your data for analysis, then subset your data as soon as possible using the subsetting IF statement. For example, if you needed observations only for females, then use the following statement in your DATA step:

```
IF Sex = 'female';
```

If you need to look at only a few of the variables in your data set, then use the KEEP= (or DROP=) data set option to decrease the number of variables. For example, if you had a data set containing information about all the zoo animals, but you wanted to look at only the lions and tigers, then you could use the following statements to create a data set with only the Lions and Tigers variables:

```
DATA partial;
   SET zooanimals (KEEP = Lions Tigers);
```

The SAS log and output also take up disk space. If you are using the SAS windowing environment, then clear the SAS log and output often.

It is also possible to compress SAS data sets. Compressing may save space if your data have many repeated values. But beware, compressing can in some cases actually increase the size of your data set. Fortunately, SAS gives a message in your log window telling you the change in size of your data sets. You can turn on compression by using either the COMPRESS=YES system option, or the COMPRESS=YES data set option. Use the system option if you want all the SAS data sets you create to be compressed. Use the data set option when you want to control which SAS data sets to compress. For example:

```
DATA compressedzooanimals (COMPRESS = YES);
   SET zooanimals;
```

If you have more than one disk on your system, then you might be able to have SAS store its working files in a different location where there is more space. See the SAS Help and Documentation for your operating environment.

**Memory**  If memory is your problem, then do what you can to eliminate other programs that are using your computer's memory. If you are using a windowing environment to run your SAS programs, try running in batch or noninteractive mode instead. The windows take quite a lot of memory, and it can be a significant fraction of the total available memory. Also, see the SAS Help and Documentation for your operating environment for potential ways to make more memory available on your system.

If you have tried all of the above, and you are still running out of memory or disk space, then you can always try finding a more powerful computer. One of the nice things about SAS is that the language is the same for all operating environments. To move your program to another operating environment, you would need to change only a few statements like INFILE, which deal directly with the operating environment.

" "Where observation is concerned, chance favors a prepared mind."

LOUIS PASTEUR

# APPENDICES

# Appendix A  Where to Go from Here

The goal of this book is to get you started using SAS and to teach you basic principles of SAS programming. For some of you, this book may be all you need. Others, however, may need to go beyond this book. This section lists sources for other training and information about SAS software. Contact SAS for more information on any of the following items. You may also have additional sources of information, developed locally, at your site.

## The SAS Customer Support Web Site

Like most companies these days, SAS has a very useful Web site. You can find all sorts of information there: technical information, product documentation, publications information, training information, news and events, user group information—the list is almost endless. If you have a question, and can't find the answer in this book, then try the SAS Customer Support Web site:

> support.sas.com

## SAS Help and Documentation

SAS Help and Documentation is available from within your SAS session, and can be accessed through the Help pull-down menu or by typing the word HELP in the command line area on your display. SAS Help and Documentation is your complete reference material for SAS and gives you access to tutorials, sample programs, general information, and specific syntax. SAS Help and Documentation includes material for all products and operating environments. Documentation is also available in HTML and PDF format from the SAS Customer Support Web site and some documentation can be purchased in print format.

## Books Offered by SAS Press

SAS Press offers many books written by users of SAS software. These books offer a different perspective from the SAS documentation, and topics range from very general and introductory to very specific. Some of these titles are listed at the end of this book and a complete listing can be found through the SAS Customer Support Web site.

## SAS Training Courses

In training centers around the world, SAS offers classroom-based courses on SAS software covering many topics and varying in length and cost. You can also arrange to have on-site training for many of the courses. In addition to the classroom-based courses, SAS also offers Live Web and Self-Paced e-Learning courses. Contact SAS for more information about any of these training opportunities through the SAS Customer Support Web site.

## SAS User Groups

SAS has a network of user groups which spans the globe. There are in-house groups, local groups, and regional and international groups. The regional and international groups generally meet once a year for several days. Presentations and demonstrations are given by users and SAS employees; there are workshops and training opportunities and usually vendor exhibits. The SAS Global Forum is the largest user group conference drawing SAS users from around the world. Local and in-house groups usually meet more frequently for a shorter duration. These user-group meetings can be a great source of information about SAS software. More information about the SAS Global Forum and the regional user groups can be found at the SAS Customer Support Web site.

## sasCommunity.org

sasCommunity.org is a Web site providing links to SAS related services and information for the worldwide SAS Community. This site contains discussion forums, SAS user blogs, presentations, event notices, job postings, and more.

## *sascom* magazine and Electronic Newsletters

The *sascom* magazine is available to all SAS users at no extra cost. It covers news items like capabilities of new releases of SAS software, has articles of general interest, and has some technical information. Also, SAS publishes several electronic newsletters including *SAS Business Report* for business and industry decision-makers and executives and *SAS Tech Report* for SAS software users, systems administrators, and IT staff, and *SAS Publishing News* to receive up-to-date information about new and upcoming titles from SAS Publishing. These newsletters can be accessed through the SAS Customer Support Web site.

## SAS-L

SAS-L is an independent electronic mailing list of SAS users all over the world. This group helps subscribers solve SAS problems, discusses SAS philosophy, posts announcements, and discusses whatever else seems related to SAS.

## SAS Technical Support

If you are really stuck on a SAS problem, you can contact SAS Technical Support. There are several ways to contact a SAS Technical Support Consultant including using the Web site or telephone. Before you contact SAS Technical Support, you must know certain information:

- your site or customer number
- the product name (such as Base SAS or SAS/STAT)
- SAS software release
- your operating system
- a description of your problem

To find your site number and release of SAS, just start interactive SAS or run a SAS job in batch mode. Then look at the beginning of your SAS log to find your site number and release notes.

The easiest way to ask a question of SAS Technical Support is to use their online form. From the SAS Customer Support Web site, click the link for submitting a problem, and then follow the instructions. You will receive an e-mail response confirming your submission, and giving you a tracking number. The traditional way to contact Technical Support still works well. Customers in North America can use this number:

(919) 677-8008

Customers outside North America should contact their local SAS office. To find contact information (phone numbers, mailing addresses, and Web sites) for SAS offices outside North America, use the SAS Customer Support Web site.

# Appendix B  Coming to SAS from SPSS

More often than not, the first question asked by people who know SPSS and want to learn SAS is, "How do the two software packages compare?" No simple answer is possible since both products are continually evolving, with new releases introducing new capabilities. Nonetheless, general comparisons can be drawn.

SAS and SPSS are very similar. Compared to other statistical software, these two products are similar because they are both based on languages. Compared to other computer languages such as C++, SAS and SPSS are similar because they both have powerful, built-in data handling and statistical capabilities.

Some SPSS users may not even know that SPSS has a programming language since many SPSS users use only the SPSS point-and-click interface. If you are one of these people, then you will be glad to know that SAS also has a point-and-click interface named SAS Enterprise Guide. SAS Enterprise Guide is provided at no extra charge with Base SAS for Windows. You can write and run SAS programs in SAS Enterprise Guide. However, this book focuses on the use of SAS programs in the SAS windowing environment.

Despite their fundamental similarities, SAS and SPSS have different styles. SAS offers more features. Consider the fact that SPSS offers over 70 functions, SAS over 1,000. More features mean more power to get exactly what you want. People who do really complex programming find they can do things with SAS that would be impossible to do with SPSS.

**Terminology**  Some vocabulary differences exist between SAS and SPSS. To help you translate from one language to the other, here is a brief dictionary of analogous terms:

| SPSS term | Analogous SAS term |
|---|---|
| active file | no analogous term in SAS programs |
| no analogous term | temporary SAS data set |
| case | observation |
| command | statement |
| file handle | libref |
| function | function |
| input format | informat |
| numeric data | numeric data |
| output format | format |
| procedure | procedure |
| save file | permanent SAS data set |
| SPSS data file | permanent SAS data set |
| SPSS Viewer | SAS Output and Log windows |
| string data | character data |
| syntax | programming statements |
| syntax file | a program |
| system file | permanent SAS data set |
| value label | user-defined format |
| variable | variable |
| variable label | label |
| no analogous term | DATA step |
| no analogous term | PROC step |

**Active files**  The concept of an active file in SPSS has no precise equivalent in SAS programs. When you read data in an SPSS program, SPSS creates an active system file. This active file is similar to a temporary SAS data set because it exists only for the duration of the SPSS session, just as temporary SAS data sets exist only for the duration of a SAS session. However, SPSS has only one active file at a time, while SAS can have any number of temporary or permanent data sets. When you run an analysis in SPSS, the data must come from the active file. When you run an analysis in SAS, by default SAS will use the data set most recently created. But you can easily use any other SAS data set including the permanent SAS data set you created last year and haven't touched since. In SAS programs, all SAS data sets are always active.

**DATA and PROC steps**  The SAS language has some concepts that have no parallel in SPSS, such as DATA and PROC steps. All SAS programs are divided into these two types of steps. Basically, DATA steps read and modify data while PROC (short for procedure) steps perform specific analyses or functions such as sorting, writing reports, or running statistical analyses. SPSS programs do the same types of operations but without distinct steps.

**Windows in SAS and SPSS**  When you start SPSS, the SPSS Data Editor window opens. From there you can type in data or open an existing data file. You can also open an SPSS Syntax Editor window if you wish, and any results will appear in an SPSS Viewer window. The SAS windowing environment has similar windows, but the order of appearance is reversed. You see the Editor and Log windows automatically, and can open the data editor if you wish.

Here is what the three main windows in SPSS 16.0—SPSS Data Editor, SPSS Syntax Editor, and SPSS Viewer—look like in the Windows operating environment. The SPSS Data Editor shows the active data file. The SPSS Syntax Editor window has an SPSS program typed into it. The results of the program appear in the SPSS Viewer. The SPSS Viewer is divided into two parts, the outline pane on the left and the contents pane on the right. There is no separate Log window. Program statements and system notes are interleaved with output in the SPSS Viewer window.

Here is what the main windows in SAS 9.2 look like in the Windows operating environment. Instead of having three completely separate windows (one for data, one for syntax, and one for outptut), SAS has all those windows integrated together. The screen below shows a SAS program typed into the Enhanced Editor. The program has been run so there is output in the Output window, and the Results window shows a tree diagram of output similar to the outline pane in the SPSS System Viewer. The Viewtable (data editor) window is open and appears on top of the Enhanced Editor and Output windows.

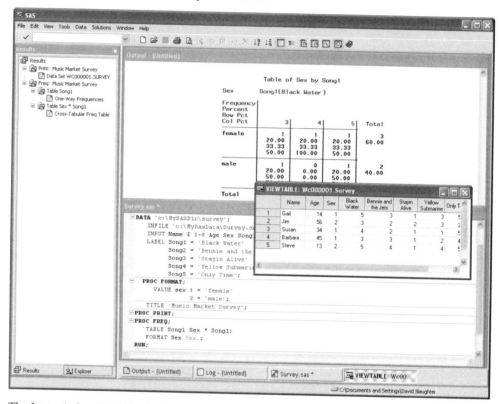

The Log window is hidden behind the Output and Enhanced Editor windows. You can bring the Log window forward by clicking its tab at the bottom of the SAS window. The Log window contains a record of program statements that have been run and notes from SAS. With SAS, output is separated from program statements and system notes. This makes the output easier to read and use in other applications such as word processors or Web pages.

**Examples**  For a comparison, we provide the following two programs that perform the same operations in SPSS and SAS. A radio station commissioned a market research company to survey listeners. Respondents were asked to listen to songs and rate them on a scale of 1 to 5, with 1 being "dislike very much" and 5 being "like very much." Here is a sample of the raw data. The variables are first name, age, sex, and the ratings for five songs:

```
Gail     14 1 5 3 1 3 5
Jim      56 2 3 2 2 3 2
Susan    34 1 4 2 1 1 5
Barbara  45 1 3 3 1 2 4
Steve    13 2 5 4 1 4 5
```

The two programs below read the same raw data file and produce the same types of reports:

**SPSS Program**

```
DATA LIST FILE =
   'c:\MyRawData\Survey.dat'
   /Name 1-8 (A) Age 9-10
   Sex 12 Song1 TO Song5 13-22.
VARIABLE LABELS
   Song1 'Black Water'
   Song2 'Bennie and the Jets'
   Song3 'Stayin Alive'
   Song4 'Yellow Submarine'
   Song5 'Only Time'.
VALUE LABELS
   sex 1 'female' 2 'male'.
TITLE 'Music Market Survey'.
LIST.
FREQUENCIES
   VARIABLES = Song1.
CROSSTABS
   /TABLES = Sex BY Song1.
SAVE OUTFILE =
   'c:\MySPSSDir\survey.sav'.
```

**SAS program**

```
DATA 'c:\MySASLib\survey';
   INFILE 'c:\MyRawData\Survey.dat';
   INPUT Name $ 1-8 Age
     Sex Song1-Song5;
   LABEL Song1 = 'Black Water'
     Song2 = 'Bennie and the Jets'
     Song3 = 'Stayin Alive'
     Song4 = 'Yellow Submarine'
     Song5 = 'Only Time';
PROC FORMAT;
   VALUE sex 1 = 'female'
             2 = 'male';
TITLE 'Music Market Survey';
PROC PRINT;
PROC FREQ;
   TABLE Song1 Sex * Song1;
   FORMAT Sex Sex.;
RUN;
```

The following table shows which SPSS commands and SAS statements perform the same operations:

| SPSS command | SAS statement |
|---|---|
| DATA LIST | INFILE and INPUT |
| VARIABLE LABELS | LABEL |
| VALUE LABELS | PROC FORMAT |
| TITLE | TITLE |
| LIST | PROC PRINT |
| FREQUENCIES and CROSSTABS | PROC FREQ |
| SAVE OUTFILE | DATA |

**SPSS output**  Here are the results from the SPSS Viewer window exported as a text file. To make the output easier to read the program commands and system notes have been deleted.

```
Music Market Survey

List

NAME      AGE SEX SONG1  SONG2  SONG3  SONG4  SONG5
Gail       14   1    5      3      1      3      5
Jim        56   2    3      2      2      3      2
Susan      34   1    4      2      1      1      5
Barbara    45   1    3      3      1      2      4
Steve      13   2    5      4      1      4      5
Number of cases read:  5     Number of cases listed:  5

Frequencies

Statistics

Black Water/DB
---------------------------
  N | Valid   | 5 |
    |---------|---|
    | Missing | 0 |
    |---------|---|

Black Water/DB
---------------------------------------------------------------------------
              |          | Frequency | Percent | Valid Percent | Cumulative
              |          |           |         |               |   Percent
       -----  |  -----   | --------- | ------- | ------------- | ----------
      Valid   |   3      |    2      |  40.0   |    40.0       |   40.0
       -----  |  -----   | --------- | ------- | ------------- | ----------
              |   4      |    1      |  20.0   |    20.0       |   60.0
       -----  |  -----   | --------- | ------- | ------------- | ----------
              |   5      |    2      |  40.0   |    40.0       |  100.0
       -----  |  -----   | --------- | ------- | ------------- | ----------
              | Total    |    5      | 100.0   |   100.0       |
       -----  |          | --------- | ------- | ------------- | ----------
```

Crosstabs

Case Processing Summary

```
------------------------------------------------------------------------------
                        |            Cases
                        |  Valid        |   Missing     |   Total
                        |  N  | Percent |  N  | Percent |  N  | Percent
      --------------------  --|---------|--- |---------|--- |---------
      SEX * Black Water/DB  5 | 100.0%  |  0  |  .0%    |  5  | 100.0%
      --------------------  --|---------|--- |---------|--- |---------
```

SEX * Black Water/DB Crosstabulation

Count

```
-------------------------------------------------------
              |         | Black Water/DB | Total |
              |         |  3  |  4  |  5  |       |
       ----   |  ------ | --- |---- | --- | ----- |
      SEX     | female  |  1  |  1  |  1  |   3   |
       ------ |  ------ | --- |---- | --- | ----- |
              | male    |  1  |     |  1  |   2   |
       ---    |  ------ | --- |---- | --- | ----- |
      Total   |         |  2  |  1  |  2  |   5   |
       ----   |  ------ | --- |---- | --- | ----- |
```

**SAS output** The following SAS output looks similar to the SPSS output. One difference is that the results of SAS procedures are written to a separate file, so you don't have to wade through the programs statements and notes from the computer to find your results the way you do with SPSS.

```
                          Music Market Survey                        1

    Obs   Name      Age   Sex   Song1   Song2   Song3   Song4   Song5

     1    Gail      14     1      5       3       1       3       5
     2    Jim       56     2      3       2       2       3       2
     3    Susan     34     1      4       2       1       1       5
     4    Barbara   45     1      3       3       1       2       4
     5    Steve     13     2      5       4       1       4       5



                          Music Market Survey                        2

                          The FREQ Procedure

                          Black Water/DB

                                          Cumulative    Cumulative
        Song1     Frequency      Percent   Frequency      Percent

          3           2          40.00         2          40.00
          4           1          20.00         3          60.00
          5           2          40.00         5         100.00


                      Table of Sex by Song1

            Sex         Song1(Black Water/DB)

            Frequency|
            Percent  |
            Row Pct  |
            Col Pct  | 3        | 4        | 5        | Total

            female   |     1    |     1    |     1    |    3
                     | 20.00    | 20.00    | 20.00    | 60.00
                     | 33.33    | 33.33    | 33.33    |
                     | 50.00    | 100.00   | 50.00    |

            male     |     1    |     0    |     1    |    2
                     | 20.00    | 0.00     | 20.00    | 40.00
                     | 50.00    | 0.00     | 50.00    |
                     | 50.00    | 0.00     | 50.00    |

            Total          2          1          2         5
                        40.00      20.00      40.00    100.00
```

## Getting SPSS data files into SAS using a LIBNAME statement
You can use a LIBNAME statement to read (but not write) SPSS data files. This method is part of Base SAS so you do not have to license any other products. The SPSS data must be in a portable file. To save a portable file in SPSS, open the SPSS data file in the SPSS Data Editor, select `File-Save As`, and then select `SPSS Portable` as the type of file to be saved. In your SAS program, use a LIBNAME statement with this form:

```
LIBNAME libref SPSS 'SPSS-portable-file';
```

After the keyword LIBNAME, put the libref which is a nickname you make up for your file (similar to an SPSS file handle), then put the option SPSS followed by the path and name for your SPSS portable file. The SPSS option tells SAS to use the SPSS data engine to read your data file.

When SAS reads SPSS files with a LIBNAME statement, variable names, variable labels, output formats, and the data remain the same. SPSS missing values (both system and user) become SAS system-missing values. However, SPSS value labels are not copied. The SAS equivalent of SPSS value labels are user-defined formats. User-defined formats are not stored in SAS data sets. If you want value labels, you can create user-defined formats with PROC FORMAT and then apply them with FORMAT statements. See section 4.7 for an explanation of how to do this.

### Example
The following SAS program reads the SPSS file created by the SPSS program in the preceding example. The SPSS file (named survey.sav) was saved as a portable file (survey.por) in the SPSS Data Editor using the Save As option on the File menu.

In this program, the LIBNAME statement tells SAS to use the SPSS data engine to read the file. Then the program does three things: it prints a simple list report of the data with PROC PRINT, it prints a report describing the portable file with PROC CONTENTS, and it uses a DATA step to copy the SPSS portable file into a permanent SAS data set named SASSURVEY in the MySASLib directory.

```
LIBNAME myspss SPSS 'c:\MySPSSDir\survey.por';
* Print the SPSS portable file;
PROC PRINT DATA = myspss.getsurv;
   TITLE 'Music Market Survey';
RUN;
* List the contents of the SPSS portable file;
PROC CONTENTS DATA = myspss.getsurv;
RUN;
* Convert SPSS portable file to SAS data set;
DATA 'c:\MySASLib\sassurvey';
   SET myspss.getsurv;
RUN;
```

In this example, the name that SAS uses for the SPSS portable file is MYSPSS.GETSURV. MYSPSS is the libref assigned to the SPSS portable file in the LIBNAME statement, and GETSURV is the member name. You can use any name you wish for the libref as long as it follows the rules for valid SAS librefs (eight characters or shorter; starts with a letter or underscore; and contains only letters, numerals, or underscores). Since SPSS files don't have internal names and never contain more than one data set, you can also use any name for the member name. Member names follow the same rules as librefs except that member names can be up to 32 characters long.

Here is the output.

```
                         Music Market Survey                              1

  Obs    NAME      AGE   SEX   SONG1   SONG2   SONG3   SONG4   SONG5

   1     Gail       14    1      5       3       1       3       5
   2     Jim        56    2      3       2       2       3       2
   3     Susan      34    1      4       2       1       1       5
   4     Barbara    45    1      3       3       1       2       4
   5     Steve      13    2      5       4       1       4       5


                          The SAS System                                  2

                        The CONTENTS Procedure

  Data Set Name      MYSPSS._FIRST_            Observations            .
  Member Type        DATA                      Variables               8
  Engine             SPSS                      Indexes                 0
  Created            Tue, April 15, 2008 02:48:41 PM  Observation Length  64
  Last Modified      Wed, April 16, 2008 09:59:39 AM  Deleted Observations 0
  Protection                                   Compressed             NO
  Data Set Type                                Sorted                 NO
  Label
  Data Representation   Default
  Encoding              Default


                 Engine/Host Dependent Information

         ORIGSOFT   SPSS for Microsoft Windows Release 16.0
         SPSSINFO   (NONE)
         COMPRESS   NO
         SPSSTYPE   PORTFILE


              Alphabetic List of Variables and Attributes

      #    Variable    Type    Len    Format    Label
      2    AGE         Num      8     2.
      1    NAME        Char     8     8.
      3    SEX         Num      8     2.
      4    SONG1       Num      8     2.       Black Water
      5    SONG2       Num      8     2.       Bennie and the Jets
      6    SONG3       Num      8     2.       Staying Alive
      7    SONG4       Num      8     2.       Yellow Submarine
      8    SONG5       Num      8     2.       Only Time
```

**Getting SPSS data files into SAS using PROC IMPORT**  Starting with SAS 9.1.3, you can use PROC IMPORT to read SPSS data files. You can also use PROC EXPORT to write SPSS data files, though this appendix covers only reading SPSS data files, not writing. Starting with SAS 9.2, you can use the IMPORT and EXPORT wizards for SPSS data files. (For more information about the IMPORT wizard see section 2.3, for PROC IMPORT see section 2.17, for the EXPORT wizard see section 9.2, and for PROC EXPORT see section 9.4.) You must have SAS/ACCESS Interface to PC Files (which is licensed separately from Base SAS) in order to use these features.

PROC IMPORT can read data in standard SPSS format so you do not need to create an SPSS portable file. Here is the general form of the IMPORT procedure for reading SPSS data files:

```
PROC IMPORT DATAFILE = 'SPSS-data-file'
            OUT = SAS-data-set
            DBMS = SAV
            REPLACE;
```

When SAS uses PROC IMPORT to read SPSS files, variable names, variable labels, output formats, and the data remain the same. SPSS missing values (both system and user) become SAS system-missing values. By default, SPSS value labels for numeric variables are converted to temporary SAS user-defined formats.

**Example**  The following SAS program reads the SPSS data file, SURVEY.SAV, created by the SPSS program in the first example in this appendix, and converts it to a SAS data set. Then the new SAS data set is printed using PROC PRINT.

```
* Import an SPSS save file as a permanent SAS data set;
LIBNAME radio 'c:\MySASLib';
PROC IMPORT DATAFILE = 'c:\MySPSSDir\survey.sav'
            OUT = radio.sassurvey
            DBMS = SAV
            REPLACE;
RUN;
* Print the new SAS data set;
PROC PRINT DATA = radio.sassurvey;
   TITLE 'Music Market Survey';
RUN;
```

The SAS data set created by PROC IMPORT will be named SASSURVEY and will be saved in the RADIO SAS data library in the MySASLib directory. Because a libname is specified, this will be a permanent SAS data set that will remain after the end of your SAS job or session.

Here is the output showing the new SAS data set:

```
                          Music Market Survey                                1

 Obs     NAME        AGE      SEX      SONG1    SONG2    SONG3    SONG4    SONG5

  1      Gail        14      female      5        3        1        3        5
  2      Jim         56      male        3        2        2        3        2
  3      Susan       34      female      4        2        1        1        5
  4      Barbara     45      female      3        3        1        2        4
  5      Steve       13      male        5        4        1        4        5
```

Notice that value labels from the SPSS data file have been applied to the variable SEX. The actual data values for SEX in this data set are 1 or 2.

**Value labels for SAS data sets**   PROC IMPORT automatically converts numeric SPSS value labels to SAS user-defined formats, and associates those user-defined formats with the corresponding variables in the new SAS data set. However, user-defined formats are never saved as part of a SAS data set. By default, PROC IMPORT writes the user-defined formats in the temporary SAS library, WORK. Any formats written in the WORK library will be lost when you exit SAS. Therefore, if you save the new SAS data set as a permanent SAS data set, and try to use it at a later time, SAS will be unable to open it because the necessary formats have been erased. In your SAS log, you will see messages like these:

```
ERROR: Format SEX not found or couldn't be loaded for variable SEX.
NOTE: The SAS System stopped processing this step because of errors.
```

There are several ways to deal with this issue. Here are three ways:

♦ Re-import the SPSS data file every time you use it. This has the added advantage that if the SPSS file is updated, you will have the most recent version. If you read the SPSS data file every time, you will not need the SAS data set to be permanent, so you can read it as a temporary SAS data set by skipping the LIBNAME statement and giving the SAS data set a one-level name.

```
* Import an SPSS SAV file as a temporary SAS data set;
PROC IMPORT DATAFILE = 'c:\MySPSSDir\survey.sav'
            OUT = sassurvey
            DBMS = SAV
            REPLACE;
RUN;
```

♦ Use the NOFMTERR system option to read the permanent SAS data set without the user-defined formats. Submit this OPTIONS statement before you use the data set:

```
OPTIONS NOFMTERR;
LIBNAME radio 'c:\MySASLib';
* Print the SAS data set;
PROC PRINT DATA = radio.sassurvey;
   TITLE 'Music Market Survey';
RUN;
```

♦ Starting with SAS 9.2, you can use the optional FMTLIB= statement with PROC IMPORT to save user-defined formats in a permanent format catalog. See the SAS Help and Documentation for more information about creating and using permanent format catalogs.

# Appendix C  Coming to SAS from a Programming Language

You can write SAS programs that do many of the tasks that standard programming languages like C++, Java, and Visual BASIC can do. There are many similarities between SAS and these languages, but there are some important differences. If you are used to programming with these types of languages, learning SAS will be easier if you remember the differences.

**Built-in loop**  The major difference is that SAS has a built-in loop for data handling. If you read data from a file, or process SAS data sets in the DATA step, SAS automatically loops through all the data. In a standard programming language, you typically need to set up an array to hold the data, then use a loop (DO, WHILE, or FOR) to process the array. You may need to know how many data elements are in the file, or check for end-of-file markers. The DATA step in SAS automates this.

While SAS processes all the data, it sees only one observation at a time. All the statements in a DATA step operate on only one observation at a time. In a standard programming language, you can see all the observations at once, by referencing the appropriate array subscript. In SAS you can simulate this using LAG functions or other techniques, but you will find that it is seldom necessary.

**Loops**  DO loops are present in SAS, but you must keep in mind that a DO loop in SAS is executed with each pass through the DATA step. So if your loop has 6 iterations, and you have 10 observations in your data set, the statements inside your loop will be executed 60 times—6 times for each of the 10 observations (assuming the INPUT or SET statement is not inside the loop). The built-in loop in SAS, in essence, puts a loop around your entire DATA step. Because of the built-in loop, arrays and DO loops are not used nearly as often in SAS programs as they are in other languages.

**Arrays**  SAS does have arrays, but they are used differently from the way they are used in standard programming languages. An array in SAS consists of variables. You use arrays when you want to do the same thing to each variable in the array, and you don't want to write a separate statement for each variable. Arrays are temporary in SAS, existing only for the duration of the DATA step in which they are defined. Arrays provide ways to shorten and simplify your SAS programs.

**Functions**  SAS has many functions available that help simplify your programming tasks. Functions in SAS are used in DATA steps and, therefore, operate within an observation. If you want to find the minimum value for an observation across a group of variables, for example, you would use the MIN function. SAS has hundreds of functions available in categories including: Character, Macro, Character String Matching, Mathematical, Date and Time, Probability, Descriptive Statistics , Random Number, Distance, State and ZIP Code, Financial, and Variable Info.

**Procedures**  While functions operate across variables, SAS procedures operate across observations. If you want to find the minimum value for a variable across all observations, then use PROC MEANS. SAS procedures can do a lot in just a few statements. Results from procedures are nicely formatted and you don't have to worry about how many decimal places to print, or where to put the results on the page. A simple PROC PRINT statement, for example, will print all the data in your SAS data set, fit as many variables as it can on a page, decide on the best format for each variable, and label each variable at the top of every page. But, SAS is flexible, so if you don't like the way SAS printed your results, you can change it.

**Data types**  Another difference between SAS and many other languages is that SAS has only two types of data: numeric and character. All numbers in SAS are assumed to be double-precision floating-point values. You don't have to declare what type of numbers you are using. You can, however, change the number of bytes used to store data using the LENGTH statement. The default length is 8 bytes, which safely stores all numbers. If you are using small integer values, you might be able to use a length of 4 or fewer depending on the computer and operating environment you are using. The SAS documentation for your host will tell you which numbers you can safely store in how many bytes.

**Program structure**  Many programming languages are particular about the layout of programs. In Python, for example, modifying the indention in a program will change the logic, and may even result in a syntax error. SAS has no restrictions on program layout. A statement can be indented, split on many lines, or on the same line as other statements. SAS simply reads a statement from one semicolon to another. In addition, SAS statements are not case sensitive.

**Compilation and execution**  Most programming languages have separate compile and execute phases. SAS does have separate phases, but when you submit a SAS program it automatically compiles and executes. It is possible, however, to save compiled SAS DATA steps and  macros if you want.

**Comparison of a SAS program to a C++ program**   The following compares a SAS program to a C++ program. Each program reads the following data from a file and prints it. The data file has three columns for the students' names, ages, and grade-point averages:

```
Mary    19 3.45
Bob     20 3.12
Scott   22 2.89
Marie   18 3.75
Ruth    20 2.67
```

## The SAS Program

```
DATA grades;
    INFILE 'c:\MyRawData\gpa.dat';
    INPUT Name $ Age Gpa;
RUN;
PROC PRINT DATA = grades;
RUN;
```

## The C++ Program

```cpp
#include <iostream>
#include <fstream>
#include <iomanip>
using namespace std;

const int N=100;

struct student
{
        char name[32];
        int age;
        double GPA;
};

void main(void)
{
        student grades[N];

        ifstream in("gpa.dat");
        if (in.fail())
        exit(-1);

        int i=0;
        while (!in.eof() && i<N)
        {
                in>>grades[i].name>>grades[i].age>>grades[i].GPA;
                cout<<setw(10)<<left<<grades[i].name
                        <<setw(10)<<grades[i].age
                        <<fixed<<setprecision(2)<<grades[i].GPA<<endl;
                ++i;
        }

        in.close();
}
```

In the C++ program, the variable's name (character array), age (integer), and gpa (double) are grouped in a data structure called student. Then, an array of these structures, named grades, is declared with an arbitrary dimension of N. Each variable in the program must be declared both in type and dimension (if an array). The SAS program has no such section. The variables are defined as either character ($) or numeric in the INPUT statement.

Next, the C++ program opens the file and uses a while statement to read the data into grades, stopping when it reaches the end of the file marker (EOF). In the same step, the C++ program writes the data out to the standard output device. In the SAS program, the DATA step sets up the built-in loop which reads all the data in the file. The INFILE statement specifies which file to read, and the INPUT statement defines the variables. The data are stored in a SAS data set named GRADES. A simple PROC PRINT prints the contents of the GRADES data set.

Here are the results of the PROC PRINT from the SAS program.

```
                        The SAS System                    1

            Obs     Name     Age      Gpa

             1      Mary      19      3.45
             2      Bob       20      3.12
             3      Scott     22      2.89
             4      Marie     18      3.75
             5      Ruth      20      2.67
```

Here are the results from the C++ program.

```
  Mary      19       3.45
  Bob       20       3.12
  Scott     22       2.89
  Marie     18       3.75
  Ruth      20       2.67
```

Notice that SAS automatically added a default title, page number, column headings, and observation numbers to its report. The way the C++ program was written, it printed just the data. Of course you could rewrite the C++ program to make the output look exactly like the SAS output, but it would take more programming.

# Appendix D  Coming to SAS from SQL

If you already know Structured Query Language (SQL), then you will be pleased to know that you can use SQL statements in SAS programs to create, read, and modify SAS data sets. There are two basic ways to use SQL with SAS:

♦ You can embed complete SQL statements in the SQL procedure.

♦ You can use WHERE statements or WHERE= data set options to select rows in standard SAS DATA and PROC steps.

Both of these features are available with Base SAS, so you don't have to license any other SAS software to use SQL.

**Terminology**  Terms such as table, row, and column that originated with relational databases are now standard SAS terms also. However, other terms can also be used with SAS. To help you understand SAS terminology, here is a brief dictionary of analogous terms:

| SQL term | Analogous SAS term |
|---|---|
| column | column or variable |
| row | row or observation |
| table | table or data set |
| join | merge, set, update or modify |
| NULL value | missing value |
| alias | alias |
| view | view |
| *no analogous term* | DATA step |
| *no analogous term* | PROC step |

SQL does not contain structures like SAS DATA and PROC steps. Basically, DATA steps read and modify data while PROC (short for procedure) steps perform specific analyses or functions such as sorting, writing reports, or running statistical analyses. In SQL, reports are written automatically whenever you use a SELECT statement; sorting is performed by the ORDER BY clause; and the operations performed by most other SAS procedures don't exist in SQL.

SAS has fewer data types than standard SQL. The character data type is the same in both languages. All other SQL data types (numeric, decimal, integer, smallint, float, real, double precision, and date) map to the SAS numeric data type.

**PROC SQL**  The SQL procedure in SAS follows all but a few of the guidelines set by the American National Standards Institute (ANSI) for implementations of SQL. One exception is that table names, column names, and aliases are limited to 32 characters in length. This complies with standard SAS naming conventions. The ANSI standard for SQL allows longer names. See the SAS Help and Documentation for more details on the implementation of ANSI standards in PROC SQL.

The basic form of the SQL procedure is

```
PROC SQL;
   sql-statement;
```

The possible values for the *sql-statement* in PROC SQL include ALTER, CREATE, DELETE, DESCRIBE, DROP, INSERT, SELECT, UPDATE, and VALIDATE statements—with a semicolon stuck on the end. You can have any number of SQL statements in a single PROC SQL step.

You can use PROC SQL interactively or in batch jobs. Unlike most other SAS procedures, PROC SQL will run interactively without a RUN statement. You just need to submit the program statements. Any results from SELECT statements are displayed automatically unless you specify the NOPRINT option on the PROC statement like this:

```
PROC SQL NOPRINT;
```

An SQL view is a stored SELECT statement that is executed at run time. PROC SQL can create views, and other procedures can read views created via PROC SQL.

**Example**　The work performed by SQL, and therefore by PROC SQL, can also be done in SAS by DATA steps, PROC PRINT, PROC SORT, and PROC MEANS. To show how PROC SQL works and to provide a comparison to DATA and PROC steps, here are programs using PROC SQL and other SAS statements to perform the same actions.

**Creating a table**　The first program uses PROC SQL to create and print a simple table with three columns. This program uses CREATE, INSERT, and SELECT statements in a single PROC SQL step:

```
LIBNAME sports 'c:\MySASLib';
PROC SQL;
   CREATE TABLE sports.customer
      (CustomerNumber num,
       Name           char(17),
       Address        char(20));

   INSERT INTO sports.customer
      VALUES (101, 'Murphy''s Sports ', '115 Main St.        ')
      VALUES (102, 'Sun N Ski       ', '2106 Newberry Ave.  ')
      VALUES (103, 'Sports Outfitters', '19 Cary Way         ')
      VALUES (104, 'Cramer & Johnson ', '4106 Arlington Blvd.')
      VALUES (105, 'Sports Savers    ', '2708 Broadway       ');

   TITLE 'The Sports Customer Data';
   SELECT *
      FROM sports.customer;
```

Notice that the LIBNAME statement sets up a libref named SPORTS, pointing to a subdirectory named MySASLib on the C drive (Windows). The LIBNAME statement may be different for your operating environment. See section 2.20 for more information about LIBNAME statements. This program creates a permanent SAS table named CUSTOMER in the MySASLib subdirectory. No RUN statement is needed; to run this program you simply submit it to SAS. Here is the output:

```
                    The Sports Customer Data                        1

        Customer
        Number  Name                  Address
        ─────────────────────────────────────────────────────
           101  Murphy's Sports       115 Main St.
           102  Sun N Ski             2106 Newberry Ave.
           103  Sports Outfitters     19 Cary Way
           104  Cramer & Johnson      4106 Arlington Blvd.
           105  Sports Savers         2708 Broadway
```

The next program uses standard SAS statements to create the same table. Notice that the LIBNAME statement, the table name, and the TITLE statement are identical in both programs. LIBNAME statements stay in effect for the duration of a session or job. So, if you ran these programs in a single session or job, you would not have to repeat the LIBNAME statement. It is repeated here only for the sake of completeness.

```
LIBNAME sports 'c:\MySASLib';
DATA sports.customer;
   INPUT CustomerNumber Name $ 5-21 Address $ 23-42;
   DATALINES;
101 Murphy's Sports   115 Main St.
102 Sun N Ski         2106 Newberry Ave.
103 Sports Outfitters 19 Cary Way
104 Cramer & Johnson  4106 Arlington Blvd.
105 Sports Savers     2708 Broadway
   ;
PROC PRINT DATA = sports.customer;
TITLE 'The Sports Customer Data';
RUN;
```

Here is the output from the standard SAS program. It looks a little different from the previous report, but it contains the same information.

```
                    The Sports Customer Data                        2

              Customer
        Obs   Number    Name              Address

         1     101     Murphy's Sports    115 Main St.
         2     102     Sun N Ski          2106 Newberry Ave.
         3     103     Sports Outfitters  19 Cary Way
         4     104     Cramer & Johnson   4106 Arlington Blvd.
         5     105     Sports Savers      2708 Broadway
```

**Reading an existing table** The next two programs read the CUSTOMER table and select one row. Here is the PROC SQL version of this program:

```
LIBNAME sports 'c:\MySASLib';
PROC SQL;
   TITLE 'Customer Number 102';
   SELECT *
      FROM sports.customer
      WHERE CustomerNumber = 102;
```

The PROC SQL output looks like this:

```
                          Customer Number 102                    3

            Customer
             Number   Name              Address
            _____

               102   Sun N Ski         2106 Newberry Ave.
```

The following program uses SAS DATA and PROC steps to select and print the same row from the CUSTOMER table:

```
LIBNAME sports 'c:\MySASLib';
DATA sunnski;
   SET sports.customer;
   IF CustomerNumber = 102;
PROC PRINT DATA = sunnski;
   TITLE 'Customer Number 102';
RUN;
```

Here is the PROC PRINT output:

```
                          Customer Number 102                    4

                    Customer
            Obs      Number        Name          Address

             1        102        Sun N Ski     2106 Newberry Ave.
```

**Using the Query window to build a query**  There is another way to write PROC SQL statements: the Query window. You can open the Query window by selecting `Query` from the Tools menu. The Query window guides you through the process of building a query.

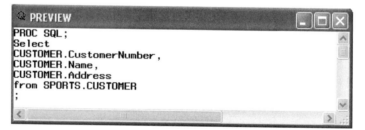

To run your query, select `Tools-Run Query-Run Immediate`. You can see the SQL statements created by the Query window by selecting either `Tools-Show Query...` or `Tools-Preview Window...`.

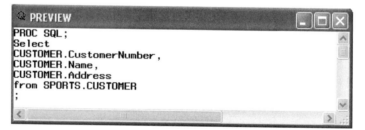

**WHERE statement vs. IF statement**  The WHERE statement in SAS is modeled after the WHERE clause of SQL, and  is similar to a subsetting IF statement. However, there are some differences in how a WHERE statement and a subsetting IF work. While subsetting IFs can appear only in DATA steps, WHERE statements can be used in DATA or PROC steps. WHERE statements are generally more efficient than subsetting IF statements, especially when they allow you to eliminate a DATA step by sub-setting directly in a procedure. When WHERE statements are used in a DATA step, SAS applies WHERE statements earlier than IF statements. This has several repercussions:

♦  The WHERE statement is more efficient than a subsetting IF because it avoids reading unwanted rows.

♦  The WHERE statement can select rows only from existing SAS tables. The IF statement, however, can select rows from existing SAS tables or from raw data files being read with INPUT statements.

◆ With a WHERE statement, you can select rows based only on the values of columns being read. With a subsetting IF statement, you can also select rows based on the value of a column created in the current DATA step.

◆ The WHERE and IF statements may produce different results when two tables are combined in a MERGE, SET, or UPDATE statement. Operations that occur after SAS applies WHERE statements but before SAS applies IF statements may cause the statements to select different rows.

For more information about subsetting IF statements, see section 3.7; for more information about WHERE statements, see section 4.2.

**WHERE= data set option vs. WHERE statement** The WHERE= data set option is similar to the WHERE statement, but is even more flexible. Both can be used in DATA and PROC steps. But while the WHERE statement affects only SAS data tables being read, the WHERE= data set option can be used both for SAS data tables being read and for SAS data tables being written. In fact, you could use two WHERE= options in the same DATA or PROC step, one selecting the input rows, and another selecting the output rows. For more information on the WHERE= data set option see section 6.13.

**Examples** To show how the WHERE statement and the WHERE= data set option work, and to provide a comparison with the IF statement, here are programs using these techniques to perform the same functions. All five of these programs read the CUSTOMER SAS data table created by the previous programs. The goal of these programs is to select and print one row from an existing SAS table. The output of these five programs is almost identical, but each method has advantages as discussed above.

**Subsetting IF in a DATA step** This program uses a subsetting IF statement to select one row:

```
LIBNAME sports 'c:\MySASLib';
DATA outfitters;
   SET sports.customer;
   IF Name = 'Sports Outfitters';
PROC PRINT DATA = outfitters;
RUN;
```

Here is the output.

```
                       The SAS System                         1

                  Customer
         Obs      Number        Name              Address

          1        103      Sports Outfitters   19 Cary Way
```

## WHERE statement in a DATA step

The next program uses a WHERE statement in the DATA step and then prints the results with PROC PRINT:

```
LIBNAME sports 'c:\MySASLib';
DATA outfitters;
   SET sports.customer;
   WHERE Name = 'Sports Outfitters';
PROC PRINT DATA = outfitters;
RUN;
```

The output looks like this:

```
                        The SAS System                          2

                 Customer
           Obs    Number         Name           Address

            1      103       Sports Outfitters   19 Cary Way
```

## WHERE= data set option in a DATA step

The next program uses a WHERE= data set option in a DATA step and then prints the results with PROC PRINT:

```
LIBNAME sports 'c:\MySASLib';
DATA outfitters (WHERE = (Name = 'Sports Outfitters'));
   SET sports.customer;
PROC PRINT DATA = outfitters;
RUN;
```

The output looks like this:

```
                        The SAS System                          3

                 Customer
           Obs    Number         Name           Address

            1      103       Sports Outfitters   19 Cary Way
```

## WHERE statement in a PROC step

The following program uses a WHERE statement directly in PROC PRINT:

```
LIBNAME sports 'c:\MySASLib';
PROC PRINT DATA = sports.customer;
   WHERE Name = 'Sports Outfitters';
RUN;
```

Here is the output:

```
                    The SAS System                        4

               Customer
       Obs      Number         Name            Address

        3        103      Sports Outfitters   19 Cary Way
```

## WHERE= data set option in a PROC step  This program uses a WHERE= data set option in PROC PRINT:

```
LIBNAME sports 'c:\MySASLib';
PROC PRINT DATA = sports.customer (WHERE = (Name = 'Sports Outfitters'));
RUN;
```

Here is the output:

```
                    The SAS System                        5

               Customer
       Obs      Number         Name            Address

        3        103      Sports Outfitters   19 Cary Way
```

Notice that the row number (labeled Obs) for the first three reports is 1 while the row number for the last two reports is 3. This happens because the first three programs create a table with one row and then print it. In contrast, the last two programs never create a table; they simply read the existing table searching for the right row, which happens to be number 3.

# Index